Rudolf Lå

An Extraordinary Life

Rudolf Laban

An Extraordinary Life

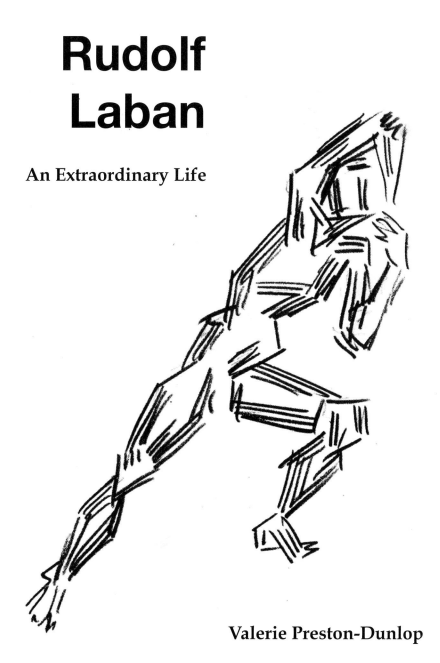

Valerie Preston-Dunlop

DANCE
BOOKS
Alton

First published in 1998,
this edition published in 2008

Dance Books Ltd
The Old Bakery
4 Lenten Street
Alton, Hampshire
GU34 1HG

© 2008 Valerie Preston-Dunlop

ISBN 978-1-85273-124-3

A CIP catalogue record for this book
is available from the British Library

Design: Sanjoy Roy

Printed and bound in Great Britain by
Latimer Trend, Plymouth, Devon

Contents

Illustrations vi

Introduction and Sources ix

1 **Early Influences** 1
Austria-Hungary, Munich, Paris, and Vienna 1879–1910

2 **Finding a Direction** 17
Munich and Ascona, 1910–1914

3 **The Nightmare Years** 37
Zurich, 1914–1919

4 **First Footholds** 53
Nuremberg, Stuttgart and Mannheim, 1919–1922

5 **Striding Out** 72
Gleschendorf and Hamburg, 1922–1924

6 **Artist and Researcher** 97
Hamburg, 1924–1926

7 **The Double Edge of Success** 119
America, Wurzburg, Magdeburg, Essen, and Berlin, 1926–1928

8 **Accolades at Mid-Point** 139
Vienna, Bayreuth and Berlin, 1929–1930

9 **The Nazification of Culture** 165
Berlin, 1931–1934

10 **Survival** 183
Berlin, 1934–1937

11 **The Will to Rekindle** 204
Dartington, Newtown and Manchester, 1938–1945

12 **Post-War Avenues** 233
Manchester and Addlestone, 1945–1958

13 **No End** 270

Glossary 276

Writings by Rudolf Laban 280

Bibliography 286

Index 291

Illustrations

Between pp. 82 and 83

1. Field Marshal Rudolf Laban in his final command for the Austro-Hungarian army as Governor of the Turkish Provinces Bosnia and Herzegovina.
2. Rudolf Jean Baptiste Attila Laban, aged three.
3. Laban as a teenager.
4. Laban in his atelier at 132 Boulevard Montparnasse, Paris, in 1903.
5. Laban in his atelier, dressed probably for some Rosicrucian activity, 1903.
6. Laban in the Bois de Vincenne at St Maurice, Paris, where he sketched with his daughter Azraela, 1905.
7. Drawing for a theatre for dance, the original drawing believed to have been submitted as the entrance examination to the Prix de Rome class of the School of Architecture at the Écoles des Beaux Arts, Paris, 1903.
8. Laban outside his house in St Maurice, Paris, c.1905.
9. School Laban de Varalja in Munich, 1913, in 'spatial group from concentrating to spreading.'
10. Laban's sketch entitled 'Music and Movement', depicting his wife, the singer Maja Lederer, and his lover, Suzanne Perrottet. Munich, 1913/14.
11. Laban's notes on *Ton* (sound) and *Tanz* (dance), 1913.
12. Mary Wigman as a student of Laban de Varalja, in 'double tension upwards and downwards', 1913.
13. The *ménage à trois* of Suzy Perrottet, Laban and Maja Lederer, 1914.
14. Laban's summer season at Ascona.
15. Laban in Zurich, 1915.
16. Open class at the Seehofstrasse Laban school in Zurich, c.1915.
17. Dada poster including a billing for Suzanne Perrottet playing Laban's piano and violin compositions, 1917.
18. Dussia Bereska in 1919.
19. Laban in 1919.
20. Kurt Jooss in 1921.
21. Poster for the Nationaltheater in Mannheim for Laban's first production in a major theatre, *Epische Tanzfolge*, 1921.
22. *Epische Tanzfolge* presented in 1922 as *Die Geblendeten*.
23. Gleschendorf summer school, Laban taking class with percussion, 1922.
24. Men's group at Herta Feist's Laban school in Berlin, 1923.
25. Herta Feist, Martin Gleisner, and a student, Berlin, 1923.

Between pp. 146 and 147

26. Members of the Laban Movement Choir, Berlin, run by Herta Feist, 1923.
27. *Gaukelei* (Jugglery), a dance tragedy, 1923.
28. Hamburg Movement Choir in Laban's *Agamemnon's Tod*, 1924.
29. Men's Group of the Hamburg Movement Choir.
30. Hamburg Movement Choir.
31. Hamburg Movement Choir in Albrecht Knust's *Erwachen* (Awaken).
32. Laban with Gertrud Loeszer on their duo tour on Wagner themes, 1925.
33. Laban in publicity material for the Hamburg Volksoper, January 1925.
34. Laban, Dussia Bereska, Robert Robst and a movement choir in *Don Juan*, 1925.
35. *Narrenspiegel* (A Fool's Mirror) in rehearsal, 1926.
36. *Nacht* (Night), presented at the Dancer's Congress at Magdeburg, June 1927.
37. *Ritterballett* (Ballet of the Knights), presented at the Dancers' Congress at Magdeburg, June 1927.
38. Figurines of Laban's choreutic scales made for the 1927 Theatre Exhibition, Magdeburg.
39. Choreographisches Institute, Gillstrasse, Berlin-Grunewald, 1927.
40. Group work with Martin Gleisner, 1928.
41. 'Procession of the Corpses', from *Die Grünen Clowns* (The Green Clowns), 1928.
42. Laban's early notation, c.1917.
43. A later notation for a space study of six dancers, c.1926.
44. A third version of the notation used for writing space harmony exercises.
45. Photocall for the Choreographisches Institute teachers and master students after the Second Dancers' Congress, in Essen, 1928.
46. Choreographisches Institut dancers demonstrating the new notation, 1928.
47. Poster for *Titan*, the first work reconstructed from the Laban movement notation score, by Albrecht Knust, 1929.
48. Designs by Laban for the decorated floats for the *Festzug der Gewerbe* (Festive Procession of Crafts and Industries) in Vienna, 1929.
49. The Ringstrasse in Vienna during the Festzug, 9 June 1929.
50. Photograph in studio clothing of Laban at the time of his fiftieth birthday, December 1929.
51. Fiftieth birthday publicity photograph of Laban.
52. Laban's 'Bacchanale' in Wagner's *Tannhäuser*, Bayreuth, 1930.
53. Laban with the soloists of the State Opera Berlin, September 1930.
54. Laban's movement choir *Tauwind und der Neuen Freude* (The Spring Wind and the New Joy) in the Dietrich Eckart Freilichtbühne, Olympic Games complex, June 1936.

Between pp. 210 and 211

55. The Dietrich Eckart Freilichtbühne with the Olympic Tower under construction in the background.
56. Laban on his visit to Lea Daan's school in Antwerp, 1938.
57. Laban in his work room at The Barton, Dartington Hall, 1939.
58. Laban with Lisa Ullmann, c.1939.

59. Lisa Ullmann and Laban, with Joan Goodrich and Diana Jordan, at Rock House, Newtown, at their first holiday course, summer 1941.
60. Movement choir at the Modern Dance Holiday Course at Moreton Hall, 1942.
61. Modern Dance Holiday Course, Sheffield, January 1945.
62. Effort graphs developed by Laban for Paton Lawrence & Co., 1942.
63. Notation and linear effort graphs for the analysis of the manual processes in wrapping Mars Bars, 1942.
64. Exercises in Laban/Lawrence Industrial Rhythm, Manchester, 1947.
65. Class at the Art of Movement Studio, Manchester.
66. Geraldine Stephenson demonstrating choreutics in the icosahedron, 1947.
67. Art of Movement Studio students in the garden of Myfanwy Dewey, 1948.
68. Sylvia Bodmer's Young Dancers Group, 1948.
69. Men's creative movement course led by Joan Russell, August 1950.
70. Modern Dance Holiday Course class at Dartington Hall, 1952.
71. Laban at the Modern Dance Holiday Course at Dartington Hall, 1952.
72. Group work at the Modern Holiday Course, Dartington Hall, 1952.
73. Modern educational dance in a Lancashire secondary school, late 1940s.
74. Movement at a primary school in Manchester, c.1950.
75. The Saltarium of the Art of Movement Studio at Addlestone, 1955.
76. Laban at Addlestone, 1957.

Drawings by Laban

77. Group movement seen as spatial form.
78. Labile figure of a man.
79. Stable figure in a dodecahedral form.
80. A three-ring harmonic form danced by three figures within an icosahedral framework.
81. Group of six dancers oriented in an equator, a space harmony form, surrounded by a twelve-ring of alternating labile transversals with stable peripherals.
82. Dancers converging and diverging in spatial counterpoint.

On p. 252

83. Notation score of *Teufel im Dorf* (The Devil in the Village), ballet by Pina and Pia Mlakar, written by Albrecht Knust in 1942, and presented to Laban for his seventieth birthday, 1949.

Introduction and Sources

Researching Laban's life has been a jigsaw. Luckily I had started amassing the materials while curating the Laban Collection for the Laban Centre for Movement and Dance, London, long before I had any idea of writing a biography. My first interviews were with elderly Labanites, some of whom have since died. Käthe Wulff, whom I visited twice, was with Laban in Ascona in 1913 and during his Zurich years where she performed enthusiastically with the Dada group. She gave me a private lesson in her Basel studio, aged ninety-six, beating on her tambour and gong for basic spatial and dynamic exercises. Herta Feist, who joined Laban in Stuttgart in 1921, was interviewed in her retirement home in Hanover. Sylvia Bodmer, who joined him in 1922 and worked with him again in Manchester from 1942, was a fount of information on the Gleschendorf summer school and the early years of the Tanzbühne Laban in Hamburg. In the year just before her death I recorded her dance studies with the Laban Centre dancers, assisted by her trusted collaborator Enid Platt. In Lisa Ullmann's last years she directed me to contacts she had made in Austria and Germany. In Vienna, Fritz Klingenbeck shared his enthusiasm and his personal archive with me. Having been with Laban from the mid-1920s for ten years, his special interest in the decisions made on notation and on life at the Choreographisches Institut were invaluable. Alfred Schlee talked to me in the offices of his erstwhile place of work, the Universal Edition publishing house. It was a great pleasure to have his enthusiastic support for my collaborative translations, with Susanne Lahusen, of articles from *Schrifttanz*, the journal that he edited in collaboration with Laban from 1928 to 1932. Gertrud Snell's close association with Laban from 1926 until 1936 gave me insight into some of the political pressures on them all in those difficult years. She generously conversed with me at her home in Hanover on more than one visit. Ilse Loesch, a radical Choreographisches Institut dancer from 1926, I sought out in East Berlin, crossing through Checkpoint Charlie on one visit and Friedrichstrasse Station on several more. More easily, last year we dined together in a free Berlin. Beatrice Loeb, a student with Dussia Bereska at the short-lived Rome Laban School of 1924, and a Labanite thereafter, I met in a hotel in Baden during her retirement and again in the seclusion of a religious house in Rome. Aurel Milloss I spoke with in his magnificent book-lined study in Rome. His studentship with Laban in Berlin from 1927 to 1928 and his passion for Laban's choreological practice had, he said, enabled him to innovate in his career as a ballet choreographer in the major European opera houses. Lola Rogge, Laban's young collaborator with the movement choir in Hamburg, I visited at her long-standing school there. I met Greta Wragge von Pustau, who danced at the Olympic Festival of 1936, near Nuremberg where she had taught Laban material for years. Irene Steiner, a Wigman student, allowed me to watch her amateur classes in her school in Winterthur. Simone Michelle, later Sigurd Leeder's chief assistant, and Jeanne Brabant of Antwerp, were both students at the Jooss/Leeder school in Dartington Hall and spoke to me of the difficult years of 1939. Willi Soukup was there too at the time of the internment of aliens. I first met Albrecht Knust in Essen in 1952 but never thought to ask him about his early days with Laban from 1921 to 1936. His archive, now cared for by Professor Roderyk Lange in Jersey, has been a rich resource on matters connected with Hamburg and with the development of notation. Correspondence between Knust and various Labanites was useful. Liselotte Diem, widow of Carl Diem, who masterminded the 1936 Olympic Games in Berlin, discussed with me Laban's impact in Germany in the 1920s and 1930s. Helen Priest Rogers, whom I met by chance in England, was also at the Olympic Games and witnessed the ill-fated performance of Laban's last work in Germany.

Of the British Labanites, Barbara Cox (on the years in Newtown) and Marjorie Bergin (on the Laban Art of Movement Guild) were most helpful. Lorna Wilson and Lorn Primrose, being early recipients of Joan Goodrich's teaching, and encountering Laban and Ullmann as students, were able to help with the atmosphere of those early days. With my fellow students at Manchester – Warren Lamb, Mary Elding and Geraldine Stephenson – I have reminisced on the early radical years of the Art of Movement Studio, and I talked with Jean Newlove. Leni Heaton, a mature student there who retired to Switzerland with Adda Heynssen, I met again in Vevey to talk about it all. Hilary Corlett, a student at Addlestone, and Dorothy Madden coming there as an American visitor, were able to add touches from their personal perspectives. So too was Yat Malmgren, who also gave supportive information from his time in Berlin. Marion North's close association with Laban in his very last years added insight to my own knowledge of the man at that time.

I spent many hours with the Perrottet family, especially with Julia, the widow of Allar, who was the son of Laban and Suzy Perrottet, and with Oliver Perrottet, Suzy's grandson. Suzy's extraordinary passion for keeping every piece of paper and for writing notes on every class proved a rich resource. The personal letters that passed between her and Laban in the first years of their love affair are unique, and enabled me to follow Laban's thoughts on the revitalising of dance. Roland Laban, Laban and Maja Lederer's youngest son, and his wife have generously shared with me their knowledge and archives. The papers and photographs collected by Laban's mother, later carefully looked after by his sister Renée, were a treasure trove which I was able to study on Renée's death, through Julia's generosity.

The first archives studied in depth were those of Kurt Peters in Cologne, now a public archive but at the time of my visit still his personal and unique collection. Together with his wife Gisela he guided my hand through shelf after shelf of precious materials from the 1920s and 1930s. Gisela enabled me to watch her children's classes in which she gave a Laban barre and choreographic studies in the Laban manner, training young dancers to perform with the kind of commitment typical of Laban's work. It took years for a Westerner to gain access to the collection of Laban's papers, now housed at the Leipzig Tanzarchiv, the problems of a divided Germany making it impossible until two years ago. The story of that collection, housed by Marie Luise Lieschke at Plauen for Laban from the time that he was appointed to the Staatsoper in Berlin in 1930, is an extraordinary one. Thought to have been lost during the war, Lisa Ullmann searched for it with great difficulty, Plauen being in the Russian Zone. She failed to find it, but John Hodgson succeeded. The problem of how to get at it, what to do with it, is a story that is yet to be told. Suffice to say that one half is now in London in Hodgson's care and the other is at Leipzig. The latter looks to be what Laban had in his desk and cupboards when he left his office at Gillstrasse on ceasing to be self-employed. It is rich in late 1920s material, especially Kammertanzbühne data.

The Laban Archive at the National Resource Centre for Dance is largely post-war material. Laban's papers and Ullmann's careful collection of every scrap of evidence have been being catalogued for some years, and are now mostly available for study. They, together with the Lisa Ullmann archive and the Art of Movement Studio archive, are a rich resource on Laban's time in Britain.

The Mary Wigman Archive at the Akademie der Kunst in Berlin holds much of both a professional and a personal nature on her connection with Laban. Being in West Berlin it was much easier to study there than in what was the Akademie der Kunst in East Berlin. At present, through the amalgamation of collections from East and West, it is not always easy to know in which buildings things are now housed, and in what state of retrieval. The Bauhausarchiv and the Landesarchiv, always in the West, are rich in specialist data, on Schlemmer in particular for the purposes of this book, and on political data respectively. The Werkbund Archiv, in what was the East, has specialist material useful for Laban's connections in Munich. Munich Libraries offer both newspaper data and collections of letters as well as contextual information on the very lively arts period there before the First World War. The libraries of Berlin are sources of newspapers, journals and films. For Laban's employment in the Nazi period the Bundesarchiv has detailed resources, the Nazis being capable and keen documentors. Originally in Coblenz when I first researched them, the holdings are now at Potsdam. The archives of the Staatsoper in Berlin were not easy to find, no one seeming to know where they had landed after they left the opera house itself. Eventually I tracked them to the Geheim Preussische Archiv in the Berlin suburb of Dahlem. Also just becoming available is the theatre collection of the Markische Museum in the eastern half of Berlin, which holds programmes and some memorabilia.

In Vienna my institutional searches took me to the Wiener Neustadt Military Academy where Laban was a cadet, to the various city libraries and archives for evidence of his father's military postings, of Laban's famous Festzug of 1929, and of his many visits to the city for lectures, as well as for the dance culture and general culture of the years in question. Nuremberg elicited prime sources on the exhibition of Laban's drawings held there in 1920, Wurzburg on the Choreographisches Institut's short time there in 1926 and on the city's disapproval of him. Bad Mergentheim city library had evidence of Laban's performances there in 1927. The Bucherei in Leipzig holds many of the articles on dance documented by Kurt Peterman in his copious *Tanz Bibliographie*; and the Book Fair held there, which coincided by chance with my visit, elicited information on the more esoteric aspects of Laban's quasi-religious interests. The City Museum in Bayreuth holds data on the productions at the Festival Theatre and the museum near Schloss Banz has evidence of the children's artwork that attracted Laban there in 1937. Hamburg, a city I visited on several occasions, is rich in material from the Weimar Republic period, the communist Ernst Thälmann having an archive collection in his name, and the university-*cum*-state library holding a good newspaper stock. The Theatermuseum and the Pressdokumentationen und Archiv in Hamburg also have some data, and miraculously some of the buildings Laban used are still there. Dortmund holds a large collection of Workers' Literature useful for its arts data and its socialist perspective.

From Laban's time in Paris I had to search for scraps of evidence, eventually locating his house in St Maurice through first finding, in the local Mairie, the birth registration of his daughter born there in 1902. The Écoles des Beaux Arts had no knowledge of their own records, and it took some persistence to find them in the Bibliothèque Nationale. Laban's Rosicrucian connection was also not easy to trace, though I eventually found enough material in the Gustave Moreau Museum, the Bibliothèque de l'Arsenale and the Rosicrucian Centre in Crowborough, to make a guess at what must have occurred. The Bibliothèque de l'Opéra holds considerable German dance materials, especially those in the collections of the Archives Internationales de la Danse from 1932. Further Archives Internationales materials in Stockholm, especially on the Dancers' Congresses and Kurt Jooss, proved helpful.

In Britain, city museums and libraries in Newtown, Manchester and Bradford contain references to Laban. The Dartington Hall records are rich in data both on the years when Laban was there (1938–40) and on the continuing connection between him, the Elmhirsts and the Withymead Centre. The Laban Art of Movement Guild magazines contain reports of courses and articles by Laban.

On many of these curating visits over the years I have been accompanied. On the German trips usually John Dunlop came, he being especially good at German gothic script and German institutional ways of going about things. Dorothy Madden came on my first searches in Zurich and Cologne and on one of the Vienna visits, as well as to the records at Dartington Hall. Susanne Lahusen came to Berlin and made a trip on her own to Dortmund, while Claudia Jeschke assisted me on my first search in Munich. For the Paris trips Dorothy Madden has often accompanied me, she being a better French linguist than I, and there we have had the help of Roland Fortin and Mireille Delsout. I am indebted to Laura Delfini for researching the 1924 presence of Dussia Bereska and the Kammertanz Laban in Rome, and to Charlotte Purkiss, who was for a season my research assistant while we were looking at Munich. Hilary Corlett has assisted me in locating evidence of Laban's presence in some of the Physical Education Colleges and courses. Glenn Willson has kindly let me read the drafts of his research on aspects of the Art of Movement Studio and the Laban Centre for Movement and Dance. I have enjoyed many discussions with John Hodgson on Labanalia. Essential family documents in Hungarian have been deciphered by John Dunlop, and he has coped with spidery handwritten gothic German correspondence on the Laban family's legal and financial affairs from the early years of the century.

Laban's own writings are a primary resource, but I have taken the view that his 1935 quasi-autobiography, *A Life for Dance*, should be read with caution. It guided me where and for what to search in the first place, but the reputation I had received of him – that he mixed fact and myth in what he said about himself – led me to be thoroughly circumspect. In the end though, I found that he had been much more to the point than his reputation suggested.

Writing about a man whom I thought I knew well proved quite strange. On first meeting – I was sixteen and he in his late sixties – he was to me a rather unusual elderly foreign man, not of great interest. Over the twelve years that I knew him my youthful and innocent opinion changed gradually and radically as something of his stature dawned on me. He never spoke about his early career to his students, and we never asked, not because no one dared but because the present was thrilling and the past seemed irrelevant. Of course it was not irrelevant, and I now muse on how different it would have been if we had had access at least to some aspects of his context. At the time I found the fawning that surrounded him quite disagreeable. To his apprentices he was a father figure, a close confidant at one moment, an austere all-knowing guru the next, a wicked debunker one moment and a deeply spiritual clairvoyant the next. In terms of sources, my own experience of the man acted as a kind of springboard against which I have interpreted both known and unexpected data.

Fundamentally, the aim of this book is to provide a chronology of Laban's life, largely from a phenomenological perspective. Without such a base, evaluations of his extraordinary output have necessarily been at a disadvantage. With my publisher, David Leonard, it was decided that to reference every piece of information would make a tedious read, for hardly a sentence was written without making use of some document or conversation. The Laban Collection holds copies of the majority of the resources, with the National Resource Centre for Dance holding further data used in the last two chapters.

1

Early Influences

Austria-Hungary, Munich, Paris and Vienna, 1879–1910

The first child born to Rudolf and Marie Laban on 15 December 1879, nine months after their marriage, was a boy. They christened him in the tradition of their Catholic faith, naming him Rudolf Jean-Baptiste Attila. Their substantial house on the banks of the river Danube, Donaulande 12, in Bratislava, with vineyards on the outskirts of the town, reflected their status as a well-to-do military couple working in the service of the Austro-Hungarian Empire. Both were Hungarian nationals. Rudolf senior's Huguenot forebears had come from the south of France in the eighteenth century, while Marie, *née* Bridling, had forebears from Yorkshire, England. Rudolf senior's career as an officer in an army that controlled large tracts of south-eastern Europe and the Balkans took him away from home for much of the year, his wife accompanying him. In her long absences, young Rudolf was looked after primarily by his maternal grandparents, his grandfather being a senior doctor in charge of the hospital in Budapest. The boy was content with them, if lonely.

Marie was young when the boy was born, just twenty-one. A handsome woman, generous, with socialist leanings, she was close to her son throughout her life, in spirit even when she had to be at some military base. His childhood letters to her, cards and drawings, witness the sense of humour they shared. He recalled her as a friend, even a playmate, and she taught him riding, swimming and tennis, all pastimes that she enjoyed herself. Two sisters, Melanie, born in Bratislava when Rudolf was two, and Renée, born in Budapest when he was thirteen, completed the family. A little girl between them died in early childhood.

Uncles and aunts featured strongly in a close and conventional family. Aunt Anna, who married Anton Sendlein, was the relative with whom the child was left most often when parents and grandparents were not available. Uncle Adolf Mylius, an actor, was the favourite, later becoming well known on the Hamburg stage. He was regarded as the black sheep of what was otherwise a traditional family whose male members were army offi-cers, diplomatic or civil servants, or doctors – 'important and dignified people' according to the young boy. Rudolf enjoyed undignified things and felt a kinship with the not-spoken-about Uncle Adolf, giving him pride of place in his imaginative play. Various other relatives, some sympathetic and others dictatorial, became his guardians from time to time.

The shifting population of adults and changing venues led the boy to rely on himself. Being without regular playmates, he turned to his own talents for entertainment. Pretending was important to him, and with his toy theatre he began the planning of his first childish dramas. Featured in them were local-life figures, peasants, wicked uncles, rivermen, Kasperl Theatre characters (rather like Punch and Judy), circus performers, gyp-sies, as well as imaginary people. These characters spoke and sang to texts written by the boy, and of course they danced, for everyone danced in those days. As he wrote years later, 'When I was a child peasant dances, religious ceremonies, court ceremonials and similar movement manifestations were still alive in my home country.' He included working movements in his plays, for occupations were still accompanied by singing, and skilled move-ments had rhythmic patterns. He wrote ballads which he presented to the household in *tableaux vivants*, with mixed enthusiasm from his guardians. Drawing was a solace. The man who taught him worked in the local theatre preparing the stage cloths there, and he sneaked the boy in to watch. But the theatre was regarded by the family, and indeed by most bourgeois families, as a dubious place for a boy of good standing to become too closely associated with: one went to the theatre, enjoyed it, but one did not work in it. Good Catholic painters existed, and drawing and painting were considered as respectable childhood occupations but definitely not as a worthy career.

From time to time the boy joined his father 'in the borderlands', the distant parts of the empire where his father was posted – Sarajevo, Mostar, Nevesinje Fort, or Constantinople. These visits began when he was twelve years old, able to ride well and to cope with the wild country and rough living conditions of military life, but still an imaginative child. He loved the excitement of manoeuvres, the discipline and pageantry of parades and musters, the adventure of forays into the mountains, where Turkish bandits lurked, and wolves and snakes surprised. While in the charge of young officers, the boy encountered danger and fear in legitimate military activi-ties. His vivid imagination translated these events into stories of goblins and giants, witches and fiends.

When alone, he explored the wilderness. Nature was physically and inventively experienced. Stones and rocks were jagged manifestations of spirits, natural cities for imagined creatures. Plants were greedy eaters with intoxicating smells, or starving weeds hanging on for dear life in the dry aridness of the stony outcrops of the Balkan mountainside. Animals, courageous and cunning, dextrous and stealthy, were spirits side by side with the plants and the rocks, inhabiting grottos and caves, ledges and clefts, gorges and lakes. These things the boy turned into dramas and songs and dreams, filling his head with a love and awe of nature, not as a world outside himself but a world with which he was one. From these experiences developed his first plans for a production, which he called *Die Erde* (The Earth), multi-media in his imagination, to be moved, spoken and sung by large masses of performers. He had neither the skills nor the facilities to try it out until years later, but these direct encounters with natural phenomena came to be a rich resource for his later creative work.

On one of his adolescent trips to the Balkans, probably to Constantinople, while under the guidance of an Imam, he encountered the Sufi brotherhood, Muslim lay brothers with special responsibilities. These were the Dervish dancers whose prayers were manifest in movement, in whirling until a trance was induced. In some instances, in states of high ecstasy, the dancer might drive long needles and nails into his cheeks, through his chest, into his arm muscles, with no sign of pain and no loss of blood. Afterwards no trace of a wound could be seen. This magic of the dance, this power of movement over man, was deeply impressive to the young Laban. He saw it as the conquest of the forces of nature through the dance. If this could apply to Balkan lay brothers, might it be possible for ordinary men and women to transcend the mundane, to find their own ecstasy in movement, not with cuts and thrusts but simply through dancing? He had as yet no idea how this might happen, or indeed if it could happen. But ten years later in Paris, in the company of spiritually aware people, he recalled again this magic and connected it with the psychic forces that he was introduced to there through his contact with the Rosicrucian brethren.

The political and religious richness and inevitable turmoil of the Balkans were realities that the young Laban experienced at an impressionable age. He drank in Middle-Eastern philosophy and sacred practices. These complemented the more Western way of thinking that the Austrian part of the empire gave him. Russian Orthodox Catholicism, Greek Orthodoxy, Turkish-style Muslim concepts and behaviour, extremist Sufi practices, as well as Catholic and Protestant Christian groups, all contributed to his awareness of religious possibilities and human behaviour.

While still adolescent, Laban was aware of a force of change on the rich movement life of the various communities that he met, and he feared it – 'the dark monster of civilisation', as he described it later. 'Drudging mechanicality' was engulfing both gaiety and 'the splendid body attitudes' of the working peasant. His sense of impending loss was to colour his later commitment to dance for all, for this became his way of combating the dark monster.

In the meantime, the mundane matter of schooling had to be endured. Rudolf was not a docile pupil. He attended middle school in Budapest and when in the top class, aged thirteen, he got himself expelled. It was his passion for dancing and his ability to get other boys to follow him that got him into trouble. He encouraged his classmates to join a youth group in the town, a forbidden act, and to participate in a festival. He himself was the lead dancer of a czardas group. He had a string of misdemeanours to his name anyway – breaking windows, for example – so this final transgression was regarded as the last straw by his headmaster. There is conflicting evidence on how long the middle schools of Budapest, *en masse*, refused to educate him, but it was probably for one year, until he was old enough to enter the Bratislava Gymnasium. In the meantime one can deduce that his fourteenth year was spent either hanging around the municipal theatre, unofficially helping backstage and playing tricks on 'stuffy' actors, or with his father, who was by now a Field Marshal and Governor of the occupied Turkish provinces of Bosnia and Herzegovina. When Laban eventually started at the Gymnasium he achieved his Baccalauréat at the usual age of nineteen, although he regarded much of what he had to learn there as of little relevance compared with his self-education.

The city theatre was a rich resource. It offered Czech, Hungarian, Austrian and Italian companies, performing opera, drama and ballet, and from the age of fourteen Laban was given permission to help there, officially. Through his art teacher's stage painting duties he learnt at first hand about design, decor and costume-making, and he became familiar with the standard musical repertoire. He was also active more generally in the town of Bratislava, not only in its theatre: he exhibited his paintings, on one occasion he entertained the provincial governor with his dramatic performances, and he founded a drama youth club.

Vienna was another city that he visited and knew well. As the cultural centre of the Austro-Hungarian Empire, it was the imperial city over which Franz Josef and his court presided with pomp and ceremony. Field Marshal Laban would have been a participant in Viennese court life, processions and military magnificence being a regular occurrence. Franz Josef, as Commander-in-Chief of the army rarely seen out of uniform, became increasingly close to the Laban family with each promotion of Rudolf senior. Invitations from Archduke Friedrich to various cultural functions can be found amongst family papers. Whether Rudolf the younger had access to any of these we do not know, but he would have been aware of his parents' entertainment and social duties. Certainly he became familiar with both court life and imperial culture. Towards the end of his career Rudolf senior was ennobled, a normal occurrence for men of high military rank. He was given the title 'de Varalja'. His son was also entitled to use the name, and did so.

Just what privileges and opportunities he would have had as the son of a military man of distinction can only be gleaned from Laban's own writings and from circumstantial evidence. Photographs of the family in Hungarian costumes of some splendour suggest an official celebration of some kind. Laban's own drawing of himself as a boy in cadet uniform confirm his personal closeness to all things military. He evidently frequented the Viennese theatre and the opera. He recalled attending the first performance of Puccini's *La Bohème* and he was well acquainted with first-class classical music and operetta. Strauss's *Die Fledermaus*, regarded as the apotheosis of Viennese operetta, illustrated the unique attitude of the citizens of the capital to the problems and vicissitudes of European *fin-de-siècle* culture. Historians describe the Viennese as seemingly heedless of the future, with no regrets for the past, living in the limbo of a carefree present that was shortly to witness the dissolution of the Empire. Café life, cream cakes, waltzing, the military band, the court orchestra and amusing performances were the popular public diversions of the day, while musical evenings constituted the home entertainment for bourgeois families. The Labans joined in, but were decidedly apprehensive for the future stability of the Austro-Hungarian societal structure.

Vienna contained an anti-Semitic element; indeed the whole empire was afflicted with racial and religious discrimination. 'Jews were to be found in every social sphere except the aristocracy, the civil service and the army,' according to the historian William Johnson. Although there is no evidence of anti-Semitic content in any document from the Laban family, Laban must have been brought up in a larger society in which those intolerances were commonly expressed.

The new science of psychology and the practice of psychoanalysis were the talk of Vienna. Sigmund Freud and his group of collaborators were prominent in the city. The new concepts of the psyche led to confusions as to what the spirit might be, what the mind might be, what consciousness and subconsciousness might be. Age-old divisions of the human being into mind, body and soul were subjected to an onslaught of questioning. Sex, sexualities and eroticism were topics discussed in quite new ways. Laban saw ethical certainties challenged in Vienna while he saw traditional values starkly maintained in the various ethnic circles of Sarajevo. Female emancipation in Vienna, the western capital of the Empire, he saw in contrast to the maintenance of female subjugation in the east. These discrepancies were the background to his own developing sense of social behaviour and his attitudes towards women and religious belief. The steady hand of his grandparents and the forward-looking views of his mother, plus the traditional stance of his father, formed the family context.

In Vienna the spirit of change was palpable in the last years of the nineteenth century in both the fine arts and the applied arts, through the group known as the Viennese Secession. Gustav Klimt became especially significant for Laban. Klimt's early paintings leant heavily towards a symbolist style. So too did those of Gustave Moreau, the Parisian painter whose influence Laban was about to experience as a student. The Secession journal *Ver Sacrum* started in 1898, and included articles, poems, designs and ideological discussions; it is the most likely organ through which Laban would have felt the reverberations of modernity in the arts. Though it was not until his return to Vienna in 1907 that the more radical elements of the Secession had surfaced, it seems impossible that he was unaware of the Viennese version of Art Nouveau in fine and applied arts, especially architecture, before he started his own art studies in earnest.

The decision to become an artist of some kind rather than follow in his father's military footsteps was made while Laban was a cadet. In 1899 he was persuaded by paternal pressure, and by a personal admiration for army adventure and manoeuvres, to enter the Military Academy at Wiener Neustadt for the training of young officers, an establishment situated a few miles outside Vienna. This institution educated the young man in advanced riding skills, in fencing, in social dancing, in the diplomatic language of French, in German, in military etiquette and nationalist dogma, and introduced him at close quarters to machinery of all sizes and complexities. The report on his progress of 1900 states that he was average overall, with good ability in things physical, but somewhat weak in German language.

Laban did not complete the course. His short stay in the army proper had confirmed his already profound anxiety that the machine would dominate man's soul to the profound detriment of human culture. While this attitude was a common one at the turn of the century, the man/machine relationship being a pervasive topic of deep and divided concern, Laban not only took sides in the debate but determined to put his body behind his words. His wish to lead the life of an artist was far from an egocentric desire to bare his soul in paint, but rather a self-motivated challenge to protect the spiritual dimension of life against the withering effect of industrialisation. He wished to join people who seemed to him to have a sense of responsibility and a means to reawaken the soul of the embattled city-dweller. The decision seriously estranged him from his father, who nevertheless gave him a small allowance and letters of introduction for his move to the German artistic mecca, Munich, and on to the European capital of the arts, Paris.

How he met Martha Fricke, a young Hanoverian art student, is not clear, but a letter shows him to have been in Bratislava writing to her in Munich in June 1900. Shortly afterwards they were married, with an address at Archisstrasse 44 in the Schwabing bohemian district, and began their art studies. The Munich Academy was probably not available to them. Like all such Academies this one was closed to women. It was also competitive, and Laban had painterly aspirations rather than dextrous skills. Several private studios flourished and were often preferred to the traditional studies of the Academy. Anton Azbe's was one of repute, but it is almost certain that Laban, and probably Martha, studied with the man dubbed the Jugendstil Renaissance man, Hermann Obrist.

Siegfried Wachmann, curator of the 1968 exhibition 'Hermann Obrist: Wegbereiter der Moderne' (Pioneer of the Modern Way) encapsulated the crucial role played by Obrist in the development of modern art in the first years of the twentieth century: 'Obrist ranks as inspirer of and commentator on the change in style in Munich around 1900.' Peg Weiss described him as a 'prophet of abstraction' in her authoritative writings on Kandinsky and Munich. That city witnessed the confrontation between the pessimism induced by the impact of industrialisation on German culture and the spirit of renewal manifested by artists in many media, both fine and applied. The result was the birth of abstract art and modernity in architecture and design. It was this that Obrist inspired in the younger generation.

Obrist was regarded by Laban as 'an old friend' in 1912 when they were together again on Laban's return to Munich. This he vouchsafed in a letter to his love of the moment, Suzanne Perrottet, suggesting that he had known Obrist for some years. Obrist had several qualities which would have drawn the younger man to him in 1900. Already well established and revered as a practitioner, teacher and theorist on new trends in the decorative arts, he was broad in his interests. Two issues immediately connect the two men: their interest in diverse art media, not only painting, and their visionary experiences. Obrist was a craftsman, sculptor, architect and embroiderer open to experimentation in all sorts of media. Laban, his direction as yet unfocused, would have had the opportunity to play with ideas under the open-minded tutorship of Obrist. Auguste Endell, some four years earlier, had been profoundly influenced by Obrist's teaching and his acclaimed exhibition of embroideries. 'He is one of the most mature artists we have,' he wrote. Inspired, Endell composed his first essay on 'Beauty of Form and Decorative Art', widely praised as setting a direction for the future. The similarity of Endell's ideas and the manner in which they were expressed in his writings with Laban's developing ideas for dance suggest that Laban must have become closely acquainted with the Obrist/Endell direction at this time. Laban's ideas, however, did not crystallise until 1912, during his second period in Munich, and are discussed in the next chapter.

As for the visions, Obrist's experiences were occasional and profound. He described in words and sketches all that he saw of these occult phenomena. He was at the time studying medicine and natural sciences at Heidelberg. He saw 'a city whose architecture surpassed everything and was different from everything' that he had ever seen. The same vision was repeated together with a voice which urged him to 'Leave your studies, go in and draw this.' The vision and the voice occurred again months later. So profound was the experience that he ended his university studies and commenced a course in craft and applied art techniques to prepare him to fulfil his calling, going on to acquire skills in marble and stone masonry, furniture-making, pottery and tapestry, and exhibiting to acclaim in these media.

Here was a man inspired to become deeply involved in art-making through disturbing spiritual experience. Laban's early encounters with Sufi rituals and his vivid imagination and sense of kinship with the world of plants, animals and inanimate forces made him a ready listener to Obrist. His occult education in Paris was yet to occur, but he was clearly susceptible to these kinds of visionary events. At which point in his life Laban became aware of two worlds, not one – the 'land of silence' and the 'land of adventure' – is uncertain. That he worked within both spiritual and material worlds is evident from his writings and his practice. He wrote in his autobiography that 'in the heart of the land of silence stands the swinging temple in which all sorrows and joys, all sufferings and dangers, all struggles and deliverances meet and move together.' Obrist wrote of another vision: 'A whole city appeared in the air. Everything in this city was in motion: the streets moved out of place, they revealed open spaces with fairytale fountains; the houses opened themselves and showed incomprehensibly beautiful rooms, mysterious equipment.' The similarities of the two men's experiences led to a rapprochement much valued by Laban.

The young man did not progress far at this time in translating of these experiences into a theory and practice of movement. It was not until ten or so years later that he decided to make movement his art medium. Suffice it to say that in 1900 Laban became aware of abstract art as a possibility, made his first abstract oil painting, and set the fundamental seeds for absolute dance as the art of movement of the body/soul. Equally significant, he had discovered that other artists deeply involved in spiritual, even occult experiences, were working and could be worked with. With this he set off for Paris later in the year with his beloved Martha, to enrol in the most prestigious school in Europe, the Écoles des Beaux Arts.

Laban arrived in Paris in the year of the World Fair, that lavish and extensive year-long exhibition and showground. Electric light was the new thing, epitomising modernity. Loie Fuller was the dance artist who became famous throughout Paris through her audacious and imaginative combination of movement, cloth and light, at the World Fair and after. Art Nouveau was the new style in architecture, to be seen prominently in the metro station entrances by Paul Guimard. Laban had just seen this revolution in applied art before he left Vienna in the work of the Secession architects Otto Wagner and Joseph Maria Olbrich, along with the early exhibitions of Gustav Klimt. But here in Paris what accosted Laban's sensibilities was the scale of sophistication and variety, the plethora of working artists and exhibition possibilities. The Cubist period, which would start in 1907 with Picasso's bombshell, *Les Desmoiselles d'Avignon*, had yet to begin. This was the era of Monet's waterlilies, of Gaugin's exotic women, of Rodin's sculptured figures and Cézanne's still-lifes. The influence of the Symbolist painters led by Gustave Moreau was diminishing, but the colourful Les Fauves epitomised by Henri Matisse had yet to find their voice. Laban arrived at a time of transition and attempted to enrol in the Écoles des Beaux Arts, where, if successful, he would have been taught the traditional skills of establishment art-making.

But enrolling was not simple. Just where he studied remains uncertain. His name does not appear in the rolls of the individual studios which constituted the School of Painting, nor does it appear in the records of the School of Architecture. Frustrating though this is to a researcher, further study reveals that in the School of Painting only the names of those who passed the competitive entrance examination to the studios preparing for the Prix de Rome are retained in the archives – that is, students in their third and fourth years of study. The preparatory classes, to which most students went, were known as the Evening School, and it is these that Laban and Martha Fricke are most likely to have attended.

The rolls of the School of Architecture are similar: only those students who passed into the upper classes are named. Laban does not appear but Martha does, in 1903, for one year in the class of Guadel Paulin. The subjects studied were mathematics, geometry, architectural history, analytical elements and perspective. In the syllabi of the Prix de Rome classes the edifices designed and studied were for public buildings. That Laban studied the elements of architecture is not in doubt. His drawings of buildings are skilful, and his knowledge of architectural thinking is evident in his writings. Especially intriguing are his drawings for a theatre for dance. These are more than elementary student material and are worthy of some study; they would be taken seriously in architectural exhibitions in the 1920s and in one in Moscow he was awarded a gold medal for the project.

The *Concours d'Admission*, the entrance examinations for each department of the School of Architecture, took place twice a year and consisted of an eight-hour time allowance to produce the necessary drawings for a stipulated building. The geometry department might require a circular stairway while the perspective department required a tomb. It was the latter department that put the design for a theatre as their advanced examination piece for 1903. It seems probable that Laban sat for the project, produced his revolutionary circular theatre for dance, but failed to get into the Prix de Rome class; or, because of the ridicule that he said he received for it, he decided to leave. One can imagine that he would have had little interest in learning how to design a mausoleum or a city fountain which, if he had passed, he would have had to do.

It was during his time at the Écoles des Beaux Arts that Laban became acquainted with Rosicrucian ideas and practices, according to his second wife Maja Lederer. That Rosicrucianism was active at the Écoles is well documented. The occult leanings of the revered teacher Gustave Moreau suggest that he was a central figure in this way of thinking. Although he died three years before Laban arrived, his legacy was very much alive. The students of Moreau's studio divided into those who embraced the concepts of idealised artworks, under the leadership of Georges Rouault, and those who broke away from the sophisticated and exquisitely executed symbolism of their late teacher to prefer landscape and naturalist methods, with Henri Matisse amongst them. The latter group shortly developed into what became known as Les Fauves (The Beasts), owing to their intense use of colour and 'wild' techniques.

The idealists on the other hand exhibited at the Salon de Rose Croix.

This salon opened through the eccentric and self-promoting aesthete, Sar Péladan, an extraordinary Parisian figure who was both lampooned and appreciated. He appears to have set up his own Rosicrucian order, L'Ordre de la Rose Croix du Temple et du Graal, with the aim to 'restaurer en toute splendeur le culte d'idéal avec la tradition pour base et la Beauté pour moyen' (restore in all splendour the cult of the ideal with tradition as a base and Beauty as a means). The cult of the ideal was concentrated in the doctrine of the order, where mystic art, beauty and idealism were preached and practised. Art was seen as the assembling of media expressive of beauty, this being regarded as the perfect balance between concept and process. Finding the ideal was the only rule in the search for beauty, illuminating the archetypal content of each form being the means. The subjects preferred were legends, myths, allegories, dreams, paraphrases of the great poets, and lyricism. The mystical proportion of the Golden Section was prominent, and Leonardo da Vinci and Michelangelo, who had both used it, were revered. Harmony was a virtue sought within the art object.

Harmony was also to become a keystone in Laban's theory and practice of movement; so too was the Golden Section. Rosicrucian subjects appear again and again in Laban's choreographic works. In what way he was part of the group surrounding Péladan must remain speculation, but that he was part of it and would have participated in quasi-Rosicrucian ritual is propounded as likely by the present Rosicrucian administration. The similarity of some of his movement concepts to those of the AMORC (The Ancient and Mystical Order Rosae Crucis) practices is hard to ignore. But since reticence and privacy are the hallmarks of the Rosicrucian brotherhood, more than speculation is difficult to achieve.

It is apparent that he had access to the psychic realm, which he termed 'the land of silence'. That he learned techniques whereby he could intensify inner energy and experience psychic events is likely. His concern with the centre of energy resonates with the Rosicrucian practice of locating and sensitising centres both within and outside the body. Listening to or intuitively becoming aware of the 'master' within each one of us, or the reality within our being, is an essence of Rosicrucianism. Laban seems to have developed the conviction that the body holds truths which, through sensitising practices, can be reached and should be sought. Movements of gathering and scattering, which any Laban student will recognise as common in his work, also have a place in the building up of energies and centres in Rosicrucian practice, which in turn lead to psychic energy flowing outwards. Profound advice is found at the centre of each individual, and focus on the centre, gathering to the centre, is one way of gaining access. Auras are familiar to Rosicrucians. Configurations in the aura are known. The aura as an egg shell around the body is one image used to describe it. Laban's idea of the kinesphere and trace forms within it and their hidden truths, described in *Choreutics*, seem close to these concepts. Visual sight and intuitive sight are contrasted in Rosicrucian practice. Laban's ability to observe people and phenomena beyond what other people could see suggests that he learned the skill or was born with the gift of intuitive visioning. Rosicrucian practice aims to bring together into perfect oneness two poles, the inner being and the outer being. Each one's personal quest is to go inward, to travel toward the innermost centre.

The mystical traditions studied in Rosicrucian learning include Hermes, Plato, Gurdjieff, agnostic writings, the ancient Egyptian religions of Amon and Osiris, Christian and Muslim texts. The writings of great Rosicrucians – Francis Bacon and Isaac Newton, for example – are studied individually, not taught as truths to be learnt but offered as assistance in the personal quest. The suppression of the ego and of self-importance, both of which decrease energy, is valued together with the certainty that all souls are equal and different. Rosicrucians are therefore not judgemental. Ritual plays a part as a form of participatory theatre through which fundamental meanings can be felt, the movement providing access to those meanings which are in any case non-verbal. Ritual is therefore a powerful way of internalising special teachings.

These ideas informed Laban's decisions and lifestyle. The evidence is everywhere in his practice and his writings. Like all Rosicrucians he did not publicise his beliefs and psychic skills: they would be seen as suspicious, even cranky, by those without access to the psychic realm and without knowledge of ancient wisdoms. The modern materialist has no tolerance for these things, so silence and continuing personal quest was seen as the wiser course.

Péladan was not recognised as a member of the regular Rosicrucian order in Paris: too many of his habits were contrary to the preferred quiet way of conduct. His style of foppish dress and exaggerated coiffure, as well as his doctrine, opened him to ridicule in the cabaret world of Paris. 'Si le Chat Noir s'en mêle la Rose Croix ne sera par sur un lit de roses' (It will be no bed of roses if the Chat Noir meddles with the Rose Croix), as it was joked in the press. At Le Chat Noir, the most popular and biting cabaret, lampooning was the sport. If Péladan's salon were taken up as an object for derision there, he would certainly not have found himself on the kind of bed of roses that he propounded as beautiful!

The young Laban became closely involved in cabaret and salon life through introductions from 'a fashionable poet' who was a distant relative. In *A Life for Dance* Laban described his initiation into the sophisticated salon of the rich aristocrat whom he called 'The Queen of the Night'. Who she was is still a mystery. His description of her seated as if on a throne, surrounded by a circle of elegant men, her slender viper-like arms fashionably covered with dark gloves reaching to the elbow, conjures up images of the well-known fashionable music hall star Yvette Guilbert, immortalised in Toulouse-Lautrec's portraits. But salons run by rich ladies were two a penny at this time. The Comtesse de Saint-Marceau, the Comtesse de Caraman-Chimay, Madame Arman de Caillaret, Madame Strauss and Comtesse Anna de Noailles are quoted in the literature as entertaining literati and anyone of fashionable interest, even dancers, regularly. We do not know to which salon Laban was invited, but that is no reason to presume that it was an insignificant one. While he could exaggerate he could also play down the eminence of his acquaintances. (In one article he wrote vaguely of 'a head of state' as being a dinner companion and it transpired that he was talking of Adolf Hitler.)

From his salon experiences Laban gained a profound dislike for socialite company and its useless pretences. 'The Queen of the Night' introduced him to cabarets, pornographic shows, political meetings, a gambling den, a mortuary, hashish, and no doubt to other dubious delights of sophisticated society. His eyes were opened to urban poverty, to the hideousness of class manipulation. While he did not wish to be part of it, he nevertheless stored up images to be used in his satires of the 1920s. In *Nacht* (1927), a dynamic 'materialisation' for forty performers, he chose 'the rottenness and decadence of our so highly praised culture' as his theme. 'The eternal hurrying ones, the rootless, the sick cry of longing for lust, a dance of alluring, seductive women, a dance of greed; a chaotic quivering accompanied by crazy laughter' was its subject.

He also discovered that the romantic ideals with which he had come to Paris and the visions of artistic plays from his youth in Hungary, even his dreams with Obrist, were considered old-fashioned, childish sentimentality. His plan for a performance of the work he had entitled *Die Erde* as an adolescent was loudly laughed out of court. His so-called new kind of theatre was equated with puerile songs and fairy tales. One can understand why he took to the idealism of the Rose Croix as his focus for the serious side of his nature while at the same time relishing the sour tastes of the city as food for his caricatures. In Paris these were expressed in colour and line and sold to raise enough money to live on; only later did he caricature through movement.

This mish-mash of experiences was the arena for his developing interest in the observation of the human being, the figure, at work and at play. He described how, with friends, he watched and sketched in the public places of the city, creating a crude way of documenting the behaviour that they observed – his first forays into a movement notation. This he did from his atelier, 132 Boulevard Montparnasse, and from the little home that he rented in Grand Rue, St Maurice, on the Marne, where his wife resided. Their daughter Azraela was born there in October 1902.

St Maurice, a suburb on the edge of the Bois de Vincenne, had an allure for painters, the riverside of the Marne being a picturesque location for landscapes. Laban and Martha's house, or part of a house, was beside the canal with a tiny garden. On the other side of the road in front of the house were steps up into the Bois, an extensive natural space in which to promenade, play and paint, an ideal location for an artist and his family. Down the road was a lunatic asylum. There Laban was able, through permission or audacity, to draw and to observe the movement patterns of the luckless inmates. The vision of his work in therapy and in acting began here. Adjacent to his house was a small bar. It is now called, ironically, Le Moulin Rouge. Was it called that in 1900? If so, the rumour that Laban appeared at the Moulin Rouge, under the pseudonym Attila de Varalja, may be true. One cannot know whether he joined other painters and portraitists in the forecourts of the big cabarets to make what money he could from thumbnail sketches and caricatures. He was good at these, so possibly he did. At any rate, he earned a meagre living from his pencil and drawing block, primarily through illustrations for stories in magazines, as well as painting and designing for himself.

Maja Lederer has affirmed that the family travelled to Nice some time between 1902 and 1904 in an attempt to sell paintings, and no doubt to make portraits of the summer visitors. In *A Life for Dance* Laban described a period when he earned money by selling newspapers at the seaside. Perhaps he did. What is clear is that the family had very little money and any way to make ends meet was used.

In Paris, Martha evidently passed the entrance examination to study with Guadel Paulin. She registered in October 1903 with an address at 11, Rue du Vol de Grace. Also in the School of Architecture was a student registered as Monsieur Morel. Could this have been the Morel from whom Laban said that he learned the movement system of François Delsarte? No reference to classes in Delsarte can be located at this time in Paris. Indeed Delsarte's work is said to have been of no interest to the French, but reappeared in the United States. And yet Albrecht Knust, in a later appreciation of Laban, wrote that Laban had studied it while in Paris. The development of his theories of movement suggest that he was aware of Delsarte's attempts to codify expressive gesture. It is interesting that he never acknowledged a debt to Delsarte although he did to many other influences. Possibly he learnt about the system and came to the conclusion that Delsarte's suggestions did not tally with his own observations. Compared with the openness of Laban's eventual theory of gesture, Delsarte's system is tight, suggesting irrefutable rules and relationships of parts of the body within a triadic numerical system. Laban developed his own methods from psychoanalytic theories, and he acknowledged that he had done so naming Freud's collaborator Karl Abraham as his source. He did not mention Emil Jaques-Dalcroze as an influence because although he saw his work he heartily disagreed with it. Perhaps it was the same with Delsarte.

One performer that he saw at this time was Isadora Duncan. She was in Paris for much of the same period that he was. She danced in the salon of the Comtesse de Greffulh and again in the studio of Madame Madeleine Le Marre. Duncan was recognised as an artist of calibre, not a 'divertissement'; as Eugene Carrière said in an introduction to one of Duncan's performances, 'it is a personal manifestation' which invokes a response in her audience. Laban was not so keen. Duncan's interest in Hellenic culture took quite a different form to his. Her highly personal form of art was not akin to his visions of cultural renewal through theatre and the arts generally. However, with hindsight and a more balanced view of her contribution to the revolution in dance, he wrote of her significant role in the introduction to his 1948 book *Modern Educational Dance*.

Laban led his life partly close to his family and partly in bohemian fashion, in a manner typical of the artistic community. His mother stayed with him in 1903, the family visited Martha's home town in Germany, and a second child, Arpad, was born to them in 1905. This birth was a tragic event. Martha became fatally ill with kidney failure. She faded over a two-year period and died in the summer of 1907. Laban, faced with two young children and the loss of the woman he loved with sincere gentleness, was distraught. The children were taken by Martha's mother. That he made no attempt to look after Azra and Arpad himself is not surprising. At that time men of his upbringing did not participate closely in the rearing of their children. One of his first bouts of depression took hold of him, and he left Paris, unable to contemplate life there alone. He returned to the parental home in Vienna, making his peace with his father. There followed a two-year period when he seems to have done little, and found no respite from his mental distress, exacerbated by the death of his father in the winter of

1907–08. With this death Laban's meagre allowance came to an end, and his mother, for whom he now felt some responsibility, found her income severely reduced. What had started as a promising beginning to a career as an artist appeared to have dwindled to nothing. And yet the seeds from which his real vocation would emerge were already sown. It was just not possible for him to appreciate that in 1908. He needed a supportive and artistic woman beside him. After the years in the wilderness he found one.

2

Finding a Direction

Munich and Ascona, 1910–1914

Laban and Maja Lederer, a singer, met at a concert that she gave at the Vienna Conservatoire. Their parents knew each other and facilitated an introduction which led to an immediate liaison. They were married in May 1910 in Bratislava and by the autumn they had made their home in Munich. It was to remain their base until the outbreak of war in 1914. They lived at Hohenzollernstrasse 120, in Schwabing, the bohemian quarter of Munich in a northern suburb near the University. Schwabing provided a climate for Laban to indulge the many sides of his artistic personality. Spoken of as an island of international culture, in historian Robin Lenman's words, it formed an oasis of anti-authoritarian thought and easy-going tolerance. Traditionally Schwabing had attracted bohemians from Austria and the Slav provinces as well as Russia. This flourishing community proved important for Laban, enabling him to inform himself of a wide range of current artistic philosophies and offering a fertile ground in which he could try out his emergent ideas in a practical way. As yet he had not found a focused direction for his life, but engaged generally in the artistic whirl of Schwabing.

During the next four years Laban continued the bohemian lifestyle that he had enjoyed in Paris. At that point he had had an allowance from his father; now, at thirty, he was ill-prepared for, and inept at earning a living. He was never in regular employment, but worked freelance when he desperately needed the money, earning as a graphic artist by producing posters and paintings. Maja was able to teach singing from time to time to aid their finances, but the birth of their first child, Johanna, in October 1910, curtailed her freedom of movement. They were permanently in debt. Illustration work was easy to come by, and for the firm of Uhlfelder Laban created an advertising symbol of a little monk, a cartoon character (his daughter Etelke described it, years later, as 'so full of movement'). Hans Brandenburg, a poet and novelist friend, visited Laban's Munich flat in the winter of

1913–14 and commented on the early Expressionist paintings and excellent designs for department store advertisements that hung on the walls. Laban occasionally managed to publish cartoons and caricatures in the widely read and lavishly illustrated satirical magazines. He succeeded primarily in *Die Jugend* which, together with *Simplicissimus*, a more humorous publication, was at the centre of the controversies concerning art, morality and freedom for which Munich/Schwabing was notorious.

He had some artistic contacts in the city from his brief period as an art student *en route* for his stay in Paris. His friendship with the artist Hermann Obrist was important, providing Laban's earliest documented link to the wider Munich cultural environment. In 1901–02 Obrist had opened a school at Hohenzollernstrasse 7a, next door to Wassily Kandinsky's Phalanx school, which began taking students in the same winter. Obrist, together with his colleague Wilhelm von Debschitz, called his establishment the Lehr- und Versuchs- Ateliers für Angewandte und Freie Kunst (Teaching and Experimental Atelier for Applied and Free Art) aiming at a rapprochement between teaching and experimentation as well as between craft and fine art. In a letter to his mother written early in 1912 when he was again ill, Laban wrote that he was so grateful 'to Obrist who has renewed my faith in the body's ability to regenerate itself'. The indications that Obrist was Laban's confidant on both a professional and personal level are confirmed by a letter in which Laban discussed with Obrist his creative experiments and accepted his advice on which sanatorium to visit for a cure.

The flowering of Munich as a *Kunststadt*, a city of the arts, had taken place in the late nineteenth century, and it enjoyed a reputation for its active promotion of both experimental and academic arts. It was, according to Hans Brandenburg, 'a city which like no other in the world possesses enthusiasm and understanding of the art of dance'. The quantity, quality and variety of theatrical and dance performances in Munich in the years that Laban resided there were copious. Rita Sacchetto danced regularly, Alexander Sacharoff's first recitals were there. We know from Maja's reminiscences that she and Laban regularly attended performances throughout the years 1910–1914. Munich was becoming the centre of a new kind of dancing, of which Laban became a part. The city was the arena for theoretical and practical experiments in a kind of theatre that placed an unparalleled emphasis on dance. The Munich trend can be seen as a striking contrast to the innovations in ballet initiated by Diaghilev for his Ballets Russes in Paris at much the same time. There the chic and the shocking joined forces for opera audiences, whereas in Munich simplicity and corporeality were the call.

Schwabing's kaleidoscopic café culture, with its practical experiments in living, its merry-go-round of artistic activity in the form of cabaret, carnival balls, *variétés*, puppet theatre, and above all its constant hum of conversation, was itself like a gigantic art work, a *Gesamtkunstwerk*. This term described a genre of works in which all manner of art media and art happenings joined. The mix was seen as the embodiment of the artistic spirit of the time. The focus of philosophical interest amongst thinkers, critics and artists working actively in a variety of fields was undeniably spiritual. Mystic spirituality permeated the fabric of Munich's post-Nietzschean artistic climate. Perhaps the most radically utopian and visionary expression of this was Kandinsky's treatise *Concerning the Spiritual in Art*, written in the period just prior to Laban's time there and published in 1911. That Laban read it and was thoroughly familiar with Kandinskian thinking is evident from the similarity of their language and of the artistic problems they both tackled.

The idea that a new spiritual age was dawning pervaded the large Munich art circle. It centred around two intellectuals, Karl Wolfskehl and Stefan George. These two gathered together the artistic and literary intelligentsia at Wolfskehl's Schwabing house, where lively discussion took place and large festivities of a liberated sort were planned. Some of these materialised as part of the Fasching carnivals (public festivals which started in November and went on to the beginning of February), while others were contained for the immediate circle of Wolfskehl and George. There is no evidence that Laban was part of the latter – indeed there is no reason to suppose that he would be, for he had not emerged yet as a person with a point of view to be reckoned with. But his more established acquaintances were involved, especially Obrist, and it is quite possible that Laban was employed by Wolfskehl to put into effect one of his more dashing carnival ideas, for that is how Laban earned his living during the carnival months.

The Cosmic Circle, a group of theosophists, were typical of several groups who engaged in mystical activity, Dionysiac and pagan in spirit, physically and sexually liberated in practice. Ludwig Klages was a member. He later published *Künstlerische Körperschulung*, proposing an artistic education for the body with ideas which corresponded with Laban's concepts, albeit within a more limited scope. The link of the body with mysticism was central to Munich's cosmically orientated culture. Madame Blavatsky, author of *Key to Theosophy* (1889), was a central figure not only in Munich but internationally. Rudolf Steiner had lectured in Paris on anthroposophy while Laban was there and visited Munich regularly in the years just before the First World War. Laban was interested in his ideas on the spiritual and artistic dimensions of living and of education, but did not himself become one of the many followers of Steiner's ideas. Rather, they sparked in him an awareness of the need for a stronger relationship between corporeal experience and the spirit than Steiner proposed. Marie Steiner's Eurythmie, a system of simple movement expression that echoed the rhythm of the breath and of words, Laban found interesting but inadequate as a basis for what he wanted, namely a renewal of bodily expression. For him, movement did not need to be a mirror of anything else. It was itself, with a far broader base than words and breath.

Kandinsky, in *Concerning the Spiritual in Art*, tackled head-on the problem for an artist in a period in which the photograph and the film had upset the role of representation in painting and Nietzschean philosophy had questioned religion and all things moral, ethical and spiritual. His treatise on the direction that he believed modern painting should take towards fulfilling 'the inner necessity' of the artist and of the age – that is, the expression of the spiritual impulse by means of non-representation – revealed the extent to which theories of art and quasi-religious beliefs were seemingly inextricably entwined at the time. In his final statement of the book he maintained that 'spirit in painting stands in direct, organic relationship to the creation of a new spiritual realm that is already beginning'.

The sixth section of Kandinsky's treatise, entitled 'The Language of Forms and Colours' deals with the essential creative thinking required when representation is removed as an aim of painting. The contemplation of the medium takes on quite another role: it becomes the crux. The means to achieve art 'in the absolute sense' are, he wrote, colour and form and the 'inevitable relationship' between them. Colour can never exist without form, while form can exist independently. Form affects colour. Colours are grouped in pairs of opposites, and linked to neighbouring colours by gradual transitions.

According to Kandinsky's concept, the medium itself has expressive powers, making so-called abstract painting meaningful: non-denotive meaning refers to the spiritual, and is made visible through the properties of the medium. The link between Kandinsky's concepts and those which pervaded Laban's life work in movement is almost direct. Laban described the medium of dance, untethered by its traditional limitations, as movement. He believed that this medium must have a syntax, for dance is always meaningful. It could not be totally abstract, for the body is the constant reference point of meaning. For Kandinsky, representation was the tether to be removed. For Laban, in relation to dance, representation was not the problem, but music and a set vocabulary of steps were. They must be removed, to reveal the medium – movement – in all its potential. A close relationship can be seen between Kandinsky's theory of colour and form interdependence and Laban's emerging rhythm and space theory for movement, soon to become his new dance subjects, eukinetics and choreutics.

The outer form of representational art, and the outer form of virtuosic dance, contrast profoundly with Kandinsky's vision of the inner necessity of the artist and Laban's developing ideas on the 'inner attitude' of the dancer. Laban coined this phrase to describe dynamic changes in expressive movement which can only occur through the dancer's inner commitment. He incorporated the 'necessity' of 'inner' dynamics to distinguish the quality of dancing from that of simply moving. He avoided an approach suggested in Kandinsky's theory that separates the mind and body, for Laban knew that in dance they are the same thing, the minded-body, and that the oneness was crucial for humanity.

Also in Munich was the Viennese avant-garde composer Arnold Schoenberg, a friend of Kandinsky. The rejection of traditional harmony in music was the concept that Schoenberg focused upon for his revolution in musical composition. Harmony was a general topic of conversation amongst Schwabing's artistic community. Harmony was taught by Obrist and Debschitz to their students of painting. For them the abstraction of the essential spirit in nature should be observed and expressed according to 'its harmonic linear relationships, linear rhythms, rhythmic harmonies'. Harmony had also been a concept central to Laban's Rosicrucian experiences in Paris. He now focused on it, asking himself what harmonic structures there might be in movement and in dance, what traditional dance harmonic structures might be and how he, like Schoenberg, might question their relevance. He did not know the answers, but he set about looking for them.

Between 1910 and 1912 Laban absorbed himself in the *Körperkultur* approaches of Bess Mensendieck and Rudolf Bode and with the Eurhythmics of Emile Jaques-Dalcroze, for thinkers in Munich were engrossed in the human body's spiritual and physical dimensions. But what consumed him more than body culture systems and therapies was *Kunsttanz*, dance as art, including its history. In pursuit of this he studied Noverre's *Letters on Dancing and Ballet* and dug out old dance notation scripts which he unearthed in the libraries of St Gallen and of Munich University.

While educating himself and pursuing these absorbing quandaries with all his forces, he had to earn. His first full carnival season in 1911–12 consisted of arranging lavish parties and outlandish costume entertainments, word having got around that he was a capable movement director. It was a hectic day-and-night job, and by Rosenmontag (the Monday before

Lent, a mad, celebratory day) he was exhausted. Maja could do little to help him, for in March their second child, Renate, was born. Ill, or rather burnt out, Laban took a cure at the Weisser Hirsch Sanatorium outside Dresden, a place renowned for its alternative approach to health. Overwork, a perpetual state with Laban, led to persistent and insidious stomach troubles and depression. Coincidentally he was invited to the dress rehearsal of the Dalcroze school's opening of their new premises, purposebuilt in the garden suburb of Dresden-Hellerau. This was a grand occasion of great interest to the dance community of Europe, people coming from England and further afield to see the first performance in the magnificent surroundings of what was regarded as the most significant new school of movement of the day. To have been invited implies that Laban was already a recognised figure in the arts. While the reports of the performances were glowing in the reviews, and Laban was full of praise for it, he saw no future for a successful way forward in dance while it remained tied to music, as it was in the Dalcroze method. In fact this performance spurred him on to bypass Dalcroze and to try to find his own way towards a revolution in dance.

The six-week cure he undertook at the Weisser Hirsch was described graphically in a letter to his mother. Equally reviving was his meeting with a Dalcroze star pupil and teacher, Suzanne Perrottet, also taking a cure. He was profoundly attracted to her and they began an all-absorbing relationship. Perrottet's practical knowledge of Dalcroze methods enabled Laban to have a direct model against which his own ideas could be seen. Dalcroze believed that the rediscovery of rhythm would regenerate man as a social being and that this was the precondition for the higher development of society as a whole. With his emphasis on festivals and his concern to find the natural rhythms of the body, his aim could be said to overlap with Laban's. But there the similarity ceased, for Dalcroze turned to the rhythms of music and Laban to the rhythms of the body itself and its movement.

From the Laban–Perrottet correspondence it is apparent that Laban did not discuss his developing thoughts with Perrottet, but rather chose to tell her of them after he had first worked them through. He regarded her fundamentally as a good teacher and an accomplished musician, although he was always curious to know of her reactions to his ideas. The letters between them were prolific in the year 1912–13 when she was under contract to the Dalcroze school in Vienna and their affair was at its height. From their letters we can learn of the massive progress he was making towards establishing his basic theory of human movement. Perrottet was keen to leave Dalcroze and to begin working with and for Laban, for both professional and personal reasons. She wrote, 'I was dissatisfied and looking for a way to pure movement, not regulated and dictated by music. When we got talking and Laban told me about his ideas I knew I had found what I was looking for.'

Maja was aware of Laban's relationship with 'Suzy' and tolerated it. The two women discussed the situation, Maja making it clear that she, with her marital status, had the prior claim. While she was broad-minded, in line with Schwabing's swinging climate, she drew the line at divorce because she and Laban already had children. Nor did she want divorce for it is clear from her interviews that her devotion to Laban continued through to her death, despite his roving eye. The letters from Laban to Perrottet are adorned with illustrations, some about his work, some commenting satirically on their amorous activities. Maja he drew in code, as a cat with a long tail and sharp teeth, while Suzy always appeared with a long nose, copious hair, and curves.

It was not until July 1912 that Laban irrevocably centred his attention on movement and dance as the prime focus of his energies. The accelerated pace of his endeavours into a raging torrent of experimentation is evident in letters and from oral reports of the period. From this time on he no longer described himself as a painter but by various titles, all associated with dance festivals and dance theatre.

His response to a performance of Ellen Tels and her group in Munich on 12 July 1912 proved important. He was excited. He found that her work contained 'marvellous things . . . it differs from my ideas, it contains too much literature but I see from the audience's response that they are ready for my things'. This was the encouragement he needed. The phrase 'impressionism to expressionism' appeared in Tels' publicity material to explain her method. Laban immediately saw the significance of it for his own studies.

He began his impressionism/expressionism experiments not in movement itself but in the relationship of music to movement. 'Exercise + rhythm = expressionism,' he wrote, with the rhythm of music in mind as he had seen at the Dalcroze school's Hellerau performances. Dance of that sort is an 'impression of the music'. As long as dance gives an impression of the music it cannot be expressive in its own right, was his view. The expressiveness of the movement itself, separated from music must be found. The *psychische* in movement had to be studied, he wrote, to add to the rhythmic elements of the movement. The relationship of inner intent to movement itself, well known to exist, had at that time never been researched. Laban started at that moment on the long process.

It was on the rhythm that he concentrated first. 'Musical rhythm is foreign to the human body ... The division of time in the natural movements of the human being has nothing to do with metric rhythmic systems. They follow another law.' From this moment on, when he thought of rhythm it was non-metric, uncountable, the rhythmic flux of movement.

He needed to experiment practically, so he gathered together a small group of students on an *ad hoc* basis. Perrottet described them as interesting people who were out of the ordinary: artists, actors, 'and a baroness'. They worked on sections of *Die Erde*, the trilogy that Laban had first conceived in his youth in Bratislava. He had tried it before, in Nice apparently. Rehearsing this second version enabled him to see how much further forward he was in understanding how to embed an idea in movement. The process encouraged him to try to form a regular Munich dance group. He advertised for dancers in the *Münchener Neueste Nachrichten* on 28 November. He told Perrottet that he had secured a place to rehearse, a *Gartenhaus* at Theresienstrasse 132. His painting, he said, would from now on be mainly for pleasure, and he packed away his canvasses to make room for movement classes. He used some of his designs to decorate the space as an attraction for students. They were indeed interesting, many being colourful working designs of his thoughts on the relationship of bodies and space. Geometric concepts of space and ideas of the crystalline structures of space were linked to ideas of a spatial harmonic system which might have a connection with the ratios in the human body. These were illustrations of what he called *meine Sache* (my things) – his Rosicrucian insights which he was to develop as choreutics, his spatial theory/practice for dance.

Already in October 1912 Laban had made the first radical attempt in practice towards 'freeing dance from the tyranny of music'. Until this time his workshops had always had musical accompaniment, which proved a difficulty. He had no money to pay a pianist and no time to train one in his requirements. He played himself and used the talents of Maja. But the available musical repertoire proved unsuitable to his experiments. The metrical rhythms, the even phrasing, the melodic harmonies all held him back. He wrote his own music, basing it on movement rhythms and phrasing and abandoning traditional harmony. These results were crude; more significantly they were far too time-consuming to create and to notate. The whole process held him up. He wrote that of the two prime concerns of music, melody and rhythm, it was the latter that mattered for dance, for 'melody gives only the feeling'. 'It is better if the melody and the movement don't go together,' he wrote.

He decided to abandon melody and to accompany his workshops with a tambour. He found this 'excellent', for it freed him to move about as he played and gave a simple sound to match his search for simple elements in movement. He was transformed by his new mobility. Not only himself but his dancers could make 'music' while they danced. He and his dancers were now improvising, with percussion and voice, but he wrote that 'for an audience, music is still essential'. He did not yet present musicless dance, but composed his own accompaniment for demonstrations and performances.

In the next month, November 1912, he turned his attention to the narrative content of movement and the relation between dance and 'literature, dramatic action, mime'. They were all expressive, but he set out to discern the true difference in what they expressed and how they did it. *Die Welt des Tänzers*, his first book, which he was beginning to write at this time, would reveal his findings. Dance, he wrote, reaches the dream world; it is the way in which the human being reaches the deeper levels of consciousness. The rhythms and patterns of the dance mirror the rhythms and patterns of the mind and the spirit. They do not depict or denote but neither are they meaningless. Images of the dream world, things larger than life, smaller than life, faster and slower than life, more brutal and more feeble than life, are the dance image. Primordial forces, not the forces of daily life, are the dance subject, he wrote. By 1921, almost ten years later, he put these ideas into his first major theatre work, the dance poem *Die Geblendeten*, created for the Mannheimer Nationaltheater.

In considering dramatic action and characterisation, he wrote that dance characters were archetypes, not the real people of dramatic action. They were modern-day *commedia dell'arte* figures. His characters were 'the tyrant', 'the juggler', 'the princess' and so on, as his later major dance dramas show (*Gaukelei*, from 1923, for example). Action in dance drama, he wrote, concerns the build-up of tensions and their resolution just as straight drama does, but the tensions are of archetypes and of a primordial kind, not those of specific places, people, times, situations. For that, he wrote, words were needed.

A further kind of kinetic material he found while studying the dramatic content of movement was the behaviour patterns of everyday life. His flair for drawing caricatures was found again in his incisive portrayal of human weakness and foible in movement. His corporeal wit was to become famous. He began now to combine acute observation, mimetic replication and dream-like deformation to produce the first examples of the grotesque material which was later a feature of his repertoire.

In November he turned his attention for the first time to the dance of the ordinary citizen by attempting to promote his idea of *Freier Tanz* (free dance) to the Munich public. He regarded this as a new form of social dance, dance for all, for which he was writing a 'marvellous prospectus', so he informed Perrottet. He made an impression in the city with a poster campaign, calling for reform in social dance. Hans Brandenburg later recalled this as his first encounter with the name 'Laban', which was plastered all over the city. The practical work of creating posters, paying for them to be printed, rushing around the city pasting them up on billboards, took his energy. But he returned straight away to his theoretical problems.

It was on the further clarification of the differences between rhythm in music and rhythm in the body that he concentrated early in 1913. He described movement rhythm as 'the poetry of bodily tensions'. It included play between equilibrium and counterweight in constant flux, and dealt with the struggle between time and 'the exuberance and range of volume' in movement, its plasticity. Spatial form was expressed through movement rhythm, he wrote to Perrottet. He was adamant that to want to express a polyphonic work through movement was 'perverse', referring to Isadora Duncan's use of Beethoven and symphonic music. Her solution for the dance of the future was no solution at all, he wrote. 'Polyphony of the body' was a Dalcroze phrase. Laban's opinion was that such a thing did not exist as a natural phenomenon in movement. The body could not follow two trace forms in space with clear intention. Such co-ordination, beloved of Dalcroze, was an exercise. By May he felt that he had uncovered essential polarities as elements of movement rhythm. As yet, however, he had no able performers to try out his ideas adequately, let alone demonstrate them successfully in public.

He also had to spend time in the winter of 1912–13 earning money through the Munich carnival celebrations which, as before, seemed to be an almost constant run of balls and events in November, December and January. Robin Lenman describes how Munich carnival was becoming increasingly commercial, with throngs of tourists integrating with the street processions. Laban used his charismatic personality to organise enthusiastic amateurs to participate in pantomimes and dance entertainments, his small group of students acting as soloists. But the massive call on his energies taken by dealing with large crowds of overexcited participants while at the same time struggling non-stop with his researches made him ill again. He could not teach in the Theresienstrasse studio, so lost some of his students. The recurrent saga of his inability, through illness, to pay his creditors meant that he was turned out by his landlord. He moved his headquarters to Klarstrasse 11, calling it his Atelier für Tanz und Bühnenkunst Rudolf von Laban-Varalja, his studio for dance and theatre art.

His attempts to establish any teaching on a regular basis were fraught. Throughout his life he needed people to work with him, to provide a reliable support for his own innovations and to act as equal collaborators, people with whom he could share his ideas and get a response. He was fundamentally a unique mix of creative artist and avid researcher, irritated by administration, an inspiring guru, never a daily teacher. Together with these temperamental difficulties, his poor health, his antipathy for doing anything purely to make money, his constant worry over how to support his family, meant that he never got his Munich school work going in any thing other than an *ad hoc* chaos until the autumn of 1913. By then Perrottet was with him to be the reliable support, and Marie Wiegmann (later Mary Wigman) had joined him to become the collaborator.

As carnival 1913 came to its climax on Rosenmontag, Laban wrote, 'It drives everyone crazy . . . they are starting to point me out as "the dancing master".' It would seem that his carnival performances were attracting more attention than in the previous season, but personally he was frustrated with having insufficient resources to ensure their success. Two seasons of carnival commissions were enough. Laban was eager to move his work away from the trivial cabaret atmosphere. He was dissatisfied, feeling that he somehow achieved a 'practical way of working without a method' and that his performers were unresponsive when he pushed them intellectually. On the bright side, he vouchsafed to Perrottet that he was making progress on *meine Sache*. These were spilling over from the esoteric into a practical theory of the body's space. He wrote that he was working on 'something else that would include all that I have learnt this winter'. This surely was the beginning chapters of *Die Welt des Tänzers*.

He also told Perrottet that he had met a musician 'with a strong rhythmic facility' who wanted to work with him, and an architect 'who does good decor in theatres'. Who they were we do not know, but these contacts may well have been through the Artists' Theatre, newly opened in Munich as a place of experimentation. Laban may also have begun his contacts with the Munich Werkbund fraternity of applied artists, which included leading architects Henry Van de Velde, Peter Behrens and Bruno Taut, all acquaintances of Hermann Obrist. Hans Brandenburg, who was beginning to be seriously interested in Laban's ideas, had connections with the Werkbund also. Although not a member himself, his wife Dora was. This organisation provided the main meeting ground for architects, and Laban, with the model of a revolutionary theatre for dance submitted in his student days in Paris, must surely have had entry to that community.

The exhausting winter season over, Laban went on a speculative visit to Monte Verità in early May 1913. By that time the 'Mountain of Truth', near Ascona in the foothills of the Alps in the Swiss canton of Ticino, was established as a centre for experimental living according to artistic, spiritual, and anarchistic principles. It had arisen as an antidote to the bourgeois intellectual society of *fin-de-siècle* Europe. In its promotion of alternative ways of living and thinking, Monte Verità shared a common philosophy with Munich/Schwabing as a place where life was lived in the spirit of the artist's life, life itself becoming a work of art. The original group, among them the Belgian Henri Oedenkoven, had met in Munich in 1900 to finalise plans to purchase the land in Ticino in order to set up a colony amongst the various and somewhat scattered groups of people who were settling there away from the suffocation of metropolitan life. Nature cures, vegetarianism, psychoanalysis, a refreshing look at the body, nudism and sexuality, together with various approaches to spirituality, including freemasonry, were all flourishing by the time Laban explored possibilities for his work there. Visitors and settlers had come and continued to do so from all over Europe, but the connection with Munich was particularly lively. Schwabing was well represented there, and Laban's choice of Monte Verità was an obvious one.

He went, he said, in order to explore possibilities for establishing a permanent school there. He had as yet not succeeded in doing so in Munich, and thought that Ascona might provide a supportive environment, both spiritually and financially, in which he could really get his work started. By mid-May plans for a *Schule für Kunst*, a School for the Arts, were in place, and also for his family and his somewhat *ad hoc* Munich group to join him, at any rate for the summer season.

Oedenkoven discussed Laban's role with him and embraced his ideas. It was agreed that he should arrange and organise the spiritual life of the colony through the arts. He should do it following his own religious conceptions. It is clear that the School for the Arts was more than its name implied. It constituted a vehicle for spiritual education and festive celebrations of the spiritual dimension, not only for the students of the school but for the whole colony. He was given the opportunity to try out his growing belief that everyone should dance, could dance, and that a renewed form of community dance should be sought.

Laban's 'religious conceptions' combined his own ideas on the spirit with those of three sources, the Muslim Sufis, the Rosicrucians and the anthroposophists. From the Sufis he had formed a firm belief that he expressed to Perrottet: 'dancing has a power over man'. This power, this magic, he saw as 'choreosophic'; that is, as embodying primordial wisdom through dance ceremonial. From the Rosicrucians he had also learnt esoteric wisdom and skills to make use of psychic energy. Although Laban had no direct link with Gurdjieff, the latter's writings describe sacred practices that have similar sources to Laban's and give some insight into Rosicrucian and Sufi ritual. The purpose of their trance-inducing practice was to transcend the space/time limitations of the present and to gain a 'power of attention' and 'degree of control over the state of consciousness', as John Bennett put it in his writings on Gurdjieff. Thirdly, Laban was familiar with the Eurythmie of the anthroposophist Marie Steiner. Out of these experiences and his own researches he had to find his own method for his artistic colony.

His group began to assemble in June, to find lodgings in the ramshackle summer bungalows dotted on the hillside. Suzy Perrottet, who had spent a few weeks only as a student in Munich, was allotted the task of apprentice teacher of music, Maja was in charge of singing, and Karl Weysel, an artist friend and student, became the assistant for painting. Also with them were Lola Zimmermann and Betty Baaron Samao, his children's young minder.

Mary Wigman joined the school as a pupil. She had learnt from a painter acquaintance, Emil Nolde, about the movement workshops and innovative methods of Laban. She knew too of Perrottet's decision to leave Dalcroze's employment to study the new ways. It was here on the Mountain of Truth in June 1913 that the two monumental figures of the future new German dance began their collaborative years. As Laban recalled in 1935, 'there was also the young artist who is today considered the greatest dancer in Germany. Her tremendous gift of capturing something of the forces of nature in her dances was brought to a great height through our work together, and we looked forward with pleasure to the effect this would have.' In June 1913 she was simply a new student.

Living in harmony with nature and the cosmos were essential features of Laban's spiritual sources and of Oedenkoven's philosophy. They achieved it through living the simple life absolutely, growing their own vegetables, cooking their own food, weaving plain cloth and making it into simple saris and cloaks. They danced outside, shoeless or with soft home-made sandals in order to feel the earth, minimal clothing and sometimes none – although Laban himself was never naked, nor did he regard it as necessary. The ground was to be touched, the air to be breathed, the wind to be felt on the skin, the night sky to be danced with. Every day had a festive moment in which the spiritual attitude filled the dancers with what Laban called a sense of mutuality and an appreciation of the personal integrity of each individual.

Not that all was serious on Monte Verità. Laban's wicked sense of humour was never hidden for long. Caricature and mime were his means, thumbnail movement profiles of fellow colonists and of each other threw them all into joyous hilarity. His personality was charming, his interest in each one was disarming, his charisma was mesmerising, his sheer getting-to-the-crux-of-it was overwhelming. Most people fell under his spell, although a few were disenchanted by his sexual appetite, which even in an atmosphere of free love was disconcertingly copious and eclectically satisfied.

Mary Wigman's very personal diary reveals her agonised feelings towards the intimate relationship of Laban and Suzy. She found herself not only enthralled by Laban's working methods but by the man himself. She craved his attention, she desired him, and like most women her soul was inflamed by him. But he had eyes only for Suzy. Wigman suffered tortuously, as much because he would not look at her work as not look at her as a woman. She could not bear to see how Suzy devoured him, left him weakened, and was, as she saw it, unreasonably demanding of him, both in private and in public, and how he was besotted with her. It was not Suzy's artistry but her body and their mutual eroticism that satisfied him. The Laban–Perrottet correspondence includes spiteful caricatures of Wigman's earnestness, but it also contains derogatory sketches of Laban and Suzy, sometimes Maja.

Though this unhappiness might have been a simple and passing case of young jealousy, it was in fact much more significant, for Laban spurned Wigman's womanliness, while casually slipping in and out of the arms of other women. It set up in her a deep hurt which surfaced as a dangerous force throughout the years that they led German dance. If she could not equal Perrottet on an intimate level (and it is possible that in her more reflective moments she did not want to), she would surpass her professionally. If she could not reach Laban himself on intimate terms she developed a determination to equal, if not surpass him, as an artist. This determination, starting as an incentive to wonderful experimentation, was to turn gradually into an uncontrolled sense of injustice during the next twenty years. In fact Laban needed her, admired her, and eventually taught her what she vouchsafed she needed most: to stand on her own artistic feet. But in 1913, her torment was real, and, I believe, damaging in the future to German dance, as will be revealed.

The experimentations in dance took place from June. Throughout the season, the *Schwungskalen* (literally, swinging scales) were his basic training method, together with dynamic improvisations, group studies and individual creative enterprises. A *Schwung* was a movement with momentum and energy, not a pendulum swing but a large movement involving the whole body. A scale arose when the end of each swing became the preparation for the next. The first scale he used, the five-scale, was a series of swings which returned to the starting point on the fifth, swinging through forward to upward, to down, to across, to open, to back (across the body), and repeat. This series he described as arising naturally, in fencing and (on a smaller scale) in behaviour, rather than being artificially devised by him. The dimensional scale (six swings) and the diagonal scale (eight swings) were the next forms to be decided upon, with the octahedron and the cube being the body-sized spatial scaffolding imagined around the mover, so giving the swings a directional framework. He chose the term 'scale' to parallel musical practice. His scales were the way in which his dancers warmed up daily, and developed their technique.

During the summer two of Laban's first works were created. *The Dancing Drumstick*, a sequence of dances, used the language of ancient Mexican drum messages as its source. Laban saw all sounds as the result of movements. He did not believe that primordial rhythmic messages of drummers communicated phonetically, like present-day Morse code, but were rhythms of the body made audible. While modern man tried to understand audible and kinetic gestures, explain them and interpret them verbally, primordial man possessed the sensitivity to comprehend meaning through bodily experience. To them explanation was superfluous. 'True dancers are biological innocents', he avowed, and have that sensitivity. *The Dancing Drumstick* explored that primordial comprehension.

The second work, *Ishtar's Journey into Hades*, had a narrative starting point. The Queen (Ishtar) removed an ornament or a garment at each gateway until she stood naked at Hades' gate. Laban translated these ideas into archetype and dream-world symbols. He described how she cast off not worldly garments, but 'the crown of pride, the cloak of hypocrisy, the sceptre of violence, the necklace of vanity, the veil of selfishness, the girdle of cowardice and ended, purified, with a noble dance'. With this work he began to form one of his choreographic methods: specificity combined with freedom. In this case parts of the dancer's body were connected with behavioural images which were specified and focused upon, in sequence, each starting point being transformed into spatial/dynamic gestural phrases.

Laban made *Ishtar*, he said, to present to his dancers his credo of utter simplicity and rejection of superficiality. It presented his belief in them as artists, able to take on a bodily limitation to their movement and able to maximise their own creativity with that limitation. It was this no-nonsense attitude that Wigman found releasing, together with Laban's welcome to all individual differences of physique and personal movement style. His Rosicrucian belief in the value of a non-judgemental attitude to people and events was a lived truth for him.

For the dancer the body took on a new significance through Laban's lived assertion of the power of the unified human being. He implicitly denied Cartesian dualism. Body–mind oneness was found in its essence in the dancing dancer, the lived body, the dynamic person. His problem was to find adequate words for his work, for no verbal language existed that could capture the unity, or the flux, or the dynamism of the dancer. 'Step', 'quick', 'arm' – such words describe an objectified body, but no words capture the lived experience of stepping out, the excitement of quickening, the sensation of swinging arms. Spurred on by this problem, he returned daily to his stressful search for a symbol system that could capture movement on paper, a *Tanzschrift*, a dance notation.

The first season at Monte Verità ended, having established Laban both in his own eyes and those who worked with him. His name started to spread as a teacher with something quite astounding to offer. He, Maja and their two children moved back to Munich to a new address, Maximilianstrasse 24. Suzy came with them and a *ménage à trois* was agreed on. They planned and advertised the opening of the Munich school for Tanz, Ton, Wort (Dance, Sound, Word), now at a studio in Schwanthalerstrasse 37. By the end of October Wigman had arrived as a student and Karl Weysel returned as an assistant/student. Wigman's ambivalent position as an exceptionally talented person and erstwhile student of Suzy's at Dalcroze, though a much better dancer, made for a slightly charged air in Schwanthalerstrasse.

The autumn began with quite another feeling for Laban than the chaos of 1912. He felt he could really progress and went at it with tumultuous energy. The school attracted a few students almost immediately. One was Jo Meisenbach, who was to remain a supportive friend of Laban all their lives. A series of lecture-demonstrations was rehearsed and given to publicise the school, with Wigman, Perrottet, Weysel and Laban leading the cast. One at least was at the Bayerische Hof Hotel. Munich felt that something strange but notable was happening.

The season's carnival work began again, but this year Laban's productions were sufficiently accomplished and successful for there to be notices in the press. On 23 January 1914 he produced *In the Grove of Aesculapius* for the Munich doctors' carnival celebration, the Ballo Medico. It was a wild comedy that took place 'in the shade of trees before the altar of the god of physicians'. Basically a spoof on medical methods, the piece experimented with group forms and group ceremonial, with outrageous props and costumes. A week later he gave a serious lecture-demonstration at the City Museum before an invited audience, including Hans Brandenburg. 'Four women and two men' illustrated his talk, and demonstrated a crude notation system. The event was well but politely received, according to the *Münchener Neueste Nachrichtung*, but earned him nothing. With the birth of his and Maja's third child, Georg, in February, the budget was tighter than ever.

Shortly afterwards, Laban organised the Munich Press Carnival festival as a 'Wallhalla Ball' in which a burlesque, *The Birth of the Dance in Hell*, was the entertainment danced primarily by his group. The chaotic rehearsals, costume making and fitting, props and set creation, and necessary cajoling of vast numbers of amateur performers is described in *A Life for Dance*. The live orchestral accompaniment had also to be produced. One day the orchestral parts were missing as the players sat down to start the show. Panic? No. The solution? Laban asked them what they could play by heart. One half knew *The Merry Widow*, the other a Wagner overture. All played, simultaneously. It was greeted, so Laban wrote, as a tremendous modern composition. Laban claimed it as his own 'Barbarian Symphony'. The spirit of improvisation, of tongue-in-cheek fun, was never far from carnival, nor from Laban, ever.

He continued his hectic programme with a school performance of *Der Freie Tanz* – dance freed from musical constraint and from a set vocabulary of steps. On 11 February 1914 two students gave a public performance. Ymelda Juliewna Mentelberg was to have given it alone but she asked Mary Wigman to help her. Wigman created and danced *Lento* and *Hexentanz* (Witch Dance). For the latter she wore a mask, her black hair wild behind it, a shapeless garment disguising her person. The convulsive figure, moving with a dynamic strength never seen before, squatting, slapping, grasping, vibrating, commanded the space, and demanded the percussionist's sporadic outbursts. The audience were riveted by her hideous but compelling performance. With *Lento* she showed her fluidity and delicate passion. Mentelberg got hardly a mention.

Wigman's first performances were highly significant for her and also for Laban. It was she who took Laban's ideas a step further than he could at this point, namely into the theatre. Her stunning ability, her uncompromising compositions, her courage to present musicless dance in the theatre began to establish a reputation not only for herself, as one might expect, but also for Laban. Both were seen as forces to be reckoned with in the theatre. With Karl Weysel as a partner she presented what Laban had not quite been able to present: the absolute dance, the autonomous dance. What Laban had inspirationally prepared through workshops, in lecture-demonstrations, on the hilltops of Monte Verità, she brought into the full glare of a theatre audience. And won. She danced her first full evening, with Weysel, on 28 April 1914 and received from the critic Rudolf Delius unequivocal recognition of her promise as the new figure in German dance.

On 30 April advertisements for the second summer school at Monte Verità appeared. As well as the classes in the 'School of Art for Dance, Sound and Word' there was to be a major production of Hans Brandenburg's *Sieg des Opfers* (Victory Through Sacrifice), on which rehearsals would focus. Brandenburg's *Der Moderne Tanz*, written before he knew of Laban's work and so too late to include him, had just been published. But his support was influential for Laban's attainment of a public profile at this point. He helped Laban by assembling and commenting upon critical reviews of all mentions of his work, turning them into a publicity brochure. He recognised the full importance of Laban's innovations during their 1914 collaboration. By describing them as stemming from 'necessity and inner force' he linked Laban with the art movements of the day, especially the Blaue Reiter group under Kandinsky. The second edition of *Der Moderne Tanz*, published in 1917 but written in 1914, confirmed and emphasised the transformation of the modern dance scene which Brandenburg saw had been brought about by Laban's revolutionary methods. It was not until the third edition in 1921 that an entirely new section on 'The Laban School' could be included.

Laban recalled how Brandenburg 'saw in our group the perfect instrument for the realisation of his poetry' in *Sieg des Opfers*. It was to be performed in Cologne. The historian Joan Campbell, in her discussion of the politics of reform in the applied arts addressed by the members of the Deutsche Werkbund, outlined the significant exhibition mounted in Cologne in the summer of 1914 by the Werkbund. The city mayor, Konrad Adenauer, was instrumental in enabling a large site to be available for the buildings, which included Van de Velde's theatre as its centrepiece, with its modern design with Art Nouveau interior and use of the new industrial materials steel and glass. It was to be the venue for performances throughout August. A vibrant sculpture of intermingling figures by Hermann Obrist stood on its forecourt. Hans Brandenburg's choric work for speech and movement was planned as the opening production. Writing this work with the innovations in dance in Munich in mind, Brandenburg asked Laban to produce it with his young artists. So it was that the second summer sessions on Monte Verità included a rehearsal schedule for this performance opportunity.

Laban had corresponded with Brandenburg in Munich on the matter of casting. While he could provide movers for all the roles, he had difficulty in finding movers who could also speak well. The character of the Father in the play was the problem. Possibly Brandenburg had expected Laban to take on the role himself, but he did not. A bearded figure, awesome, and central to the narrative, the role required vocal capacities and a presence that his male students did not have. He turned to his most forceful student to fill the role, Mary Wigman, who reluctantly agreed to try. The established actress Gertrud Leistikow was engaged by Brandenburg for the female lead.

Notable students for the season included the Falke sisters, Ursula and Gertrud, young dancers with traditional training. They were to find Laban's ways little to their taste and later became known as a partnership performing dances of a more decorative kind. Käthe Wulff, who became a life-long Labanite, was of quite another persuasion. She had heard of Laban and decided to leave her job as a graphic artist in Hamburg and try his mode of expression for herself. A determined woman, dismissive of convention, she hiked, pack on back, to Monte Verità with no money. There she made a primitive home for herself in a large packing case and so survived the season. Sophie Täuber, a painter with broad interests in art-making, soon to be part of the Zurich Dadas, joined too, as did the dancer Laura Oesterreich.

Laban, Maja and the children set up home in one of the community's wooden cottages, bringing their maid with them from Munich – a much more comfortable accommodation than the previous year. Laban's mother and sister Renée stayed at the colony's hotel. Perrottet, Wigman and Weysel were the assistants for the dance farm. Some twenty-five people formed the permanent core of students. There were classes in the meadow, gardening, clothes-making, in an atmosphere of impecunious festivity, combining deeply felt involvement in art-making with jollity and amorous activity.

How conscious any of them were of the pending catastrophes in Europe triggered by the assassination on 28 June 1914 of Archduke Franz Ferdinand, the heir presumptive to the Austrian Emperor Franz Josef I, is open to speculation. Writings suggest that they were all taken by surprise when the inevitable war actually began in the first days of August. That the shooting took place in Sarajevo must have been registered by Laban, and surely his mother was alarmed. But the history of continual unrest, local wars and invasions, treaties and treason, may well have inured them to news of a murder.

Their immediate problem in July was their production, which did not run entirely smoothly. Although the experimental way of working with the text was successful, the players were an assorted lot, inexperienced, and ill cast with Wigman both female and too young to achieve the difficult transformation into the mature, bearded and evil Father. But the performance was never to be. Suddenly one July morning no one was there to rehearse. It must have been the 31st, the day that Germany issued an ultimatum to Russia and to France to halt mobilisation, for by 1 August Germany had declared war on Russia, and by 3 August on France. The escalation followed quickly as treaties of support had to be upheld, bringing in Great Britain to the defence of the invaded Belgium. Austria-Hungary, Serbia, Montenegro joined the fight and Japan. The international members of the Monte Verità colony fled in an attempt to get home before the borders closed. All the dancers left except Wigman. Suzy remained, but was professionally marginalised. Maja, the children, and Laban's mother and sister stayed on.

Through this unexpected loss of his artistic world Laban was forced to think about his work, his hopes, his life. He learned from the difficulties of the production that to achieve a work in his mode of expression a sustained training programme would have to be set up. Summer schools could not develop performers with the artistry he wanted. Long-term plans were needed, and a clarification of method. The beginning of a World War was not a propitious time to begin such a development, but in this instance one advantage presented itself: Laban and his outstanding student, Wigman, were artistically isolated, together on the Mountain of Truth.

3

The Nightmare Years

Zurich, 1914–1919

With the departure of the international dance community of the summer months, Laban had no employment, and so no commitments to disturb his concentration. Instead of leaving the mountain for the winter as intended, he stayed with Wigman and worked on. Space was not at a premium, for the whole colony had been more or less abandoned.

Wigman has described their daily work together. It was fraught with argument, with passionate outbursts on both sides. Together they built on the intense study that Laban undertook on his own, namely his continuing attempts to discover what he firmly believed to exist: a rule-governed base to movement as one of man's fundamental modes of communication. In 1928 he was to give this side of his work the name 'choreology' but he had not reached that point in 1914. Suzanne Perrottet did not participate in the crucial daily work. With her strong Dalcroze background and musical skills, she assisted Laban instead with his attempts at musical composition, and in his work on a new tonal scale, on harmonic clusters and instrumental improvisation.

The man's ever-present financial problems were compounded by the war. His domestic arrangements were complex and inevitably costly with by now three very young children to support and house, as well as his wife. Should he return *en famille* to his apartment in Munich, to a country in conflict, or should he stay in Switzerland, a neutral country, and work on with his able colleague? His position was further complicated by the need to assist his mother and younger sister. They had been at the Monte Verità hotel, on holiday, accompanying Laban during the summer festival, but at the commencement of war Excellenz Marie von Laban Varalja was cut off from her pension as the widow of a Feldmarschalleutnant in the Austro-Hungarian army. Her Austrian kroners could not be transferred to Switzerland. She had no wish to return to wartime Vienna and lose contact with her son. She, and her youngest daughter Renée, aged twenty, were left with barely sufficient means to remain self-supporting. They became dependent on Maja and Laban for meals, although they were able to remain in the hotel as a place to sleep. Lengthy negotiations ensued to enable some finance to be transferred through the Viennese War and Interior Ministry, but it took time. Well into 1915, Laban and Maja had somehow to pay their rent.

For the winter season of 1914–15 Laban had planned to open a school at Baden-Baden, financed by Baronin Porembsky, a wealthy admirer of his work. Their plans were well advanced to build a theatre there, and to start a centre for the new dance culture on a much larger scale than his Munich studio allowed. No doubt he had Dalcroze's facilities at Hellerau in his mind. The war turned that into an impossible dream. Laban had therefore no immediate plan. He had no ready alternative that he could put into effect. He had somehow to accommodate four burning needs: his onerous responsibilities as a parent, husband and son, his all-consuming passion for dance and movement, his need for valid papers to remain in Switzerland, and the problem of impending military service.

He was asked by the Hungarian consulate to join the army voluntarily. He was not a pacifist; his family's army background and his own cadetship in 1899 had in fact given him an admiration for military discipline and energy. But he had already abdicated the army once when he gave up his cadetship to be an art student. Now he did not see himself either surviving or being useful as a soldier, because of his permanent poor physical health and his intermittent but ever-returning depressive illnesses. His reluctance to join up could be interpreted as cowardly, egotistical, and vain, but that would not provide a true picture of the situation. He was convinced, one might say clairvoyantly, that he was destined to contribute significantly to the development of human culture. He sensed that he could give humanity more through his pioneering movement work, his vision of harmony for men and their environment, than by providing the army with a sick body or an early fatality. He therefore did not volunteer, and when called up early in 1915 he was in any case rejected on medical grounds.

A home for his wife and children was a necessity, but the difficulties of finding somewhere and paying for it were immense. To this end he tried to find a sponsor for his work, and found one in Frau Gebhardt, a wealthy pupil and admirer whom he had helped therapeutically at Monte Verità. He planned and published his ideas for the 'Labangarten', his own version of a kindergarten, no doubt with some inspiration from Rudolf Steiner's ideas. It was to be a live-in school where children could learn to express themselves artistically, become skilful in the crafts of living, sewing, shoemaking, cooking, moving towards a self-sufficient and creative life-style. Zurich was the planned location, with land provided by Frau Geb-hardt. But she was unable to get her money out of Germany, and the plan fell through.

Maja responded by returning temporarily to the Munich apartment with the children, while Laban decided to leave for Zurich by himself and managed to rent a studio and secretariat, at Oetenbachgasse 24, off Bahn-hofstrasse in the city centre. He advertised it immediately as a *Schule der Bewegungskunst*, translated directly as 'art of movement school', but de-scribed by Laban in his 1951 curriculum vitae as a 'dance-dramatic school'. He advertised himself as a *Festspiel-Regisseur* (Producer of Art Festivals). Very slowly he began to attract students. One, on hearing of his family's housing predicament, recommended Laban to her father, a farmer, who had accommodation to rent. And so it was that in March 1915 Maja, the children, Laban, and Suzy Perrottet moved into an old farmhouse 'Im Hinterholz' in the hamlet of Hombrechtikon, some thirty kilometres south of Zurich. They occupied the ground floor while the farmer lived above them.

This was probably the first time that free love, advocated and practised at Schwabing and Monte Verità, had been brought to the rural conserva-tism of this Swiss canton. Laban's *ménage à trois* was flagrantly unconven-tional. Soon, both women were pregnant. To live, they contributed what they could, growing vegetables and making clothes, which they were able to sell, and husbanding vines. Self-sufficiency was the plan, but in truth they were often hungry. Laban worked with Wigman in the city at Oeten-bachgasse on his researches and dance-making, and lived there much of the week. Suzy joined him there from time to time. She could help him as a teacher for the amateur and children's work which he had begun.

In April they gave a public presentation of their work as the 'Laban-schule'. This consisted of a lecture surveying dance history by Laban in the Kaufleutesaal, followed by Mary Wigman's dance to excerpts from Nietzsche's *Also Sprach Zarathustra* and several ensemble pieces. The press reviewed it with considerable interest. He immediately advertised a 'Laban course' for the summer season under the title 'Tanz – Ton – Wort' (Dance – Sound – Word). He had to pay for the publicity and preparations of the course, but had no money. To get enough together to persuade the printer to do the job, he resorted to illustrating books and designing adver-tisements from his old employer Uhlfelder in Munich. Laban's publicity material, written by Hans Brandenburg, explained how the school's ap-proach to movement education was 'through each individual finding his own movement rhythms, through the principles of swing, tempo, beat, order, structure.' The method was described as 'quite different from Dalcroze's early eurhythmics, where the body submitted to musical rhythms, a pedagogical method inadequate for the human body's dance, sound, and word expressiveness.'

By the next month, Laban expanded his work by hiring extra premises for his school at Seehofstrasse, and planned a rural dance farm at the Hombrechtikon home, to be run by Maja. With three premises, his team was stretched to the limit, Perrottet, Wigman and himself hurtling from one to the other. Unable to pay the hotel bill for his mother and Renée to stay in Ascona, he housed them temporarily and uncomfortably in his secretariat at Oetenbachgasse.

His great problem was how to balance the complex forces around him. On the one hand he was desperate to earn money, first to feed his family and his assistants and to pay his own rent, and second to be allowed to retain his permit to stay in Switzerland as a self-financed person. To do this meant publicity, but that drew attention to his ability to work successfully and therefore to be healthy enough for military call-up again. As he commented to his mother in a letter, no Swiss was going to part with money in advance for a man they thought likely to leave for the battlefield.

Laban's health was a major issue in these years. He was continuously ill with lung, heart and digestion problems, exacerbated by poor living conditions, inadequate food, and worry. Wigman was almost as sick, having to stand in for him as well as coping with her own work in poverty-stricken circumstances. Nevertheless they staggered on.

Slowly his work took root and he hired another studio at Seegartenstrasse by July 1915, with studios on the ground floor and an apartment above it where Wigman lived for some time. People began to listen to him, attend his lectures, come to his children's and women's classes, and to a men's drama class. The eight-week lecture series publicity shows the breadth that he covered: 'Historical and ethnographic overview of the sacred and profane in theatre art and festive culture. The education of the body, costume, make-up and decor in olden and present times. The spirit of the festival, and the performing arts as mirror of our time.' But with his permit to stay in Switzerland valid only till December, and with the military again on his heels, the whole enterprise was in permanent jeopardy.

In November, Isadora Duncan was in town. He wrote that it was hard to bear that she stayed in the city's grand hotels, the Dolder and Bauer au Lac, attracting a large adoring entourage. But he saw her dance and was 'quite interested', although his own work was on quite another tack. Later

Laban acknowledged that Duncan had given 'modern artistic dance its first impulses'. He regarded her as having opened people's eyes to new possibilities, new ways of looking at dance, and for this he was full of praise. Their views parted on how to provide a substantial basis for twentieth-century dance. He described her return to the Greeks as 'imitation', which provided an immediate, albeit romantic form, but one which could not give a founding philosophy valid for this century. He too returned to the Hellenic period, but to Pythagoras and Plotinus, to look again at the roots of musicology, systems of harmonic relations, and to a culture in which choric dance played a role. He believed choric artistic activity to be essential. Duncan's solo dances, however praiseworthy, were individual events to be watched, not the beginnings of the new dance culture he envisioned, in which all could participate.

His Hombrechtikon plans did not work out. His ideas for an amateur dance circle, Der Orchestische Bund, and for the Labangarten children's residential school to be established there had to be put aside. It was hardly surprising. Suzy's and Maja's evident pregnancies can hardly have encouraged the conventional locals to send their children. The new attitude to sex and feminism which these enterprises offered was a threatening one. To live in such a rural and isolated spot was uneconomic; he realised that it could never provide enough income to cover domestic costs and so leave him free to finance his research and artistic work in the city.

Maja's fourth baby, Etelke, arrived in December, and Suzy's son Allar was born a month later. The women were in no position to work as assistants. Laban could not pay the rent. He searched for other properties with land, found one near the Simplon and another at Stein-am-Rhein, but neither place had a population big enough to provide students. Maja and the four children temporarily went to Lausanne to camp out with Laban's mother, who now rented two rooms in a pension there. By April he found a villa in Dietikon. It had no land for self-sufficiency, but it lay on the railway line to Zurich, so making commuting possible. Maja and Suzy returned with the children and apparently Maja managed to find work as a singer. Her voice had ripened and she had some success, Laban told his mother.

Meanwhile he successfully obtained his papers from Hungary to allow him to remain in Switzerland. His work for the dancers, for performances, his writing, his lectures, his costume designs and choreography, his research for a notation consumed him, in and around the domestic upheavals. In February, Wigman, with a leading student, Clara Walther, performed at the opening of the new museum in Winterthur, and again at Bern. Her 'dance-poems', especially *Die Malerie* (Painting), *Die Plastik* (Sculpture) and *Die Musik*, were described as a delight for the eyes and something quite new. At St Gallen and Zurich she danced in the Laban School demonstrations. Hans Brandenburg continued to write programme notes for all these performances, educating the audiences and presenting Laban's profound ideas and Wigman's concepts of dance artistry. All endeavours to find sponsors had proved fruitless and the costs of these performances took all the money that they earned. Clara Walther could be found teaching the Tango and the Boston at Seegartenstrasse as a way of paying the landlord.

In March *Der Spielmann* (The Fiddler) was rehearsed, Laban's largest work of the year, for the April end-of-term concert. *Der Spielmann* was an allegorical dance play for which Laban wrote the music and designed both costumes and movement. The sources of the dance were archetypal characters: 'Unkebrunk, the tyrannical King of the toads', 'shaggy grinning treacherous mandrakes with green grey bodies', 'the innocent young girl, with hair and dress covered in long silvery threads', and woodland creatures. He wrote of it in *A Life for Dance* in terms of its sound content: singing, whistling, the tinkling of silver bells, buzzing, humming, calling, shuffling, and a fiddler playing. The costume designs had the names of the performers attached to them: Perrottet, Wiegmann, Mohr. The unfamiliar mix of dance, sounds and words, performed by both men and women in deeply committed performances, caused a stir amongst the conservative Zurich audiences.

From the scenario in *A Life for Dance, Der Spielmann* sounds childish, but the surviving costume designs and musical fragments suggest that the abstraction was such that it was not a narrative work but rather the forerunner for *Erste Epische Tanzfolge*, his 'dance symphony' of 1921, that being his first major work based on textures of movement qualities. Laban wrote to his mother that his work was beginning to be recognised not just as a local dance school but as a trend towards the renewal of cultural life with universal potential, for which much larger vision and support was needed. This comment constituted his earliest declaration of his belief in his own mission and its scope.

A substantial fillip to Laban's morale was the receipt of the text in 1915 of F. H. Winther's book *Körperbildung als Kunst und Pflicht* (The Education of the Body as an Art and as a Duty, eventually published in 1919), in which the 'Schule Laban de Varalya in Zürich' was included. Laban's sister Melanie, in Budapest, let it be known that the book changed her view of her brother's aspirations. The women of the family had laughed at his plans on many occasions. They had seen them as irresponsible and impossible dreams, but were now reassured by Winther's inclusion of his school which emphasised the importance of the body's expressiveness for both physical and emotional health.

While Laban's work was developing in Zurich, another avant-garde group gathered, who would become the Dadaists. Hugo Ball, with Emmy Hennings, opened the Cabaret Voltaire in the centre of Zurich's old and rather seedy quarter on 1 February 1916. The venue lay just across the Limmat river from Laban's Oetenbachgasse headquarters. Ball, earlier in Munich, showed an interest in the concern for abstraction that the Schwabing artist community were exploring. He commented in his diary, 'The human countenance has become ugly and worn', while considering whether the portrait had any further place in the modern painter's repertoire. He continued, 'Objects in the environment have become repulsive', and questioned whether the still-life, also, had a place. As a poet, his struggle lay in how to accommodate the new abstractionist methods to his own art form. Kandinsky hid the human form and objects; his paintings arose from within himself, through a feeling response to events and people, expressed as colour and form, as non-bodies. Ball began to present language as non-sense, as sound patterns devoid of denotive intent. This he did in his Cabaret, as recitation, to an astounded audience.

While Ball was an innovator with a wish to disconcert his audience, he was fundamentally a thoroughly civil man. Hennings, a volatile diseuse, supported him with similar material, presented more dynamically. Three weeks later a very different, anarchic Romanian individual arrived at the Cabaret, Tristan Tzara. His aim looked far more radical than Ball's: to present not art but anti-art, to break every rule of presentation, of content, of audience contact, through the employment of language, as sense and non-sense, as a weapon, supported by his body. For Tzara the body consisted of a series of orifices: it was a subversive object, it shat, pissed, farted, it was susceptible to syphilis and diarrhoea. For Ball, the body had possibilities that could surprise, but he did not present it as coarse. By the end of February 1916, the two poles of Dada were in place, Tzara doing everything shocking he could think of with his body to underline his verbal abuse of the confounded audience, while Ball supported his own nonsense phonetic poems with bodily exploration and feeling.

Where did Laban fit in, with his aspirations for an organic use of the body harmoniously related to the cosmos? For him, the word and the body were expressions of the human soul. Was he clinging to outmoded romanticism? He was certainly poles apart from Tzara.

Tzara, Ball and Hennings became the core of the first Dada group, soon joined by Marcel Janco, the mask-maker, his brother George, Hans Arp the visual artist, and Hans Richter. All became avid contributors to the Cabaret Voltaire. Laban was intrigued, as was Wigman, but as spectators. They were noted in the audience as 'Laban and his ladies'. Incidentally, another spectator was the studious and quiet Lenin, elsewhere found working in the Zurich City Library, alongside Laban.

The Labanites and Dadaists did not remain unconnected for long. Sophie Täuber was the first link. A teacher at the school of applied art in Zurich and a visual artist in her own right, she had enrolled in the Laban School, displaying a natural talent for expressive movement and costume-making. Hugo Ball described her dancing as full of invention, caprice and fantasy, dazzling and penetrating, at once mysterious, grotesque and ecstatic. She became amorously and artistically attached to Hans Arp and gradually most of the male Dadaists found their way into the 'hallowed halls' of the Seegarten Laban studio, there to engage in sometimes fleeting, sometimes more or less permanent liaisons with the dancers. Richter described Laban, with some deference, as 'stern', likely 'to spring out from some hiding place' and shunt the visitors out of the dance studio into the costume-making domain of Täuber and Maja Kruscek tucked behind it.

The Dadaists did not find many dancers with similar views to their own, for Laban's students were deeply involved in his credo. Yet they were all innovative, daring, and prepared to break rules. Perrottet played Laban's musical compositions in the Cabaret along with Schoenberg's early pieces. Laban dancers began to participate in the Cabaret, especially after the return from Hamburg of the daring Labanite Käthe Wulff. She and Täuber choreographed dances, abstract in character and written down in Laban's early notation method. But these dances were of another order compared with the improvised chaos of Tzara and his confederates. Janco's primitive head and body masks provided the performers with a non-face, to accompany the non-sense of the poetry. They inspired a spontaneous response 'bordering on madness' in the wearers. Masks empower: they cause the wearer to lose the self, to become another. The Dada men found themselves helplessly moving in a 'bizarre tragic-absurd dance', 'festooned in improbable objects'.

Ball described the fragments of this improvised movement in his diary. What was expected as dance at that time, that is motifs and phrases with development and repetition, to music, was not on offer. Terse convulsions of masked bodies replaced the harmonious whole of ballet. The developed, passionate, dynamic force of a Wigman work was replaced by clumsy snatches of isolated actions. The discontinuity of a swing, a turn, a collapse, a crouch, a step forward, in non-sensical rhythm, to shrill noise, was the dance of the male Dadaists, unskilled but empowered by Janco's masks.

The Dada message (or rather messages, for the manifestos proclaimed a series of disorganised non-credos), was nihilistic – a transient, potent protest at the mess the world had got itself into and the impotence of the artist within it. Laban protested too, but instead suggested an alternative way forward, rooted in a free body. Tzara's freeing of it focused on those parts usually kept private: anus, penis, vagina, nipple, armpit. Laban's method removed the corsets, tore down the decorous social façade and encouraged a flowering of the public parts, the torso, shoulders, legs, hips, in expression. He welcomed both the satirical and the decorous, the mystic and the grotesque, focusing on the body as a means to free behaviour in art-making, as his 1916 work *Der Spielmann* showed. For the Dadaists, all was transient, spontaneous happenings, which they threw out and threw away. In contrast, Laban's spontaneity led to finding fresh movement and forming it into repeatable studies and theatre works.

Although Richter wrote that the whole of the Laban School became involved in the Cabaret happenings, he also vouchsafed that Tzara took up with Maja Kruscek, George Janco with Maria Vaneselow (who later threw him over for Richter himself), Arp with Täuber, and so on. 'Into this rich field of perils we hurled ourselves as enthusiastically as we hurled ourselves into Dada,' he wrote. 'The two things went together.' They did for the male Dadaists, but apart from Wulff and Täuber, the Laban dancers were participants in Dada fundamentally by virtue of amorous relationships, not through love of the chaotic and abusive performance material of their lovers. Seegartenstrasse was a 'celestial headquarters' while the 'terrestrial base', the Odéon Café, was where the real Dada brainstorming took place – without the women. Janco voiced the respect that the young men felt for Laban, 'the great dancer with the Assyrian beard', while Hans Arp called him 'the grandpapa of all dancers, male and female'.

Other people known to the Laban circle visited the Cabaret. Alexander Sacharoff and Clothilde von Derp, who attended the Laban School classes from time to time, were there, along with the painters Marianne von Werefkin and Alexei von Jawlensky from Munich. Augusto Giacometti (uncle of the sculptor Alberto Giacometti) assisted with decor from time to time. In March 1917, the Grand Opening of the Galerie Dada was a typical event, the Laban soloist Clara Walther leading 'four hundred people in a celebratory dance'. Who those people were was never stated. Throughout 1917 the dancer–Dada cohabitations and co-performances continued. On 14 April the Cabaret included a *danse nègre* in a style of studied and deformed ugliness, Maja Kruscek leading a group of five women in long satin kaftans and masks. On 28 April Perrottet played Schoenberg's piano and violin solos and improvisations of musical themes of Laban's. On 25 May Käthe Wulff recited intentional garble at the Galerie Dada. On 26 June Hugo Ball performed a 'Bizarre Dance'.

Laban's own work was not only complementary to the Dadaists, but also to the *Einzeltänzer*, the solo dance recitalists. These individuals, mostly women, toured dance work in their own style, with a range of technical ability from very little to excellent. They constituted an equivalent to the recitals of singers and musicians, or *récitateurs* in the society salons. Niddy Impekoven was one who came to Zurich from time to time; Alexander Sacharoff and Clothilde von Derp gave solos and duos; Isadora Duncan was an outstanding example; and, to start with, Wigman followed in that trend, although presenting a much darker side of life than the others. Laban's work was in another vein, for groups rather than soloists, while he and Wigman shared experimentation without music, just with words and poems, offering dance movement with unfamiliar rhythms arising out of the dancer's passion and danced with an unfamiliar fervour and commitment.

The programme for the end-of-year performance of the professional part of the Laban School, given on 27 June at the 'grosse Saal zu Kaufleuten', reveals that the school's departments collaborated in short works which included poetry recitation, dances with spoken poetry, dances with and without music accompaniment, modern, baroque, romantic and opera music all appearing. A mimic-dramatic scene and a 'film-mime' by Laban were given. The departments were named as offering 'Dance, Sound and Word' led by Laban, Wigman, Perrottet, von Langwara and Walther; 'Pantomime' led by Laban, Wigman and Mohr; 'Harmonic Education' led by Laban, Wigman, Wulff and Barmel; 'Form' led by Laban, Täuber, Chruchez, von Ruckteschel and Wulff. The school's teachers performed together with other adult students. At least half of the named performers continued on into a career in the arts, either with Laban or on their own account.

In August 1917, after the summer schools advertised in the performance programme, Laban and his dancers returned to Monte Verità. The draw was the ten-day meeting of the Ordo Templi Orientis (OTO), a freemasonry organisation. Laban's freemason membership in Switzerland is known to have started in 1914, when he joined the Vera Mystica lodge, founded in 1913 by Theodor Reuss at Monte Verità. It was a lodge of the OTO, not a regular masonic lodge, but one which combined Rosicrucian and freemason symbols with the 'cult of Mary' and the 'mysteries of sex'. Membership by men and also women was allowed, an unusual practice.

On the evening of 18 August Laban's group performed *Sang an die Sonne* (Song to the Sun), a dance hymn, on the Asconan hillside. At 6.30 p.m. there was a 'Dance of the Setting Sun', at 11 p.m. 'Demons of the Night', at 6 a.m. the next morning 'The Rising Sun'. It was an extraordinary event, a mixture between an open-air theatre work and a ritual, with the sun, night, stars, and moon acting as the scenery, the audience sitting on the hillside. Laban described how they had erected a fireplace of boulders. After a solemn *Reigen* (choric round dance) around the fire, a speaker, accompanied by attendants, came up the slope. The moment when his head appeared over the edge of the bank was exactly timed so that the lower rim of the setting sun was just touching the horizon. Standing there, he spoke the first lines of his poem. The connection between mankind and universal forces was overtly made. The spectators were led away from the meadow. Shortly before midnight, a group of dancers with drums, tom-toms and flutes assembled them again, torches and lanterns lighting the way to a mountain peak where bizarrely shaped rocks looked down on a circular meadow. Here five blazing fires were lit and a group of dancers dressed as goblins performed leaping dances around and through them. Performers in body masks of twigs and grass approached, what seemed like witches and fiends crept out, tearing the masks away and burning them in a wild scene. The dance at dawn took place on the eastern side of the slope, the rising sun visible through the silky garments of the dancing women as they surged up and over the hillside in a joyous celebration of renewal.

This would seem a fitting work for the Vera Mystica. Nowhere else could Laban have created such a ritualistic happening, and he never attempted one again; but its flavour was not lost in his later choric dances for the city movement choirs all over Germany and beyond.

He followed *Song to the Sun* four days later with a performance of *Die Wunderblumen* (The Miraculous Flowers), a perfectly ordinary group dance work, first performed in Zurich a month earlier with Clara Walther as the main collaborator. Mary Wigman gave a solo performance, and Laban, with his students, gave a demonstration of 'Ancient Rites and Dances' from Mexico, Africa, Babylon, Egypt and the Orient. He seems to have shifted between the occult and the mundane, his imagination and research gliding from one to the other.

It is possible that these performances drew Dussia Bereska finally into partnership with Laban, for it was a month later, in September, that he and

Suzy Perrottet travelled again to Ascona to be followed on the next train by Bereska. A Russian, or possibly Polish, she had arrived in Zurich sometime in 1917 as Olga Feldt. She appeared as an unfeatured student in the school concert of 17 June, bringing with her a reputation of having trained in Russia. Whether she was widowed by the war or the revolution, or possibly had left her husband, indeed who he was, is not known. A private and perceptive person, reserved offstage, she had a charismatic and dynamic performance style. Laban was strongly attracted to her. Suzy recognised that her time as Laban's number one love was over. Bereska was to have a remarkable partnership with Laban lasting until 1929, during which she acted as his co-choreographer, co-researcher, co-teacher, as well as personal confidante, lover and mother of his child.

It was during this visit that Laban decided to found his own lodge in Zurich, the Libertas et Fraternitas/Johannisloge der alten Freimaurer von schottischen und Memphis und Misraim Ritus im Tale von Zürich (Libertas and Fraternitas/Johannes Lodge of the ancient Freemasons of the Scottish and Memphis and Misraim Rites in the district of Zurich). In fact on 20 October 1917 the contract was made with Reuss, and paid for, that 'Laban de Laban-Varalya, holder of the VI grade' of the OTO was permitted to found his own lodge. He became a Grand Master immediately, with a Herr Hilfiker as his number two. The founding meeting was held on 3 November at Möhrlistrasse. Members named included Olga Feldt, Perrottet, Wiegmann, Wulff, Maja Lederer, and the Laban student Oskar Bienz. Also members were the director of the City Theatre, Herbert von Bomsdorff-Berger, and his wife, plus others to make six brothers and ten sisters. Shortly another lodge joined them with a further seven brothers.

One cannot ignore the esoteric sexual behaviour of this group. They inaugurated and participated in 'sexual magic' as part of the OTO craft. They appeared not only to believe in occult powers but to experience them in the body through sexual rites. While history does not relate just what these were, there is enough evidence in the archives of the OTO to confirm these practices. This sexual freedom spilled over into the dancers' work as increased bodily confidence, especially in Wulff. A feminist and iconoclast of women's norms and restrictions, she went on to participate wholeheartedly in the Dada anarchy, as poetry declaimer, negroid dancer, maskwearer and audience abuser. It seems likely that the main body of the Laban School pupils knew nothing of these meetings.

There is scant chronological evidence for Laban's activities during the first half of 1918, but it is clear that by 1919 several strands of his work had progressed. His problems persisted, but despite being hounded by creditors, bureaucracy and the military, he must have continued his mission vigorously. Apart from teaching and inspiring, writing his work on notation was pursued with no respite. He tells us in *Die Welt des Tänzers* (1920) that he studied the early notation systems of Zorn, Saint-Léon and Feuillet, the dance theories of Blasis and Noverre, and also the work of Faulmann and Kleinpaul on language, writing and signs, for he believed passionately that the problems of dance literacy must be solved before dance could stand as an equal with her sister arts. His first crudely workable system had already been used in 1914, and Täuber and Wulff are known to have used another one for some of the Dada dances; and he continued to work, reject, and review until 1927, the final breakthrough date.

Mary Wigman tells us that by 1918 Laban had fully established his *Schwungskalen* to use as his training method, based on choreutic and eukinetic findings. The octahedral space model was already there; so too was the icosahedron as a basis for mapping personal space. *Kraft, Zeit und Raum* (force, time, and space), *Spannung und Entspannung* (tension and release), *eng und weit* (narrow and wide) were all present as basic ways of finding and defining human expression.

Why was all this so fascinating? Why did people who came in contact with Laban become life-long devotees of his work? Much later Wigman was to write: 'Laban had the extraordinary quality of setting you free artistically, enabling you to find your own roots, and thus stabilised to discover your own potentialities, to develop your own technique and your individual style of dancing.' She went on: 'What years later was to become his dance theory and was called his dance philosophy was at that time still a free country, a wilderness, an exciting and fascinating hunting ground, where discoveries were made every day. Every new phenomenon was looked at with equal curiosity only to be jammed into one big bag, where it had to stay, to be studied, to be analysed, to be worked on later.'

Through all the horrendous financial, health and legal problems of these Zurich years, one might have expected both Laban and his students to lose heart. Wigman again: 'And there was always Laban, drum in hand, inventing, experimenting. Laban, the magician, the priest of an unknown religion, the worshipped hero, the Lord of a dreamlike and ever-so-real kingdom. How easily he would change from the gallant knight into the grinning faun! . . . And this was the best of all, and perhaps the greatest of all pedagogical achievements: to be given not only one's artistic independence, but to be forced into an absolute self-responsibility.' And so they did not give up. Everyone surmounted the problems.

During this period Laban became aware of the work of psychoanalyst

Carl Gustav Jung who, having recently parted from his teacher Sigmund Freud, had set up his own establishment in Zurich. In *Die Welt des Tänzers*, Laban mentions the psychoanalyst Karl Abraham and also Jung. Jung's work on archetypes and on the four functions of the psyche — intuition, sensing, thinking, and feeling — struck a profound chord in Laban. That functions of the psyche were discerned in behaviour was one focus of the new psychoanalytic methods. Laban's insight led him to propose that there existed a direct relationship between psychic function and the four motion factors that he was by now certain were the crucial framework of movement: time, weight, space and flow. Although Laban's definitions of the four functions were not identical with Jung's, they served between them as a working model for the oneness of the body/psyche in human movement expression. Other writers that Laban studied in Zurich and mentioned in his book *Die Welt des Tänzers* were 'Harless and Kollmann on plastic anatomy for artists' and 'Faulmann and Kleinpaul' on the history of words and writing. On behaviour he studied Charles Darwin and Wilhelm Wundt. Together these led to the theoretical basis for his later diagnostic work in therapy, and much later, in Britain, in his ergonomic work in industry.

Laban's architectural and space studies, first started in Paris, were now put to use for the development of his revolutionary design for a dance theatre, for which Käthe Wulff was his able helper. As she remembered, writing in 1929, 'Laban storms into my room to discuss with me his plans for our Dance Theatre, and leaves with me heaps of drawings and notes which take me several days to sort out. But at last the model of the so-called Dance Temple is built. The dancers were to enter the six-cornered stage from behind pillars standing at the six corners. Both light and music came from above the stage. The musicians were not to be seen. Laban knew all about the laws of acoustics. This temple would have been the ideal building since the audience was to be seated so that every spectator could see every dance from top to toe. But, alas, it has yet to be built.' (It is possible that this episode took place in 1914, not 1918, while they all rehearsed for the performances at the Deutsche Werkbund Exhibition at which architecture was very much in evidence. We may never know.) Over the next fifteen years Laban's designs were accepted at architectural exhibitions and competitions in France and America, while in Russia in 1926 they were said to have earned a gold medal.

Laban's first book, *Die Welt des Tänzers*, a visionary work in 'Fünf Gedenkenreigen' (five thought-rounds), was nearing completion. There could be no possibility of getting it published during the war. He knew that he would have to wait until he could get back into Germany. It was an extraordinary book, in which he set down in a unique format his philosophy for dance and dancers in human culture for the future, drawing on a wealth of sources which no dance person had attempted before. It was chaotically organised, written in chunks as he made each fresh discovery. Influences from the natural environment of his youth, his architectural knowledge and Rosicrucian beliefs were all in it. So too were the spiritual experiences of Ascona and the down-to-earth teaching and festive culture of Munich, as well as the historical and choreological researches of Zurich. The completion of the book took place under great difficulties, for by the autumn of 1918 Laban was desperately ill with the killer *Grippe* (influenza), an epidemic of gigantic proportions which ravaged Europe, causing more deaths than the war itself.

He was taken to a sanatorium in Klosters, moving in and out of hospital all winter with disastrous financial impact. His family had to move to a cheaper apartment in Altstetten, a suburb of Zurich. He could not keep his school together, nor provide his personal and professional dependants with money to live on. His whole work seemed to be falling apart. As ever, he succumbed to a severe bout of depression. Desperate, he negotiated to sell the Laban School to Suzy Perrottet. By the agreement she would teach the children and amateurs, with Käthe Wulff as her partner, while Wigman would keep the 'art classes' – the professional work. Such an arrangement could never have lasted given three such diverse and strong personalities, and it did not survive beyond 1919.

Herr Gams, his landlord at Seegartenstrasse, loaned him money against security offered by Marie Laban, over and above what Laban already owed him in unpaid rent. In spring 1919 Laban was still seriously ill, in company with several thousand others struggling with the same lethal virus. His continued decline gave him ever greater financial problems. He could neither pay the doctor's bill nor the sanatorium to which he was moved, in Lugano.

The last straw for him was an attack on his leadership of the Seegartenstrasse OTO lodge by von Bomsdorff-Berger, who published a tirade with anti-Semitic content purporting to reflect the views of the Lodge as a whole. Laban found this intolerable. In his debilitated and bed-ridden state, Laban could not counter him, and he decided to resign from the Lodge, and from the OTO. He longed to get out of Switzerland as soon as he could, to rid himself of 'the bad dreams of these last years', as he described them to his mother. But how?

Laban's erratic and ineffectual attempts at domestic responsibility finally collapsed. Maja left him 'to his wandering life', taking the five children (Roland had been born in 1917) with her back to Munich in April 1919, hoping to return to her career as a singer. One might have expected her to be bitter, but she simply recognised his need to struggle on without the family, admiring him, even loving him, till her death in her nineties. His other women co-operators in Zurich, Käthe Wulff and Mary Wigman remained his long-lasting colleagues. The relationship with Suzanne Per-rottet was not broken off entirely: they remained friends all his life. But she was not a sounding board in the way Wulff and Wigman were, and in the way Dussia Bereska was about to become.

4

First Footholds

Nuremberg, Stuttgart and Mannheim, 1919–1922

It was Jo Meisenbach who determined to help Laban. A student in Munich from 1913, not of long standing nor of notable talent, Meisenbach had left the group on the outbreak of war and was not heard of during the nightmare years in Zurich. Yet he must have kept in touch, for he was aware that Laban, the master, was in dire financial trouble. The extensive medical bills amassed relentlessly as Laban lay still tormented by the *Grippe*. Meisenbach remembered Laban's drawings of the harmony of movement and of crystals as some of the most beautiful he had ever seen. The young man, whom Laban referred to as my 'spiritual brother', may have been a freemason, and so, duty-bound to give succour to a fellow brother, as well as wanting the public to be aware of the spatial drawings he so admired. He sought to arrange in Nuremberg, his home town, for Laban's works to be shown in the first post-war exhibition of the Albrecht-Dürer-Verein. A German-wide association of artists and craftsmen, the Verein was closely linked with the Deutsche Werkbund, its professional counterpart. The Verein had open membership, aiming to give opportunities for artists of all persuasions to exhibit and share their work. While not a Masonic organisation, it is known that Dürer himself was in his time a Nuremberg freemason, and a contemporary lodge dedicated to Albrecht Dürer was instituted there in 1900. The golden section and spatial harmonies used by Dürer, whose work Laban admired, were an appropriate topic for Meisenbach to bring to this exhibition, showing the affinity between the two men's ideas.

Laban lay collapsed in the Monte Bre Kurhaus in Lugano when Meisenbach made contact with him, but he was without his drawings. The ever open-hearted Maja was despatched to Munich in March to retrieve the early drawings stored there to add to those in a suitcase in Dietikon. For those he sent Suzy; she was asked to go through the bundles, to shake them out in case there were 'love letters and bills from creditors' mixed in with the drawings. Maja he entrusted to collate them and get them to Nuremberg in time for the opening 13 April 1919.

The exhibition of some fifteen artists, held in the Kunsthalle am Marientor, was open for a month. Meisenbach had hung twenty designs and contributed the introductory remarks in the catalogue. He quoted Laban's extraordinary statement: 'I don't understand anything about painting in itself. Every landscape is an attempt by me to express space, every figure is a dancer, every scene a dramatic situation.' The designs were study materials made by Laban in Munich during the period of his intense search for 'the substance and laws of movement'. They were never made with the intention to sell as art works. Meisenbach described Laban as a reformer of theatre. His artistic material, he wrote, was not colour but 'mankind'. Today this reads as somewhat sweeping but in the German *Kultur* of the time – with its layers of Nietzsche, nationhood, Freud and the expressionist arts – references to Man, the Soul, Community and Renewal came off the tongue rather freely. With people, Meisenbach wrote, Laban creates 'Dance, Sound, Speech, total art works for a celebratory culture'. Stage scenes, the architectural drawings for his dance temple-*cum*-theatre, landscapes, and dance masks were among the exhibits. The critics found his unusual offerings difficult to discuss, but critical acclaim was not the aim of the endeavour. To make some essential funds was, and in this it succeeded: he sold enough to raise 2000 Swiss francs. At any rate he was able to pay 600 francs to 'my financier' (probably Gams), one of several with whom he had taken out loans.

While the wretched Laban lay in the grip of a life-threatening, chronic disease, other dance people were flourishing. Mary Wigman, after a year's absence in seclusion, returned with a freshly created independent programme given at the Zurich Pfauentheater on the 31 March. She was heralded in the theatre's publicity material as 'the most excellent and unique artist in the area of modern stage dance today'. The writer Otto Flake, a participant in Dada events, provided an introductory article on her. Contrasting her with other more conservative women dance artists, he stressed that she had no intent to present a womanly quality, but an impersonal, neutral one, realising an idea, a purpose. 'Dance is to her a religious art.' Flake picked up the Kandinskian concepts of the media of abstract arts to discuss the medium of the new dance as 'gesture, the body, and spatial line', writing that Wigman had no aim to charm but rather to deal with the material of the dance. The spectator was required to think not about the story but about the way the gesture, the body and its spatial lines spoke. 'She seeks a communion with space as if with God.' References to the soul, to space as a religious medium, were not limited to Wigman. The Blaue Reiter group and Schoenberg were also seeking ways to express spiritual feeling, insights and aspirations – beliefs shot down by the Dadaists, Nietzsche and Freud.

Wigman's programme offered four 'Dance Songs', then 'Shadows' from her *Dances of the Night*, a 'Temple Dance' and 'Adoration' from her *Ecstatic Dances*, and ended with four Hungarian dances with Brahms piano accompaniment. The *Neue Zürcher Zeitung* critic was full of praise: 'Rhythm is in the feeling body, the soul of this artist . . . Without musical accompaniment, nevertheless a musicality was achieved.' The applause of Alexander Sacharoff and Clothilde von Derp in the audience must have heartened her as well as the genuine reception by the spectators, he commented.

It was common knowledge that Wigman had started her career as a Laban pupil, so her acclaim would benefit him by association. With her personal talent, she was presenting to the public in her dancing body what Laban was saying in his classes, in his lectures and his books, but was not equipped to present with his own body. The actuality of the moving body communicated dance concepts and beliefs far more directly than written or spoken words. He knew it. She knew it. The public perceived it.

She performed again in May, and this time the programme's introductory remarks contained Laban's appreciation of her dance where he emphasised the rhythm of bodily movement, different but equal to that in music and speech. Even with musically accompanied works, the movement was in control. The music adapted itself to the dance, Laban wrote. The dance was freed. His explanation addressed the term *Freie Tanz* used by Wigman and himself and easily misinterpreted as 'free-to-do-whatever-you-like-dilettantism'. He meant, as did Wigman, freed from the bondage of music visualisation. Again, in this performance her success was clear to all. 'With bouquets and applause was the artist thanked for her rare talent,' lauded the Zurich press.

Sacharoff and his wife von Derp, being Zurich regulars throughout the war, were highly appreciated in the press too. 'A triumph', their 'wonderful spirit-rich dance art' was noted. In contrast to Wigman, their art had a conventional relationship with music. It must have been easier on the spectator, through familiarity with the kind of accompaniment the pair used, which in this performance was Chopin. They were elegantly costumed and some works referred to historical periods which an educated audience could recognise. Riding on the wave of success, the Sacharoffs went off to America. Wigman went off to Dresden. Laban was stranded in Lugano sanatorium.

Between Wigman's two appearances the final Dada 'Grand Soirée' took place at the Saal der Kaufleuten in Zurich. The mixture was as before, but more so. Tristan Tzara marshalled his forces, and the audience responded with ever-increasing outrage, as was expected. Suzanne Perrottet participated in the first part, dancing in a negroid mask by Janco to Schoenberg and Satie piano music, but the spectators let that occur peacefully. Käthe Wulff recited sound poems by Richard Huelsenbeck and Kandinsky with a waste-paper basket over her head, to catcalls and laughter. Next, Tzara's simultaneous, non-unison reading by twenty people of sound poetry caused the anticipated uproar. In the evening's second half, Hans Richter harangued the audience with a speech 'against, with, for Dada'. Perrottet danced to the 'anti-tunes' of Hans Heusser, and Hans Arp rubbished the audience verbally. Elegant Walter Sterner abused them with an anarchic manifesto accompanied by a tailor's dummy to which he had presented a bouquet. The expected happened: the audience behaved like a destructive mob. Tzara triumphed because 'the cretinisation of the public' had been achieved. After a calming pause, the third part ensued uninterrupted, including the *Noir Kakadu* danced by the Labanites in Janco masks and depersonalising costumes. Tzara commented in his diary: 'Dada had succeeded in establishing the certainty of absolute unconsciousness in the audience, which forgot the frontiers of education, of prejudices, experienced the commotion of the NEW. Final victory of Dada.'

Apparently the contrast between the aims, processes and products of Laban and Wigman with Tzara could hardly have been greater. And yet Laban was about to shock, and Wigman to present new perspectives for dance as an art. All three were vigorously denying the old. Laban's immediate goal was not to outrage, but his long-term aim was certainly to shift society's values radically. How to make it happen was his next problem.

While Wigman performed in Munich in September, Käthe Wulff's adventurous soul revolted against Perrottet's supposedly Laban-influenced but also Dalcroze-influenced Eurythmie School, and she left Switzerland. Laban underwent surgery which finally cleared his compounded medical problems, at least for the time being. Eventually he found ways around his financial debts, physical weaknesses, his spiritual depression, and his bureaucratic visa confrontations. By October he prepared to leave behind the 'bad dreams' of Switzerland, to set out for Nuremberg, Dussia Bereska and a fresh start.

Difficult though it had been to get permission to stay in Switzerland, it was to prove far more problematic to get out, and even more difficult to stay in Germany. The political chaos and boundary complexities arising out of the various end-of-war treaties meant that Laban was regarded either as stateless or as a Czechoslovak – Bratislava, his birthplace, having ceased to be in Hungary. To leave Switzerland he had to exit by the same border control through which he had entered. That meant retracing the Ascona–Munich route. But Bavaria was not keen on Czechs, who had fought against Germany. Laban sought the aid of Hans Brandenburg and Jo Meisenbach – but separately, for Brandenburg apparently had a dislike for the young man from Munich days. Laban was required to have a permit to enter Germany, for which again he had to have a profession and be financially self-support-ing. The latter he clearly was not, and the former was difficult to argue. In the event he managed a fourteen-day visa, as a writer, and got into Nurem-berg by November 1919, taking the completed text of *Die Welt des Tänzers* with him and as many of his papers as he could. And Nuremberg was not welcoming.

He had to find somewhere to work, and rented an unheated room, at Josephplatz 10, in which he attempted to camp out. When that became intolerable he slept in the station waiting room. Eventually he obtained a room in a boarding house where Dussia Bereska had found herself accom-modation. It was possibly easier for Bereska to have entered Germany – her other name, Olga Feldt, suggests German nationality which she might have had as the estranged wife, or widow, of Herr Feldt.

The instability of the political and cultural situation in Germany, and in particular in Stuttgart, became the context in which *Ausdruckstanz,* and especially Laban, took tentative root in the post-war period. The Treaties in 1918 and 1919, the requirement in them for reparations, were seen as grossly unfair by the Germans, depriving them of land that they regarded as rightly theirs, insisting on their guilt, which they did not feel, maintaining that they had lost the war, which they denied, and demanding that they should pay the victors, which they resented. However, seen in conjunction with the earlier Brest-Litovsk Treaty, made between Germany and Russia during the war, it could be said that Germany came off comparatively lightly. In Lenin's view the Russian revolution of 1917 could only succeed if the hostilities between Germany and Russia ended, so when Lenin insisted on the collapse of the Russian front in 1917 and the consequential inevi-table defeat, the reparations went in favour of Germany, who demanded both land and capital. In the Treaty fifty-six million people, mostly Slavs, found themselves Germans, and six billion Marks was the ransom paid. Less than two years later the border changed again. With the Versailles Treaty, Alsace-Lorraine was restored to France, Eupen-Malmedy to Bel-gium, Schleswig to Denmark, most of East Prussia to the newly-created

Poland. Hungary lost Austria, which became independent, and Slovakia, which eventually became part of Czechoslovakia, and its own southern territories which Laban's father had governed. These became Yugoslavia.

Laban and his family's situation became particularly complex. His nationality as a Hungarian was uncertain, since he was now Slovakian on the map. His mother was a Hungarian with a pension from Austria. His sister Melanie was a refugee, Hungarian-born, now Slovakian, living in Budapest. His wife was German-born, married to a Hungarian-*cum*-Slovakian with children born in both Germany and Switzerland. From the point of view of visas, passport and finance this developed into a maze through which Laban had to navigate. In Bavaria, in which Munich and Nuremberg lay, the political leaning was conservative, anti-Prussian and anti-central government, while Württemburg, with Stuttgart, was strongly socialist. The Kaiser abdicated, so that anyone with monarchic leanings was distressed, while the communists gained strength and recognition in the various elections, which alarmed the majority of the population. The anxiety, anger and aspirations of the extreme right and left gave rise to the Freikorps reactionary volunteers. 'Forces of counter-revolution', they took defence against communism into their own hands in street riots. The demobilisation sent thousands of shell-shocked and maimed men into civilian life, with inadequate job and care possibilities. Both workers and soldiers banded together in violent protest. Caught up in this chaos was Albrecht Knust, a war-shocked young man, a survivor of three hellish years at the front, who was recommended to Laban, more or less for therapy. Originally a folk dancer, he became a student and thereafter a staunch life-long worker for Laban's cause.

Jugend (youth) was a word on everyone's lips. Youth was seen as a problem and a challenge. Adolescents too young to have fought but old enough to have experienced family separation and loss of parents were in a majority in the population. *Jugend* became synonymous with the breakdown of social culture; *jugendlich* (youthful) connoted irresponsibility; *jugendlich Arbeiter* suggested aggressively socialist young workers. Youth clubs and organisations, already plentiful before the war, increased as a solution to the problem. Youth groups in which songs, open air and hiking were a focal point had long been a feature of German life. The Wandervögel was such an organisation. The *Bewegungschor* and the *Sprechchor* and the *Singchor*, radical art movements for amateur youth to dance, to declaim and to sing together, would become the alternative. Germany was sufficiently Central European still to have a strong folk culture ethic, but folk dance and folk music were rapidly declining. Social dancing was no substitute, especially the imported American dances, the Shimmy, the Tango, the Charleston. They were fun, but had no spiritual content, which community dance had always had, celebrating special occasions, weddings, births, and seasons. Urban German youth therefore received no art culture, something which formerly would have been handed down to them through their community.

The lack of art culture could not be ignored. It had to be mourned as a loss or somehow be turned into a gain. Laban resolved to tackle it, as one of his self-imposed tasks, by putting amateur dance forward as an art form, and by supplying dances to be danced by amateurs, young men and women as well as boys and girls. He needed helpers, for which Knust would prove invaluable, and he also needed to be better known in order to attract students. This he now set out to do.

Throughout these uncertain months he concentrated on the ever-lengthy processes of publishing. *Die Welt des Tänzers* was completed in text, but he needed illustrations. Wigman had somehow managed to lose the planned photographs while *en route* from Munich when she came to perform at the Intimes Theater in Nuremberg. Laban was dumbfounded. The only solution was to ask Perrottet to send two photographs of her Laban/Eurythmie schoolchildren, one of herself and one of Wulff, while he and Bereska hastened to get additional studio-based shots, which were poor substitutes. He was concerned with the use of Eurythmie as a title for Perrottet's school, which was nominally a Laban-based school presenting his curriculum. Perrottet's Dalcroze background and musical abilities had led her to consider the term 'eurhythmics', but she could not use it since it was clearly only applicable in a credited Dalcroze school. Rather confusingly, she adopted the term that Rudolf and Marie Steiner used for their movement work. So long as 'Eurythmie' was used only for amateur and children's classes Laban tolerated it, but he made his opinion clear when he wrote, 'I myself am now fully in theatre art, which has nothing to do with Eur-education.'

His contacts with his publisher on visits to Stuttgart strengthened his desire to leave Nuremberg, 'a shabby, lonely, hard place', but he had no way of doing so immediately. In the meantime he continued work on completing *Choreographie*, in which he explored the grammar of dance and a script for it, and which he was hoping to publish straight after *Die Welt des Tänzers*. While continually working on a definitive solution to the problem of how to write movement on paper, he was aware that other people were tackling it too. He studied Olga Desmond's 'Rhythmographie', a notation written with a mannequin on music notation paper. He found it far too complex, taking ten minutes to read one movement. He was concerned that neither written symbols nor film recorded the dynamics of movement sufficiently well, so he invented an 'instrument' that he called a kinetoscope to cope with the problem. He made detailed drawings of a projector with mirrors and light sources which somehow gave a three-dimensional image, and looked for a patent on it and a means of selling it; but no more was heard of the idea, so it must have come to naught.

He was pursuing the possibilities of film as a new medium for dance. Russian film had made an impact during the war which the German art world was now appreciating. Lenin, in the early days of the Russian Revolution, through his Commissar for Education and the Arts, Anatoly Lunacharsky, had supported the avant-garde and Soviet cinema in particular. Film was new and Laban was curious about it. What was more, Wigman had been filmed, so Maja informed him. Laban, wasting no time, gave a lecture in Nuremberg in January 1920 on 'The Art of Movement and Cinematography', with slides, and in April, with Universal Film of Berlin, he gave a lecture in the Hotel Goldene Kranz. He was already planning how to use film to illustrate his notation ideas.

But above all he was searching continuously for a way of working practically with dancers. Since he was no soloist at this point, he could not do what Wigman was so successfully doing. He needed a company, but Nuremberg could not provide one. Possibly Stuttgart could. In April he managed to move there to a room in Eugenplatz 5, despite restrictions on his movements through his alien status.

His urgent need was to get residency. For that, he still had to prove his usefulness. It was not until July 1920, after eight months of renewing visas, each valid for two weeks only, and twice being expelled from Stuttgart into Bavaria and *vice versa*, that his publisher Seifert, through the company's agent Herr Weber, succeeded in assuring the authorities of Laban's status as a *bona fide* writer and abilities as a professional.

With bureaucracy overcome, he explored the possibility of a job as a *régisseur* or choreographer at the Württemburg Stadtstheater in Stuttgart. It was a staid institution with a staid ballet-master, Fritz Scharf. Although some headway was made, and at least one soloist, Albrecht Burger, showed interest in Laban's ideas, there were problems. Scharf was due to celebrate forty years as ballet-master in 1921, and he could not therefore be replaced in 1920 with any decorum. At the time, Burger and his wife were working with a master art student on the latter's preparation for a dance performance in which the costume design was the prime innovation, the space a special feature, and the movement simple. The artist was Oskar Schlemmer, a post-demobilisation mature student at the Akademie der Bildenden Künste, soon to become an influential figure of the Bauhaus as well as a scenic designer of acclaimed originality. Schlemmer lived and worked first in Stuttgart, and then from 1920 in Cannstatt, a suburb. Was it here that Laban and Schlemmer first met? They were certainly well known to each other by the mid-1920s. Was Burger the contact, for he had a studio for social dance classes in the same building as Laban? At any rate, however much Burger pushed his Württemburg employers for Laban, the Stuttgart theatre job was not made available.

While negotiating with Stuttgart Laban took a close look at the possibilities of a typical opera-ballet's soloists and *corps*. He compared what he wanted to create with the capabilities and adaptability of this kind of dancer. Could he ever get from them what he needed in terms of commitment, expressiveness and spiritual content, for the *Freie Tanz* that he had in mind? He hoped that he could, but was not confident, and so decided to concentrate on building up a professional training school with young men and women whose ideas were compatible with his own. Herta Feist, later to become a passionate teacher and amateur leader, joined him early in 1921. He began to give classes and to recruit by making himself known to the young in Stuttgart. With Dussia Bereska at his side, and Knust and Feist to perform too, he started a lecture-demonstration series by 25 April 1920 in the Falkenschule Turnhalle, a gymnasium, and also gave classes, talks and demonstrations in the Zentralstelle für Beratung in allen Künstlerischen Angelegenheiten (Central Office for Consultations in all Artistic Affairs) at Paulinerstrasse 40. The space proved too small for the number of students he succeeded in attracting, so the city authorities allowed him to use the larger Blaue Saal in the Kunstgebäude. When the Stuttgart theatre residency failed to materialise, Laban researched the possibilities of work in other cities, and eventually accepted an offer from the Mannheim Nationaltheater. Although some sixty miles away, he decided to commute from Stuttgart rather than to move. In this way he could complete his publication commitments near his publisher and also build on the contacts he had already made in the city and strengthen his professional training school.

Through his Werkbund contact with Eugen Diederichs in Munich, Laban had begun writing for Diederichs' *Die Tat*, a journal devoted to future German culture, including arts, community and spiritual concerns. Diederichs, regarded as an imposing intellectual, humanist and Nietzschean, used his journal to promote 'inner renewal through humane values' for all people. For the December 1919 issue he had already accepted an article by Laban on 'Symbole des Tanzes und Tanz als Symbol' (Symbol of Dance and Dance as Symbol), following it in June 1920 with 'Kultische Bildung im Feste' (Ritualistic Education in Celebration). It was this article that made Laban known in the Frei-deutschen Jugendbewegung (Free German Youth Movement). A young music and drama student was attracted by what Laban wrote, being already much interested in rhythm, dance, and exercise. This was Khadven Joos, later Kurt Jooss. He had read about Laban in Fritz Winther's book *Körperbildung als Kunst und Pflicht*, and using his initiative, went to the publisher of *Die Tat*, Diederichs, and asked for Laban's address. The young man enrolled as a student in Laban's small but enlarging class. Julian Algo joined at about the same time.

Fest is a word used in several articles in *Die Tat*. It can mislead modern readers, for it is often translated as 'festival', where 'celebration' is perhaps nearer the intended concept. *Kultische* is also a problematic word. Laban wanted to discuss spiritual education, especially corporate spiritual education. There was no word for it. But it was not intended to convey concepts associated with narrow religious sects that may be associated today with the word 'cult'.

Laban envisioned future art works, dance works, verbal works, musical works, total art works, which would not be performances by artists to audiences, but would be celebrations in and of themselves. He was not suggesting that the celebratory act should replace theatre performance, but rather supplement it as a way in which ordinary people could engage in a corporate act of value. Two things were to be celebrated: the art work itself, the symbols of the human spirit contained in its form; and the community feeling of the people who danced, sang or spoke it. The symbols would not be storytelling symbols, or narrative, but layers of human feelings and aspirations, turbulences and peace, struggles and resolutions, which could best be expressed in abstract forms and dynamic rhythms in any art medium. The term 'ritual' was used in this connection, and again can be misunderstood. In a sacred context the ritual is a means of venerating a god of some kind, a spirit 'out there'. For Laban, a ritual was an event in which each celebrant participated as an informed equal with others. In the new German culture the celebratory ritual was to be an event in which all participated rather than observed; all were fully informed and fully committed to the artistic content of the work and to the human spirit symbolised in it.

Stuttgart itself was a turbulent venue in which to plan anything, as Oskar Schlemmer's diary reveals. Students, referred to as *Jugend*, demanded that professors be elected by them on short-term contracts, not appointed by the central authorities with tenure. The conservative/modernist confrontation exploded in militant action wherever educational and political institutions were involved. The old guard attempted to resist change, while the young attempted to oust them. Anyone living in this city was aware daily of the conflicts and of the 'spiritual chaos', as Laban called it, from which arose the energy for renewal, or its contrary, the defence of tradition. Laban was in contact with other cities, Berlin included, and must have been aware of the communist-inspired riots there and of the support to them given by the Berlin Dadaists, George Grosz, John Heartfield, and Erwin Piscator for example. Munich was torn by riots as the socialist Workers' Council attempted to get its voice heard. Laban was aware of the predicament of his sister Melanie living in an abandoned railway truck in Budapest. Budapest was rife with civil war between the newly-appointed Soviet who nationalised the media as well as land, and the invading Romanian counter-revolutionary forces who entered Budapest. Refugees from both extreme right and extreme left were an everyday sight.

Amidst this chaos, Hans Brandenburg pursued his ideals for a renewal of German theatre through his proposed publications for a 'Bund für das neuen Theater'. A *Bund* was an organisation that had an element of crusading for a cause, and a commitment to a spiritual concept; perhaps 'guild' is the nearest translation. The Werkbund in Munich that Laban was acquainted with, and to which all the avant-garde applied artists belonged, was a *Bund*, mostly male, with a suggestion of an elite. Hans Brandenburg's work towards the formation of a Theaterbund carried such a connotation. He wanted Laban to be a co-director. Though Laban declined, he recommended to Brandenburg the following as 'stimulating for your theatre studies': 'all areas and methods of psychoanalysis, freemasonry and Rosicrucianism, oriental ritual in addition; with regard to harmony and the like, the book of crystallographer Prof. Goldsmidt from Heidelberg.' It was clear in these recommendations how deeply Laban's spiritual influences had become embedded in his work. The problem of what 'spiritual' should be, or might be, at this time was addressed by many writers, Diederichs foremost amongst them. Laban offered to Brandenburg what had provided at least some coherence and sense of continuity to himself in response to the spiritual chaos of the times.

The two men worked closely together, albeit by letter only, since Brandenburg was in Munich and Laban had neither a permit to travel there nor the money for the fare, for he was penniless; the correspondence details thwarted plans to meet. While Laban was sympathetic, even supportive of Brandenburg's aims, he determined to remain independent and not to co-edit the proposed publications for the Theaterbund, for he felt that he could give more weight to his own ideas by speaking as a private individual. Brandenburg oversaw the third edition of his successful book *Der Moderne Tanz*. For the first time Laban was to be featured in this edition. He urged Brandenburg to include Wigman in the chapter on 'Dancers of the Future', as she was having such outstanding success with her tours. He provided photographs of his work for Brandenburg's book, and got on with the proofs of his own *Die Welt des Tänzers*, having just completed, he told Brandenburg, the text of *Choreographie* (not published, however, until 1926).

Die Welt des Tänzers needs some comment. Years later Laban said that its main content was the important inner adventure manifest in movement which he found from movement observation. It was 'the result of the first ten years of my experimental work in movement.' He dated the beginning of his observation from his Paris days, for he had completed the text by 1914 and had to wait for the war to end to get it published. In a rather desperate letter to Brandenburg, when he still had not achieved residency in Germany, when the political situation was volatile, and at the time that Wigman had lost the photographs, he spoke of its content: 'Two important trains of thought permeate the general part of my book. The first is to give to dance and to the dancer the appropriate value as an art and as an artist, and the second to emphasise the influence of education in dance on the stressed psyche of our time.' He went on to share with Brandenburg his outrage at the dismissal of dance and dancers by the intellectuals and the bureaucrats. 'It is incredible that today, when we already have an increased number of significant kinds of dancer, and where the educational element of artistic body movement is encouraged in schools, we still come up against the resistance of the "authorities", and of the general public, when it comes to dance.' The lack of comprehension of the power of dance feeling and of the insight gained through the experience of moving with inner commitment and from inner vision was an acute frustration, a daily wound to the man. 'Poets, painters, musicians, etc., are recognised as cultural factors. The dancer always still encounters the damned equivocal smile.' He was determined to change the attitude of this 'stiff gang' in his lifetime. He picked out especially the self-congratulatory academics, 'philosophers, theologians, dreamers, scientists, and sociologists who believe they have the tenancy' of the realm of comprehension of higher things. For Laban the mover had an equal insight, an equal right to that tenancy. He longed for dance and the dancer to be accepted as the equals they were because 'the gestures of the soul of the body' could be within the experience of every-one, if only it were recognised. All people were potential dancers, as he understood it – not potential performers of steps, but potentially in touch with their own souls through the experience of gesture and moving.

He explained to Brandenburg that movement was the root of sound differentiation, of concept-building, of word-making, of the plastic arts, that this was the true root of dance and dancing. He deplored sexually motivated movement, mistakenly named dance; it was idiotic, he wrote. All dancers were discredited because of it. In *Die Welt des Tänzers* he had set out 'to illuminate the nature of universal dance, of the dancer, of the dance-like art studies in dance, sound, word, and form.' He repeated his urgent message: 'The experience of the spatial tensions of form, and of the changes of forms (that is, movement) is the foundation of all awareness, all sensitivity, of all knowledge and of all ideas . . . Human movement is the archetype of all the tensions that thoughts, feeling, acts of will, etc., are and produce.' 'Tension' is an inadequate translation of *Spannung*. The word encompasses a positive, fluent and balanced meaning, something like 'ten-sioning/releasing'. 'Sound is the spatial tensioning/releasing of the atom,' Laban wrote, using his understanding of acoustics acquired from his archi-tectural studies in Paris. Sound 'has a sad or cheerful psychological effect according to whether its atomic tensioning is deeply heavy or lightly lengthened. A body is also sad or cheerful according to its positioning' – uplifted, sagging, tight. Thoughts were also changes of tension, he wrote, and were therefore movement-derived.

All this he had attempted to unravel and to express in the book. What a task, especially when verbal language by its very nature is inadequate to communicate polykinetic flux. The problem of the discrepancy between the discrete nature of words and the continuous, multi-layered nature of move-ment was addressed in the book. It was only solvable, he felt, through developing a movement script, and he was determined to produce one – his *Tanzschrift*.

Fritz Hanna Winther, in reviewing *Die Welt des Tänzers*, evaluated it as 'a work of genius', stating it contained a dancing view of the world; that is, the dancer's insights into the tensions and flux, in macrocosmic and micro-cosmic terms, organic and inorganic, in things spiritual. Through his bodily experience of movement, which is the common denominator of all things, the dancing person is given a power of affirmation, something only dance can give. Winther commented: 'It is impossible to give a review of this book and of its chaotic contents, one would hopelessly fray apart its riches, its inspiration, and if one were to list the couple of hundred headings of the sections, that would be a threadbare extract from abundant splendour. The book not only gives, it serves up, it radiates turbulence in endless multiple directions — there can be no conclusion.' On the disorganisation of the book, hearsay has it that Laban confessed to Jooss that he had cut up the text into short sections and thrown them in the air, to land as the fancy took them (no doubt a Dada method executed in Zurich!). That, at any rate, was one way of (dis)organisation which solved the difficult problem of order. Winther vouchsafed that the book made demands on the reader, and certainly all attempts to translate it adequately have foundered to date.

That it was received with acclaim is clear. Laban became not only an interesting person of the future, with a talented colleague, Wigman, but *the* current figure to be reckoned with. Between them, Wigman and *Die Welt des Tänzers* put Laban at the head of the *Ausdruckstanz* movement. The astounding point for other artists and literary people, who regarded dance people as of no intellectual consequence, was that this man demonstrated that he, a dance person, was well-read, verbal and insightful. The book was published in October 1920, and, with his residency settled, things began to look at least more stable, if still financially barren and artistically only at embryo stage. He needed the royalties badly, for performance and lecture expenses. The book went into a second edition in 1921, but Gams, his Swiss financier, threatened legal action unless Laban repaid his debts, so all royalties had to go to Gams.

Laban showed his socialist inclination by writing in the new journal *Die Fahne*, published in January 1921, on 'The art of movement and the new theatre'. He argued that the spoken word, presumed to be the principal carrier of a play's message, is less able to than the accompanying gestures and movement tensions of the actors. These provide the essential subtleties of changing moods and relationships, which vocal inflections can only suggest. He set out the development of expressive movement that an actor required. Not only pleasant suppleness but a refined sensibility to movement was needed, and could be obtained through the bodily experience of moving rather than simply learning moves. The psycho-physical was essential. Actors should be able to improvise in movement and develop a detailed movement memory. The psycho-physically sensitive actor was also economic, Laban suggested. A stage needs fewer well-trained players than those who move emptily: the message can be got across with less elaborate costume and decor. This article suggests that Laban already had a basic curriculum for actors' movement training by 1921, and that acting as well as dancing was his domain of activity.

People were beginning to write about Laban, Wigman, and the emergence of the new dance. Paul Nikolais named three outstanding female dancers, 'the grotesque Valeska Gert, the happily youthful Niddy Impekoven, and the rhythm-intoxicated Mary Wigman', who were emerging from the spring cleaning of the old theatre dance — the present 'agonising of stage dance'. Wigman wrote on Laban's teachings in the same journal. Because ballet no longer sufficed for the modern artist as an expressive form, new ways had to be found, she wrote. The question was, could dance be an absolute art, in its own right, equal to other arts? Only if it found its own language and through that could reform itself. Dance was not only movement, not only musical rhythms, or intellectual mime: it had its inherent life, its own form of expression, its 'being' in space. Laban's creative talent, relentless research and tireless energy had enabled him to propose a harmonic theory for dance space on a par with musical harmony, and a theory of dynamics. This, Wigman wrote, he furthered into a training method for the dancer. She discussed his status *vis-à-vis* Isadora Duncan, the Sacharoffs, Dalcroze, and the *Körperkultur* teachers, as the only one who dealt with the form of dance itself, not confounding it with music, history or physical health. She described his dance symphony *Die Erde*, his dance sketchbooks, full of costume designs and choreographic notes, and his 'great instrument, the dance ensemble', the 'orchestra made of people'. She discussed his *Gesamtkunstwerk* ideas, his concept of thinking, feeling and willing in dance, sound, word and form, and told of how his school taught costume and stage design, applied to opera and acting as well as dance. She included his idea of festive and celebratory dance as well as dance performance. He would be the key figure and fighter for the dance of the future, she ended.

This ecstatically expressed appreciation of his endeavours from the outstanding young dance artist of the day must have been helpful to Laban, linking him with Wigman in people's minds. Wigman had nearly been given the job of ballet-mistress at Dresden. Although the advisers recommended her, the conservative administration demurred, then declined. The public and local writers attacked them as Philistines, but to no avail. However, her talent enabled her to start her school there and her own acclaimed ensemble would follow.

Laban, on the other hand, was offered the Mannheim job, as a guest choreographer for the 1921–22 season. His students increased, Jens Keith and Edgar Frank being notable additions, and Friedrich Wilckens became his musician. Laban concentrated on the growing group of dancers, gradually developing their skills of body dexterity and confidence in dynamic expressiveness in space through the daily *Raumlehre* (space studies) and eukinetic exercises. They stayed with him, entranced, as he taught courses throughout the summer at Cannstatt am Neckar. One was for the members of the Mensendieck *Körperkultur* group, who together with members from similar groups based on other systems were led into the experience of dance. These other groups were from Loheland, Bode and Medau groups, with established exercise methods, usually performed in unison. Laban minimised any antipathy or rivalry between the groups and emphasised that people from systems which were individual and clearly defined could still work towards a shared goal, that of experiencing the dance. He did not shield the participants from a full spiritual involvement, taking them away from gymnastics into celebratory dance. One course was given for the state-employed teachers of physical education and many private pupils joined the courses too.

At the end of the Volksschule (secondary school) summer semester a special course for young people was offered. Entitled 'The Ethical and Social Significance of Physical Culture', the course led into a 'Reigen festival' held in the Bopfer open-air theatre. A hundred dancers, led by Laban's own people, were brought to an experience of 'marrying themselves to beauty, to profundity, and significant depths', an ecstatic state which the Laban group already knew well. He told them that festival, celebration, and theatre works were all worthwhile experiences.

By the autumn Laban turned his attention to his next endeavour, co-operation with the Mannheim Opera's *corps de ballet* for the *Tannhäuser* 'Bacchanale', the Paris version. He was also given the opportunity to mount a *Tanzabend* (dance evening) for which he could create his first major choreographic work. He confided to Brandenburg that he was in a high fever of anticipation, planning how he could make a breakthrough to work with 'the old theatre', that is, the opera establishment, since to work only in the new was financially impossible.

It proved to be a fearful struggle. The task was to apply his new theatre ideas, his ways of working together and inner intention in performance to the old. Both in constructing the 'Bacchanale' and in performing it, the *corps de ballet* found that alarming demands were made of them. In the first place they were asked to co-operate with *Freie Tänzer und Tänzerinnen*, the new breed of dancers whom they regarded as beneath them, as students rather than as professionals. They made difficulties, they pulled rank. Artistically they could not do what Laban wanted them to do. He offered extra rehearsals to which they would not agree but simply quoted tariffs. A joint performance was finally achieved, on 4 December 1921, but some dancers were berated by the press for being unconvincing.

But the 'Bacchanale' itself was seen as very different in form and concept from previous productions. 'What he did not achieve was outweighed by it not being the usual conservative stuff,' was the final consensus from the press. His work was 'unusual', 'well-grouped', 'with great variety of movement', a 'wonderfully soft colourful group dance dissolved in movement, rhythm and physical culture', and 'so different from the conventional Venusberg [the opening danced scene of *Tannhäuser*]'. In the *Badische Landeszeitung* the work was seen as the beginning of a brilliant dance poet's renewal of theatre arts. The freed, enlarged, strengthened movement of the ballet *corps*, said the critic, who had lost their stiff backs, enabled them to begin to move with rhythm in their bodies and to interpret the rhythm of the music.

The Dance and Pantomime evening given on 20 December was another thing altogether, for Laban had created *Die Geblendeten*. There was no way that the *corps de ballet* could take this (Lisa Ullmann's note in *A Life for Dance* that the opera dancers joined in was not the case, according to the programme notes). Instead they offered *Elfenreigen*, a piece for eight solo elves and a group of little elves, joining with their free dance rivals in a *Hungarian March* to end the programme. That was difficult enough. Herta Feist commented that the prime problem was the completely different philosophy of life of the two groups: for one dancing (and life) was routine, for the other both were a thrilling adventure.

Erste Epische Tanzfolge (First Epic Dance Sequence) was the title in the programme for the main work of that evening. *Die Geblendeten* (The Deluded) was its title for the second performance. With this work Laban first presented his vision of the integration of a class-ridden society and its replacement by a sense of community. He used a 'multi-armed glittering idol', created by a close group, as a symbol of an establishment held together by pomp. The form they made was described by a critic as a demonic superman, a multicoloured dancing devil. The 'idol' kept disintegrating into individuals, each with his own agenda – 'violent, senile, dreaming, searching, raving, paralysing' – and then reforming again. Although Laban wrote in his autobiography that the roles were not titled, in fact they were for the first performance, though subsequently not. Kurt Jooss was the King, Esther Smolova the Queen, Dussia Bereska a Princess, the group were Lunatics, and so on. However they were not costumed as literal representations, but given movement material as archetypes of their roles. Through four sections the dancers played out their individual differences, the dance culminating in an ordering and structuring of their qualities and spatial patterns into one harmonic whole. A musicless work with some percussion, it was astoundingly innovative and surprisingly well received. 'Lively ... like quicksilver ... with enjoyment ... on fire ...

energetic, shining' were some performance qualities remarked upon. 'Eroticism, cruelty, myth, worship' were episodes noted.

After five further performances of *Tannhäuser* in repertory, the group
left for Stuttgart to give a sold-out morning performance of *Die Geblendeten*
as the completion of a lecture-demonstration by Laban. The critics praised
them, the group was overjoyed and strengthened in their determination to
stay together. In fact the dancers had to put on the performance almost by
themselves, for Laban succumbed to fatigue and burn-out, ending up in
hospital.

A few weeks later they performed again, a full evening to a sold-out
house with a new humorous work *Himmel und Erde* (Heaven and Earth)
also turning up later as *Oben und Unten* (Above and Below). This had a
narrative of three scholarly star-gazing astronomers meticulously measuring the heavenly bodies, 'moon, evening star and comets', who performed
on the upper half of a divided stage 'dancing their undeviating rounds'.
Making use of his sense of caricature, Laban gave the three astronomers
material that ridiculed scholars, full of mimetic and comic relief as they
measured and observed the immeasurable and unobservable while the
astral figures used spatial scales in continuous repetition, coolly distant.
This was classic choreutic and eukinetic stuff. Each character had a leitmotif which could be developed as the interaction took place. Friedrich
Wilckens, whom Laban had met in Mannheim, improvised the accompaniment as the piece was being created. An opera chorus *répétiteur*, Wilckens
took admirably to Laban's way of working.

'Effectively amusing, original fantasy', 'such a thing has not been seen
before', was the press comment. Kurt Jooss was particularly noticed, so
too was Bereska as the moon and Hildegard Troplowitz as her daughter
moonlet. *Die Geblendeten* and *Himmel und Erde* introduced contrasts in
Laban's choreographic output, the one an epic dance sequence carrying a
political vision, the other made to be enjoyed and for laughter, but also
with a satirical undercurrent. Both styles demanded an intelligent response
from the audience, where hitherto simple entertainment had been considered appropriate for dance.

Laban had been expected to stay on at Mannheim to choreograph the
dances for *Scheherazade*, but he withdrew. He told Brandenburg that
although artistically there were no problems with working in the mainstream theatre, 'the *régisseur*, intendant and soloists recoil' at what confronted them, making it an extremely uncomfortable environment in
which to work and an impossible one in which to include his group. He
decided to go it alone and turned down further offers from the Stuttgart

opera and from Berlin. It must have been a hard decision, for he needed the money badly, as well as the opportunity; but he realised how circumscribed he would be. To conform or to compromise were not in his nature. To do one thing at a time was not his way either. He needed the freedom to explore all the avenues he saw opening out, although that meant financial vulnerability.

After being released from hospital at the beginning of March, Laban planned a two-month summer school and a speculative tour of the 'Laban Tanzgruppe' taking in northern seaside towns, some on the Frisian Islands, places where there would have been many summer visitors. How much of that tour was undertaken is not clear. Herta Feist mentioned dancing in forward-looking towns in south Germany at this period, but made no mention of the north.

What had Laban achieved in Germany so far? He was now well known, indeed famous in the south. Wigman's successes and her magnanimity towards him as her mentor had contributed to his aura as a leader and teacher with a method and vision. He had published, he had lectured, he had been employed in a major opera house. He had survived considerable hardship, coped with illness and penury yet again. He had a reliable and loving lieutenant in Dussia Bereska and intellectual sympathisers in Brandenburg and Diederichs with whom he could discuss his ideas. He had made the decision to be his own impresario, to be self-employed, with all the hazards which that would involve. He had a musician with whom he could experiment. Ongoing was the research for the notation and the need to establish a wider sphere of operations, beyond the south.

Most important of all, he had gathered around himself inspired, faithful, talented dancers with a wish to form a company and embody his concepts. Julian Algo, in part of a tribute for Laban's seventieth birthday, wrote 'in those decisive years about 1920 . . . we were a multicoloured flock, a somewhat gypsy-like lot, we Labanites, and soon we became the terror of Stuttgart's bourgeoisie. Laban thought us grand, and so we thought him.'

To Brandenburg he asked what he should call his company: Freie Tanzbühne Rudolf von Laban (but to North German people *frei* meant *nackt*, naked)? Or Neue Tanzbühne Rudolf von Laban, or Neues Ballett Rudolf von Laban, or Ballet Rudolf von Laban? 'Please take the baby out of the font,' he requested, and with that he left for the north.

5

Striding Out

Gleschendorf and Hamburg, 1922–1924

Although Laban was said to be apolitical by Lisa Ullmann in her retrospective appreciation of Laban's work and purpose, it is difficult to see how her opinion applies to his output from the 1920s. Laban's 1922 article 'Festwille und Festkultur' published in *Die Tat* was not an apolitical article, nor did Laban see it that way. The community, the bond between ordinary men and women within it, was profoundly important to him. His experience of Parisian élite culture and dilettantism had had the effect of bolstering his admiration for how the proletariat cope. His mourning for the loss of the community culture he had known in his youth in Hungary spurred him on to suggest an alternative. He wanted to supply a vision to which men and women could affiliate. In 'Festwille und Festkultur' he put forward his key ideas. The rational person, he suggested, has propounded physical culture, sport and gymnastics as a way of providing what the body needs in an age of mechanisation. But, Laban wrote, the *Festwille* (the will to celebrate) is a natural drive, combining enjoyment of splendour and of play, and implicitly he compared these with the exercise-based concept of his *Körperkultur* compatriots. Lonely people, people denied communal cultural activities of any significance, epitomised the longings of modern man to participate together in symbolic activity, for the will to live is bound up with the will to live together, he wrote, and is given form in community action, whether in family, religious or political groups, as children and as adults.

The place for celebratory community action was the theatre, the concert platform and the open space, Laban proposed. The people who would find a way to make this happen were the artist, capable of creating symbolic forms, together with the arts enthusiast in the community, who could organise and galvanise the participants. Laban saw that people were searching for new ways to fill the gap of old rituals. They turn to other existing forms, old church customs and masonic lodges, he suggested. But these would not satisfy the need. Social activity, whether organised or improvised, was a human requirement. The present culture had no provision and yet the will to find one was evident everywhere. It would come, he said, through artistic forms of a profane cultural togetherness.

This article was published in February 1922, and written a year earlier. Laban was beginning to find and to build up the symbolic form that he could offer for community celebratory action: the *Bewegungschor* (movement choir). He had to experiment with it further than he had done already in Ascona and in Cannstatt, by creating dance works which were within the capabilities of the amateur. They had to be symbolic of human tendencies, able to be performed by large groups, economically, and be within the scope of community expectations and facilities.

Eugen Diederichs, through *Die Tat*, continued to be supportive of Laban's ideas, and of Brandenburg's, for the renewal of theatre for the community. In December 1922 he published Arthur Jacobs' compatible views on proletarian schooling, which proposed an education with culture as the focus. Party political pressures on education were a real problem in Germany at this time. Local governments financially supported schools, art colleges, teacher education, universities, and were funded according to the political colour of their councillors. The Bauhaus is a well-known example of a college tossed from one side to another by politicians. Jacobs propounded a plan which transcended party politics; Laban and Brandenburg would agree with him. Each of these men was promoting the arts, especially the performing arts, rarely prioritised by any school funding body. It was not science, technology, engineering that they promoted, but speech choirs, community music, choric dance works. They were proposing to make focal the spiritual development of the young and the opportunity of spiritual fulfilment by the proletarian community – not material gainfulness for the individual or the state, not intellectual prowess, but art.

Later in the same issue of *Die Tat*, Laban put forward several key issues for the future success of the emerging new dance culture, in the form of a discussion between a 'Dancer' and a 'Dance Enthusiast' (quoting the text of a lecture he had given earlier in the year at the Stuttgart theatre). First he propounded that not only amateur celebratory dance but dance as an art is necessary, and for that dance theatre needs its own space, its own form of theatre building and theatre organisation. The priorities of opera houses and concert halls work against dance, for existing auditoria with their footlights and prompt box, cut off dancers at the knees. The three-dimensionality of dance was not well served by the proscenium. He clearly had in his mind his own architectural design of a theatre for dance, though he did not mention it. Should speech and music not appear in a dance theatre?

asked the Enthusiast. It should, was the reply, but only in service to the dance, to support it. Would the public not want the usual theatre offerings? Laban insisted that the 'old' had had its chance. He laid out what the new performance art would contain: an empty space (not one full of complex sets) organised by multikinetic gestures of individuals and groups (not spoken texts or sung lines), subject to laws within a vast range of possibilities (not according to the conventions of yesterday), controlled and supported by the ebb and flow of forces that could only be expressed in human movement, forces which speech and music could not utter. The dancer should be dressed, not dressed up, the space be filled by bodies. Carried objects, danced-with objects, were preferable to static props. In addition, ethical elements would be essential to the works, and spiritual values would be expressed with both harmonious and disharmonious movement forms. The spectator should be able to recognise universal forces in the dance which speak of the human being, of being a human, within laws of space and time that have existed since time immemorial.

These visions, these plans, he took with him in June for a summer at Gleschendorf, a village in the district of Holstein in north Germany, with open spaces on the shores of Lake Ponitz, not far from Lubeck. It was a holiday place, a weekend place where people swam and walked in the summer months. The dancers at Gleschendorf were the Stuttgart performers already committed to working with Laban: Dussia Bereska, Albrecht Knust, Kurt Jooss, Julian Algo, Edgar Frank, Herta Feist, Gertrud Loeszer, Edith Walcher, and Gerd Neggo were named participants. New recruits with similar aspirations joined them. Sylvia Bodmer, Mine Mempoteng, Ingeborg Roon, El Corret, Hildegard Troplowitz, Ida Urjan, Jens Keith, Lotte Müller and Helmi Nurk were mentioned. Other dancers passed through, spending their holidays in dance as recreation. In *A Life for Dance* Laban described, somewhat vaguely and with hindsight, the rugged working conditions of their summer-long experiments. Sylvia Bodmer recalled the thistles underfoot and the uneven surface of the rehearsal meadow, the Klingberg, one end much higher than the other.

Photographs of their workshops cannot fail to communicate the involvement, freedom of expression, courageous abandon and sensitivity to each other which this summer session developed in the new recruits. Laban knew that working outside made the dancers 'healthier, more beautiful, and freer', which they undoubtedly became, so Herta Feist noted. Also from time to time at the Gleschendorf summer workshops there were children and teenagers. Feist taught them, and surely so did other dancers whom Laban saw as gifted in that direction. Laban himself was no children's teacher, but he had passionate and clearly defined ideas on how children should be engaged in dance as a means of education. Herta Feist wrote that by 1922 he was convinced that taking part practically in group dance, dancing with other people as a group endeavour, gave people a beneficial strength. It educated socially, spiritually and physically. It was an integrating activity – self-integrating as well as socially integrating.

Der Schwingende Tempel (The Swinging Cathedral) was the work which Laban was forming with the committed young performers. Starting as workshops in the meadow, he began to see how it could become a major work. At first he trained the dancers in the open air, for all the beneficial reasons already stated, and then moved inside to a local hall, probably one connected to an inn, to start work seriously on the five acts which the dance contained by the end of September.

The wet weather was partly the reason for the number of dance studies for small groups. Laban described how, to avoid the rain, they split up, finding rooms to rehearse in the neighbouring inns. Each group, led by the dancers who worked with him in Stuttgart, created chamber dance sketches. These he looked at, threw out, kept or developed as he saw fit. By the end of July they had enough material to make a programme and sufficient performing skill to present it in Munich. Encouraged, he negotiated with agent A. Bernstein for a tour to Hanover. Seifert provided publicity material combining photographs of the open-air workshops at Gleschendorf, newspaper reviews from Mannheim and Zurich, and advertisements for *Die Welt des Tänzers* and for other Seifert books on theatre.

One of Laban's students from Stuttgart, Edith Walcher, also taught a Laban-based summer school at Blaubeuren, near Stuttgart. It was the beginning of a trend as Laban schools began to open, or rather, existing schools changed their traditional curriculum to *Freie Tanz*, coming under Laban's jurisdiction. Martin Gleisner, an actor who would become a key figure in amateur dance, commenced his training at Walcher's July and August workshops.

The impact of Laban's inspirational way of working had its inevitable result, for as the summer progressed the dancers wanted to stay together. They were convinced that they had a way of working which was profound, both for each one of them and for the public, as Sylvia Bodmer recalled. At a time of German demoralisation and general spiritual chaos in Europe, this international hotch-potch of searching individuals became one body with one voice, one value system. But how to achieve their aims was another question. Where? With what funds? They looked to the master to find a solution.

At some point during the summer months Laban met Dr Emanuel Benda, a lawyer from Lubeck, who became enthusiastic about what he saw at Gleschendorf. The two men must have talked over what possibilities might be found for the future, for Laban had nowhere to go for the autumn. Benda introduced him to a Hamburg banker with whom Laban discussed the possibility of bringing his dancers to that city, of forming a school, and of touring an experimental dance company from there. It sounds, from Knust's brief notes, that the three men planned and budgeted the minimum necessary to enable Laban to start. Post-war inflation had already escalated. Although not yet at its height, it was clear that the Reichsmark was a weak currency, and any financial undertaking would be a risky task. The banker was able, somehow, to donate a substantial sum of money in dollars to Laban. Dr Benda became the honorary secretary-*cum*-financial manager. By the beginning of October most of the dancers, the key figures – between twenty and thirty at any rate (although Laban wrote that there were fifty) – moved with him to Hamburg.

While the financial negotiations were still going on, the group began work. A rehearsal room was found in the municipal recreation centre at Barmbeck, a suburb of Hamburg. School premises had to be rented for amateur classes to bring in fees, and for training classes for the group. A studio was found in Tiergartenstrasse; Laban and Bereska could live there, but lodgings for the dancers had to be found. Through local supporters, possibly through the large folk dance community that Albrecht Knust knew before he came to Laban, all were accommodated. With the name Ballett Laban, Gruppe für neuen Bühnentanz, they began to become known.

The Deutsche Bühne support organisation promoted Laban's new work and undertook to present the first performances. In the meantime, with the banker's gift, Laban was able to negotiate a contract for the use of the main restaurant of the Zoological Garden. Bookings for wedding receptions and local jollifications that used to fill this restaurant had started to fall off due to the inflation, so the zoo authorities were keen to have the place smartened up and used by the public again. Laban designed a stage for it and the management began restoration and building works for him. The company moved there in the spring of 1923.

In the meantime Laban continued giving lecture-demonstrations. In October 1922 one was given in Berlin with his men's group at a Gymnastiksbund day course. In early November they put together a programme under the title *Mosaik* and tried it out at the Frankfurt Opera House and in Lubeck, to sold-out houses.

'Filled with a new vision of the life of a performer, I could only consider the fostering and adapting of the old-style theatre as a sideline. Over and over again I felt the urge to create an independent dance theatre.' These words, written in the 1930s when Laban was in the midst of the 'old theatre' as choreographer at the State Opera in Berlin, express exactly how he felt in 1922, having tasted enough of the old at Mannheim. Between October and December, working with the kind of passion engendered by commitment to a cause, the dancers and the 'dancing master' confronted the accepted rules of theatre dance and broke them, challenged the bourgeois aesthetic of Hamburg theatres, and prepared to shift both while upgrading their own technique and expressiveness in an attempt to match their vision with skills. By December 1922 Laban had his first Hamburg season ready, and presented on alternating evenings *Der Schwingende Tempel*, *Fausts Erlösung*, and *Die Geblendeten*.

They danced in the performance space at Conventgarten, with production assistance from the Schauspielhaus and lighting hired for the purpose. *Der Schwingende Tempel* was described as a *Reigenwerk*. Laban wrote, 'It is just as difficult to explain the content of this work as it is to explain the content of pure music.' It was an interplay of bodies in movement, their patterns in space and rhythms in time. They touch on the energy which lies behind all material things, a forgotten and hidden landscape that he called 'the land of silence, the domain of the soul'. In the middle of this land stands 'the swinging temple', a swaying, swinging, turning, pulsing temple of people. This is the realm in which true dancers live – not those whose 'lamentable prancings and contrived hollow gestures' often pass for dance, but those who seek by experience to perceive the deeper energies of life.

From studying the extant notes on the work, it appears that each *Reigen* represented a different dance temperament, by dancers working as a group, each with its own colour: yellow, red, green, blue, white, black. The movement material was built up from group improvisation and organised around three movement types: high dancer, medium dancer and low dancer (similar to soprano, mezzo and alto, tenor, baritone and bass voices). The *Vorreigen* was the expression of chaos, primordial stirrings developing into rhythmical impulsive motion. Each group was given a rhythmic structure to work in, one in 6/8, one in 4/4, one in 3/4, one in 5/4. Their material was developed as two group statements of spatial harmonies, using Laban swings as a basis. The first *Reigen* developed out of this as a 'bacchantischer Aufschwung', in which kinetic interplay of the four rhythmic structures and the two spatial structures developed with surging bacchantian energy. It was vigorous in rhythm and broad in space, with a combative undertone.

In the second *Reigen*, a reconciliation of the colour groups emerged, with each group stating their own material followed by the men of each group dancing developed material. Laban used his A and B scales as a source. The overall feeling was of a ritual. Circles developed and led gradually off stage, the *Reigen* ending calmly. After the interval, the third *Reigen* opened with bizarre motion, strictly organised in spatial and directional disharmonies. Exactly what was danced here is not stated, but in other work he took movement ideas from interpersonal behaviour, especially of eccentrics, and placed them together in caricature-like statements. The *Reigen* ended in sad solemnity as the groups took over from the bizarre soloists in a satirical comment on the ridiculousness of some human endeavours.

The fourth *Reigen* began in a dreamlike atmosphere. It developed into automaton-like motion, machine-like, which became disharmonic and jarring in its complexities. This resolved into rhythmically and spatially restrained movement when both the individual dancers' motion and the motion of the group were designed in harmonic relation to each other.

The work was called 'a dance symphony'. It was constructed on similar lines to a musical symphony in that there were movement motifs which were developed, altered and reiterated, through classic choreographic devices. No story was told, but each *Reigen* had clear moods and tempi which were expressive, broadly, of being human.

The sound score was experimental, much of the dance being without music at all. Some of it, such as the opening 'chaos' section, they danced with drums and gongs. Friedrich Wilckens wrote the music as the dance evolved, on a rhythmical outline provided by Laban, the movement always arising first in all parts of the dance.

Der Schwingende Tempel presented a quite new brand of art, the plotless dance as a full-length work. It presented group movement as thematic material; no 'stars', no technical brilliance. Laban's original sketches for the groupings and pathways emphasise choric dance material. The accompaniment, three different kinds of sound, simple melodic line, then percussion, and then silence, with only the bodily sounds of the dancers confronting the ear. By emphasising the movement and giving the music a diminished role than had hitherto been usual, the spectator was forced to see dancers dancing rather than music visualised.

The *Hamburger Nachrichten* review vouchsafed that the premiere was given to a sold-out house and 'won a really great success.' The writer was familiar with the Laban style already, for he described these new *Reigen* as 'typical'. They were 'exceedingly ambitious and interesting in invention

and underlying idea'. Laban clearly succeeded in arousing intellectual interest as well as confronting the audience with a language they had never seen
or heard before.

It is from this review that we learn that Goethe's colour theory was seen
as relevant to the work. Possibly the colours of the costumes, organised in
groups, were related to the 'temperaments' which Laban had in mind as a
source for the choreography. That colour theory interested him can be
traced through his correspondence and writings. In Munich he had studied
Kandinsky's colour theory, and his own idea on vibrations and oscillations
of forces had resonance in colour theory. Laban admired Goethe, so it
seems likely that the costumes' colours, designed by Laban, were carefully
chosen with these concerns in mind.

The overall theme that came across to the reviewer was 'the gradual
change of disharmony to harmony, of chaos into cosmos'. The qualities he
enjoyed were that Laban, 'a finely inspired producer', never lost the direction and leadership of the groups, but moved 'unerringly to his goal'. Laban
obviously gave him confidence that the work had a coherence, that the
experiments were paving the way to an arresting renewal of the 'stage art of
our time'. The work needed some tidying up, he thought: one *Reigen* should
be shortened, one transition altered, the chaos was a bit too chaotic. Comment was also made on the inconsistency of performance, from time to
time, by some members of the company; some dancers were not quite up to
the standard of others.

The next evening *Fausts Erlösung* (The Deliverance of Faust) was given,
for which Laban had co-operated with Wilma Mönckeberg-Kollmar. She
was a lecturer at the University in *Sprechkunst* (the art of the spoken word),
and also ran amateur speech choirs for young workers and students. The
speech choir was a popular art medium in the 1920s, accessible to all
manner of people. With no need for dancing skills, singing skills, instrumental skills, it provided an opportunity for everyone to join in community
art-making. The socialist poets of the day, Bruno Schönlank for one, used it
as a means of involving young people in political action and political
propaganda. In Hamburg particularly, communist writers employed this
medium, and the public were familiar with it.

Laban offered Mönckeberg a commitment to a choric celebration in
movement, a radical concept. She offered him production experience in
choric speech. Both were Goethe devotees, as were the majority of Germans at the time. They were joined by Richard Goldschmidt, a pianist
acquaintance of Laban from his Vienna days. Their co-operative effort was
an adventure, and brave; some said 'impudent', for a dance to Goethe

would have been analogous to the first musical about Jesus Christ, sacrilegious to many. But they risked it.

The performance, arranged by the Deutsche Bühne, used the Ernst-Merck-Halle, which Laban altered to give an enlarged apron stage, which pushed right out into the auditorium. The spectators sat on three sides, but with no tiered seating. The speakers were out of sight in the gallery. Not only did the dancers have to master this expansion of their relationship to their audience, but all knew that the audience would have to respond with a new attitude.

The pre-performance announcements in the Hamburg papers sound thoroughly doubtful. Speech choirs were regarded as 'the painful child of the stage, the producer's worry', and the proposed movement was an unknown quantity. The whole thing must be regarded as a tentative experiment only, they warned.

Nevertheless, the hall was full. The *Hamburger Nachrichten* reviewer, Max Alexander Meumann, was somewhat confounded. This work had no precedent, he wrote. That the rhythm of Goethe's words and the rising and falling melody of the voices might be as significant as the ideas carried by the words, was unforeseen. That the rhythm and melody might be transformed into dances with rhythmic-spatial form as their content was confusing to him. Something to hold on to was the division of the speakers into high, middle and deep voices. That high, medium and deep dancing bodies might exist too was a new idea. But they did, visibly, and could be a lifeline to the viewer, through analogy. But the reviewer was keen to learn new ways of looking and listening, new responsiveness, he said, and he recognised that the work was contributing to the urgent call for renewal, for modern means in theatre for modern Germany.

Several factors worked against the performers. As Meumann recorded, the acoustics were evidently poor, the lighting designers had not coped with the thrust stage, and there were visibility problems. The speakers were insufficiently expert and unable to cope well enough with the music. The movement was not always as unison as intended. Despite these problems, and his own sense of inadequacy to the newness of the occasion, Meumann supported it. 'Strong and clear effects emanated from it. It is gratifying that Hamburg is the city where these new initiatives are taking place.' Prolonged applause and great public support ensued.

The *Hamburg Echo* reviewer was confounded, but confounded with admiration. Using a vocabulary which suggests that he was an intellectual, he reviewed all three Laban works, *Faust*, *Der Schwingende Tempel*, and *Die Geblendeten*. Opening with a general declamation, he said that standard criteria could not be applied to the works of this creative pioneer. Any judgement of the façade of the works missed the point, for here were offerings which were engrossing to the soul, unsettling, and which smashed down received values. What might appear to be presumptuous in the topic could be seen as an attempt to oppose worship of the dollar with that of other gods, namely with the spiritual burgeoning of culture.

Laban had taken Goethe's almost sacred concepts on Faust and presented them with his own concepts to the forefront as 'The Deliverance of Faust', the reviewer wrote, creating an 'astonishing, epoch-making' combination of word and dance, with sections of separateness and prominent moments of unification when Mönckeberg's disciplined verses, Richard Goldschmidt's piano, and Laban's dance corps synthesised. The dancers, depersonalised, worked as one body, each limb of which contributed to the harmonic impression of this extraordinary performance. The third *Reigen*, 'a masterly creation in itself', presented the ecstatic dance of primordial people at a level never reached before. One left the hall as if leaving a religious service, he concluded.

The dancers' view of the performance was expressed by Herta Feist: 'An unbelievable enthusiasm was produced by this dance. With it we conquered Hamburg.' With success and controversy ringing in their ears, the inspired and strengthened group faced the rigours of 1923.

In the new year the theatre in the Zoo Restaurant was ready. For the first time Laban had his own performance space, his own dancers, his own musicians to work with, and he started on an unbelievably fluent year of experimental theatre. The incredible speed of the spread of his ideas was boosted by Herta Feist, who left the group to open a Laban school in Berlin, with Laban's curriculum, and with theoretical studies from her partner, Fritz Böhme. It became an influential school with a performing movement choir. Martin Gleisner, who would be a tower of strength for amateur dance in a year's time, enrolled there.

At the same time there was economic hyperinflation, and an increased threat of revolution throughout Germany. It is almost impossible to imagine the enormous scale of the weakening of the Mark, the daily rise in prices. One could not buy a theatre ticket for the following day, for by then the price might have doubled. The modest magazine *Junge Menschen: Blatt für Deutschen Jugend*, to which the Laban group contributed, cost 500,000 Marks in September. People were seen carting wheelbarrow loads of paper money to buy provisions. The historian John Willett quotes '10,000 marks to the dollar in 1919, to 25,000 in April 1923, 110,000 in June, 4.6 million in August and so on down.'

In Hamburg, Ernst Thälmann led a communist rising, and for three days Hamburg was in turmoil before the police suppressed the rioters, imprisoning many of them. It was not possible for any of the dancers to avoid political awareness. In a chaotic Germany, urban Hamburg was no idyllic Gleschendorf. Street violence, crowd riots, transport strikes, food queues, official and unofficial military groups were daily evident in the city. The inflation caused untold hardship. Anyone on a fixed income was made a pauper. In the main it was the middle classes, used to living on income from investments, who found themselves, as a class, dispossessed. Every German became a worker, everyone was anxious, longing for a solution, looking to right and left for leaders to find a way through the political, social and economic chaos that the Weimar Republic had produced.

Theatres generally were failing everywhere. No one could afford to attend, no one would finance a production. The city governments took over most private theatres and performance spaces as the only means of making them viable. Laban's situation was not as bad as some, for his small theatre had been finished before the worst of the inflation, and he still had some of Dr Benda's dollars. He had very modest requirements for his productions: movement in itself was not expensive, he had no orchestra, no lighting crew, no backstage hands. He could cut his coat according to his pfennigs. However, an immediate problem as the year progressed was temporary hunger. His dancers could not afford food. It was Knust's family, old Hamburg residents, who helped feed them, by supplying soup in quantity.

In this turmoil, Laban created dances. No wonder he cast a Tyrant and a Beggar in *Gaukelei*. No wonder *Der Schwingende Tempel* started in chaos. For an allegedly apolitical man, he was certainly involved in politically charged libretti. He was clearly political through his work, but without any party allegiance. Rather he was an optimist: he hoped, he believed that solutions could be found. He had a belief in his own destiny; he would find new theatrical means, he would show people through dance how community feeling could triumph. He would alleviate human greed and aggression through art making. These hopes he expressed in his writings and attempted to realise in his practice, by putting his head on the line and presenting his beliefs immediately and consistently in the Hauptrestaurant of the Zoological Gardens. That was his positive response.

Concurrently he expanded the school. Dr Krieg, a family friend of the Knusts, owned premises at Schwanenwik 38. He rented the building to the school some time in 1923 when Albrecht Knust became the school's administrator, and it became a stable home for Laban educational work for more than ten years. Note the delegation. Knust had been with him for two years

1. Field Marshall Rudolf Laban in his final command for the Austro-Hungarian army as Governor of the Turkish Provinces Bosnia and Herzegovina.
(Laban Collection from Excellenz Marie von Laban Varalja's estate.)

2. Rudolf Jean Baptiste Attila Laban, aged three.
(Laban Collection from Excellenz Marie von Laban Varalja's estate.)

3 (left). Laban as a teenager.
(John Hodgson collection.)
4 (below.) Laban in his atelier at
132 Boulevard Montparnasse,
Paris, in 1903. (Laban Collection,
gift of Fritz Klingenbeck.)

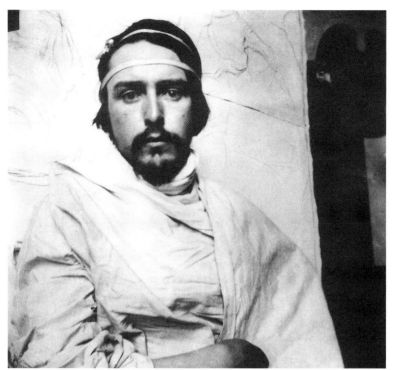

5. Laban in his atelier, dressed probably for some Rosicrucian activity, 1903. (Laban Collection, gift of Fritz Klingenbeck.)

6. Laban in the Bois de Vincenne at St Maurice, Paris, where he sketched with his daughter Azraela, 1905. (Laban Collection, gift of Fritz Klingenbeck.)

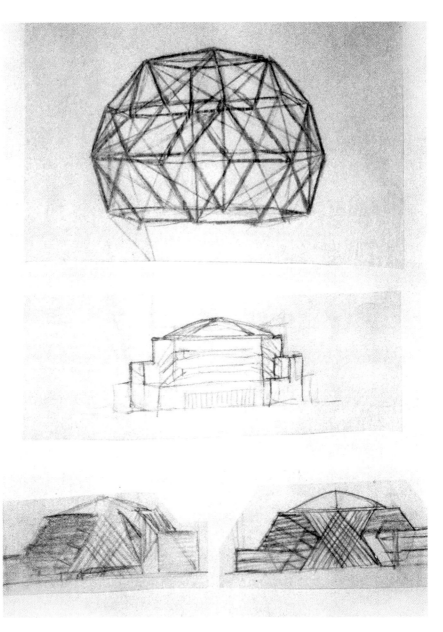

7 (above). Drawing for a theatre for dance, the drawing believed to have been submitted as the entrance examination to the Prix de Rome class of the School of Architecture at the Écoles des Beaux Arts, Paris, 1903. (Laban Archive, National Resource Centre for Dance.)

8 (opposite, above). Laban outside his house in St Maurice, Paris, c. 1905. (John Hodgson Collection.)

9 (opposite, below). School Laban de Varalja in Munich, 1913, in 'spatial group from concentrating to spreading'. From left: Karl Weysel, Betty Baaron Samao, Suzanne Perrottet, Mary Wigman, Johan Adam Meisenbach. (From F. H. Winther's *Körperbildung als Kunst und Pflicht*, 1919.)

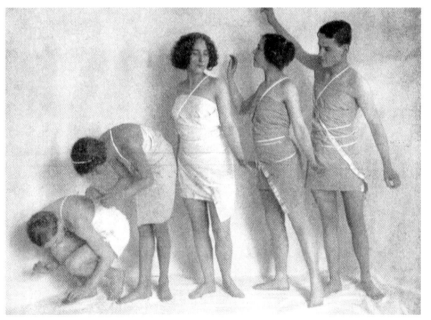

10. Laban's sketch entitled 'Music and Movement', with his wife, the singer Maja Lederer, depicted as a cat, and his lover, Suzanne Perrottet, always caricatured with a long nose and copious hair. Munich, 1913/14. (Laban Collection from the Suzanne Perrottet estate.)

11. Laban's notes on Ton (sound) and Tanz (dance), 1913. (Laban Collection from the Suzanne Perrottet estate.)

12. Mary Wigman as a student of Laban de Varalja, in 'double tension upwards and downwards', 1913. (From F. H. Winther's *Körperbildung als Kunst und Pflicht*, 1919.)

13. The *ménage à trois* of Suzy Perrottet, Laban and Maja Lederer, 1914. (Laban Collection, gift of Julia Perrottet.)

14. Laban's summer season at Ascona. From right: Laban, Betty Baaron Samao, Maja Lederer, Käthe Wulff, Suzanne Perrottet, Karl Weysel. (Photo by Johan Adam Meisenbach, Laban Collection, gift of Oliver Perrottet.)

15. Laban in Zurich, 1915. (Laban Collection, gift of Sylvia Bodmer.)

16. Open class at the Seehofstrasse Laban school in Zurich, c.1915. On the right, Clothilde von Derp and Alexander Sacharoff. (Photo by Schwabe Zürich, from Laban's *Die Welt des Tänzers*.)

GALERIE
D A D A

Samstag, den 28. April, abends 8 ½ Uhr findet in den Räumen
der GALERIE, Bahnhofstrasse 19 (Eingang Tiefenhöfe 12) als
III. geschlossene Veranstaltung ein

ABEND NEUER KUNST

statt

PROGRAMM:

I.

S. PERROTTET: Komposition von SCHÖNBERG,
R. VON LABAN und S. PERROTTET. (Klavier und
Violine).

Es war Klavier solo = Violin solo

F. GLAUSER: „Vater", „Dinge" (eigene Verse).

LÉON BLOY: „Extraits de l'exégèse des lieux-
communs", übersetzt und gelesen von F. GLAUSER.

TRISTAN TZARA: Vers.

HUGO BALL: „Grand Hotel Metaphysik". Prosa, in
Kostüm.

II.

MARCEL JANCO: Ueber Cubismus und eigene Bilder.

S. PERROTTET: Komposition von SCHÖNBERG,
R. VON LABAN und S. PERROTTET. (Klavier).

EMMY HENNINGS: „Kritik der Leiche", „Notizen".

HUGO BALL: Eigene Verse.

TRISTAN TZARA: „Froid lumière", poème simultané
lu par 7 personnes.

III.
(Unterhaltungsprogramm)

„CHANSONS IN MASKEN"; HANS REIMANN,
Die Beleidigung"; JULES LAFORGUE, „Lohengrin";
„MUSIQUE ET DANSE NÈGRES": ALPHONSE
ALLAIS, „Le petit veau"; MAC NAB, „Le fiacre";
LICHTENSTEIN, „Dämmerung".

Mittwoch, 2. Mai

AUSSTELLUNG NEUER GRAPHIK.

17. Dada poster including a billing for Suzanne Perrottet playing Laban's piano and violin compositions, 1917. (Laban Collection.)

18. Dussia Bereska in 1919. (From Laban's *Die Welt des Tänzers*.)

19. Laban in 1919. (From Laban's *Die Welt des Tänzers*.)

20. Kurt Jooss in 1921. (Sigurd Leeder Archive, gift of Grete Müller.)

NATIONAL THEATER

1

MANNHEIM

116. Vorstellung 1921—22
Dienstag, den 20. Dezember 1921
21. Vorstellung in Miete, Abtlg. A
(für 2. Parkett A 17)

Zum ersten Male:

Tanz und Pantomime

Entwurf und Einstudierung von Rudolf von Laban. Musikalische Leitung: Paul Breisach

Ouvertüre zu „Donna Diana" von E. N. von Rezniceck

1. Elfenreigen Friedrich Klose

Dargestellt vom Tanzchor des Nationaltheaters

Erste		Liesel Gerlach
Zweite		Gretel Heiss
Dritte		Anna Hohmann
Vierte	Elfe	Betty Sauter
Fünfte		Luise Weber
Sechste		Liesel Schmitt
Siebente		Käthe Pfeiffer
Achte		S. Landschneider

Elfengruppe:

Margarete Kersebaum, Rosel Möhring, Else Seufert, Maria Dietrich, Ria Fessle, Anna Ziegler, Helene Bannholzer.

2. Epische Tanzfolge in vier Reigen

Dargestellt von den Meisterschülern Rudolf von Labans

König		Kurt Jooss
Königin		Esther Smolova
Tanzpriesterin		Dussia Bereska

Erster Zweiter	} Tempeltänzer		Hubert Frank / Otto Precht
Erste Zweite	} Tempeltänzerin		Karola Berlio / Ines Royon
Tempelrichter			Edith Walcher
Tempelhüterin			Gertrud Löser
Herold			Vera Carus
Wächter			Emila Török
Trommler			Julian Algo
Gongschläger			Albrecht Knust
Irrwische			Jutta Buchholz / Liesel Eisinger / Herta Feist / Eellen Kreba / Elisabeth Lang / Jerda Neggo / Inge Tess

3. a) Sylphentanz Hector Berlioz

getanzt von Dussia Bereska

b) Ungar. Marsch Hector Berlioz

Dargestellt vom Tanzchor des Nationaltheaters und den Meisterschülern Rudolf von Labans.

Pausen nach der ersten und zweiten Abteilung.

Manuheimer Nationul-Thenters „Rheinische Thalia" enthalten. Diese
ist durch den amtlichen Zettelverkauf vor und im Theater zu haben.

Inhalt vom Heft XVI:

Julius Maria Becker (Aschaffenburg): Carl Hauptmann; Hans Johst (Oberallmannshausen): Am Grabe Carl Hauptmanns;
Friedrich Castello (Breslau): Erde halb -- und halb auch Träume. Hans Christoph Kärgel (Dresden): Die arm-
seligen Hexenbinder. Otto Schabbel (Hamburg): Ein Brief von drüben. Paul Dubray (Frankreich): Brief an
Carl Hauptmann. Gillis van Rappard (Holland): Einige Worte über Carl Hauptmann. Richard Benz (Heidelberg).
Emil Alfred Herrmann, Notizen—Bildbeigaben.

Preis des Heftes mit Theaterzettel und Inhaltsangabe des zur Aufführung gelangenden Stückes 1 Mk.

Das Personal ist angewiesen, während des Orchester-Vorspiels Niemand den Zutritt

21. Poster for the Nationaltheater in Mannheim for Laban's first production in a major theatre, *Epische Tanzfolge*, 1921. (Archive of the Nationaltheater, Mannheim.)

22. *Epische Tanzfolge* presented in 1922 as *Die Geblendeten* (Illusions, or the Blinded Ones). From left, unidentified, Sylvia Bodmer, Dussia Bereska, Edgar Frank, unidentified. (Photo by John Thiele, Laban Collection, gift of Sylvia Bodmer.)

23. Gleschendorf summer school, Laban taking class with percussion, 1922. (John Hodgson Collection.)

24. Men's group at Herta Feist's Laban school in Berlin, 1923. (Laban Collection, gift of Martin Gleisner.)

25. Herta Feist (right), Martin Gleisner, and a student, Berlin, 1923. (Laban Collection, gift of Martin Gleisner.)

only, but was given the responsibility of 'administrator', a challenge for the young man, a risk for Laban.

Laban established the Hamburg Movement Choir as the amateur performing arm of his company. He was seeking to set up by the end of 1923 a similar institutional complex to the one he had in Zurich: a conglomeration of an amateur school which had to be financially profitable, a dance company which could earn by its performances, an amateur group which paid its own way, an office and secretariat where he could work on his books, his lectures and his movement research, and a room 'over the shop' where he could live.

The balance between these activities shifted each year. In 1923 the accent was on dance-making and theatre experiments, while by 1926 the research side expanded to become the Choreographisches Institut. In Zurich, emphasis had been on teaching and lecturing. There was no fixed plan, for Laban was pragmatic. Whatever became possible he did, with his whole being, for everything, somehow, had to be forwarded.

Laban's primary resources were his dancers. By now he himself was forty-four, broadly built and thoroughly male. No acrobat, he nevertheless commanded the stage space with his sheer personality and intense performance. He did not perform in the December 1922 season, but he would do so later. Dussia Bereska, in her mid-twenties, was a 'eukinetische' dancer. The expressive range of movement qualities was her strength. Gertrud Loeszer was choreutic, inspired in space. Kurt Jooss and Sylvia Bodmer were his strong deep dancers, whose qualities were earthy and forceful. Others he saw as high dancers, elegant and lifted, while the middle dancers were gifted at swinging with momentum. He looked at their personal profiles, their potential, their unique movement voice, and worked with that. Although he stressed that everyone has maleness and femaleness within, he felt the need to emphasise manliness, to attract men to dance. He had a fine resource in Jooss, Algo, Keith, Knust, Frank, Mario Volcard, and would be joined during the year by Martin Gleisner and Karl Bergeest.

For his improvisatory style of choreography to function, Laban's dancers needed to be skilled in working together, and sensitive to each other. To this end Laban encouraged, and indeed reinforced, a communal mode of living. His valuing of individuality bred mutual respect for each other. The usual jealousies and rivalries between performers fell away as meaningless. His expressionist style required utter commitment, utter conviction, utter *Erlebnis* of the movement content (that is, living the movement as it is experienced) which depended on a positive self-image to succeed. This was balanced by the need to conform, for he used unison work which they achieved through intensive kinetic empathy for each other. He needed his dancers to be athletic, well-sprung, supple, with a dynamic range from demonic intoxication to spider's-web fragility, and with a sense of timing based on acute awareness of kinetic change. By this means they built up skills of memory, accuracy of phrasing and quality, all in free rhythms. They needed metric exactitude and musicality, and an ability to play percussion instruments while moving and to use their voices in all manner of unprecedented ways. Above all they had to be able to invent movement, to work creatively.

These needs, emerging from Laban's preferred way of making dances, dictated his training programme. So his dancers had daily classes in body training, choreutics and eukinetics followed by rehearsals both individual and communal, with Bereska, his assistant-in-chief, always at his side.

The Kammertanz dances that Laban provided were partly his own and partly, as at Gleschendorf, his dancers', moulded by him from their personal improvisation in response to his 'near hypnotic stimulation', as Sigurd Leeder described it. He divided the repertoire into five categories: ornamental dances, designed to be appreciated for their beauty; ecstatic dances for the way they reflect spiritual vision; rhythmic dances for their ability to excite; grotesque dances for both comedy and comment; and style dances, historically and nationally flavoured dances, for their traditional qualities. These divisions, he wrote, simply emerged; they were not planned. The longer works he called dance poems, dance dramas and dance comedies. Within each category the company could offer variety. Solos, duos, a quartet, a men's trio, a women's group dance, were listed. Bereska was his leading woman. He was himself the main male soloist, with his younger men sharing the roles that required greater dexterity and athleticism.

Not enough is known about the form of these 1923 dances to give an adequate description. What is known is that Dussia Bereska developed a set of solos, for in each performance she danced alone and was almost always reviewed with acclaim. By 1923 she had *Orchidée*, in the ornamental category, as a well-known solo. A film clip of it remains. She is seated, cross-legged, wearing the standard bloomers, but in gold lamé, covered with transparent baggy trousers, nude from the waist up. The movements are exotic, subtle and intricate finger and arm gestures, reminiscent of opening petals of a bizarre flower. This dance was seen by the group as a symbol of the burgeoning of 'the spirit of our theatre'. *Krystall* Laban described as a dance 'which divides the space in hard, severe lines', based around his tetrahedral and dodecahedral orientations in space, while

Rosetten was surely based on the volutes of the choreutic scales, the rounded female movements which surround the body's centre from all sides, as a rosette. She danced a 'style dance' in *Alte Tanzvisionen*, which must have been based on a pavane or *basse-danse* or the like, and she had a comic dance, *Interpunktiontanz*, which played on the movement possibilities of question marks, exclamation marks, commas and so on.

Individual members of the ensemble each had a solo. Kurt Jooss made his own *Cyclops*, Jens Keith danced *Erbisches Thema*, Gerda Scheck danced *Bewegtes Thema*, Hildegard Troplowitz danced *Basso Ostinato*. In another programme, Edgar Frank and Jooss danced *Vogel* (Bird), of which a brief film clip exists, Keith danced *Peitschentanz* (Whipping Dance), Loeszer danced *Phantasmagorie*, and Ingeborg Roon danced *Elegie*. No trace of these dances remains except their titles.

Because Laban used the same themes in developing solo dances in the late 1940s a little more is known about the following works. Laban danced *Marotte* himself, which Aurel Milloss recalled, and *Mondäne*. *Marotte* (The Quirky One) was in a rondo form with a circling arm movement, repeated again and again like an obsession, as the main theme. As verses, different gestures of people possessed were danced into a climactic nightmare. Laban spoke about his observations at the lunatic asylum in St Maurice, Paris, which he visited in 1902 to widen his understanding of harmonic and disharmonic movement patterns; *Marotte* was based on this experience. *Mondäne* (The Chic Thing) drew on his Parisian experiences too, his dislike of all things sophisticated and over-cultured. *Homunculus* (The Artificial Man) took a look at depersonalisation, how modern values mechanised men, and this was taken further in the more bizarrely mechanistic *Robot*. In contrast, *Mönch* (The Monk) was an ecstatic dance using the religious forms of blessing, obeisance and praise, with which the three spatial planes are connected.

Laban created duos for himself and Bereska. *Gebet* (Prayer) and *Mosaik* (Mosaic) are nowhere described. *Lustleid* (Joy–Grief) he said was 'representative of inner stirrings; that is, almost abstract, but whose rhythm and dynamic connote the changing tensions between joyous and grieving feelings.' He created duos for two men: *Schatten* (Shadows), *Ifriti*, and *Dithyrambus* were the titles.

In *Zaubergarten* (The Magic Garden) he created a trio for himself, Bereska and one other woman. It was an ornamental dance, a development for three of the motifs in *Orchidée*. *Tempeltanz* was a trio for himself, Bereska, and one other man. He used the prayer gestures of the religious ceremonies he had seen in Sarajevo and Constantinople in his youth, and the turning motif of the Dervish priests. *Drachentöterei* (Slaying the Dragon) was a light-hearted pantomime. A film of it shows the gallant Prince, the innocent Princess, and malevolent Dragon in conflict and resolution. Group dances for the newer company members came in the Style Dances category: a Hungarian, Slav, and Romantic dance, a Schottische and a German dance were in the programme.

Performances started as soon as possible. Their first was on 11 January 1923 when they gave a matinée and late night show, sandwiched around a performance of G. K. Chesterton's *Magie* at the Schauspielhaus. Solos, duos and 'grotesques' were included. This audience had no idea what to make of it. There were interruptions, laughter and derision. The *Nachrichten* reviewer liked one solo 'because it was precise' and a duo because it was 'simple to understand'. He was glad that here there was 'real dancing' compared with the 'Dance Symphony' (presumably referring to *Der Schwingende Tempel*).

Kammertanz performances at the zoo restaurant theatre began on a regular basis and the Deutsche Bühne was a considerable help. As a support organisation aiming to promote performances and with the ability to underwrite them financially, it was able to lower seat prices so that the *Arbeiter*, the workers, of Hamburg could afford to attend. Membership encouraged regular audiences for the Kammertanzbühne in the small theatre in the Zoological Gardens. They toured locally as well. *Drachentöterei* had its premiere in Oldenburg in April, *Zaubergarten* in May at the larger Conventgarten theatre in Hamburg. The group dug themselves further into the community by performing in the annual May Day festival. Dussia Bereska increasingly had to take over responsibility for the zoo performances – and she proved her worth. Typically Laban was earning elsewhere, in Rostock for example, arranging dances for which Tchaikovsky's *Serenade* was the accompaniment.

The usual pattern of work was getting under way: Laban had the imagination, the vision, faced the initial problems, solved them to his own satisfaction, and passed the realisation on to someone else. He chose Bereska for the regular productions, and Knust for the leadership of the school. When an opportunity was no longer a challenge, he saw no need to occupy himself with it – in fact was irked by it – and turned his talents to the next practical challenge while continuing the fight for dance in print, and seeking solutions for the notation.

He gave public lectures in the Bans Gesellschaft in Hamburg, a series between 10 and 12 March 1923 under the umbrella heading of 'The Nature and Purpose of Dance'. He opened with an 'Introduction and History', followed by 'Dance Teaching', then 'Dance and the Stage', and finally 'Festive Culture', prefaced by a demonstration 'to give people a visual image'. He proved his point in practice time and time again.

Laban was urgent in his desire to get people thinking about the role of dance in their own lives and about the status of dance people. He wanted his school to attract students, both as potential teachers and as performers, and to build up an understanding of what a movement choir might be before he launched the first one in May. *Die Tat* carried an article on the Tanzbühne performances in March too, and Laban wrote in it 'A Word about Dance Theatre'. Dussia Bereska and Mario Volcard appeared as 'Rudolf von Laban Tanzbühne soloists' in the Opera House production of Richard Strauss's *Josephslegende*, a new departure, and primarily a means of earning. Laban saw that his dancers were wanted by other producers, which was both gratifying but also dangerous, for he could not offer salaries to his dancers, only expenses and pocket money. They could be lured away.

Simultaneously he was occupied with the launching of the Movement Choir. He had worked regularly with eighty amateur dancers, both men and women, over the spring to create a work, *Lichtwende* (Dawning Light). In *A Life for Dance* he remembered the simplicity of the movements, 'with common swinging, leaping, measured slow stepping we conquered space', 'interweaving paths in common rhythms'. The public were excluded to start with as the group simply performed the dance for their own enjoyment; but then, with confidence, they decided to open it to an audience. So on 24 and 25 May 1923 it was shared. Knust and Mario Volcard were *Vortänzer*, lead male dancers. Käthe Wulff had joined from Switzerland, Lotte Wedekind (Frank Wedekind's daughter) was a leader, and so too was Margarethe Schmidt. All three women, working as apprentices on this occasion, were about to run successful schools with a Laban curriculum and start movement choirs in their own cities.

The dance, in five *Reigen*, started with solemn stepping in subdued sadness as the participants felt the gradual awakening of the revitalising capacity which exists within each one of us. The dance was built around Laban's idea of tropism. As he wrote in *Die Welt des Tänzers*, under a paragraph entitled 'Tropism', just as the flower turns towards the light, the animal approaches its food and takes it, so the dancer turns towards and reacts against the many influencing experiences of *Spannung* (tensioning). He referred to the action/reaction rhythm in movement, the natural counterbalancing effort in gesture, attraction towards and away from gravity, towards and away from other people, towards and away from one's own body, opening to the light, closing away from it. In *Lichtwende* the experi-

87

ment lay in the audacity of the simple movement, danced by young adults with total commitment, in 'turning to the light'. Additionally, it was without music, and with one *Reigen* which was only percussion-playing, no movement.

Karl Bergeest was typical of the young participants. He described himself as having been a lively member of the 'free proletarian youth culture', interested in political engagement of some sort, for which joining a performers' group was one solution. *Wandervögel* or folk singing could have been his choice, but he heard of Laban, saw his work and joined the new Hamburg Movement Choir for its first season and presentation of *Lichtwende*. The sessions took place in the midst of mounting inflation and rioting. The hopeful affirmation of *Lichtwende* took on a political meaning, and a deeply spiritual significance in that troubled context. Bergeest was one of several performers set on a life's career in dance by *Lichtwende* and the Hamburger Movement Choir commenced a decade of flourishing and satisfying amateur dance. To accompany the launching of the choir, Laban started an occasional publication *Tänzerische Zeitfragen*, from the Tanzbühne Laban. The first leaflet, summer 1923, was *Vom Sinn der Bewegungschöre* (On the Idea of Movement Choirs). Dance it, see it and read about it was Laban's method.

Typically, Laban was creating another major theatre work concurrently for a May production the week after *Lichtwende*. Choreographed with the Tanzbühne dancers, it was *Gaukelei* (Illusions). He was absorbed in its creation because it required new solutions, being his first major dance-drama. The title suggested that juggling had gone on, through which illusion or disillusion arose. In *Gaukelei* Laban was making visible, and commenting on, the social and political turbulence of his time. He described it in *A Life for Dance*. 'The basic idea behind *Gaukelei* is a social experience. An individual, who rises to power over a community, all too easily becomes a slave to his own might. In the same way, rebels who rise up against authority are rarely capable of becoming true leaders. They mostly succumb to cynical pessimism when personal experience and the defects inherent in their environment either arouse their suspicions or depress them. In the end, they lose faith in their own ideals and condemn their achievements as useless and vain. From this springs hatred of people which leads to tyranny.' The detailed scenario, as written, seems over-complicated, with a plethora of small scenes; but it must have worked, for not only was it well received and toured in the 1923–24 season, but it was also remounted by Jooss on his company in 1930, and by Aurel Milloss at the Dusseldorf opera in 1935.

The story was only too topical, for rebels abounded in Germany, in Russia, in Hungary. Laban had sat next to Lenin both in the City Library and in the Café Voltaire in Zurich, and he had experienced Tristan Tzara's rebellion at the Dada Soirées. He might well have known what problems Tzara had had in Paris, where, awaited as a saviour by would-be French Dadaists Francis Picabia and André Breton, he had proved a grave disappointment to his disciples. Tzara was no tyrant, but he did lose faith in his own nihilism and was certainly incapable of becoming a long-term constructive leader.

The rehearsal film snippets extant of *Gaukelei* show the exaggerated declamatory motifs of the Tyrant, played by Laban himself at the premiere. With a frenetic dynamic and commanding the space, he used a majestic tall-backed chair as a perch above the people, from which he could exhort and swoop on his fellows. The range of dynamic was the character's play from extremes of domination and arousal to vain and chaotic gestures. He created the persona out of eukinetic elements, never 'steps', which enabled him to play with subtle developments of attitude. There were no acrobatics, no virtuoso turns and leaps, but instead virtuoso command of dynamic phrasing.

The Beggar was the grotesque figure, played by Sylvia Bodmer, working near the ground in jagged and irregular turns and twists, contorting her body. The *Gaukler* or Illusionist was the main male dancing role, given to Kurt Jooss (still 'Khadven Joos' at the premiere). His job was to entrance the crowd on behalf of the Tyrant. It gave Jooss plenty of room to improvise in rehearsal and find ways to develop his character and his 'business' which suited his body. Jens Keith was cast as the Hangman, forbidding and unmoved. Hildegard Troplowitz as the Jester had to amuse, in contrast to the *Gaukler*'s manipulation. Clare Therval took the female lead as the Tyrant's Daughter, archetypically a figure who longed for happiness and harmony. Her material included soft gatherings and fluid extendings. Various lesser roles were created, with an important dramatic part for a group, who responded to the central figures in improvised interactions.

The work was clearly an expressionist piece but the costumes suggested a more constructionist aesthetic. Laban's designs played with head coverings and simple arresting lines of light against dark. Angularity and geometry showed his participation in the changing aesthetic of the *Neue Sächlichkeit* (New Objectivity) with which the Bauhaus, and Oskar Schlemmer in particular, were concerned. The critics approved of *Gaukelei*. It put Laban and his Tanzbühne firmly on the map as innovators of considerable interest.

The summer months of 1923 were especially difficult, with inflation really biting. Despite being hungry, they must have kept on with classes for the repertoire increased; but some young dancers returned to their parents when the deprivation got beyond bearing. In July the company managed a performance in Munich at the Hotel Vierjahreszeiten, and one in Stuttgart. September was the height of the Mark's disastrous inflationary spiral, but they put on shows at the zoo theatre nevertheless, and on 25 September gave *Gaukelei* at the Sagebiel Marmorsaal in Hamburg. A more topical work one could hardly imagine: it underlined the perception of Laban as an artist working centrally with the problems of his time, an astounding position for a dance person. By surviving and performing topically he gained many supporters for dance in general, as well as for his own work.

The younger dancers wrote in *Junge Menschen*, the communist youth journal, which devoted one September issue to dance, Mary Wigman being featured on the cover. Their words were full of fire and affirmation. 'Through dancing, a person states: "Here I am, world." Dance plays with the stars and is the brother of all creatures. Dance gives testimony of the rhythm of the earth and speaks from the soul; that, every child understands,' wrote Erich Lüth. Jooss wrote on dance as art; Dussia Bereska discussed manly dance: our men don't dance a dance, they dance manliness, masculinity, she wrote.

In the autumn, supposedly with their dollars still holding out, they were able to create *Casanova* (also performed as *Komödie*), with a subtitle 'an affair in very many acts', a light-hearted work to tour with the heavy drama of *Gaukelei* and *Die Geblendeten*. While the dance still embodied 'characters concerned with the problems and aspirations of our time, ethical values and attitudes', it included people's ridiculousness, their pettiness as well as their nobility. Its amorous plot gave Laban's wit an opportunity to flourish. Bereska played Frau Venus, supported by Three Graces: Kurt Jooss was Capitano Casanova, Laban played his all-knowing servant Sokrates, and Gertrud Loeszer played Fräulein Giftpilz (Miss Poisonous Mushroom). These were the main participants in a full evening of laughter, with eighteen performers and a pianist. The set, extremely simple as it must have been for financial reasons, had to evoke a street scene, Frau Venus's domain, and the Burgermeister's home ground. It took place 'on a well-known planet', the time 'as always'. Its purpose was to show another side of humanity's 'aspiration' and a lighter style of Tanzbühne artistry, and to give the audience a chance to smile in a very tough real world. Laban was funny. He was a wicked mimic, and so was Jooss. They gave *Komödie* first in Hamburg and straight after in Hanover.

Laban then decided to risk Berlin, the capital, the ultimate arbiter. He took the Philharmonie in Berlin for three nights in November, a performance space of good standing and size used more often for concerts than dances, but with an excellent reputation. But the Berlin trip was a financial disaster, hit thoroughly by the height of the inflation. With it Laban's last dollars were used. However, they fulfilled a commitment to give *Die Geblendeten* at Munster later in the month, and a lecture-demonstration at Lüneburg at the beginning of December. Then home to Hamburg, to earn if possible.

Bereska had continued with Tuesday, Thursday and Saturday performances of the chamber group, the Kammertanzbühne Laban, in their zoo restaurant theatre since October. Because of the number of performances to regular audiences, they had to think of new ways of presenting their repertoire. They showed the same solo performed by different dancers, repeated a woman's dance with a change of costume, or let one of the men dance it. They strung different excerpts of dances together, giving them the title *Arabesque* or on another occasion *Schwingende Gewalten* (Swinging Forces). Between them they earned enough to keep going. Laban was hired by the Deutsches Schauspielhaus to arrange the incidental dances to Shakespeare's *A Winter's Tale*. He managed to organise a contract with the theatre's intendant for all the Tanzbühne dancers to be hired to participate in the *Weihnachtsmärchen*, a Christmas fairytale.

In the meantime, the Movement Choir premiered a new work, *Prometheus*, in the Ernst-Merck-Halle exactly a year after *Faust*. Once again Laban co-operated with Wilma Mönckeberg and the speech choir of young workers and students. They were visible in this production, darkly clad and clumped together on either side of the stage. Laban decided to provide a danced prelude 'portraying the fetching down of fire from heaven and the chaining of Prometheus to the rock . . . A huge vulture, danced by three people, threatened the demi-god.' He described how dancers with percussion instruments, grouped on the steps between the stage and the auditorium, accompanied the fire-bringers with a sound score composed by himself. On a cue, they rose up and processed solemnly across the stage, there to play again, repeating this several times 'to give both visual and sound three-dimensionality'.

The speech choir took the stage for the actual rendering of the Aeschylus tragedy, Prometheus himself being played by Ernst Stattler, a professional actor from the Deutsches Schauspielhaus. Presumably one of the reasons for employing him was the problem with audibility that Mönckeberg had had in *Faust*. But Stattler was only a partial success, for beside the lively and dynamic movement choir, his declamation appeared 'wooden and inhibited'. The choir itself was rehearsed to give a good rhythmic and musical account. As they returned to their seats, the dancers took the stage, giving a concluding *Reigen* with the release of Prometheus as the theme. Through the group rhythms Laban attempted to show the awakening of the people in Prometheus's care to true cultural values rather than simply miming the act of release. The piece ended in a mood of 'radiance and redemption'.

Because Laban had already accomplished one co-operative work with Mönckeberg, he prepared *Prometheus* for an apprentice to produce. He envisioned the whole concept and planned it in detail with Knust, then allowed the young man to bring the plans to life, giving him full responsibility. Working through apprentices became a consistent feature of Laban's method. He had the ability to see what a young person was capable of achieving and setting him on his way to what usually became a successful career. It certainly was successful for Knust: he was far better at this than at running the school.

Laban also decided to use the production as a qualifying examination for Knust, who wanted to use Laban's work with amateurs. Knust's final hurdle before being awarded the Laban Diploma was to show that he could actually put *Prometheus* on stage. He did, with flying colours.

Prometheus took place just after the Berlin debâcle with the Tanzbühne. The company was from then on in real financial trouble. The decision was made to undertake a gruelling tour in an attempt to earn money. To do this, the School had to be catered for, for Bereska and Laban would join the company. Knust was the only person with experience, so he had to take over the School completely, and ran it as his own Labanschule, alongside the Movement Choir.

On 3 January 1924 the Tanzbühne company set out to Brunswick, Mühlhausen in Thuringia, Görlitz and Halle, returning to Hamburg before going off again to Magdeburg and Lubeck. After a week back at base, trying out new works in their own zoo theatre, they toured in February to Berlin, Munich, Stuttgart, Wurzburg, Nuremberg, and back to Hamburg. In March they stayed at their own theatre, made twelve new Kammertanz works, and played the large Tanzbühne works at the Schauspielhaus and the Kunsthalle. It was a gruelling schedule.

Laban could not work at this pace without burning himself out. Additionally, he was harassed by problems with his passport. He wished to retain Hungarian nationality, not Czech, for which he needed to gather all his papers from his mother. Leaving Bereska in charge, he went 'to the

South to convalesce', to get well enough to undertake a planned Balkan tour.

Why the Balkans? It seems a hazardous route to attempt with a group in the uncertainties of 1924. Did he have a longing to show his work in his own country, within his own ethnic culture, to prove to his family that their teasing of him as a youth was unnecessary, that their belief that his way-out ideas could not take root was unfounded? The ever-present need to bolster his self-doubt surfaced in his life several times, and this appears to have been one.

In April, having obtained his passport, Laban himself arranged the tour details, writing from Zagreb to Hans Brandenburg about his hopes. The father of a company member, Vera Milanovic, director of the Royal National Theatres in Yugoslavia, assisted in the organisation. The tour started in May, but without Jooss who had accepted an opportunity to be movement *régisseur* in Munster. This was a blow, for Jooss had a much-used talent. His parts were learned in three weeks by Karl Bergeest, a new recruit from the Movement Choirs now in the professional school. As a deep dancer, he had, potentially, a similar style to Jooss. He wrote that it was a dream come true, but that he did not succeed. He was too much of a beginner to dance well, too green for international touring. He divulged that the rest of the company gave him 'a rough time', having to cover for him both on stage and socially.

With fourteen dancers, a musician, and three programmes, they set out. The tour took in Leipzig Altes Theater, Prague, the Opernhaus in Graz, then Halberstadt Stadttheater, and on to four days in Zagreb. They had great success, but even so they earned insufficient foreign currency to cover the costs of touring such a large company. They were due to go on to Belgrade but nobody had the funds to buy rail tickets, no one could pay the hotel bills. One can imagine the agonising discussions, recriminations and frustrations, the questions as to whether Laban or Milanovic was to blame. The difficult decision was made to abandon the southern half of the tour. They were literally stranded in Zagreb without enough money to get home. The Tanzbühne Laban was at an end. They split up, and dispersed as best they could.

It is difficult to imagine the impact that this short-lived company's work had on European dance. The reviews on the Balkan tour continued in the Hamburg vein: 'astounding', 'topical', 'audacious'. As so often before, Laban's work touched some individuals in the towns that they visited sufficiently to give them a life's direction. Ana Maletic in Zagreb was one. She determined to learn Laban's method and to introduce it to Croatia, combining it with her own dance education. Her school and company thrived. The same happened in Graz. The same in Prague.

Bereska's response to the Zagreb collapse was to gather round her a small group of the most experienced of the company dancers: Jens Keith, Edgar Frank, Hildegard Troplowitz and Ingeborg Roon. She was determined to keep dancing. They formed their own Kammertanz Laban and looked for places to perform. Where they went immediately is not known, but by 31 August, as the Balletto Laban, they were dancing at the Teatro Nationale in Trieste. The work was entitled *Il Balletto della Stella* (The Ballet of the Star), surely a version of *Himmel und Erde*. Bereska soon founded a Laban school in Rome, attempting the frustrating task of introducing German dance to what proved to be reluctant Italians.

As for the other company members, Sylvia Bodmer and Lotte Müller opened a school together in Frankfurt-am-Main. Karl Bergeest went back to Hamburg, to study further at the school, and he and Ida Urjan assisted Knust with the Movement Choir. Aino Siimola joined Jooss. He and Sigurd Leeder had set out on their own. They had studied ballet for some months in Vienna, toured as a duo, eventually starting the Neue Tanzbühne in Munster with the assistance of the intendant Hanns Niedecken-Gebhardt.

Laban himself did not (or could not?) remain in Zagreb long enough to help his company members. He had a commitment in Halle on 1 June where the first movement choir for children was to demonstrate with Jenny Gertz, their inspired teacher/choreographer. Laban gave an introductory lecture to her morning presentation in the Thaliasaal. Gertz was to promote his work for children and adolescents with renowned success and brave innovation until well into the 1930s.

Laban was expected to go back to Hamburg, where an ambitious movement choir work there was already half completed. Concurrently he republished 'The Idea of a Movement Choir', to be used as an aid to the growing number of group leaders who needed to be able to answer: 'What is a movement choir?' The Hamburg choir was under the regular leadership of Knust, but this work, *Agamemnons Tod*, was rehearsed by Raja Belensson as apprentice. Laban needed a strong person for the more mystic style of this work, and Belensson, a Russian, was such a one, having been with him at Ascona and a participant in the *Song to the Sun*. The named parts were taken by erstwhile Tanzbühne dancers, Gerda Schenk as Klytemnestra, Gerd Neggo as Elektra, Knust as Orest, Belensson as Kassandra and Grete Beckman as Iphise. Laban should have played Agamemnon, but was apparently not there for the performance; Knust had to perform this role as well as his own. Each soloist led a group, identified by colour – brown, yellow, violet, blue and light and dark green. The colour theory in *Der Schwingende Tempel* seems to have reappeared here. Taking Noverre's concept as a starting point, Laban transformed the tragic story into a four-*Reigen* work for groups, each of which took on the characteristics of the person they embodied. It was the characters' ethical attitudes that dictated the groups' movement qualities. Of Agamemnon himself he wrote: 'What is important is the king and leader; he forgets and neglects his own private life in his struggle for law and order. He cuts himself off from the desire for home and love, and for the sake of fighting he renounces everything that leads to the appreciation of purely human and personal ties.' One cannot fail to make the connection between this view of Agamemnon and Laban's own life, his struggle for dance and what he saw as his renunciation of family life for his cause.

Laban had little to do with this production beyond the planning. Did he intend to dance the role of Agamemnon himself? It looks as if he did, for he danced in the September performance. The wretched Knust was given a bad press for his poor rendering as the substitute in the June premiere. With his slender physique and light dynamic, he was hopelessly miscast.

The back of the programme for *Agamemnons Tod* listed twelve Laban movement choirs established and working by the end of 1924. The spread of his work was astoundingly rapid and immediately successful. His ideas were seen as a godsend to the *Jugend* clubs and organisations in their search for spiritually significant occupations for the young. His dance leaders were adequately trained and conspicuously inspired to make dance for all successful. The newly formed groups were located in Vienna under Margarethe Schmidt, in Lubeck under Senta Pander-Gellmitz, in Berne under Emmi Sauerbeck, and in Budapest under Emita Török. The leaders had all danced in his works and trained in the school or at Gleschendorf, where they had learned to create works for amateurs, to teach and to dance well themselves.

By the end of the summer of 1924, Laban was established as the unchallenged leader of the new dance, with his pupil Mary Wigman regarded as the unchallenged female dancer. Both were assembling a group of dancers who were devotees on both a personal and professional level. Wigman orchestrated what became a personality cult in her choreographic ensemble: she was the leader, they her followers. Laban was a natural magnet, powerless to stop his attraction to women, many of whom who adored him, and to men who admired him, almost one and all. The two groups would become more and more partisan, the jealousy not essentially between Laban and Wigman but between Labanites and Wigmanites. It took a few years to erupt, but erupt it would.

Laban had lost his ensemble, and for the moment he had lost Bereska. He needed to take stock of his achievements and present challenges. He had schools beginning to open and movement choirs in major cities, plus a working base at Hamburg. His book *Choreographie* was not as yet published. His solutions for notation were still developing so that he had to resolve the problem that the text was soon out of date. He had published copiously on his beliefs for renewal through dance. Now he had to write on his teaching method, both to safeguard it and to make it available. He prepared to write two books: *Gymnastik und Tanz* and *Des Kindes Gymnastik und Tanz.*

His plans for performing were uncertain. Who could replace Bereska? Possibly he already envisaged a partnership with Gertrud Loeszer for she had not disappeared to start a school or a company of her own but was still wanting to perform with him. Who would replace Jooss as chief choreographic apprentice? Jooss, having joined up with Sigurd Leeder, was branching out on his own. Laban's ability as a catalyst, while evidently successful for the individuals he taught, sometimes had a boomerang effect on himself. His students became so self-confident that they felt able to start out on their own. He had difficulty in keeping a stable group of assistants. Wigman went, Jooss had gone, Bodmer, Wulff, Gleisner, Feist, and others, were all now independent.

How he spent the summer months of 1924 is uncertain, for there is no sign of a summer school. Did he holiday with Bereska and their little daughter? Did he concentrate on writing the two books? Did he discuss the progress of the notation with Jooss and Leeder, both keenly interested? Whatever he did, by September he was back in Hamburg, in full swing.

6

Artist and Researcher

Hamburg, 1924–1926

The season began amid political readjustment. The Mark had been stabilised, but political leaders were toppling. 1924 saw two general elections,
with the more middle-ground socialist democratic parties taking votes from
the extremes of both right and left. It was in 1924 that *Die Neue Sächlichkeit*
(The New Objectivity) became a catchword for the stabilisation and ration-
alisation of the post-war traumas and birth pangs of the Weimar Republic.
The concept took root as shifts in emphasis within the arts, especially the
visual arts. Laban's verbal language lessened its religious overtones, but
the body, its experiences and its spontaneity, remained a central theme in
his work.

As always, Laban was engrossed in several endeavours simultaneously.
His first lecture-demonstration was with the Hamburg Movement Choir. He
talked on the idea of the movement choir again, this time to the public. He
addressed first his concept that contemporary physical culture needed to be
artistic; the movement choir was the form of art proposed, with its central
aim of a festive, joyous dancing experience. He supported this proposal by
citing the longing within physical culture circles for a healthy, strong and
lasting foundation for their work with a bodily, spiritual and mental basis.
His stand was clearly put that recreation is achieved through a creative,
artistic, integrated experience shared with other people, and he compared
it, uncritically but definitively, with gymnastic exercise. He illustrated his
view with extracts from *Agamemnons Tod*, performing the title role himself. The able delivery of his lecture and the 'strong concentration' of his
performance impressed the reviewer of the *Hamburger Anzeiger*. He had
replaced the Tanzbühne dancers, who gave the premiere, with young movement choir members, and their immaturity was noted. Nevertheless the
reviewer congratulated the choir, and Laban, for lifting amateur work from
the realm of play into that of art. 'Is that important?' he asked. Yes, for
these young people live in a difficult time. They could become resigned, but

Laban lifted them out of this world into another, one in which 'pain and weakness are put beside strength and happiness, melancholy beside joy.' The value of this amateur dance was obvious, he wrote.

It was important to Laban that his vision of the movement choir should succeed in practice. He saw the combination of professional soloists with amateur corps, influenced by the way singers are combined in cantata performances, as a possible way of performing in the future, for both artistic and financial reasons. It worked with *Agamemnons Tod,* and would have worked even better if the female soloists had been professional, too. He decided that improving the training of the choir should be a priority, so he separated it from the main school, giving Knust the job with the amateurs. The school he handed over to Ida Urjan, a dancer with him since Stuttgart, well able to deal with professional students. Karl Bergeest, although still a Tanzbühne *Eleve*, became an assistant teacher, no doubt with the men's training in mind. Since the June disbandment of the Tanzbühne, Laban was short of trained men, who were all dancing for other people, especially with Bereska and with Jooss. Unlike Wigman, Laban attracted a continuous flow of male dancers – amateurs in considerable numbers, but professional students also.

Work was offered at the Schauspielhaus which was producing *A Midsummer Night's Dream*, for which Laban directed the incidental dances, using ex-Tanzbühne dancers. But it was a bread-and-butter affair. He needed his own dancers for his Kammertanz performances, so after the premiere they taught the roles to a selected group from the Movement Choir. To pursue his own experiments, he decided to work with Gertrud Loeszer, while Dussia Bereska was in Rome. He questioned what could be done as a duo beyond the expected *pas de deux*, the traditional love duet. He settled on Wagner, the idol of German culture second only to Goethe, as a starting point. Could he take Wagner's themes, Wagner's characters, without Wagner music? This risky concept was what he chose. He and Loeszer started rehearsing duos on Tristan and Isolde, and on Klingsor and Kundry, in silence, for a December premiere, concerning themselves with ways of playing with the traditions of both Wagner and the *pas de deux*.

In the meantime Laban turned his attention to his writing. He signed a contract with Gerhard Stalling of Oldenburg for a book for teachers on children's work. *Gymnastik, Rhythmik und Tanz für Kinder* was the provisional title. *Gymnastik* cannot be literally translated as 'gymnastics', for it does not include *Turnen*, apparatus work. *Gymnastik* is best translated as 'exercise' or 'body training', or simply 'movement'. *Rhythmik* in this connection denotes movement to music or to percussion sound. These two words were the customary pair used in school syllabi of the day. Laban added 'und Tanz' and set about documenting his credo and his method for *Freie Tanz* for the young. Just how interested he really was in the minutiae of children's work is not clear. He never taught children's classes although he enjoyed playing with children, his own included. It is more likely that he had to fill a gap, had to provide his students with a text. Not only was one needed to inform, but also to protect his own ideas from plagiarism: plenty of *Körperkultur* teachers from Bode, Medau, Loheland and Mensendieck, and students with one week's summer school participation, were ready to set up classes for children using Laban's ideas as a form of physical culture. He needed an apprentice to deal with the book's details. Jenny Gertz was to hand, with her successful school for children's dance, and she could also supply excellent photographs.

The second book contract was for *Gymnastik und Rhythmik für Erwachsene*. It became a best-selling text for dancers in general, under the title *Gymnastik und Tanz*. He needed these two to be published as soon as possible, to cope with the demand from teachers. Who helped him with this is uncertain – probably Herta Feist. German was not his native language, nor even his second. He always depended on someone to help edit his texts, and to cope with the time-consuming essentials of book publishing.

The book had to compete with others, and to follow on from pre-Weimar publications on movement teaching. F. H. Winther's *Körperbildung als Kunst und Pflicht* (Bodily Education as Art and Duty) gave an overview of the different schools. Although published in 1919, Winther's book, like Laban's *Die Welt des Tänzers*, was delayed because of the war. The concepts and illustrations were old-fashioned by now, when the New Objectivity had taken over from Expressionism and Romanticism. It contained pictures of Laban's first group in Munich. The young Suzanne Perrottet and Mary Wigman, and two young men, Karl Weysel and Jo Meisenbach, were illustrated in Greek-inspired tunics, or nude. Their movement looked tentative and ill-formed compared with current photographs. Winther's book would do Laban's work no good in the 1920s except to show the reader how rapidly and spectacularly he had developed.

Each *Körperkultur* group had its own specialist literature with prescribed exercises, although some included little conceptual background. Rudolf Bode, in *Ausdrucks – Gymnastik*, published in its third edition in 1926, described 360 exercises and gave an introduction on the psychology of bodily education, quoting from Goethe and Schiller. The psychologist Ludwig Klages was the major theoretical source, especially his concepts on rhythm and expressive behaviour. Bode's work was for 'German youth' and

'German *Volk*'. No artistic content was suggested, and the exercises were described specifically for women with others for men. His work was not only for healthy functioning of muscles and bones, but for the link of mind and body. More functional was Alfred Müller's *Rhythmische Gymnastik*, published in 1926, approved by Dr Diem of the Deutsche Hochschule für Leibesübungen (High School for Physical Exercise).

Laban wrote his new book with these others as a context. Since the book embodies central arguments relevant to the 1920s public, and which run continuously through his work, it is useful to summarise its contents. In *Gymnastik und Tanz* Laban started his discourse just as he did his workshops, with practices familiar to his public. He led his reader gradually through concepts that they knew, towards his new vision of *Bewegungskunst* (the art of movement) as education. He was at pains to value all forms of movement exercise, not only his own. He did not proselytise, but informed.

He started with 'free-standing exercise', which, he said, was the focus of all movement work. Movement, or gymnastics, had several forms of development which he discussed by considering their goals. One was for skilled work on apparatus, *Turnen*, where the goals of courage and contending with objects were added to those of body strengthening and control in gymnastic-oriented free-standing exercises. Another development was theatre dance, in which communication with the audience through the symbolic content of the movement became the aim. Another development was the religious ceremony, where the movement became the means of prayer and adoration, adding to the spiritual nature of free-standing movement. Yet another possibility was in movement therapy, where the goal was to cure, to counterbalance an imbalance. At the centre of all these developments stood the person, moving, in space, rhythmically, free-standing. Laban then looked at the confusions which teachers and students of free-standing exercise might meet. Were pupils dancing or doing gymnastics? Was it hygienic exercise (the term used for both health and therapy)? Did the movement have spiritual content? Some gymnastic exercises were performed to music, and that could lead people to think that they were dancing, which they were not.

This confusion went away, he wrote, when one clarified the source of the movement, its aim, its natural development, its grammar, and its social significance, plus the philosophy of life of its practitioners. He took each of these themes and led his reader towards a thorough conceptual grounding in the 'new art of movement'. In the early part of the book he called it the 'new gymnastics', bringing *Bewegungskunst* in gradually.

The aim of the art of movement was both simple and deep, as he described: to become aware of, to feel and to enjoy the free-standing body relating to the surrounding space, and the feeling of the changing qualities of time and dynamics. No more and no less. That was sufficient. No external goal was necessary, no body strengthening, no communication to an audience, no therapeutic aim, no religious one. And yet by this awareness there occurred an integration of body, mind and soul.

Laban took many pages to try to express the inexpressible – kinetic feeling – to try to convey that alongside the valid goals of applied motion there is another: simply awareness of bodily movement. He used *Erlebnis* in preference to *körperlich*, to get at the lived experience of the body rather than the body treated as an object, moved by the individual.

The language of the book is restrained until the last chapter, when his *Die Welt des Tänzers* writing style creeps in: 'The flood gate of inner-movingness is opened when the soul swings/participates in action plays,' for example. These rhapsodic tones, his way of expressing the phenomenal experience of dancing, were needed to lead the reader into the 'land of silence', just as he would lead the practical student.

Laban discussed the source of the movement material in free-standing exercise. There was not one but several, he wrote. Gymnastic exercises use idealised movement: they do not incorporate ugly, grotesque gestures, but clear lines, completed positions. But the dance turns to gesture for one of its sources, to behaviour, which gymnastics would never use. Dance presents the ugly as well as the ideal, untidy everyday movement as well as the neat. The free-standing exercise leading to liturgical processions and religious ritual had particular sources, handed down from earlier times: gestures of blessing, of prayer, of adoration, of supplication, addressed to an outer being. Similar movements might be used in the art of movement, he wrote, but their goal is not religious observance but deepening awareness of universals. Working movement, movements from martial arts, are sources for gymnastics. The dynamic range of these encompasses cut and thrust, push and press, he said. The art of movement uses those too, but also soft strewing, scattering flickers, sharp tapping, which counterbalance aggressive and contending qualities.

Laban attempted to get his readers to see that it was not only the selection of actions which distinguished one kind of free exercise from another, but the intent behind it, and that intent was not idiosyncratic but an inevitable outcome of recognising the source and embodying the aim.

He next turned his attention to the social relationship between movers. In gymnastics the possible interaction of people is wide but circumscribed. Gymnasts move alone, in unison with others, or in competition with others. Gymnastics' associated realm of sport is dominated by competition or even fighting with others, while in religious exercise the ritual is communal rather than co-operative, related to an outside ideal figure. In theatre the focus is to the audience. It includes all manner of human relationship: fighting, competing, laughing, teasing, loving. In the art of movement, partner and group relationships of all sorts are included because social education through the art of movement is an important aspect of it. Movement art includes the experience of fighting but also of resolution, deriding but also supporting, both following and leading, being alone and co-operating.

Laban looked at the philosophy of life of the adherents to the various forms of free-standing exercise, which were diverse and based on their own history. Modern sport, although concerned with co-operation, teamwork and personality development, ultimately saw the world as a place in which to be in control, to fight and to win; it had a highly competitive element, which the original Olympics did not have. The religious dance, having its roots in primordial ritual and ceremony, had a philosophy of life in which eternal forces and a god figure were central. The hygienic exercise teacher saw the world as a place with disharmonies to be eradicated; its history lay in the history of medicine.

While it was not difficult for Laban to give a historical base for well-established practices, he had to do the same for the new developments that he proposed. He was in no doubt about their roots, but they would be news to many of his readers, and controversial. He wrote that the art of movement could trace its history in Plato's *Timaeus* and the writings of Confucius. There, movement experience was valued for itself, and the strong and supple body was not advocated for purposes of fighting but for beauty and self-worth, for spiritual content.

Any free-standing exercise, even gymnastics, could become valuable when imbued with a life philosophy, Laban wrote; not only the art of movement, but any movement without a philosophy was arid. While a philosophy gave an over-arching purpose to a movement practice, the detailed content of each movement phrase could only be achieved through awareness of its syntax. The grammar of each free-standing form was distinct, for each was a language that derived meaning through its own grammar, and that could be discovered through a study of its history and the source of its movement material.

Laban then discussed some of the grammar of behaviour, the rules of gesture through which people understand each other socially. 'Gesture and posture do not lie,' he wrote, while words could and did. He put forward the grammar of the art of movement, based on harmonising principles, on the balance of opposites. Gathering is balanced naturally by scattering, strong by weak, wide by narrow. Curved and straight, action and reaction, fight and co-operation, off-balance and on-balance, asymmetry and symmetry – all balance each other. This balancing propensity is innate to the body, mind and spirit, and is what makes sense of bodily movement. Nonsense movement does not conform to the grammar. Without awareness of this grammar, exercises are without meaning to the mover, and do not integrate mind, body and soul, or person with person.

He continued over many pages to show how the art of movement would lead into dance-making and described the movement choir as one form for the reader to use, the *Reigen* being another and dance theatre a third. In the back of the book he included a fold-out description of beginners' free-standing exercises. Read on their own they present limited material, but with the book in mind they make sense.

Laban illustrated *Gymnastik und Tanz* with photographs from both accredited Labanschulen and schools using his ideas. Emita Török, leader of the school in Budapest who had been in the Stuttgart *Bacchanale* and *Die Geblendeten*, gave photographs which showed her school's clear focus on dance as art. Her teaching went beyond free-standing exercises into dramatic content. Her pupils included both men and women, some working in the nude. The photographs from Margarethe Schmidt, who gained her diploma through leading *Agamemnons Tod*, leant towards a movement choir style for both men and women.

The vigour, freedom, exhilaration and personal movement language of each dancer were shown in the images from Herta Feist's school and the Hamburg school. The contrast between Toni Homagk's gymnastic school and Berthe Bartolomé Trumpy's could not be lost. Homagk's were in unison, earthbound, young girls in neat costumes using idealised movement. On the next page, the school of Trumpy, a graduate of the Zurich Laban school and a Wigman colleague, showed three freely leaping, expressive women. The Hamburg Men's Movement Choir, Feist's Berlin school, Käthe Wulff's in Basle, and Martin Gleisner – all illustrated the applicability of Laban's art of movement to men. A Mensendieck school was illustrated by nude young women in soft poses; the Menzler school for 'healthy and artistic gymnastics' had figures reminiscent of ancient Greek vase paintings.

Throughout the book, Laban insisted on the *art* of movement, the *art* of dance. Although he participated in gymnastic-related conferences, he had to underline his own artistic intent. The book focused on that point and illustrated it soundly. Nevertheless, in 1926 a Deutsche Gymnastiksbund was formed, by the Kallmeyer, Gindler, Mensendieck and Loheland groups which Laban joined, according to the magazine *Die Schönheit*.

A demonstration by Rudolf Bode and seven of his young women students in Hamburg in November 1926 illustrates the confusion that Laban was addressing. Bode, who was not a dance person, nevertheless used the term *Bewegungskunst* in his talk. The *Hamburger Nachrichten* critic picked him up on it. The 'art' of Bode's girls was like a nightingale, he wrote: natural, but quite different from the 'art' of Mozart, linking the Mozartian concept with Laban's 'art' work in Hamburg. They are both beautiful, he wrote, but no bridge can be built between them. The problem was, in 1926, and later in Britain, that the gymnastic people could not distinguish the nightingale from the Mozart aria, nor see that the bird who tried to sing Mozart was in the wrong place.

The number of Laban schools increased in 1925–26, as the advertisements in *Die Schönheit* show. Herta Feist's brochure, a typical example, included professional training for both men and women as dancers, and as teachers of dance and gymnastics. The prospectus emphasised Feist's connections with theatre performances and her own performing experience with Laban. In addition, classes were offered for lay people, 'as a balance to the mechanisation of working life', and for housewives, mothers, and children. The chance to perform in the Movement Choir was offered.

Des Kindes Gymnastik und Tanz was published simultaneously with *Gymnastik und Tanz*. In it Laban was more aggressive towards *Gymnastik*, attacking its inadequacies as a form of bodily education for 1920s children. 'One must always think about the basic concepts of gymnastics. It is not play, it is not art, both of which children need, but rule-governed bodily function. *Gymnastik* has an aim to arouse and enliven atrophied life energy and to maintain and increase it. But there is no expression in *Gymnastik*, which children demand, and this is a pathological limitation, which with our way, is removed.' He expressed his approach to children's dance by discussing it in topics, one of which was *Schriftzeichen*, signs for written language. These, he said, were originally depictions of gestures, actions, which expressed not one sound, as letters do, but rather a thousand unsayable things and passions. Children learn letters and words now, but the non-verbal content had gone from them. But the content in the gesture is there in dance. He brought the discussion to the struggle for *Tanzschrift* or *Choreographie*, that is for the written sign which would capture the movement, the non-verbal. He wanted his script to contain the passion which letters could not contain, for that he saw as essential to dance.

He discussed the movement choir for children as their introduction to modern cultural education. He included photographs of Jenny Gertz's children's work, young boys and girls, nude, dancing together in group play with clear sensitivity and intent, and with bodily freedom and confidence. He cited the need for the whole personality of the child to be involved 'to break through the barrier between us and our real selves'. He spoke out against 'drill', and insisted on the importance of experiencing the movement process. He concentrated on the skills of expression which a dancing child acquired. 'The stream of inner mobility breaks forth when the soul opens itself in the dance,' he wrote. The forms of culture, forms of art, spoke of their era. Gothic arches, baroque curves, Hellenistic pillars speak of the soul of their times, but today architecture and dance have to speak of the twentieth century. The harmonic balance between the stability of the weight, with its verticality as in architectural buildings, and the positive impulse to move on with off-balance mobility, could be expressed in movement, in the dance. These were the experiences children needed, not drill. He had in mind his whole choreutic material, but he did not attempt to describe it – an impossible task in any case.

The problem for teachers using his work for children in 1925 and 1926, as later for teachers in Britain in the 1950s, was that a sufficient understanding of the work, such as Laban or his Tanzbühne dancers possessed, could not be acquired quickly. To use his work well, teachers had to learn movement sequences to pass on, to learn their grammar, their source, their development. They had to learn how to free the life energy of children, how to give that energy form, how to guide them to play with movement, how to create dance works for them to participate in. In 1926 it took a talent such as Jenny Gertz's, but many would-be teachers did not have the talent. Laban paid little attention at this time to the problem, but by 1929 he recognised the uneven results, and, with Mary Wigman, besought the government to support a High School for dance training. But that was already too late, for many inadequately trained teachers were already in place.

Laban's concentration on writing these books on education was disrupted by an invitation to put on a late-night *Phantastische Revue* at the Deutsches Schauspielhaus in Hamburg, for a fun November evening in 1924. Little did the administration realise what they might get. It was a burlesque to end all burlesques, with numbers like *Death of Cleopatra*, *Cocaine Dream*, and *Wax Figures' Closet*. His Dada and caricature background combined to give the Schauspielhaus audience too much of a jolt. 'The whole thing was a mistake,' he commented later, 'and lost us a lot of friends.' The *Hamburger Anzeiger* reviewer found it 'unbelievably tasteless'. Only the *8-Uhr Abendblatt* thought it 'mature art, hitting at the world as it is'. But the audience felt themselves to be the subject of the parody, and the Laban of *Der Schwingende Tempel* to have betrayed himself. The only good to come out of it was Loeszer's reception. Laban saw that her dancing had another side, 'erotic/exotic/ecstatic', which could be used in the Wagner programme. He added the words 'Burlesquen, Satiren, Grotesken' to the publicity material, and on 1 January 1925 announced in the *Hamburger Fremdenblatt* that he had a new partner, Gertrud Loeszer, and would undertake a duo tour with her immediately. Karl Bergeest was another beneficiary. His hidden talents as a comic performer were noted. 'Laban set me off at this point on a future career as a character dancer,' he wrote later.

Laban's urgent concern was money. With the dollars finished and no city subsidy, he was on his own, and the *Phantastische Revue* had done him no good. He had to turn his mind to his least favourite topic, raising money. The growing number of schools using his name, and for whom he was writing, could be a source of income by the publishing date in 1926. But more immediate had to be the means of earning. Loeszer and Laban had given a preview of their Wagner presentation at a matinée at the Stadttheater, Aachen, on 14 December 1924, and opened their spring and summer touring season with an evening in Hamburg. They offered 'Scenes from *Rheingold*, *Tristan und Isolde*, *Parsival*, and *Götterdämmerung*', without music.

Laban, despite his lack of traditional dancing skills, was resoundingly well received. Time and again the reviews remark on the 'power of his personality': 'he always imbues the movement with a manliness' . . . 'the most masculine of dancers, the one to be taken most seriously' . . . 'the most fruitful leader of the modern dance' . . . 'behind these performances is a fiery artistic will.' Loeszer was also noted: 'the elasticity and energy of this young dancer' . . . 'this lithe young woman is the most mature performer we have seen in Hamburg this year' . . . 'a bold temperament' . . . 'a magical technique'. So wrote the critics in Halle, Leipzig, Stuttgart and Hamburg. Between the two of them they caused a stir. The choreography was said, in the Munich press, to be 'the most unusual and daring experiment, it bordered on the phenomenal.'

Gustav Grund, writing in the Hamburg newspaper *Der Kreis*, was more perceptive. He commented on the way in which the Wagner characters and the underlying meaning of their relationships were abstracted to give only the kernel; it was so clear that the spectator, used to the pampered *Gesamtkunstwerk* productions, received a new vision, and understanding. As so often with Laban, he wrote, it was the underlying significance which was brought out. The ideas of *Leitmotif* and counterpoint were made visible, especially in the heroic Siegfried, fiery Wotan, and Loge. He delighted in the characterisation of Alberich and Mime, a 'grotesque'. Other solo dancers should free themselves from dependency on music, he suggested.

The duo tour had to choose its venues carefully. Whereas the variety of the Kammertanz repertoire, with its grotesque wit, and number of short items, could entertain a broad public, here the most traditional theatre-goer would be nonplussed. 'Unusualness' can arouse many responses, and Grund warned that the 'Bayreuthers' would be horrified. In retrospect, Laban wrote that he had misgivings about the Wagner experiment, but that through it he came to understand and appreciate Richard Wagner's concept of movement in theatre. Despite these experiments, or perhaps because of them, he was hired to work at the Bayreuth Wagner Festival for the 1930 and 1931 seasons, by Siegfried Wagner, the great man's son.

While Laban and Loeszer performed from time to time, the Kammertanzbühne Laban, 'with selected soloists from the movement choir', began a series of evenings in Hamburg at the Volksoper, from January, under the title 'Orchestik'. The publicity pointed out the company's financial problems, and in order to keep Laban in Hamburg, asked for support for the series through prompt ticket sales. 'Orchestik' kept them going. Kurt Jooss and Sigurd Leeder gave two guest performances in the series, in March 1925. Two male dancers were a novelty, and their varied programme was both humorous and sensitive. Their reception was enthusiastic, '*stürmisch*', but attended by a scant audience. Financially they were no help to the 'Orchestik' series, but Laban was surely delighted with their audacity and evident artistic success.

Special inexpensive weekend performances were given by the Kammertanzbühne, by 1924 nicknamed 'Katabü', in halls in the Hamburg suburbs, with youth groups and the unemployed in mind. These were no earners, but fulfilled Laban's desire for *Tanz für Alle*, to bring dance to everyone. His ideals remained, but his financial acumen was barely adequate to support them. Possibly he felt this gesture might brighten his tarnished image with the authorities. To accompany the performances he wrote in *Der Spiegel*, the local newspaper for youth, on 'Vom Geist des Tanzes' (The Spirit of Dance), that the new dance art is not about the dancer, nor about physical beauty, nor yet personal self-expression, but artistic expression in a new medium: movement. He knew that the readers would be familiar with expression in singing and in speech choirs. He went on: 'Movement rhythm and movement harmony are the strongest expressive media of all.'

To bring new dancers into the Katabü, 'a fresh repertoire of 32 dances' was rehearsed for this 1925 season, for the solos of Jooss, Keith, Troplowitz and others needed to be replaced. With Bereska still in Rome, Loeszer had a double role as Laban's Wagner partner, and main female performer in Katabü performances. While Loeszer was a talented dancer, she was young, without the authority of Bereska to lead the group. Laban had to do that himself.

Bereska was stated as leader of the Movement Choir in Rome in their 1925 publicity, and in *Gymnastik und Tanz*. Jens Keith and Edgar Frank who were with her in Rome in the autumn of 1924, were no longer there by February 1925, but intended 'opening their own school'. Bereska had difficulties in introducing *Freie Tanz* to the Italians. Newspaper articles and performance reviews illustrate her problem. Her quartet – Keith, Frank, Ingeborg Roon and herself – appeared in January in a series of concerts at the Independi, a theatre in Rome directed by Anton Guilio Bragaglia, a central figure in the cultural life of the city at that time. Giovanni Miracolo, writing in *Comoedia*, took the view that the theoretical stance of northern Europeans, epitomised by Laban, was not to the taste of the southerners, for whom inspiration, novelty and improvisation were preferred. They appreciated Niddy Impekoven – she was free of national spirit (implying German spirit), more international. But Bereska's true rival seems to have been the dancer Jia Ruskaya, whom Bragaglia favoured and promoted. 'Passion, spirit and inspiration' were how Ruskaya described the content of her work, and the Romans loved her. Laban's image as a German theoretician could not compete. Wigman as well as Bereska were given a cool reception. It is no wonder that Keith and Frank decided to leave Rome, Frank to join up with Sylvia Bodmer and Lotte Müller in Frankfurt. Italy was a relatively new country, and critics may have been keen to establish an Italian style, not an imported one seen as alien to the fire of southern people.

Bereska must have been thoroughly disheartened, for she was not German in nationality or outlook. She would have been aware of Loeszer, who, unless Laban's amorous behaviour had changed, was surely his lover of the moment. Bereska, always a private person, was nowhere to be found in the Hamburg literature in 1925, until the autumn, when she is fully back as the collaborator he needed. In the meantime he had to cope without her.

The movement choir work expanded during the 1924–25 season. Martin Gleisner, first an actor, then a Herta Feist student, briefly a Tanzbühne Laban *Eleve* in the Balkan tour, took a job as leader of the *corps de ballet* at the Reussisches Theater, Gera. Concurrently he managed to start a Laban-style movement choir at the Volkshochschule, a strongly socialist institution, much to Gleisner's taste. He began to give regular classes, and with Laban and Knust's assistance, put on an evening with dances from *Licht-wende*, a *Gruppen Grotesque* from Knust, and his own first dance work, *Spiel für sieben Paare in fünf Reigen* (Play for Seven Couples in Five *Reigen*). He managed to arrange a Laban/Loeszer performance at the Reussisches Theater too. A man with vision and talent both as a performer and an organiser, Gleisner then worked on a combined evening for his more able dancers and Katabü. They gave *Drachentöterei*, and Laban created a dance version of the Mozart *Les Petits Riens* for them, using Noverre's original idea. This was Laban's second use of Noverre. He liked to work as part of an ongoing dance history, which not all *Freie Tänzer* did – Wigman especially, for she saw herself as breaking with the past, not as a natural development of it as Laban did.

The significance of Gleisner at this point was that he opened up possibilities for Laban's belief in soloist/amateur collaborative works. These he saw as educationally inspiring for the amateur, financially helpful for the theatre producer, and choreographically challenging. The programme in Gera was repeated in February with the Berlin Movement Choir, under Herta Feist, but more ambitiously as a festival over several days. She was, after all, more firmly established. Excerpts from Laban's *Prometheus*, *Lichtwende* and *Agamemnons Tod* were given, together with the Knust work. Feist was a fanatical Laban supporter, running a first-rate school. She brought the fiery spirit of Stuttgart and affirmation of Gleschendorf to her leadership and her own performance. The professional/amateur collaboration was fully operative in her festival. The Hamburg Movement Choir followed suit and they performed at the German Teachers' Conference in June, dancing the prologue from *Prometheus* and a new work of Knust's, *Goetzendienst* (Tribute to an Idol). Knust had particular talent for group movement, group canons, group forms and shapes, and their spiritual content, building up a strong men's group within the Hamburg Choir. This kind of performance, at a conference, was particularly useful in that it stimulated interest in possible students and in Laban's future books.

Gleisner encountered Eugen Diederichs in Jena, where Diederichs' publishing house operated. The latter was in close touch with the Laban group through their writings in *Die Tat* and through his agreement with Laban to publish *Choreographie*. He was also well established as a Jena socialist entrepreneur of cultural events. Diederichs was influential in promoting Gleisner's politically motivated dance-making, by arranging for a festival in the open-air theatre in Gera. Impressed by Gleisner, he helped him to start a larger regional movement choir, more ambitious than the Gera

Hochschule group, in Jena, a neighbouring and equally industrial town. This became the Thuringer Movement Choir, primarily a workers' group, with young men predominating. Gleisner became a key, even fanatical figure in the Laban fraternity, contributing to Laban's image as a spiritual and socialist artist. Diederichs' annual summer festival, where Gleisner's group presented Ida Seidel's *Planetenspiel*, a work with the quasi-religious tone of many of Diederichs' publications, ended a stimulating season.

The summer months were complicated for Laban by conflicting needs. His focus had to be on the publication of *Choreographie*, as well as on the two teaching method books. *Choreographie*, written by 1919 but not published until 1926, needs some explanation. Far from being a textbook on notation, as it was first intended to be, as the companion text to *Die Welt des Tänzers*, it was both far more and far less – less, because the problems of the notation were still not solved and because various schemes for analysing and writing movement were contained in it, none of which constituted a usable system; more, because it contained choreological concepts, showing how he came to his decisions on movement analysis, and more significantly, on the theory of dance form, a first attempt at a morphology of dance art. These he applied to ballet and to folk dance steps using his own choreutic scales as archetypes of dance form. In the summer of 1925 the text, illustrated by diagrams, needed careful graphic preparation and detailed proof-reading. Neither of these being Laban's forte, an apprentice was used, as always. This was Gertrud Snell, a student and an occasional Katabü dancer with a particular talent for the notation and analysis side of his work. It was she who was elevated to become his assistant on all matters of the presentation of notation, starting with *Choreographie*. Her surprise was immense, and her confusion complete, for to her Laban was 'the master'. No longer. She had to neaten his drawings. He required a workable notation system urgently, in which to write the movement choir parts, and also the schools' studies. The need was no longer theoretical or political, but a practical essential.

The number of new schools opening forced Laban to consider legal and financial consequences. Although pleasing, this success obviously had its problems. He had inspired these people, who taught a curriculum based on his work, and it would be very easy for him to have no benefit and to lose control through their proliferation. An accreditation system was arranged whereby for a school or movement choir to call itself a 'Labanschule', it must specify in its publicity that its leader had the Laban Diploma. The Diploma had to be kept up to date by attendance at the annual vacation courses, and the examinations of professional students ready to gain the

Diploma had to be held by Laban himself. Schools also offered private lessons by Laban personally. In this way he attempted to safeguard the quality of the schools and provide himself with some financial reward.

The Diploma was not easily gained. Students had to dance, to create, to know choreutic and eukinetic theory and practice, and to write notation. The notation was still in flux, and choreutic and eukinetic theory developing; hence the need for keeping up to date via the summer school. In whatever branch of his work they wished to qualify, the candidates had to act as apprentices somewhere, somehow, for some event.

This organisation proved a heavy burden. Laban spent many hours travelling to cities for examinations for which he had to set up criteria, and to provide examination exercises. But it was also highly successful in keeping a Laban community feeling, a sense of belonging to a concerted epoch-making contribution to the cultural life of the times.

It also meant that he must run a summer school. He did not in 1925, possibly because he was overwhelmed with publishing, and partly because Bereska was not there to teach. He ran an Easter course instead, in Berlin, organised by Feist. Many new people attended – ballet-masters, solo dancers, teachers, as well as his regular Labanite group. In a two-week course Laban's magical qualities could set people on a life's odyssey. The summer validation programme did not commence until 1926. While Snell's notes are ambiguous as to the year, it seems almost certain that in the summer vacation of 1925 Laban joined up with Dussia and with their daughter Little Dussia. The photographs in *Des Kindes Gymnastik und Tanz* are surely Little Dussia, for the likeness to her mother is unmistakable. Did Bereska have the little girl with her in Rome? Although Little Dussia was fostered soon after birth, Snell recalled that Laban went on holiday with the child. That must have been 1925, for in 1926 he was in America. Possibly both 1924 and 1925 were summers when they all holidayed together, and in between Bereska attempted to combine motherhood with teaching and dancing in Rome. By the autumn of 1925 she returned, without Little Dussia. In any event, as an adult Little Dussia utterly rejected her mother and father. She preferred the *petit bourgeois* upbringing with her loving and consistent foster parents, and disowned her natural parents whom she learnt to regard as immoral.

The 1925 autumn season began with Laban in Paris, invited by Rolf de Maré, who later founded the Archives Internationales de la Danse, to participate in the theatre section of the Exposition Internationale des Arts Decoratifs on 22 and 23 September. The role of the decorative and applied arts in theatre was the topic for which a Théâtre de l'Exposition was temporally created. The modern scenic arts were presented as elements of theatre in maquette form, and experiments on the integration of these elements were undertaken. Quite what Laban did is unclear, but he was billed as dancing duos with Madame Madika-Szanto, choreographed by her, with Monsieur Szanto providing the music. Why he joined this couple remains a mystery. On his return to Hamburg, the home season started with renewed energy. Encouraged by the imminent publication of *Choreographie*, by Bereska's invaluable contributions and critical advice, and by the prowess in notation of Gertrud Snell, Laban decided to raise the profile of the choreological research side of his work. For this he created the Institute for Movement Notation and Movement Research, housed in the Schwanenwyk school building in Hamburg. He directed it, putting in enormous energy to get the final breakthrough on the script, while Snell administered it. For the Diploma examinations, notation reading material and choreutic/eukinetic study materials had to be prepared. Snell was the apprentice who did this. She admitted asking foolish questions of Laban while he was busy on tour. With more confidence, she could perfectly well have answered them herself. He wired her: 'Snell is a silly goose'; and she got on with the job.

Bereska's autumn return to Hamburg was welcomed by a burst of creative output. Laban, having finished his part of the preparation of his teaching books, started choreographing immediately. They began the creation of two major touring works, *Don Juan* and *Terpsichore*. Concurrently he created *Dämmernden Rhythmen* (Dawning Rhythms) for the Hamburg Movement Choir, with Knust's assistance, a group work in three *Reigen*, named *Dumpf* (Muffled), *Unruhig* (Unquiet) and *Ausgreifend* (Striding Out). With percussion accompaniment, it featured one solo male dancer, Knust in the first performance but then Edgar Neiger, a promising Movement Choir member subsequently. Laban continued lecturing as usual, this year on 'The new art of dance in Rome and Paris', taught regularly and inspiringly in the Hamburg school, and worked on the notation and choreology.

Bereska did not return alone. She brought with her the Kammertanz group that she had formed and performed with towards the end of her stay in Rome. Hermann (Robert) Robst, Motta Nolling, Gretl Berner were full members, while Elso Lembke and Beatrice Mazzoni were *Eleven*, student dancers. These were added to continuing members of Katabü to make a strong and able group who could tour with small works, and also with Laban and Bereska in the new large productions.

They engaged an agent, Herr Leonard, and created a version of *Die Geblendeten* for a smaller group which they entitled *Schwingende Gewalten*

(Swinging Energies). In September they played it at the Schauspielhaus in Mulhausen. With Bereska back, Laban was contemplating a more ambitious programme, requiring professional musical forces and stage design. They created *Terpsichore* as a vehicle for Bereska. She played the muse of the dance, with Handel's music as her partner, so to speak. Apollo was a soprano sung part, Erato an alto. A Young Man (Robst), Graces, and a Faun accompanied her changing moods and fortunes. The piece required professional singers, an orchestra and a solo pianist. The premiere was not appreciated by the *Hamburger Anzeiger* reviewer. Always a ballet-lover, and quick to note weak technique, he compared Bereska's Terpsichore with that of the Diaghilev company. A Terpsichore who only moved her shoulders, more or less, was unimpressive. 'Hail Pavlova!' was his ironic note. Quite what Bereska intended remains unknown, but it suggests an experiment which misfired.

Don Juan was a vehicle for Laban, demanding five good soloists and a dance chorus. He played the well-known figure; Bereska played Donna Elvira. Gluck's ballet music and Angiolini's ballet concept formed the core of the work around which the production was made, with the plan to present it in cities where a movement choir was already adequately trained. With these works, he and Bereska experimented with how to work in the mainstream theatre. Its full resources, the expectation of its audiences, and the clutter of its traditions had to be anticipated. They were a long way from the group spontaneity of *Die Geblendeten*, from Bereska's *Interpunktion* comedy, from *Gaukelei*'s avant-garde socially conscious political dance-drama. Here they attended to another challenge altogether, that of how to evolve a contemporary dance theatre, related to its own history.

In the accompanying prestigious brochure, Laban contributed an article on 'The Classical and Romantic Dance Art'. In it he attempted to locate Handel's music and Bereska's choreography in relation to mainstream art developments. He discussed traditional ballet as an example of classical form, Russian developments of ballet as the struggle to leave the classical and embrace the romantic, and Wigman as an example of romantic feeling. His own work and Bereska's he saw as neither classical nor romantic, but, like Bach's pre-classical music, as pure art. As an explanation of what he meant, he wrote, 'Pure dance is the expression of the urge to movement. Those spiritual impetuses that lead to action, to *practical* movement are in dance balanced against each other, are played off against each other. They stimulate, cancel, confuse and dissolve, and before our eyes there is revealed a world of inner drives, which we scarcely suspected would be so deep in its variety, power and beauty.'

113

Artur Michel, esteemed critic of the *Vossische Zeitung*, gives us an idea of Laban's *Don Juan* at its third performance in Berlin, with Herta Feist as Donna Elvira, and the Berlin Movement Choir as the supporting *corps*. Fritz Böhme's review in the *Deutsche Allgemeine Zeitung* of the same programme was ecstatic. Between them, and John Schilkowski in *Vorwärts* and Willy Bastor in *Tägliche Rundschau*, we can get a fair view.

After commenting with satisfaction that contemporary choreographers were reminding themselves of their predecessors, Michel continued: 'Laban's staging, that he undertook with the dance group of his student Herta Feist, also imparted graceful life to the work. Exactly what the original work required: the movement full of expression, the speaking dance gestures have reached their objective in Laban's creation. So for the public it was astonishing and impressive that, without drastic, naturalistic, everyday mimicry, the sense of the events was revealed simply from the movements of the soloists and of the group, movements changing in a purely dancing way. The events *spoke*: that they could and should have spoken more powerfully, more passionately-splendidly, more emphatically, more colourfully, remains by comparison a secondary question. Laban had no suitable soloists available for the performance.'

Bereska, whose performance of Donna Elvira at the premiere had been well received, was performing with the Kammertanz soloists in another city. While Feist was just adequate for Michel, the dancers in smaller solo parts were not. Michel continued: 'He [Laban] himself certainly danced Don Juan only because he had no adequate dancer for this role, although he knew that for this character he lacked the range of dancing.' But Laban danced Don Juan himself everywhere, to great acclaim, despite his lack of acrobatic dance skills. Possibly he did so because he loved performing it, possibly because it was economically better if he did, and possibly the range that Michel expected was in fact never in Laban's mind, ever.

In all the reviews the group scenes were of special interest. Michel wrote, 'One was reminded of Laban's best work by some of the colourfully moving group scenes, if not always firmly enough structured. Artistically the high point was constituted by the third part: the party in the graveyard with the visit of the three dead. Here he succeeded, in a sequence without music of group and solo dances, in evoking the eerie atmosphere that the apparition of the two ghosts required.'

Böhme was much taken with the spiritual layers of the piece as a whole: 'This Don Juan is not merely the seducer, but the powerful person who leads the person enraptured by him to a more powerful liveliness, to an experience of bodily rapture, to the expression of inner powers of form . . .

In this dance poem the spiritual elements of human community experience, the magical, and the ecstatic, are so distributed that they become visible in completest, effective vividness. And that produces the magnitude and the power that emerges from this creation.' He described Laban's nuance of character: 'A person's path, a being, a destiny arises before the spectator in a passage of gigantic intensification; starting from the light tempter, losing itself in the staggerer, the equivocator, the scorner, raised into the mocker, the destroyer, and finally as a body destroyed by the powers that have been summoned up but which can no longer be controlled. The magician dies in the glow of the blaze from himself.'

He summed up: 'The whole was a performance (also happy in the costume provision and flowing in the collaboration of music and move-ment) of gripping and thrilling power, which released from the spectators a storm of applause that did not wish to end.' Michel found this performance of the last scene 'too harmless': it 'denied the ending the necessary eleva-tion to the grandiose.' The Berlin Movement Choir was not quite up to it, in his view. But, apparently, the Hamburg choirs were and the Nurembergers, and the Jena group and the Essen group in their turn, as the press reports there testified, though perhaps without Michel's criteria.

This piece was toured to acclaim, at first with *Terpsichore* and later with the newest work *Narrenspiegel*, through 1926 to 1927. These two full-evening dances were hugely successful everywhere. To tour profitably, Laban needed at least two major works to alternate with the Kammertanz pieces. *Narrenspiegel* (The Fool's Mirror) he created for January 1926. In it, he wrote, he set out 'to portray the world through the eyes of a fool.' Of its two acts 'one could be called the dance of life and the other the dance of death.' Each character had two faces. In his mind these were pride/humil-ity, joy/grief, love/hate, although those titles were not listed in the pro-gramme. He vouchsafed that the idea for the dance came from childhood enjoyment of the *Kasperltheater*, a kind of Punch-and-Judy roadside show. He played the Fool himself, Bereska was cast as the Enduring and Forgiving One, Loeszer as the Careless One, Robst as the Solemn One, who becomes the Death figure. Rudolf Wagner-Regeny was the pianist hired for the sea-son to play Liszt's piano pieces as accompaniment. The publicity described the piece as 'surging between the ideal and real life, purity and beauty, profundity and greed, between flight-from-the-world and love.' *Narren-spiegel* was toured between January and May 1926, and again from Septem-ber through to April 1927. It was reasonably economical to tour, needing four good performers, and two small parts, played by *Eleven*, plus Wagner-Regeny, no set being required. *Don Juan*, which also toured in 1926, was far more expensive, requiring an orchestra and a set. Both works had appealing music; as Laban said much earlier, in 1913 in fact, 'audiences need music, we don't.' Certainly these musical works were sought after and much enjoyed. They earned well, and Laban was able to afford to pay for the assistants he needed on the serious research for the notation and choreology.

Mary Wigman was also touring, and in February 1926 Laban and the Rome Katabü preceded Wigman by one week in Hamburg. Gustav Grund compared the two under the intriguing heading 'The Laban–Wigman Problem'. Inevitably these two great artists were compared, in Hamburg, but also in general, by the public, by each other's followers, and by the critics. There was a growing tendency for a 'for or against' mentality to emerge. Grund rose above such short-sighted partisanship, and saw Wigman as a huge personality, dancing with a chorus of trained (some said regimented) young women behind her. In contrast was the self-affirmation of each member of Hamburg's Movement Choir, and each Katabü dancer. Both concepts were possible. Grund discussed theatricality against confession, those being two perfectly good qualities in performing arts, pointing out that both artists had both qualities, but also presented polarities. He juxtaposed Laban's *Die Grünen Clowns* with Wigman's *Totentanz*, the one an ironic comment on human behaviour, the other a powerful communion of the soul and death. While Grund admitted that he preferred theatricality, he wanted to promote a broader appreciation of the art form of both dance leaders by all audience members.

Wigman was famous. She had been touring as a soloist for seven years, and with her women's ensemble. Her school based in Dresden was supported by the local government, and she had developed a technical training which was providing her dancers with expressive skills and a Wigman style markedly distinct from Laban's. Her ensemble, begun in 1923, gave her opportunities for group choreography, in which she was customarily a solo figure. She excelled as a teacher, trained many dancers who became successful soloists in their own right. By 1926 Gret Palucca, Max Terpis, Hanya Holm, Vera Skoronel, Yvonne Georgi and Harald Kreutzberg were with her. Her philosophy and Laban's diverged in that she saw herself as establishing a clear break with ballet, with folk dance, with anything in dance that had gone before; instead she erected her Absolute Dance. Laban, on the other hand, saw himself as a reformer, but following in the traditions of the innovative dancing masters Jean-Georges Noverre and Gaspero Angiolini. She was an independent choreographer, he a socially engaged artist/researcher. She developed finesse within her style, he continually moved on to new challenges. Each had supporters and students who were devotees. While she was ready, both earlier and later, to give Laban credit for freeing her, enabling her to find her independence and giving her the strength to use it, in the mid-1920s partisanship increased. She had to forge her own place in German dance, and possibly eventually become its leader. By 1926 these rumbles were to be heard, to surface unhelpfully at the three Dancers' Congresses of 1927, 1928 and 1930. The critics were divided between their respect for her choreographic and performing prowess and their respect for Laban's spiritual leadership of the whole dance revolution.

By 1926 Laban's ex-student Kurt Jooss was also well established with his Neue Tanzbühne in Munster, where Hanns Niedecken-Gebhardt was the supportive intendant. Tanzbühne Laban dancers, including Aino Siimola and Jens Keith, became part of his company of three men and four women, together with the independent dance artist Sigurd Leeder. Although Jooss's movement style in 1925 still remained close to Laban's experimental work, as photographs of *Larven* and *Groteske* show, his growing sense of overall design was already evident in *Herakles*. Jooss moved more than Laban towards an aesthetic of technically based line, which his brief studies of ballet in Vienna and Paris enabled him to do. He was by 1926 becoming known, having built up his artistic team of able dancers, plus Hein Heckroth as designer and Fritz A. Cohen as musician. With his individual choreographic voice more and more in evidence, as *Kaschemme* showed, the Neue Tanzbühne, with twenty dancers including ex-Laban dancers Ingeborg Roon, Edgar Frank, Ida Urjan, and Werner Stammer, gave guest appearances across Germany. Although Jooss was increasingly independent in style and purpose, he was a close ally to Laban, integrating the choreutic and eukinetic practices that he had learned with classical work for his dancers' training. His commitment, and Leeder's, to the notation was profound. In 1925 and 1926 the three men and Bereska met on and off, but with intense discussion, Jooss being especially influential in nudging Laban to expand the application of his theories of movement analysis to all forms of dance.

Very much on the sidelines at this time with the dancers and dance public was Oskar Schlemmer, working in the Bauhaus Theatre Department. His *Triadic Ballet* was performed from time to time. Dancers and critics were too indoctrinated with valuing bodily experience to tolerate his work. where design of costume and space was prioritised over movement, which had to serve its purpose rather than be the central core of the work. But in 1926 he and Laban were known to each other without rivalry.

During the year the plan to upgrade the Institute for Movement Notation and Movement Research moved on. Laban's books, published in the spring of 1926, and his touring successes, his increased number of students, allowed him to spread his influence and finance his dearest concern, 'Choreographie' and 'Choreologie'. With the school self-sufficient, there was no reason for him to remain in Hamburg; indeed it would be beneficial to have a change of town for local performances. When Wurzburg City Council invited him to establish a school there, he considered it seriously. Wurzburg was Gertrud Loeszer's home town. Her mother lived there, and her younger sister, also a dancer. Through them contacts, premises, and an open-air training space could be found. Laban negotiated for a more ambitious institution, calling it an Akademie der Tanzkunst. By May it was settled that he and key staff would move to Theaterstrasse 24, Wurzburg, by the autumn. Loeszer herself had been teaching at the El Corret Laban school in Munich from time to time during the year between tours, and opened a studio there for occasional classes for professional dancers. Loeszer and Bereska were rivals for Laban's attention, whatever form that might have taken. Each was important to him, for Bereska was the intellectual stimulus he always needed and the mature colleague and performer, while Loeszer was the athletic youngster, and a bright young star and teacher.

It was also finalised that a 'Labanbund' should be instituted, an organisation for all the growing number of people engaged in Laban's work, a way of keeping together and of expressing the corporateness of being a Labanite. The suggestion had come in the autumn from the professional students and administrators of the Herta Feist Berlin school, Dr Buchholz, Lotte Auerbach, Fritz Böhme, Anny Fligg and Hans Rausch. Laban agreed, and the legal necessities were set in motion. By April 1926 the Labanbund was in place, in time for the year's examinations.

For the summer months Loeszer would lead the summer school at Wurzburg in the Waldkolonie, the open-air colony on the edge of the town. Bereska did not feature in the summer school, so possibly she again went to her little daughter, but she was also advertised as running a school, or classes, for *Eleven* in Berlin. So too was Snell, but separately for *Tanz-schrift*, probably both in April and during part of the summer months.

Laban himself was billed to be personally present at the Easter course but not in July. After an exuberant May festival of the Laban schools in Munich, supported by a lecture on 'Moderner Tanz im neuen Theater' given by Hans Brandenburg and combined no doubt with the qualifying examinations for the prized Laban Diploma, Laban sailed for America 'to undertake ethnographic research.'

7

The Double Edge of Success

America, Wurzburg, Magdeburg, Essen and Berlin, 1926–1928

Laban's American visit is something of a mystery. Why he went, how he paid for it, even where he went, is difficult to establish. What is known is that he appointed a personal agent, Herr Mayer, before he went, and when he returned Mayer had set up an extensive lecture tour. It had the dual advantage of giving him an opportunity to talk about his experiences, and also to pay for it.

The purpose of his trip was referred to in the press as 'ethnographic studies', and he was certainly interested in how cultures outside Europe manifested community dance. A further aim, he wrote in his 1951 curriculum vitae, was to establish a kinetography centre in New York. This may have been an exaggeration, but certainly Irma Otte Betz organised a lecture in June 1926 in a hotel in New York for him to talk about his work. Her translation of *Bewegungschor* as 'moving chorus' and the language used to introduce his work suggests that she was not used to German/English translating. Laban knew very little English, and travelled in New York with an interpreter, but was soon able to communicate unaided. His own descriptions of the press interest in his notation, its commercial and sensation value, have to be read with caution, but it seems that he was greeted as a celebrity. Americanism was a catchword in Europe for all things modern. Possibly modernism was what attracted Laban to visit the States, but he was not prepared for the onslaught of what he called 'American zeal'. He saw press coverage as exploitation and enthusiastic interest as a 'wind force ten' storm. He found the response to be the 'crazy high tension of over-excited human brains.' This reads as unappreciative of the efforts made by well-wishers to promote his work and of the genuine reception his notation ideas received, as the journalist Courtenay Davidge reported. He was used to working solidly over years on his notation, for the sake of dance, while here quick results were not only wholly alien but certainly shocking to him. Davidge's remark that 'for years he has twinkled in the theatrical firmament of Hamburg, Paris, Prague, Rome and Belgrade' – is an example of the culture gap. If he had any intention to sound out emigration possibilities (and his writings are ambiguous on the point), it was no longer there by the end of the first week.

He took off for the West Coast and there he was escorted, as he said, 'by an acquaintance of mine, a technical director of a Hollywood film company.' This suggests that he had introductions through UFA, the Berlin film-makers with whom he had recently co-operated, with others, on a film later circulated as *Neuer Weg zu Kraft und Schönheit* (New Way to Strength and Beauty). He travelled to Los Angeles and encountered the Hispanic, Chinese, and Indian cultures in San Francisco, New Mexico and Arizona.

In *A Life for Dance* there is an unexplained visit to a lavish 'mission inn', a quasi-religious meditation centre of some kind. Did it hold interest for him through his Rosicrucian background? Why did he describe it so extensively and so vividly in his book? It would appear that he wanted to express his distance from the moneyed element of American culture of which this 'inn' was an exaggerated example. That he visited Arizona and witnessed American Indian ceremonies is not in doubt. They impressed him greatly, just as they did the American dance pioneers Martha Graham and Louis Horst at a similar time. He was inspired by the relatedness of man and nature, and of art, ritual and life in Indian culture. The striking scarlet costume designs for *Titan* (1927) were inspired by his Arizona experience. He saw, too, Chinese theatre performances in San Francisco, looking at it all from the ethnographic point of view. He visited Chicago, though the reason why is unknown.

Who were the 'young Americans' Laban worked with during his trip, with whom he studied a sword dance and fragments of *Der Schwingende Tempel*? Where did he go 'along the Mississippi' to witness 'Negro dancing'? He does not vouchsafe.

Lisa Ullmann, in a footnote to the 1975 edition of *A Life for Dance*, wrote that he had to cut short his trip because of his mother's death in October 1926. In fact he was back in Wurzburg opening his lecture tour 'Tanz in Amerika' by 16 September, dancing *Don Juan* in Berlin on 23 September, and speaking at a Labanbund evening on 26 September. Excellenze Marie Laban died in Geneva in October, leaving Laban's favourite younger sister Renée with whom she had lived, and with whom 'Rudi' kept in contact, irregularly but nevertheless with great tenderness. In 1926 Maja obtained a divorce from him, a fact that was not made public by Laban. He kept the myth that he was still married as a defence against the many women with whom he had, or who wished to have, amorous contact.

Indeed it was not until his lost archive was found in Germany well after his death that the divorce came to light. So it was with his family commitments increasingly diminished that he returned to the new premises in Wurzburg.

The Choreographisches Institut opened in September, in Wurzburg at Theaterstrasse 24, just opposite the city theatre, amidst continuing rumbles from the Catholic community, who in June had loudly objected to his coming. A reputation for nudity preceded him, no doubt through the number of nude photographs in *Gymnastik und Tanz* and even more in *Des Kindes Gymnastik und Tanz*. Possibly, too, one of the 1926 issues of the magazine *Die Schönheit* devoted to dance, containing similar photographs, had been seen. Gertrud Snell regarded the balance of clad and unclad dancers in *Die Schönheit* as atypical of Laban's work, but commented that he had perhaps had to agree to it to get his work into the magazine with such a copious spread. A closer look reveals that it is Feist's and Gertz's male and female dancers who are nude, together with women from the *Körperkultur* schools. The only Laban dancers with any nudity are Bereska and Loeszer, whose upper bodies are bared. The *Würzburger General Anzeiger* carried arguments against the Institut opening, and the Burgermeister defended the decision to support it. The Loeszer-led summer school in the open-air colony in the Gullenberg woods on the outskirts of the city, in grounds made available by the sculptor Arthur Schleglmuenig, may also have contributed to the furore, for the colony did have a nudist section. How unclothed Loeszer's students were was not revealed, although students at other Laban summer schools were always adequately if briefly clad. What enraged the church was the suspicion of unethical freedoms, which the conservative element in the town also pounced upon.

The incident was not unique. The question of the body in Weimar culture was topical, linked with several concurrent and polarised arguments. The traumas in German value systems, from the turn of the century, focused on the body as a symbol. The sexual freedom promoted in the Wilhelmine time was tempered by the new rationalism which emerged in 1924 at the time of the relative calm that followed the hyperinflation chaos. Science was brought to bear on family life, sex education promoted hygienic and safe practices against venereal diseases; the body should be exercised, given fresh air, and regarded as an object of beauty. *Die Schönheit* was a journal of this ilk. The more anxious voices taking this line of argument to the body concerned themselves with *Volkstod*, the fear that Germanness was being lost through the genocide of the war, and through the low birth rate in the educated and intellectual classes. They feared that the poor, ill-educated immigrants from the east, with considerable Slavic and Jewish numbers and large families, would so change Germanness as to obliterate it. Socially responsible behaviour was promoted as essential, and discussion of eugenic engineering appeared as a means of safeguarding lineage. The body, *Körperkultur*, and through that to dance, all seen as evidence of hygienic and ethical values, were inevitably caught up in these discussions.

On the other hand, arguments based on current psychoanalysis, Jungian and Freudian particularly, whose focus was the individual and the need to unlock the unconscious, were also regarded as scientific and fact-based. Freedom from outmoded prudery, sexual enlightenment and individual responsibility, based on the recognition of the idiosyncratic nature of each soul (and body), led to a tolerance of diversity, of homosexuality (at any rate in Berlin), and of racial differences. These ideas were given corporeal reality again in dance and physical culture. Laban, as always, sought balance, harmonic equilibrium, between enjoyment of diversity of personality and of body build, of movement characteristics, while also seeking ethical community behaviour through movement choirs and platonic relationships within the dance community. Several small instances which came to light in the 1930s suggest that he was somewhat homophobic, perhaps because he so wanted to re-establish the male element in dance art, as it had always been and still was in folk dance.

These tensions surrounded Theaterstrasse, Wurzburg; but the Choreographisches Institut got on with its job of being a centre for 'Choreographie, Choreologie und Choreosophie'. This could be done with support promised from the Theatre and the University, and with a staff of Laban as director, Bereska for eukinetics, Loeszer for choreutics, Snell for theory and practice of notation, and Hermann Robst for training, everyone teaching choreographic studies.

Choreographie was described in their brochure as the study of 'the effective structure of movement, with the aim of notating both educational exercises and works of dance art.' *Choreologie* was 'the study of the governing laws of the dance event as the synthesis of space and time experiences.' In *Choreosophie* the ethical and aesthetic effects of the cultivation of movement and dance art in the service of community culture and education were studied. We might now call these three dance notation and reconstruction, dance morphology, and dance sociology and ethnology. The three were offered as core studies for training dance artists, dance teachers, and amateurs. Overarching it all was composition through *Choreographie*, *Choreologie*, and *Choreosophie*; that is, through interconnection of the laws in dance with 'free intuition'.

To publicise precisely what the Institut was offering, and why, a pocket-sized brochure was written. It focused on the new research into dance as art, and on the dance knowledge undertaken there, with dance script as a central source. It explained that the language of movement, which is unconsciously present in everyone, must be made known to all people and races, while forms of art applicable to the present day must be found as an adequate means of expression. The Institut was intended for all interested in mastering movement, in observing and understanding it, in writing it; that is, for dancers and dance masters, for dance researchers, dance writers, dance inventors or *régisseurs*.

Teaching at Theaterstrasse had to take place spasmodically around theatre performances, for Katabü toured from the end of September. Primarily Bereska's affair, the company's full title was now given as Kammertanzbühne Laban–Bereska. They premiered the season's programme, with added material made mostly during Laban's time away in America, at the Volksbühne in Berlin, returning to Wurzburg for a month of teaching. From late October to December they were on the road, mostly in mid-sized town theatres, good earning venues – Harburg/Elbe, Bremerhaven, Elmshorn, Stetten, Freiburg, Magdeburg, Hanau Wiesbaden – ending at the opera house of Frankfurt-am-Main. Laban joined them, so far as one can discern from his archive, from time to time to give his popular lectures with demonstrations by the company members. Bereska was clearly a good manager, for the receipts of outgoings and statements on the nature of their reception in each town were neatly typed out.

Don Juan and *Narrenspiegel* were in rehearsal with Laban and played at the Neuen Theater am Zoo in Berlin in November. A booking for one noontime meant a lecture plus performance, while six further evenings alternated the two works, one being followed by an additional late night performance. Both works were given at the Wurzburg Stadttheater, but the 15 December booking of *Don Juan* at Nuremberg was never forgotten. At its most dramatic finale, Laban leapt off the raised stage as usual into 'hellfire', but no mattresses were in place to cushion his fall. He hit the ground hard, seriously injuring himself. Concussed and in acute pain he could only listen to the applause, realising even then that he had given his last performance. Indeed he did not dance again, the luckless Katabü *Eleve* Fritz Klingenbeck having to attempt to take his role of the Narr to fulfil the January engagement for *Narrenspiegel*.

The news of Laban's retirement spread immediately, and *Don Juan* had to be dropped, for no one could replace Laban's spellbinding stage presence. Instead, they somehow resurrected the 1923 piece *Komödie*. From

January 1927 on, it was the smaller works only that they could tour, and they did this copiously and with laudable success. Between 16 January and 5 May they gave 51 performances throughout Germany, including bookings in Switzerland, Poland and one in Amsterdam with Laban's name blazoned on all the posters.

For Laban, January started with far too many things happening at once. Still recovering from his injury, he had a commitment to arrange the dances for a Hamburg performance of Gluck's *Orpheus* for 11 January, for which the Movement Choir provided the Bacchantes. Classes had to be given in Wurzburg, and, with Katabü on tour, he had to teach many of them. His 'Dance in America' lectures continued, his notation was crucially on the point of a solution; but the new idea that now filled his imagination was the preparation of a congress for dance people of all kinds, to be held in June.

The idea behind it was to forge together the disparate parts of the dance community in order to forward the place of dance and dance people in society in general. While this was Laban's personal odyssey, it mirrored the way in which German workers were confronting their difficulties in all spheres and industries. No trade union for dance people existed, no safeguards, no way of bargaining fees and contracts. Dance people lived with constant work insecurity, and with their dismissal by the authorities as unimportant members of society. Something had to be done. The memories of the hardships of unemployment in the 1923 hyperinflation were ever present, as well as the uncertainty of public sponsorship of schools, of colleges, of theatres. Between 1918 and 1923, the chaotic years, industrial barons had retained a co-operative attitude to their work force, an *Arbeitsgemeinschaft* existed; but with the stability started by the 1924 currency reforms, wage disputes erupted as each group tried to gain financial ground and more job security. The Weimar republic had accelerated the introduction of the welfare state which had started before the war. Insurance, pensions, welfare assistance and health provision were written into the republic's constitution. But they could only function where the state had sufficient funds, and the state had conspicuously failed to cope with demand during the 1923 crisis. The gap between goals and what was actually given out was huge. Twentieth-century industrialisation had brought into language and to consciousness the idea of the 'mass', in contrast to the individual. Mass culture, mass media, mass production and the introduction of Taylorism (stopwatch time-and-motion study) into the industrial workplace lessened individual worth and power. Benign togetherness, much promoted in youth camps, and certainly in movement choirs and in the Labanbund, was matched by aggressive togetherness, a kind of link-

124

arms-and-face-the-enemy outlook. Both were necessary to survive in a time of political, social, moral and economic instability.

The large Theatre Exhibition, organised for Magdeburg from June to September 1927, was one way in which theatre people were promoting both these forms of *Zusammenheit* (togetherness). Laban and Oskar Schlemmer were individual dance people invited to exhibit because they both had visual materials, Laban with his figurines, his icosahedra and his choreology drawings, Schlemmer with his costume designs and stage sets. Laban had the idea that a *Tänzerkongress* (Congress for Dancers) could take place during the exhibition. As always, Laban turned a contained idea into a massive undertaking, with utopian goals. He gathered Hanns Niedecken-Gebhardt, intendant of Munster and a strong supporter of Jooss and Laban, and his dramaturge Alfred Schlee, to negotiate with Paul Alfred Merberle, the Theatre Exhibition's administrator. Laban masterminded the four-day event, aiming to bring together as many dance people as possible, with a view to 'linking arms' and showing the world a strong united front. Fritz Böhme and Ludwig Buchholz, associated with the Feist school, joined the organising group.

The way they divided their responsibilities proved problematic. Merberle and Buchholz took on the preparatory organisation and recruiting of participants, Schlee and Böhme the lecture programme and the control of the dance evenings, Laban and Merberle acting as overall decision-makers on all points. In the event, Merberle seems to have been overwhelmed by the job, and, notwithstanding assistance from Böhme, failed to inform applicants whether or not they could perform, for how long, or on what day, misjudging crucial needs and personalities. Wigman, invited along with the rest, was piqued that Laban had been allocated a whole performance evening, with expenses paid for fifty dancers, while she had not. Neither had she been invited to exhibit by the Theatre Exhibition administration (understandably, for she had no static visual materials). From the correspondence it is clear that Merberle did not treat her in the way that she regarded as her due, did not negotiate with her or try adequately to placate her. It would seem that Laban was not involved in the correspondence. While the row could have been seen as a short-lived jealous spat on Wigman's part, unfortunately it developed into a far more serious, deeply felt problem, begun already in 1913, to surface again and again. In 1927, Wigman stayed away, telling all her close-knit partisan followers to do the same. She apparently recognised Laban's achievements for modern dance, but she needed to demonstrate her equal place as co-author. She could not achieve this by attending, but she could by withdrawing.

It was caused, sadly, by no more than slack administration, and its ripples jeopardised Laban's overall goal of unity. In the meantime he had to prepare for the exhibition. *Choreologie*, *Choreosophie* and *Choreographie* were his themes, for which E. W. Moll was commissioned to make figurines to illustrate the spatial bodily tension of his choreutic scales. Laban placed them to give a sense of how one figurine's position moved into another. Costume designs, possibly those for the dances he was to present, were to be exhibited, along with his books and drawings. Oskar Schlemmer's materials on his *Triadic Ballet* would be there too. Laban must have been aware of their extreme visual interest.

For the performances, Laban decided to offer three works which showed a range of his choreographic styles and methods. He was committed to a commission to make a dance to open the new Kurhalle at the Bad Mergentheim to be performed one week before the Congress. This, together with *Titan*, a choric work inspired by his American visit, and *Nacht* (Night), a grotesque work using his caricature and Dadaesque aesthetic, constituted the threesome. The Mergentheim architecture provided the idea, centred on a Teutonic castle imbued with the history of medieval knights. Laban, with the Katabü members just returned from touring, and Choreographisches Institut *Eleven*, took up residence and rehearsed in the halls of the castle to create *Ritterballett* (Ballet of the Knights). The programme notes explain that Beethoven's youthful suite for a *Ritterballett* was the central musical score chosen, one of the reasons being that Mergentheim was celebrating a Beethoven festival at the time.

Organisation for the rehearsal of the three pieces centred on the need for them all to be rehearsed together, with preparatory creative phases completed at Wurzburg. They required large forces of dancers, sixty in all. Looking at the cast lists, it is possible to see that in each piece Laban worked with groups. In each group there were *Meisterschüler und -schülerinnen* from the Choreographisches Institut or Katabü dancers. He would have created the dances with them first, using them as apprentices, then worked the material with the less experienced group members at the castle venue. He had used this method for *Der Schwingende Tempel* and *Faust*, and would do so again in post-war Britain, passing it on to his apprentice, for his movement work in the York Mystery Plays.

Ritterballett was a suite of dances created out of his response to medieval images, stories, and archetypes. It included Knights, Poltergeists, Pages, Ladies, peasant girls and nuns; Hunters and peasants; with two solo characters, the Witch and the Grandmaster of the Knights' Order. Having advised Hans Brandenburg to make use of the rituals of freemasonry, there

126

is little doubt he used it here. The work was non-narrative, but the audience were given the following scene titles and introductory programme notes as an aid:

'Scene One. The wild dance of the pagans and the witch, interrupted by the solemn procession of knights, the conversion to Christianity of the pagans, and general joyous thanksgiving.

'Scene Two. The grotesque dance of poltergeists, pages, and peasants; a decorative rondo for noblemen and pages, who join into an excited parade of knights to a tournament.

'Scene Three. A riotous peasants' rebellion, contrasted with a procession of holy women, who are assaulted by the rioters and finally rescued by the courtly knights.

'Scene Four. Hunters, tender games of love, an eerie night of ghosts, ending with dreams of roaring witches and black horsemen.'

It sounds like a popular piece made for a general audience at a spa, decorative, and balancing decorum with wild fantasy. The costumes and banners were based on the 'mighty coats of arms' in the halls of Schloss Mergentheim, with their 'authoritative cross, in black and white'.

Titan was described by Laban in *A Life for Dance* as a 'dance-play, telling of the strength of the common hope which lies in a common will to achieve something better.' A statement such as this is easily picked upon as an example of how *Ausdruckstanz* was used with ease by the Nazis to express their kind of 'will' and conception of 'better', only six years after the Magdeburg Congress. What has to be clearly understood is how Laban's concept of 'common' was fundamentally at odds with regimentation. He continues in *A Life for Dance* to say straight out: 'The purpose of life, as I understand it, is to care for the human as opposed to the robot; a call to save mankind from dying out in hideous confusion; an image of a festival of the future, a mass of life in which all the celebrants in communion of thought, feeling and action, seek the way to a clear goal, namely to enhance their own inner light.' How were these strongly felt goals embodied in a movement choir work? First, through a common aim – but not a common action to express that aim, not a robotic movement in unison, and certainly not a militaristic one; rather, an individual expression of that aim 'through their own light'. Second, through individual responses that are not idiosyncratic or for selfish enjoyment but 'in communion' with others, implying a harmonic (not simply harmonious) blending of one person's action with another's. That blending is not achieved through an intoxication of common feeling, but through thought as well as feeling and action, echoing the Nietzschean call to value both Apollonian and Dionysian expression. If ever there was an embodiment of sociologist Emile Durkheim's theory of a community's 'organic solidarity' it was in Laban's choric works for movement choirs, where the sense of responsible and responsive togetherness was given artistic form in the variety of group actions, group tensions, group resolutions, group forms, group timings, group weight sharing, and so on. *Titan* was such a dance, created primarily for the participants as a celebration of community – or rather communities, for *Titan*'s forms and costumes and sounds contained Laban's response to America: 'the Indian', 'the African', 'the Caucasian', 'the Asian', and the feminine and masculine. The scarlet and yellow costume designs evoked Arizona. Simple sounds of the hollow kettledrum, the woodwind melody, and silence, arranged by Wagner-Regeny, evoked open spaces. Twenty-five named dancers and forty further dancers from the Hamburg, Gera, Berlin and other movement choirs participated.

The Intermezzo for soloists in *Titan* was an unusual insertion in a choric work. It was danced by the soloists of Katabü, Bereska, Loeszer, and five men, Laban himself, Robst, Klingenbeck, Heinz Effner and Heinz Landes, with music from Beethoven's Septet in F-major. Laban wrote nothing about it. Was it a balancing contrast of 'individual inner light' to the 'communal purpose' of the main work? Did he want to include his best dancers in the Congress? Did he want to show himself as performer as well as lecturer and organiser? No clue is given.

Nacht was the third work, representing present-day modern man where *Titan* expressed hope for the future and *Ritterballett* enjoyment of the past. The present-day modern man was shown as singularly nasty. Laban wrote that the work was 'an absolute flop', producing abusive comments from the press and a startled audience. The contrasting statements of the utopian *Titan* on 17 June with the Dadaesque *Nacht* the next day must have taken some creating, and performing, as well as demanding a complete shift in expectation by the spectators. Called 'a dynamic materialisation' rather than a dance, the only clue for the audience was a Goethe quotation: 'What in man is unconscious . . . wanders through the labyrinth of the breast in the night.' The characters were 'men' and 'women' and three icons, and forty further dancers. Recreations of some of this work were included as part of a 'day of dance' in London in the 1950s and Laban used similar scenes for workshops with his British students. This side of the man erupted from time to time throughout his productive life, ranging from wicked lampoons in his drawings, on a par with those of Otto Dix, to almost cruel ridicule. It had happened in his *Phantastische Revue* of 1924 and here it was again in *Nacht*. The dancers' view, according to Gertrud Snell and Ilse Loesch, was that it was a fantastic, avant-garde propaganda piece which they loved.

The persona were 'Everyday people – of Our Time – Timeless – United in a more colourful society – Men and Women from different worlds – Children and adolescents – Living-for-the-past people. Thinkers – sportsmen – chambermaids – pageboys and maniacs'; in other words, anybody and everybody. Loeszer was the *répétiteur*. It had an original sound composition by Erich Itor Kahn, played by him and Wagner-Regeny, which included motorbike hooters, and indeed a motorbike was ridden across the stage. The icons, if Laban was true to form, would have been Money, leading to exploitation of the poor; Sex, representing exploitation of one another; and the Machine, with its inevitable annihilation of the soul. He had a particular dislike for stockbrokers, for cocaine addicts, for pornography, for *petit bourgeois* prejudices, for male chauvinism, for female flightiness, for religious bigotry, for class snobbery. These ideas he put into the dance, with gesture as his main vocabulary, bizarre ugliness as the consistent aesthetic, eye-opening shock as the means, audience awakening as the aim. He commented later that perhaps he had put 'excessive hatred' in it, for he knew that the public was unready to appreciate such confrontation. That aesthetic reappeared years later in Pina Bausch and Reinhild Hoffmann in their *Tanztheater* productions. In a letter from 1957, he wrote with hindsight, 'I think it was my best theatrical work.'

Oskar Schlemmer's performance was cancelled through the same administrative bungling that had led to Wigman's withdrawal. He commented in his diary on the event as a whole: 'Laban is a good man (the only one of the committee besides me to come)', referring to the absence of Wigman and Pavlova. 'Still, this committee will remain in existence for future undertakings, congresses and such.' An entry, mid-May 1927, shows that his primary involvement was in the Theatre Exhibition: 'Our booth was the most modern in the exhibition, which is not saying much at such a second-rate affair.' He went on: 'Still, instructive and a chance to see all sorts of things I had not seen previously.' While Laban was eclectic in style and message, Schlemmer was not. In the same diary entry he wrote, 'Gropius is doing a theatre project with Piscator, who might collaborate with me, but if he tries to bring in politics while excluding modern form, I shall have to decline.' Schlemmer's strength lay in his consistent attention to man's relation to space, *Raummensch*, to perfect a 'modern form' of production, while Laban exploded with spatial analysis, spatial scales, space as cosmos, spatial requirements of a dance notation, the experience of man in space and of space in man, and more. His copious ideas acted electrically as a catalyst for a diversity of people, but it opened him to the accusation that not one of those things, whether dance, book, school and so on, was ever perfected.

The productions at the Theatre Exhibition included one day of celebratory choric works. Bruno Schönlank's poetic work for speech choir and movement choir *Der Gespaltene Mensch* was given by the group from the Berlin Volksbühne under the choreographic leadership of Vera Skoronel. The Trumpy/Skoronel dance group worked alongside the movement choir with *Erweckung der Massen*, and the Chemnitz groups gave Werner Illing's *Aufbruch des Geistes*. The titles illustrate the serious agenda of these committed, amateur performances. While exact translation is inadequate, the overall topics were: mankind split, divided by the political and cultural dilemmas of the times; the awakening of the mass of ordinary people from the sleep of years to the realities of the present; and the presence or departure of the spiritual/intellectual dimension of action. These pioneering and inspirational works expressed the desire to engage in and initiate debates of the day, illustrated by the journal *Die Tat* and writers like Laban and Brandenburg, playwrights like Bertolt Brecht, and art movements such as the short-lived German Dada groups.

Notwithstanding the Wigman problem, the Dancers' Congress was regarded as an event to be repeated, for it succeeded in the end in giving a shared platform to artists and groups from almost all other modern and classical persuasions. It also achieved a mixing of theory and practice, for not only did dance scholars attend and speak, but discussion took place in which writer and performer debated together. The choice of speakers showed the scope offered. Oskar Bie, an academic historian, André Levinson, a critic with a leaning towards classical ballet, and Fritz Böhme, a historian interested in the new, shared the same platform. Musicians Egon Wellesz and Alfred Schlee, psychologist Dr Liebermann and critic Hans Fischer contributed their supportive ideas. The relation of dance and the theatre was the topic for presentations by Hans Brandenburg, Niedecken-Gebhardt, Schlemmer and Kurt Liebmann. The practical problems of the day for dance people were discussed by Laban as choreographer, Max Terpis as *régisseur*, and a Walter Howard, with a panel discussion on notation, which became a major topic of the Congress. The sectional discussions were divided under 'artistic questions', 'organisational questions', and 'pedagogic questions'; small groups took specialist topics which focused the debates. Far-reaching aspirations emerged and at the closing discussion, chaired by Laban, two significant changes took place. First, in order to include professional dancers of all styles, 'ballet' was replaced with 'dance' in the name of the only organisation available for dancers, which now became 'The German chorus–singer association and dancer association'. Second, Laban pushed the discussion on even further to the need for a broader-based dance association concerned also with artistic and educational issues. It led to the first suggestion that a High School for dance was needed, and should be furthered before the next congress. No doubt Laban had in mind, and now had the backing for, a much stronger voice from the dance domain, based on a broad consensus and tolerance of differences through two organs, a recognised union and a financially supported college.

The energy generated at the Congress spilled over for Laban into the two-month summer school held at Bad Mergentheim from 1 July to 30 August. Assembled were many Congress participants and performers for a pedagogically successful and financially viable period. After a rousing performance of *Ritterballett* and *Don Juan* at Leipzig on 30 June, Laban settled down with his closest colleagues to a final assault on the notation at the castle, the summer school going on all around them. Each brought areas of concern and special skills. Laban wanted at all costs to defend that he was writing motion, not positions. Sigurd Leeder needed the notation for practical use with professional dancers and the system had to be able to accommodate all kinds of dance. His training as a graphic artist gave him a special gift with signs and symbols. Kurt Jooss brought his expertise as a trained musician as well as a choreographer. Dussia Bereska was thoroughly acquainted with the painstaking progress that Laban had made and was especially concerned with safeguarding the dynamics and timing of movement. Albrecht Knust was the notator, the logician, the score writer, with the desire to write choric works. Fritz Klingenbeck and Gertrud Snell hovered in the background as scribes.

The final epoch-making and exhilarating breakthrough came one evening. The spatial three-dimensionality of the movement had been handled through agreement on signs which by their shape and an added dot showed the body's inclination. The shape of the movement had so far been managed through another set of signs which could be co-ordinated with the first. The moving part of the body had been coped with, broadly, through the matrix in which the signs were put, timing by the matrix being repeated at intervals across the page. But the overlapping nature of time and uneven durations had not been dealt with. Each sign was like a letter, which clustered together to make 'words'; but the flow of movement was not amenable to this mode of analysis. It was Jooss, apparently, who suggested that they should try opening out the matrix from a cross with four spaces for signs, to lines with four columns for signs. It was not long before it became apparent that the movement signs could be elongated to show how long the movement took and when it started in relation to other moves. Signs similar to the sharp and flat in music were proposed to modify a movement indication to make it large or small, to indicate a whole limb or part of a limb. One heady discussion focused on whether it was practical to write all movements as progressions in space. All agreed that they were progressions, as a *port de bras* is or as head circling is. These were easy to write if one knew the movement, but not easy to read back if one did not. Whether or not progression or tracing shapes in the air, as in arm movements and leg gestures, could be transmitted to a reader by stating the places passed through was tried out. Ballet terminology was based on that premise; fifth *en bas* is a position passed through as well as being a position held; so is *à la seconde* in *port de bras*.

The jubilation followed painful compromise by Laban in accepting that gestures were best expressed as positions passed through, while 'steps' were best expressed as motion. The essential celebration was that the flow and timing of movement was clearly stated in the system. One can only imagine Laban's relief at the completion of the crucial phase of his search for a script. It had taken fourteen years of continuous slog preceded by a further fourteen years of preliminary exploration around the idea, supported always by his colleagues, especially Bereska. Alfred Schlee, already alerted to the imminence of the breakthrough, was consulted with a view to publishing the system.

A preliminary booklet for in-house use was produced from the Hamburg *Tanzschreibstube* (Dance Notation Office) by Fritz Klingenbeck and Herbert Vogel in the autumn, while Laban oversaw the preparation of a full booklet of the principles. But Alfred Schlee was not content with simply publishing the method. He had attempted to start a dance journal as early as 1922 and had failed to get Emil Hertzka of Universal Edition interested. Now he tried again. With the notation as a revolutionary ingredient, the concepts of written dance, dance writing, literate dance, merged into a proposal for a journal centred on the new notation, called *Schrifttanz*. Having just become an employee of Universal Edition, Schlee, with the support of Dr H. Heusheimer, persuaded Hertzka to think about it. Schlee was an invaluable ally. Twenty-five years or so younger than Laban, he was of the present *Jugend* generation, a graduate and disciple of Jaques-Dalcroze, and, being a Dresdener, a frequenter of Wigman's studio. A movement person who started as a musician, he was wide in his appreciation of what was going on of interest, from *Wandervögel* to Oskar Schlemmer or Valeska Gert, and could give a dance journal a broad range. It was hoped to publish the first issue to coincide with the Second Dancers' Congress in 1928. Schlee set about pushing Hertzka to make a decision.

The Choreographisches Institut had a strengthened core with the publication and notating of dance materials, the exploration of literate dance being an available option for any dance person who wanted to use it. That, at any rate, was the belief and the concept on which progress was devised. At some point, probably around the time of the Magdeburg Congress, the Institut moved to Gillstrasse 10, Berlin-Grünewald. The reason is not stated, but the new premises were certainly more capacious, more convenient, with a garden, and on the edge of the capital city. Catholic worries about nudity could be left behind. The technical staff was expanded to take in Susanne Kabitz and Eleanor Warsitz, who had danced *Nacht*, with Margot Koch, who had assisted with *Titan* and danced in *Ritterballett*, and Annie Sauer, also a *Ritterballett* dancer, as assistants.

Since the notation breakthrough, Dr Buchholz had joined Gillstrasse and advised Laban on the legal position of a dance notation. Issues of copyright had to be considered. For that reason alone a precise and speedy publication of key concepts and signs was essential prior to wide presentation of the system. Its name had to be considered. It was a *Bewegungsschrift*, a script of movement, but the name *Kinetographie* was decided upon to distinguish it from Feuillet's eighteenth-century *chorégraphie*. The profession of dance notator was the new concept and written dance the new domain.

During the winter of 1927–28 Laban demonstrated Kinetography to a group of well-wishers, out of which was formed the Deutsche Gesellschaft für Schrifttanz (German Society for Written Dance). Its function was to market the notation, to teach it, to print it, to finance its further development and publication. Dr Ewald Moll, a Berlin privy councillor, became chairman of the society. *Schrifttanz* was to be the society's journal, which they hoped to publish through Universal Edition's publishing house. One friend and admirer, Dr Marie Luise Lieschke, from Plauen, agreed, or offered, to loan Laban money for the initial work, and this enabled him to employ Fritz Klingenbeck to teach, Snell to organise, and Knust and Susanne Ivers to notate.

The first proof of the efficacy of the system was the score of *Titan*. Knust wrote it after Magdeburg, and in January used it to remount the work with the large numbers of the Hamburg Movement Choir. On 29 January 1928 the *Titan* performance was given in Hamburg to celebrate five years of the choir. It was a grand occasion, with much city support and satisfaction –

evidence of the value to urban youth seen in Laban's work, and, to the dance community, of the usefulness of the notation. On the informal side, the dancers of Hamburg, Lola Rogge and Ursula Falke amongst them, gave a typically hilarious post-performance Labanite entertainment.

The score had proved itself, and Knust was inspired to develop the system to cope with movements of groups as well as movements of individuals, so making the script especially pertinent to movement choir leaders. By February, Universal Edition were convinced of the viability of the system and of the journal, and Laban received his first offer from Hertzka.

Concurrent with these epoch-making notation issues, the gruelling and always chaotic programme emanating from the Choreographisches Institut went on as before. Creating new dances, exploring choreutic scales, performing and improvising, teaching, lecturing and writing, all started in early autumn. New students, new premises, new courses, new ideas were the ingredients, all taking place in the typical Labanite atmosphere of excited commitment combined with an iconoclastic outlook on all things regarded as establishment, and a pioneering attitude to the future of movement, dance and life itself.

The Choreographisches Institut, although at Gillstrasse for only two years, became highly influential. Since it was located in Berlin it attracted an international and well-educated type of student. Theatre people with a feeling for modernity came, Aurel Milloss for example. At the core, the young faculty were like a family around Laban, emboldened to take on every problem and every opponent. These were two of Laban's happiest years.

The Magdeburg Congress was given a complete issue of *Die Tat*, for which all the proceedings and lectures had to be prepared for printing. A new paper, *Der Tanz*, was started with Joseph Lewitan as editor, appearing first in October 1927. Laban was invited to contribute; indeed it would have been misguided to start a dance magazine without an article by 'the spiritual leader of the German Dance'. He wrote on 'Geist und Form des Tänzes' (Spirit and Form in Dance). The influence of Nietzschean forces could hardly have been missed.

From October to December 1927 Katabü toured the customary mixed programme of small works, with Bereska in artistic charge and arrangements made by Herr Leonard, Laban no longer performing, joining them in flying visits from time to time, giving lecture-demonstrations and making contacts with ballet-masters and *régisseurs* for the notation and for performing jobs for his dance students. Occasionally everyone joined together for one of the larger works. *Ritterballett* was performed in Wurzburg on

2 October and in Hamburg it was given for three performances from 30 November to 2 December. Local movement choirs were trained to join the Choreographisches Institut, and Katabü dancers and Laban accompanied them with a lecture. A Polish tour for the company with Laban was arranged for December, but he had to pull out for health reasons, burned out once more. Katabü were playing in Lubeck, Kiel, and Griefswald, and while at Lauenburg Laban's cancellation telegram arrived. They continued on without him to Thorn and postponed the rest of the tour, to cram it into February, after which they gave a mini-season in Italy.

It was decided that the wisest course for the future of the regular performing work of the Choreographisches Institut was for Bereska and Robst to take over Katabü entirely. They were in any case all but independent. It was they who had made the new works for the tour. On 21 January 1928 Laban gave legal permission for them to run the company. Relations between Laban and Bereska were increasingly remote. They each had their own living quarters at Gillstrasse, their own artistic jobs to do, their own earning to be achieved. They needed each other less and less now that the notation was solved and Laban was no longer performing. He had an ever-present problem of attempting to do more than any single human being was capable of, with the inevitable result that he pulled out of commitments at the last moment. Bereska had an alcohol problem, mostly under control but sometimes not. She had, after all, lost her little daughter; and she was soon to leave Laban.

Laban contributed to two publications in the spring. From the Hamburg school a new magazine came out, *Der Bewegungschor*. It had a short life of four issues, but was a means of celebrating the success of the fifth year of running the general choir and the men's special choir unique to Hamburg, and the triumph of mounting *Titan* from a written score. *Die Scheinwerfer*, the newsletter of the city theatre at Essen, put out a special edition on dance in anticipation of the city hosting the next Dancers' Congress. Laban contributed, and also Jooss as the resident choreographer and key figure for the event.

Preparations for the Second Dancers' Congress were concurrent with the season's already full programme, starting immediately after the first one. It was to be at Essen and had the financial and administrative leadership of Dr Neurer, who worked with Fritz Böhme on the presentations and discussions and with Alfred Schlee and Kurt Jooss on the festival performances, Buchholz acting as link man with the city of Essen. This capable team should have been able to set in place all that was necessary for a smooth-running congress. Laban's personal focus was to present his notation and get it accepted by the congress participants, and to introduce the supporting concept of choreology as the associated theory of dance practice.

Rumbles of forthcoming troubles began in March when a further dancers' organisation, the Deutsche Tanzgemeinschaft, was created, initiated by Wigman and under her chairmanship. Wigman's focus for the Essen Congress was on establishing her equal, if not superior leadership of German dance, and this rival organisation to the one set up by Laban was her first volley.

In a letter to Fritz Böhme in early May 1928, Jooss advised him never to forget three people in his preparations: 'Laban, Kröller, Wigman – Die Götter [the gods].' Kröller, who was ballet-master at the Munich Opera, represented the classical ballet fraternity and sorority, a group always in some state of tension with the moderns. Of the other two, Laban was *in situ* as leader of the moderns and Wigman was all set to challenge him. Böhme took note, attempting to prepare a peaceable event.

However, at the commencement of the Congress, Kröller, the personification of classical traditional excellence, became the metaphorical object of controversy. Laban, together with Max Terpis, ballet-master of the Berlin State Opera, and Jooss of the Neue Tanzbühne der Stadt Bühnen Essen, favoured the development of German dance through co-operation, possibly synthesis, with ballet. This seemed to them to be the way forward into the next decade. Wigman, on the other hand, vigorously and categorically denounced ballet and promoted the modern – her modern – as the only dance form for the future in Germany.

The followers of the two sides were dogmatically behind their champions, so from the discussions on 'Tanztheater und Theatertanz' on the first day of the Congress, battle lines were drawn. Supporting Wigman were outstanding modern dancers, Valerie Kratina, Yvonne Georgi, Gret Palucca, plus Jutta Klamt and the writer Felix Emmel. To underscore the divide, Emmel had edited a journal, *Tanz Gemeinschaft*, and had promoted Wigman's new organisation, not as an equal alternative to the Chorsänger und Tänzer but as a trade union for the professional; that is, as a superior alternative. In contrast, Alfred Schlee's editorship of the new journal *Schrifttanz*, begun in 1928, promoted an organ for discussion and writings on dance with a wide subject base, topical issues arising from the introduction of Laban's notation for dance being seen as the central core.

Both positions were based on profoundly held beliefs for dance, Laban and his followers on the evolutionary renewal of all aspects of dance, with tolerance of differences and enjoyment of variety, compared with Wigman and her belief in a radical break with the past into a new excellence, the Absolute Dance Art for the theatre of today.

The topics discussed at the Congress, apart from theatre, were amateur dance and dance teaching, the latter, inevitably, becoming a polarised discussion. The planned High School for dance was equally a focus for dispute. Laban's notation, the other main topic, was by comparison an easy issue, being welcomed wholeheartedly.

Of the performances, Wigman's *Die Feier* (Celebration) for her ensemble was the high point, described as the work of an outstanding artist and reaching a level which fulfilled the hopes of all dancers regardless of their ideological differences. Kröller's traditional ballet piece *Pagoden* and Terpis's modern piece *Der Letzte Pierrot* (The Last Pierrot), both danced by major opera ballet ensembles, were performed on the opening night, giving an illustration to the question, 'where should opera ballet be going?' Bereska led the Laban Kammertanzbühne with *Die Grünen Clowns* (The Green Clowns), a satirical social comment in typical Laban style. Soloists, both German and foreign, and several folk dance groups performed on the second and third evenings to mixed but undisturbed reception. Jooss's Neue Tanzbühne, as the company in residence, closed the Congress satisfactorily.

At the conclusion a working party, including several representatives from each of the warring factions, was commissioned by the Congress participants to look into professional training and practice, the application of Laban's notation, and the proposed High School. To that extent, from Laban's point of view, the Congress was a personal success, and supportive. But the split in the dance community was severely damaging to the integrity of new German dance as a cultural force. Headlines in the press such as 'The battle for the future' were no advertisement for the unity so badly needed and eagerly sought by him. The *Westdeutscher Scheinwerfer*'s comments were a typically biased response to the overall outcome of the Congress: 'The aesthetic musicless dance has no future'. For this writer, only Terpis and the Neue Tanzbühne from Essen were on the right lines, while the notation was a non-starter. For another writer, in the *Deutsche Tageszeitung Berlin*, the notation was the high, Katabü's *Die Grünen Clowns* a superbly comic grotesque. The faction-ridden dance world was exquisitely reflected in the polarised press reports.

The incomplete training that German modern dancers received, there being no schools comparable to the classical opera house schools, was partly to blame for the tirades against them. Laban schools were insufficiently staffed for professional work, and passion took pride of place over technique. But also to blame was the almost non-existent modernisation of the traditional ballet, epitomised by Kröller's methods and works. The urgent question that emerged for Wigman, Laban and their co-artists was: whither now in professional theatre dance? For Wigman, it was the end of an era, for she had to disband her acclaimed ensemble for lack of funds at an artistic high point, a peak that she would possibly not reach again. Laban had completed his independent choreographic experiments and would go on to make work within the opera house domain. But that was as yet unknown, even to him.

8

Accolades at Mid-Point

Vienna, Bayreuth and Berlin, 1929–1930

The stability of the political environment in which the development of German dance took place was at a crucial stage in 1928–29. As the historian Peukert writes, 'The variety and dynamism of the political movements and social programmes which make the Weimar period unique in recent German history were also uniquely corrosive of the political process itself. The result was disillusionment and recoil from democracy.' While 1928 was a high point for dance as a whole, and also personally for both Laban and Wigman, it was also the height of the illusion of stability in Germany itself. While Laban continued to flourish in 1929, signs of political and economic fragility emerged all around him.

The number of political parties (at least eight), the shifts of power between them, and their compromises to achieve workable coalitions, meant that the attempts at a stable state through democratic means were foundering. The 1928 election, the fifth in the nine years since the war ended, resulted in a coalition of parties with such ideological differences and deep-seated regional and religious tensions that no workable social policy could be agreed.

The power struggle of the 1928 Dancers' Congress was a mini-version of what was happening at the Reichstag, the radicals (Laban) tolerating the conservatives (Kröller) supported by people taking a compromise position (Terpis and Jooss), rejected and opposed by a militant radical (Wigman). The dancers had only one tentative coalition *contra* one radical group to contend with, and still held to a belief that a compromise might be reached. The Weimar politicians had tried so many compromises already, and with a Communist party which would never co-operate with its social democrat left-wing colleagues let alone with other centralist and rightist groups, that a longing for strong leadership, for a single voice offering a workable social programme was beginning to emerge. It was only an inclination towards dictatorship that followed the 1928 elections; it would become a lurch by 1932 and finally a collapse into totalitarian presidential rule by 1933.

The results of the second tier of elections, that of a President, in 1925, had brought a significant ingredient to the country's mood. Paul von Hindenburg, a compromise second-ballot candidate, got in through a split vote in the opposition, between the militant but visionary communist Ernst Thälmann and the uncharismatic centre man Wilhelm Marx. Hindenburg, in his late seventies, had been the supreme commander in a war that was lost ingloriously, and was a symbol of the *passé* Wilhelmine age. He and his advisers set out to strengthen the Reich Presidency as a seat of power by exploiting the weaknesses in the ineffectual government-forming processes of the parties. Power games ensued between the President and the elected coalitions, the in-fighting ever weakening the possibility of the success of democracy. Hindenburg's right-wing, old-fashioned aura offered nothing either. The result was disillusionment – a thoroughly dangerous mood in a volatile political situation.

The crucial element of 1929 was the unforeseen economic turmoil triggered by the Wall Street Crash in New York in October, and the resultant calling in of American loans. Germans were hit hard, including dancers, ever vulnerable and expendable. Germany's dependence on foreign credits for its post-war reconstruction programme meant that major industrial, cultural and educational institutions found their foreign capital backing no longer in place. Short-time working and unemployment inevitably followed. The unemployment figures for the next four years make startling reading: 6.2% in 1927 (the years of the first triumphant Dancers' Congress), 6.3% in 1928, 8.5% in 1929 and 14% by 1930 (the year of the third and last Dancers' Congress). By 1932 almost 30% of the population was registered as unemployed. It is against these figures and the deprivation they represent that we have to follow Laban's struggles and achievements of 1929 and the early 1930s.

National insurance, introduced by the Weimar Republic for the first time, emergency benefits for stricken families, meagre local welfare assistance, degrading form-filling, led to despondent deprivation for both blue collar and white collar workers, despite strong unions. The newly formed dancers' unions, the Tänzerbund and the Tanzgemeinschaft, were too inexperienced, and in any case fighting each other, to carry any clout at all. Germans as a whole, in whatever profession, felt powerless to control their own destinies. This fearful background contributed to the increase in the support for the National Socialists under whose rule the life of everyone, including dancers, would be radically and personally convulsed.

140

Laban's story is picked up in July 1928. For him, on a high following the Second Dancers' Congress, life at the Choreographisches Institut, in Berlin, Gillstrasse 10, continued at its usual breakneck speed, with two concurrent summer schools. One, for the usual two months of July and August, was offered by the Choreographisches Institut in two venues, Gillstrasse and the Poststadion in Universitätsübungsplatz in the centre of Berlin, together with one at which both Laban and Bereska taught in Holland at Scheven-ingen. It was probably during the summer school that Gillstrasse was decorated for a 'Balabile Fest', a crazy celebratory party. With Laban's triumphs at Essen, to which everyone at the Choreographisches Institut had contributed, they had plenty to 'make whoopee' about – which they did, according to Fritz Klingenbeck.

It was decided to move the Central Laban School from Hamburg where it had been since 1923 to the Gillstrasse premises. Certainly there was a first-rate staff there for the professional students and a good secretariat from which to deal with the diplomas and examinations of all the other 'Labanschulen'. To that end, Knust, who had been its director in Hamburg, relocated it to be one arm of the Choreographisches Institut. This freed Knust to notate, a job for which he showed a natural talent. His young assistant was Azra Laban, Laban's eldest child, who also showed special ability as a scribe. The move was good for testing the notation too, for the students at the Choreographisches Institut came there knowing that nota-tion and literate dance would be part of their daily activities and would tolerate problems. The Hamburg students were more of a mixed bag, and mostly younger, so their response to reading and writing and movement analysis would be more revealing of the strengths and difficulties of the system. In fact at this point in its development the notation was very simple, one might almost say simplistic, and offered no difficulty to a Laban-trained dancer.

Laban's autumn and spring lecturing schedule took him first to Karls-ruhe, Vienna, Halle, Brunswick and Plauen. His quest was to arouse inter-est in dance as a discipline as well as an art, to make known its crucial place in cultural history, so that the proposed creation of a government-supported High School for Dance would have wide backing. To this end his targeted audience included not only dancers but influential institutions and establishment groups. Wherever possible he followed a lecture with a per-formance, or a demonstration of the notation in action, assisted by Snell. Correspondence from the Choreographisches Institut files shows how hand-to-mouth the whole organisation was. Laban and Snell had no money for the train fare from Berlin to Vienna for the scheduled lecture the next day. It was Azra who scraped together enough to get them there. Financial juggling was still part of Laban's life, even with the generous support of Marie Luise Lieschke for the promotion costs of the notation.

In February 1929 Laban was a guest in Mannheim, in connection with the Nationaltheater, giving an open lecture with the local Movement Choir as demonstrators, while on 1 March at Lessing Hochschule in Berlin he had an audience largely made up of physical training and sports professionals. In May he gave a lecture in Dusseldorf on stage in conjunction with a Kammertanz performance at the Neussisches Theater with an audience of the general public. The January edition of *Schrifttanz* carried a chart entitled 'Was tut Not? Praktisch und Theoretisch' (What is needed? Practically and theoretically) illustrating these lectures, through which he aroused further interest from other administrators who booked him for their seasons. Lectures were still the main medium for disseminating ideas, together with newspapers and magazines, radio being still too new to be an adequate substitute.

Knowledge of both notation and choreology was increased by the publication of the journal *Schrifttanz*, for which notated reading material had to be prepared for each edition as well as articles. The July 1928 edition, the first, carried excerpts from *Don Juan*, the October edition a popular social dance 'Yale Blues', while in the third, published in January 1929, the score of 'Zeitlupe' from *Die Grünen Clowns* was the supplement. Alfred Schlee was responsible for the journal, but Laban's contribution and advice were sought continually. Schlee succeeded in broadening the scope from a purely notation-oriented first edition to one of diverse interest. By the third edition, the format had settled into six or seven articles, both historical and topical, followed by discussions on previous articles, reviews of books and music, news items, and the notation insert. The Choreographisches Institut staff (in this case Gertrud Snell) contributed 'Foundations for a general theory of dance,' divided over two issues, in which she introduced to the wider reader the concepts and content of choreology. The important issue for the development of the notation was that it was being looked at and used by the profession as a whole and was seen as a natural part of dance practice and scholarship, as the news items show. Those mentioned in the January 1929 edition quoted tours by Ida Rubinstein's group to European capitals, Harald Kreutzberg and Yvonne Georgi to the USA, and Bereska's group to north Italy. Mary Wigman's premieres, the Paris debut of Vera Skoronel, and Oskar Schlemmer's performances in Berlin were all listed.

In order to copyright the notation it was essential that Laban should publish a text booklet on it, for the outline of the system in the first edition of *Schrifttanz* was insufficient. He would have regarded the preparation of such a text as a chore, but he did it, no doubt by supervising his devoted notation team who would have prepared the graphics. The booklet appeared through Universal Edition as *Tanzschrift: Methodik und Orthographie*, with a text in German, French and English (he already had notation students from abroad for whom the foreign texts were intended and seen as essential).

In each edition of *Schrifttanz*, under News Items, the proceedings of the German Association for Written Dance were always included. By the October 1928 edition this association, formed immediately after the first publication of the notation, boasted a membership by representatives of twenty-five local groups in Germany, together with one in Vienna, two in Switzerland and America, one each in Paris, Holland, Prague, Budapest, Zagreb and two in Latvia. The new text booklet was badly needed for such a far-flung flock of enthusiasts, for up till now all Laban's innovations had been disseminated primarily through the long summer sessions. Some students came from as far as America, but the organisation of an empire (for that is what it was becoming) needed further thought. In the meantime the Choreographisches Institut team coped.

The Wigman problem opened up at the Congresses continued with her insistence on being an equal part of the plans for the High School. That her input into the training would be beneficial to it, that her expertise as a teacher, and the inclusion of her well-formed technique, would contribute to the content and to the public image of the college was never in doubt. Her inability to co-operate without partisanship and rivalry was the ongoing problem. The two of them must have met to discuss their differing points of view and to accommodate Laban's insistence on a broadly-based curriculum and Wigman's insistence that the whole idea was hers. The outcome, however achieved, was an open meeting held jointly by the two of them in December 1928, in which they let it be known that they had combined to write a plan for a High School for which support was being sought at the highest level. The curriculum was published in *Schrifttanz* and signed by the two of them, not as individuals but as leaders of the two associations, the Tänzerbund and the Tanzgemeinschaft. The Choreographisches Institut documents reveal Laban's pencil notes of his search for support. They start with lists of the people to contact in the ministries – Herr Seelig, the Prussian Minister for Education, Ministerialrat Haslinde and Minister of Culture Dr Becker, and continue with the names of civil servants in the Berlin City administration and the Prussian State administration as well as the Ministry of Finance. The names of his own acquaintances who might have access to people in these elevated positions of influence were noted too. Walter Gropius, with his experience of the Bauhaus, was on the list. Whether he was actually consulted is not clear, but some names have '*Brief geschrieben*' (letter written) beside them. The evidence suggests that the implementation was well thought out and at an advanced stage. The opposition to be overcome was not only the usual disbelief in the value of anything to do with dance, but the as yet unforeseen onset of the crippling recession. Laban's image of the propaganda work to be done as a battle was reflected in the title of his lecture given in the Bachsaal in Berlin on 19 February, 'Der Kampf um den Tanz' (The Fight for Dance). As 1929 began, his hopes of success were still high.

The suggested curriculum was well ahead of its time compared with traditional dance training methods. No doubt the Bauhaus was an influential model. The emphasis on theory as well as practice was innovative, especially the addition of optional subjects listed: psycho-physiology, music theory, kinesiology and sociology of dance. While practice focused on the new German dance, ballet and folk dance, exotic dance and social dance were options, as well as practical theatre management and music for dance. A library and an archive were envisaged, with scores and films of dances and records of music, all quite new ideas for dancers' training. The curriculum addressed head on the differences between educating dance professionals, performers, teachers and administrators and training dancers for narrowly focused skills. But it never came to fruition, beaten by the economic slump rather than anything else.

Laban's own involvement in dance-making shifted gear in 1929 through two very different opportunities. The first was an approach from the administration of the Prussian State Theatres offering him the post of choreographer at the Opera House at Unter den Linden in Berlin. This was a plum job for any choreographer. The timing of this invitation is not clear, for documentation of the invitation itself has not survived. That it was highly confidential and muddled is certainly clear, for Max Terpis was still the resident ballet-master, and unaware of change brewing. *Schrifttanz* reported in May that the well-known theatre man from Munster, Hanns Niedecken-Gebhardt, a supporter of Jooss and a good friend of Laban's, had been appointed as leader of the whole of dance activity for the Prussian state and city theatres and also *régisseur* at Unter den Linden. He had been put into the organisation at a higher level in the hierarchy than Terpis, with a wider brief. A letter from Laban to the Intendant of Unter den Linden survives in which he asks about what was going on, making it clear that he did not see himself, when appointed, working under Niedecken-

Gebhardt. The next move was not until the end of 1929 when Max Terpis resigned in some dudgeon, and news of reorganisation was published. It was still not public knowledge that Laban had long since been approached, for speculation in the press as to who should fill this vacated prestigious post was copious. Wigman was the anticipated choice, while Terpis himself championed Jooss. One can imagine the dismay at the announcement that the post had gone to Laban. He superseded Niedecken-Gebhardt as movement director for the seven state theatres. The thinking behind his appointment remains a mystery. One can only speculate. Was it the width of his choreographic styles, shown to advantage at the 1927 Congress, that suggested that he might offer something that Terpis could not? Were his large theatre pieces *Don Juan* and *Narrenspiegel* the attraction? Was there a freemasonry element, or a sexual bias in favour of manly men? Did Wigman's uncomfortable radicalism outweigh her undoubted choreographic talent? Laban's appointment certainly soured relations with Wigman further. In the first instance the contract, to start in autumn 1930, was for one year only, so a certain caution may have been advised.

The second gear shift for Laban came through the opportunity to direct the Festzug der Gewerbe (Festive Procession of Crafts and Industries) in Vienna, another high-profile project, to culminate on 9 June 1929 in a huge procession to be watched by all the dignitaries of the city and thousands of spectators. The event, which took place once every fifty years, was for Laban a once-in-a-lifetime chance to test his theories on amateur dance for everyone, in a city he knew intimately from his youth and where the name Laban de Varalja was remembered through his father's fame. It was also one of the few occasions in his life that he was an employee rather than an entrepreneur of his own work, and he would have had an office and a reasonable salary. Fritz Klingenbeck accompanied him as chief assistant. From April to June he was continuously in Vienna. Concurrently he was asked to put on a large movement choir event in Mannheim as part of the hundred-and-fiftieth birthday celebrations of the Nationaltheater, where he had had his first opportunities to choreograph in 1921. However he delegated the preparations, concentrating on the Viennese experiment himself. These two events focused his mind for three months on one of the poles of his dance-making, dance for the masses, while the Berlin appointment was soon to focus his mind on the other pole, namely prestigious, even elitist, opera dance.

Laban's extraordinary vision of what the Festzug der Gewerbe might consist in a modern age, and his sheer audacity in putting that vision into practice, deserves discussion. His idea was to rekindle the interest of the urban workers in their own traditions by researching the movement patterns, and, if any, the folk dance material that included their craft. He intended that the workers should, so to speak, dance their own industry. He planned to present the different dances in the most up-to-date manner possible, including the use of the absolutely novel loudspeaker system for recorded music, also in its infancy. A marriage of tradition and modernity was his overall vision.

The director for the annual festival fortnight as a whole was the theatre director Max Reinhardt. He, together with fellow modernist performing arts personalities (director Erwin Piscator and conductor Otto Klemperer, for example), were champions of the contemporary creative artists, playwright Bertolt Brecht, composers Ernst Křenek, Kurt Weill and Paul Hindemith. Křenek's new jazz opera *Jonny Spielt Auf* was put on by Reinhardt in the Vienna festival. Max Brand, whose music was included by Laban for the Festzug, had had his jazzy opera *Maschinist Hopkins* supported by Reinhardt earlier in the year. It would seem that the Viennese authorities had engaged the two most famous men they could find for their celebrations.

The Festzug was to take place on the middle Saturday of the festival as a highlight for the general public. Laban engaged Alfred Schlee as director of music; as an employee of Universal Edition he was well able to secure music and local musicians. Gisa Geert and Gertrud Kraus, local modern dancers, he brought in as rehearsal assistants. Specialists were found to cope with the loudspeaker arrangements, and co-operation with the police and army was needed to oversee the safety of the performers and the spectators on the seven-kilometre procession. It was scheduled along the Ringstrasse, the traditional route, an inner ring road which boasted all the municipal and imperial buildings. Laban's office was in the former imperial riding school, where today the white Spanish horses and their riders are trained to display their skills. From there he masterminded the extraordinary event.

He began by contacting all the guilds and craft unions in the city and attempted, at top speed, to persuade their leaders that all their members would love to participate. On the whole they disagreed, finding his ideas 'wicked nonsense'. However, direct contact with young female workers resulted in enthusiasm, and with young male workers reluctant acquiescence. Eventually old men were cajoled into telling about their half-forgotten memories of manual skills and erstwhile festive use of them as well as their functional use.

Laban's daily challenge was to turn the workers' minds beyond simply working for hard-earned financial reward to becoming aware of the work

26. Members of the Laban Movement Choir, Berlin, run by Herta Feist, 1923. (Laban Collection, gift of Herta Feist)

27. *Gaukelei* (Jugglery), a dance tragedy. Laban, Dussia Bereska, Edgar Frank with the Hamburg Movement Choir as chorus, 1923. (Photo by R. Schellenberg, Laban Collection.)

28. Hamburg Movement Choir in Laban's *Agamemnons Tod* (Death of Agamemnon), 1924. (John Hodgson Collection.)

29. Men's Group of the Hamburg Movement Choir. (Laban Collection, gift of Martin Gleisner.)

30. Hamburg Movement Choir. Right, Lolo Rogge. (Laban Collection, gift of Lola Rogge.)

31. Hamburg Movement Choir in Albrecht Knust's *Erwachen* (Awaken). (Laban Collection.)

32. Laban with Gertrud
Loeszer on their duo tour
on Wagner themes, 1925.
(Laban Collection.)

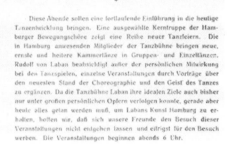

TANZBÜHNE
RUDOLF VON LABAN

Orchestik

4 Abende mit Tanzchorspielen und Kammertänzen
in der Hamburger Volksoper

(1. Abend Januar 1925)

*

Diese Abende sollen eine fortlaufende Einführung in die heutige
Tanzentwicklung bringen. Eine ausgewählte Kerntruppe der Hamburger Bewegungschöre zeigt eine Reihe neuer Tanzfeiern. Die
in Hamburg anwesenden Mitglieder der Tanzbühne bringen neue,
ernste und heitere Kammertänze in Gruppen- und Einzeltänzen.
Rudolf von Laban beabsichtigt außer der persönlichen Mitwirkung
bei den Tanzspielen, einzelne Veranstaltungen durch Vorträge über
den neuesten Stand der Choreographie und den Geist des Tanzes
zu ergänzen. Da die Tanzbühne Laban ihre idealen Ziele auch bisher
nur unter großen persönlichen Opfern verfolgen konnte, gerade aber
heute alles getan werden muß, um Labans Kunst Hamburg zu er-
halten, hoffen wir, daß sich unsere Freunde den Besuch dieser
Veranstaltungen nicht entgehen lassen und eifrigst für den Besuch
werben. Die Veranstaltungen beginnen abends 6 Uhr.

33. Laban in publicity material for dance events at the Hamburg Volksoper (People's
Opera), January 1925. (Laban Collection.)

34. Laban, Dussia Bereska, Robert Robst and a movement choir in *Don Juan*, 1925. (John Hodgson Collection.)

35. *Narrenspiegel* (The Fool's Mirror) in rehearsal, 1926. Centre, Laban and Gertrud Loeszer; right, Dussia Bereska and Robert Robst; left, unidentified. (Laban Collection.)

36. *Nacht* (Night), presented at the Dancers' Congress at Magdeburg, June 1927. (John Hodgson Collection.)

37. *Ritterballett* (Ballet of the Knights), presented at the Dancers' Congress at Magdeburg, June 1927. (John Hodgson Collection.)

38. Figurines of Laban's choreutic scales made for the 1927 Theatre Exhibition, Magdeburg, which ran alongside the First Dancers' Congress. (Laban Collection.)

39. Choreographisches Institut, Gillstrasse, Berlin-Grunewald, 1927. Dussia Bereska (left), Gertrud Snell (on floor), Laban at the piano with Beatrice Mazzoni, Eleanor Warsitz (on the piano), Robert Robst (next to the piano), and Gertrud Loeszer (right). (Laban collection.)

40. Group work with Martin Gleisner, 1928. (Laban Colllection, gift of Martin Gleisner.)

41. 'Procession of the Corpses', a scene from *Die Grünen Clowns* (The Green Clowns), 1928, choreographed by Laban with Dussia Bereska for the Kammertanz Laban tours. (Photo by Wide World, Laban Collection.)

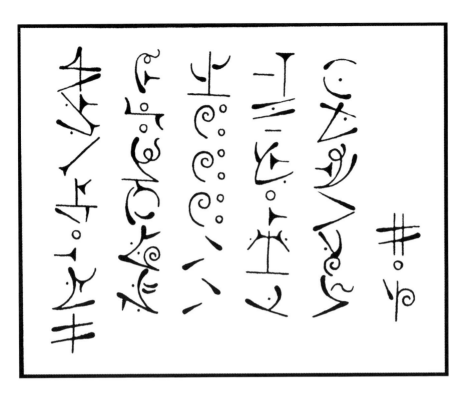

42. Laban's early notation, c.1917, based on shape of the movement and inclination in space. (Illustration in Laban's *Choreographie*, 1926.)

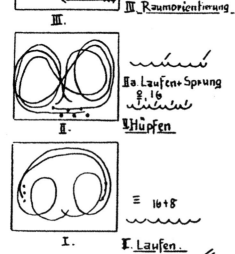

Zeichen.

⌣⌣⌣⌣ ... Rythmuslinie
◉ ----- Atmung
⊢=⊣ ----- Spannung
⊢= ----- Impuls
~ ----- Schwung
⊙⊢= ----- Sprung
• ----- tief
○ ----- hoch
•• ----- kniend
••• ----- sitzend
•••• ----- liegend
⊥ ----- vor
Ⅱ ----- rück
⊨ ----- rechts
⊧ ----- links
✓ ----- Schräge
/⟩/⟩ ----- flach hoch + tief
/⌃/⌃ ----- schwebend
// • ----- steil

3 4 ◉ ⟨ ⟩
2 5 ◉ ∧
1 6 ◉ ∨ } 4x
◉ 1x

Ⅳ. Atmung.

Ⅳ.+Ⅴ.

5 ꞉ 6 ꞉
5 ꞉ 4 ꞉
1 ꞉ 2 ꞉

Ⅱa

Ⅲ. Raumorientierung

Ⅲ.

Ⅱa. Laufen + Sprung
𝄞. 16

Ⅴ Hüpfen

Ⅱ.

≡ 16+8

Ⅰ. Ⅰ. Laufen.

Ⅴ. Abspannen (Rumpf)

43. A later notation including indications for dynamics and rhythm for a space study of six dancers, c. 1926. (Laban Collection, gift of Roland Laban.)

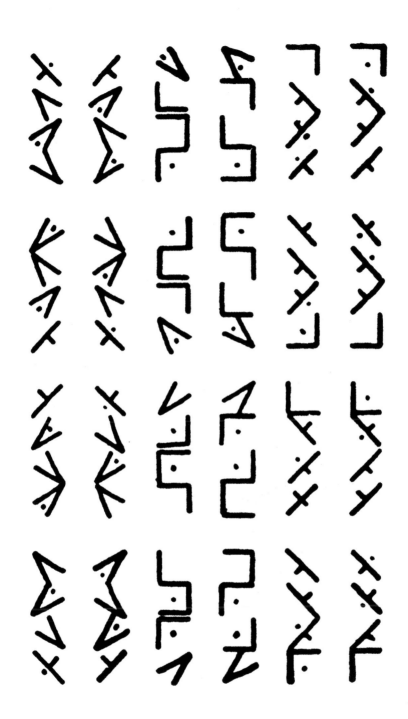

44. A third version of the notation used for writing space harmony exercises. (Illustration in Laban's *Choreographie*, 1926.)

Tänze die man lesen lernt

Es ist die Erfindung Rudolf von Labans, des Leiters des bekannten choreographischen Instituts gleichen Namens, daß man Tänze lesen lernen kann. Und zwar ist es nicht eine Reihenfolge figürlich dargestellter Schritte, durch die mit erläuterndem Text das Bild eines Tanzes übermittelt wird, sondern ein mit großer Genauigkeit ausgearbeitetes System moderner Art, das den Ausübenden in die Lage versetzt, Haltung, Bewegung und Schrittfolge von einem vorgezeichneten Muster, das sich Tanzschrift nennt, abzulesen. Die Tragweite dieser Erfindung liegt, sofern sie sich durchsetzt, auf der Hand. Der Uebermittlung von rhothmischen, gymnastischen und tänzerischen

45. Photocall for the Choreographisches Institut teachers and master students after the success of the presentation of the notation to the Second Dancers' Congress, in Essen, 1928. (Laban Collection, gift of Fritz Klingenback.)

46. Choreographisches Institut dancers demonstrating the new notation, 1928. (Laban Collection.)

47 (above). Poster for *Titan*, the first work reconstructed from the Laban movement notation score, by Albrecht Knust for the Hamburg Movement Choir festival, 1929. 48 (below). Designs by Laban for the decorated floats for the Festzug der Gewerbe (Festive Procession of Crafts and Industries) in Vienna, 1929. (Laban Collection.)

49. The Ringstrasse in Vienna during the Festzug, 9 June 1929, showing one of the experimental recorded music loudspeaker vehicles. (Stadtarchiv, Vienna.)

50. Publicity photograph in studio clothing at the time of Laban's fiftieth birthday, December 1929. (Laban Collection.)

51. Fiftieth birthday publicity photograph of Laban as the creator of the dancers' notation. (Laban Collection.)

52. Laban's 'Bacchanale' in Wagner's *Tannhäuser* at the Wagner Festival Theatre, Bayreuth, 1930. (Photo by A. Pieperhoff, Museum of the Wagner Festival Theatre, Bayreuth.)

53. Laban with the soloists of the State Opera Berlin on his appointment as choreographer and director of movement for the Prussian State Theatres, September 1930. Daisy Spies, Dorothea Albu, Eugenie Nikolaieva, Rudolf Kölling, Jens Keith, Walter Junk. (Laban Collection, gift of the Library of the State Opera, Unter den Linden, Berlin.)

54. Laban's movement choir *Tauwind und der Neuen Freude* (The Spring Wind and the New Joy) in the Dietrich Eckart Freilichtbühne, the open-air theatre of the Olympic Games complex, June 1936. (Laban Collection.)

rhythms of their trade, for which there was understandable resistance. Why interrupt a routine to make conscious an unconscious automatic act? Why try to make people co-operate with other people whom they regarded with professional jealousy, retailers with manufacturers, or manual worker with clerical worker, glove-maker with chimney sweep, right-wing guild member with left-wing trade unionist? Animosity and competition had to be changed into tolerance and collaboration, in a very short time. By the end Laban reported that around four hundred trades wanted to take part and that ten thousand people participated; no mean feat.

Makeshift workshops were created in the Riding School where Laban's designs for *Festwagen* (decorated floats) had to be turned into moving vehicles, his original designs being based on the individuality of each trade transformed into a modern look. The equestrian arenas became rehearsal halls where every evening two thousand or more young people came to learn their parts, with increasing enthusiasm, Laban and his assistants having devised the movement from their researches with the guilds. Daily, Laban and his team drove all over Vienna to smaller rehearsal sites, to decorating workshops, to costume-making halls, to musical rehearsals. Highly innovative was his decision to record the music, an absolutely new technique in 1929. Universal Edition, through Schlee, organised the recordings with Gramola-Electrola, of march-like music by Bittner, Max Brand, Ernst Křenek and Egon Wellesz.

A group of able dancers joined him as lead performers, Ruth Abramowicz, Cilly Ambor, Edith Bell, Edith Eysler, Maru Karjera, Olga Suschitzky, Ellinor Tordis, Traute Witt amongst them. Finally the whole pageant was run through in the huge courtyard of the Riding School one evening 'in moonlight', 'stepping, gliding, jumping, turning' in endless numbers. Laban was obviously bowled over by the manner in which these masses of individuals threw themselves into their task and seemed to gain a new perspective of and deference for the history of their trades. 'In those hours the dream of a dancing master became reality,' he wrote in *A Life for Dance*. It was by all accounts a tremendous undertaking. The participating groups included blacksmiths, metalworkers, cutlers, coachbuilders, furriers, garment makers, comb and fan makers, milliners, linen makers, carriage decorators, rope makers, sunshade and umbrella makers, barbers, dry cleaners and dyers, plasterers, porters, chimney sweeps and launderers, gamekeepers and foreign travel agents, coffee houses, inns, coffee bars and milk bars, bakers, butchers, confectioners and meat smokers, trade newspapers, old Vienna clubs, flag-makers, tanners, leather goods makers, glove makers, Lederhosen makers, harness makers, strap and whip makers, vehicle hirers, goods vehicle makers, harmonica makers, gunsmiths, sword-smiths, upholsterers, stove fitters, glassmakers, cardboard goods makers, photographers, antique dealers, cabinet makers, carpenters, turners, coopers, agricultural workers, foundrymen, instrument makers, coppersmiths . . . and more.

The actual event encountered all the hazards that one would expect for an open-air pageant, primarily the weather and an unpredictable public. The wind caused havoc with the loudspeakers, literally blowing the sound away so that the dancers had great difficulty in keeping together. With no modern radio communication, trying to keep the huge numbers in order and in time was attempted through runners, flag waving, 'steam sirens' and somewhat primitive telephones. By all accounts it was a chaotic affair, too long and probably too ambitious in concept, but nonetheless a triumph for the participants and their trades. Laban's description of it in *A Life for Dance* makes clear that he was profoundly moved by the whole three months.

Immediately it was over, or possibly in a rushed visit during the preparations, he took a plane to Mannheim to aid his collaborators Martin Gleisner, and Harry and Grete Pierenkämper in preparing the Nationaltheater jubilee celebration with the Gera, Jena and Frankfurt Movement Choirs. They found themselves in local political difficulties. For reasons unstated, permission was withdrawn for some young people to participate. Through Laban's contacts new dancers were found, bussed in, and rehearsed. The piece, entitled *Alltag und Fest* (Everyday and Festivity) was accompanied by a speaker and speech choir, who intoned epigrammatic thoughts on 'a homage to the theatre', its past, its present and their hopes of its future.

It was typical of Laban's festive choral works. 'The movements were simple . . . we conquered space in common swinging and leaping, in measured, slow stepping or sprightly walking and running . . . in interweaving paths,' he wrote. He described it as having 'vital dynamic movement', 'dignity and innocent enjoyment', 'a healthy delight in physical ability and in natural poise', 'states of collectedness'. 'Rhythm of Youth 1929' was the title of his article in the programme of the *Jubiläumswoche* (jubilee celebration week), in which the content of the spoken text of the dance, on the link between past, present and future was his message. Apparently the performance was marred by rain, with dancers undeterred and spectators stalwart, but the local press, already on one side or other of the local politics, was less kind. With the modernist moves in theatre, opera and concert hall, it was not surprising that Laban's insistence on keeping the same movement choir ethos that he had had for at least a decade should be regarded as inappropriate by theatre critics. But was it inappropriate to the partici-pants? While theatre fashions come and go, do the needs of the human spirit shift that rapidly? By the accounts of the Labanites, they found the experience uplifting and paid little heed to the criteria of others.

A month previously Martin Gleisner had had great success at the Social Democratic Convention in Magdeburg where he had been able to express his deeply felt socialist ideals in a choric work there. Entitled *Flammenden Zeit* (Flaming Times), the dance had been choreographed to take place afloat in boats on the lake. Always a militant man in his political alle-giances, he wrote challenging articles to underline his views. 'Enemies of Amateur Dance', in the March edition of *Singchor und Tanz*, was one such. His talent for inspiring young men and women in movement choir leader-ship was outstanding; his students were ready and able to start their own choirs fearlessly, and did so. *Tanz für Alle* (Dance for All) was the title of his later book on amateur dance. He was a true champion of Laban's ideals.

By 1929 other second generation Labanites were very much in evidence in independent and largely successful enterprises. Sylvia Bodmer and Lotte Müller, both previously Tanzbühne Laban dancers, directed their joint La-ban school in Frankfurt. They had a flourishing movement choir attached to it, which included a large group of men with whom Bodmer particularly had special teaching talent. They succeeded in co-operating with Frankfurt Opera in several performances. Gluck's *Orpheus und Euridice* in September 1929 was one, given again in January 1930; Meyerbeer's *L'Africaine* was another, also performed in January 1930. Jenny Gertz, an outstanding pioneer of children's dance and movement choirs, started experimenting with teaching notation to her young dancers in 1929, and then to children in the local state schools. Ruth (Gertrud) Loeszer had become leading dancer and dance arranger of the Dusseldorf City Opera in April 1929. By the autumn she had opened a dance studio in association with the Opera, for she encountered the same problem that Laban had in his first experi-ences at Mannheim: that dancers trained in the traditional opera-ballet school could not dance what she choreographed, not because their bodies were unable to master the steps but because their attitude to life in general was narrow. To innovation in particular they were downright hostile. Frida Holst, a Jooss dancer from Essen, directed Laban's *Don Juan* as her first production on taking charge of the Essen Tanzbühne, while Jooss created a new production of Laban's *Gaukelei* in April 1930. Many ex-Tanzbühne dancers had positions as soloists in city operas (Julian Algo, for example), and teachers of professional dancers, amateurs and children abounded. Grete Meisenbach in Nuremberg was one, Milca Mayerova in Prague was another. There is ample evidence by 1929 that Laban was indeed the father of German modern dance.

After Vienna and Mannheim the obligatory two-month Laban summer school took place, organised from the Choreographisches Institut and the Laban Central School, this year at Burg Lauenstein, in Thuringia in eastern Germany. Laban was billed to teach personally for August. The staff included the regular specialists, Bereska, Snell, Klingenbeck, Robst, Ivers, Annemarie Dunkel. Many classes were held in the open air, no doubt with memories for Laban of the creative and experimental atmosphere of the dance farm at Ascona in 1913 and 1914. It was by all accounts a joyous affair, with large numbers, including many who came regularly, some to keep their Laban Diploma's validity, some for the sheer love of dancing the Labanite way. Suzanne Perrottet attended, describing it in her diary as 'very successful'. The classes described in her papers show that the curriculum was of the standard Laban school sort, but with innovations and developments in the notation and choreutics.

Changes were afoot again in the organisation of the Central School. One key ingredient was the departure of Dussia Bereska. She had had an exploratory tour of Paris in the spring, and now having control of the Kammertanz with Robert Robst she could operate from anywhere. Just what the combinations of reasons were for her to leave Berlin and her close and erstwhile passionate relationship with Laban is not known. It would make sense that she knew of his forthcoming full-time post at Unter den Linden in which she would have no part to play. It makes sense that she was party to the imminent removal of the Central School from Gillstrasse to Essen, although which came first is unclear. She emigrated to France and opened a Laban school at 40 Boulevard Gouvion-Saint Cyr, near the Etoile, with Katrola Dessauer as assistant. She operated a small training centre and Kammertanz tours with Robst, and student dances were rehearsed there.

The removal of the Central School coincided with the city of Essen taking over the administration and financial responsibility of the dance department of the Folkwangschule, run by Kurt Jooss with Sigurd Leeder. It made sense for the Central School to gain that security, so it was amalgamated with Jooss's department and he became its director. Gertrud Snell moved to Essen to teach choreology, leaving the Choreographisches Institut at Gillstrasse staffed by Laban and Susanne Ivers with an emphasis on notation, dance theory and research. Knust returned to Hamburg with Azra Laban in time to run the summer school there. They would shortly open the Hamburg Tanzschreibstelle (Dance Notation Bureau) and focus on the development of the system, a task for which Knust was admirably suited. These moves divided the notation forces into specialist units. Snell, with Sigurd Leeder, had the task of using it and teaching it in the midst of a professional training school and company, a place essential to its development. Leeder began to make additional signs and concepts useful to that context. Laban and Ivers were on their own, mostly concerned with writing about the role of notation, seeing it not only as a recording method but as a way of understanding the basic structures of dance material, and as crucial for the recognition of dance as a literate art. Ivers was the notation scribe, providing illustrations for lectures and articles. But they were temporarily isolated from practice, for there were no students, there was no Bereska and no company – not a good context for the early development of what was still an embryonic system. Knust, with Azra, was away from professional dance too, the thriving Hamburg Movement Choir with its group movements and elementary technique being his daily contact with dance practice. He too started developments to cope with his needs. While these diverse developments enriched the system in the long run, they made for uncomfortable disagreements in the short term. It was also essential that everyone concerned should meet regularly – hence the essential role of the summer schools. But Jooss and Leeder were not at Burg Lauenstein, so Snell had to cover their point of view.

For Laban the autumn of 1929 was, by comparison with some other years, a quiet season. He published in three languages a book of short dances and reading exercises through Universal Edition, and undertook his usual lectures. He coped with bothersome officials in his battle to retain his Hungarian nationality and to avoid being classified as Czech. But the international financial crisis loomed. By October the New York banks crashed, and anxious administrators, dependent on foreign aid, scrutinised their budgets for the inevitable cuts. Luckily the Central School was for the moment safe.

The main feature of the 1929 autumn dance season was Laban's fiftieth birthday in December. It became a major celebration in print as well as in performance. Both *Der Tanz* and *Schrifttanz* devoted an issue to him, and *Singchor und Tanz* published a special issue with articles on his work. Knust wrote on Laban as educator, Gleisner on Laban as the creator of Dance for All, Hans Brandenburg remembered Laban's beginnings in Munich, Fritz Böhme focused on Laban's new generation of dancers. Hein Heckroth's line drawing of Laban was the front cover of *Schrifttanz*, and two of Laban's own oil paintings were printed while the well-known dance photographer Robertson gave a picture of a Laban hand study. Mary Wigman contributed 'Rudolf von Laban for his birthday', writing specifically on his work, not, she said, his personality. She stated, 'Present-day dancers, regardless of whether they have personally passed through Laban's school or not, respect and recognise in the name "Laban" the start of a new era in the history of European dance . . . He was the great discoverer and catalyst.' She continued with an entirely generous accolade of praise for her outstanding teacher and early collaborator. It could not have been an easy statement for her to make publicly, knowing her intense feelings about her own role. She ended with the corollary that those things which were dependent on his personality, by which she must have meant his dance works, would share the fate of all the performing arts, would die with him (as, she must have been thinking, would her own work on her death). But his great gifts as an educator and theoretician would live on. Her message was beautifully put and sincerely moving.

The birthday performance and party took place at Essen with due pomp and festivity, starting in the morning with the City Oberburgermeister and the musical director of the city opera giving the opening speeches, followed by Laban himself, who gave an overview of how he saw his own work. In the afternoon the Schrifttanz association gave him a collection of good wishes from many of his students and hundreds of movement choir members, who had signed on a roll of paper twenty metres long, the names being joined by notation phrases. The city of Essen gave a small gathering at which letters of best wishes and congratulations were read by the Minister of the Interior, Dr Becker of the Culture Ministry, and other influential civic gentlemen. An afternoon performance of Jooss's new work *Drosselbart* was given in the Opernhaus, and the whole festival ended with Jooss applauding Laban's great achievements despite all the problems that he had had to overcome. Much informal festivity followed. Several Laban schools gave their own birthday celebrations later, and Laban was interviewed as a celebrity on Berlin radio by Wolfgang Hoffman-Harnisch. All in all he was well and deservedly fêted.

If Laban knew that he was to be invited as guest choreographer to the Bayreuth Wagner Festival, he did not reveal it until an announcement appeared in the May 1930 edition of *Schrifttanz*. Also announced was that the summer school would be held at Bayreuth under Laban's personal leadership from 15 June to 22 August, using spaces in the Festival Opera House. A course for ballet masters was envisaged as well as for dancers and amateurs. This must have offered a very different draw from the previous open-air venue of Burg Lauenstein in the wilds of Thuringia. Professional dancers were the focus, adding to the ever-loyal Labanites.

Applications for the summer school were handled not from the Choreographisches Institut, nor from the Central School, but by Marie Luise
Lieschke at Plauen. This lady was becoming an important figure in Laban's
administrative arm. With Bereska in Paris and Snell in Essen, he had
accepted Lieschke's offers of assistance with gratitude. Her home, with her
husband, became a refuge for Laban to which he returned, many times
with Bereska, until he left Germany in 1937. Lieschke was a well-educated,
financially stable and politically astute woman, devoted to Laban's work
and ideas but unattached to him romantically. Having no steady amorous
partner at the moment, his reputation as a womaniser had certainly followed him to the Festzug, and would no doubt do so to Bayreuth; but not to
Plauen. In the meantime, between birthday celebrations and the spring he
undertook an 'ethnographic' trip to Hungary and Spain, according to
Schrifttanz news items, but nothing is known about it. His appointment to
Berlin he kept to himself.

As 1930 continued the economic situation worsened. The rising unemployment began to bite, people started to be fearful for the future. The 1923
hardships through hyperinflation were still fresh in people's memories. The
Third Dancers' Congress held in Munich from 20 to 25 June 1930 took place
in this uncomfortable context. It also followed the other two after a year's
lapse, but the memory of the unedifying turmoil and partisan in-fighting of
1928 could not be dispelled. Alfred Schlee anticipated a crisis of another
sort in a critical article in *Schrifttanz*, 'At the turning point of the New
Dance'. New Dance had lost its connection with other art development; it
had held on too long to expressionism and had tried to base theatre solely
on elements of ritual, he wrote. His key phrase reads: 'The New Dance is
obstinate. It does not concede to having been only an episode.' But he
added, 'As such its significance is immense.' He saw signs of change emerging but called for a clear demarcation between physical culture, the amateur movement choir and theatre dance so that each could be given its
place and its value. Theatre dance could then move forward into a post-
New Dance era. The short-lived but influential Dada eruptions must surely
have been in his mind as an episode of undoubted value which had had to
give way, to surrealism.

Schlee's mood was influenced by the turn of events in the other performing and literary arts. *Der Sturm*, the sharp-eyed monthly magazine on
expressionism in culture and the arts edited by Herwath Walden, had
closed. German socialist politics, which Walden supported, had weakened
so drastically that he saw support for the Soviets as the only way forward
and had left for Russia. *Der Krüpfel*, the satirical magazine to which George

Grosz contributed his vitriolic cartoons, had closed. New music that embraced jazz was criticised for being modish and insubstantial by the establishment writers. Playwrights were criticised for producing communist-related agitprop works, and directors, equally, for such way-out productions of classics that they could hardly be recognised as versions of the original. The silent films of the giants Eisenstein and Chaplin were seen as rivals to the theatre, so that those *in situ* had to make uneasy adjustments to this new competition. Piscator's response was one: he introduced multiple stage spaces and film clips as his stage settings, and, according to the historian John Willett, formed his theatre into a mix of lecture hall and debating chamber in an attempt to get his audience to respond and to think. The first 'talkies' appeared in 1929, further disturbing the equilibrium.

Hans Brandenburg, in a preview article, explained that the Munich Dancers' Congress, organised by the Laban and the Wigman dance associations in collaboration with the Chorische Bühne, would take place during a German Dance Week. As part of it there would be a performance by the Chorische Bühne of Talhoff's *Totenmal* (Memorial) 'a dramatic-choric vision for speech, dance and light'. A new form combining theatre and dance, Brandenburg saw it as a possible way forward out of the 'crisis' in both arts. A specialist team had been assembled, Mary Wigman as director/choreographer, Adolf Linnebach for lighting and technical arrangements, Bruno Goldschmitt for masks, and Karl Vogt for the rehearsal of the spoken parts. Certainly the outcome was anticipated with great interest and as a test of Wigman's directorial skills. Buchholz, Eckhardt, Felix Emmel and Martin Gleisner were the Congress organisers, Brandenburg playing host somewhat, being a Münchener. Unlike previous Congresses, performances formed the major part of the programme. Fourteen hundred participants attended, from both Germany and abroad.

Schlee's anxiety was well founded, for the mixture, which needed to be innovative, was the same as before, but instead of the three 'gods' being in full flight, Laban played a very secondary role, in Amateur Dance only. Kröller was as traditional as ever, and Wigman's production of *Totenmal* was described as a disaster. The speeches on the opening day on theatre offered nothing new, with Rudolf Schulz-Dornburg on 'Dance in Opera', Felix Emmel on 'Dance in Plays' and Brandenburg on the Chorische Bühne. The two rival Dance Associations were given time to discuss the issues amongst themselves, followed by a plenary session. On day two, community dance was the topic, with Gleisner focusing on the Workers' Movement, Laban on amateur dance forms in modern times, and a Jesuit priest, Pater Friedrich Muckermann, speaking on the function of amateur dance for young people for whom spiritual means of a traditional sort were no longer attractive. Again nothing new, for everything that could be said about the movement choir had already been said. On day three, Fritz Böhme spoke on the depressing social and economic plight of the dance profession. The Bavarian State Theatre gave the opening performance with a one-act opera by Puccini, *Der Mantel* (*Il Tabarro*), Kröller choreographing a ballet, *Mammon*, to a Křenek score, and mounting the safe and sure *Nutcracker*. Alternatively, for those not keen on ballet, an evening of Kammertanz performances from several groups was on offer, those of Rosalia Chladek, Heide Woog, Gertrud Kraus, Manda von Kreibig, Jutta Klamt and Wulff (who did not list her first name). Their offerings were variations on the well-tried theme of short dances, no new directions being noted. Ten further small groups performed on Saturday afternoon, followed in the evening by an amateur dance festival for Laban movement choirs from Altona, Berlin, Gera, Halle, Hamburg and Mannheim. Laban, Gleisner and Knust were in charge, percussion was the sound accompaniment. This culminating festive evening, not a performance, followed a week of working together on dances already partially learnt from the score locally. No stimulating or challenging new work had been composed, no equivalent to *Titan*. The predictability was depressing.

A professional matinée offered Margarethe Wallmann's group in a premiere of her *Orpheus Dionysos*, with Gluck's music, in a programme shared with Lizzie Maudrik's revival of *Coppélia*. Four further amateur groups offered choric dances, three on the Laban lines with the fourth, the Proletarische Laiengruppe Leipzig, waking everyone up with a satirical piece to jazz accompaniment, in similar vein to Laban's *Nacht* of 1927, but far less iconoclastic. Further professional groups from municipal theatres and from the Dalcroze Institut performed, Gertrud Loeszer offering a suite of national dances to Stravinsky, Kurt Jooss giving his version of Laban's *Gaukelei*, Gret Palucca and Vera Skoronel, good as they were, following in the footsteps of 'the gods'.

A lengthy afternoon of thirty-three young soloists preceded *Totenmal*. The necessary transformation of the theatre space for this ambitious work was not completed on time, so only a rehearsal of it could be shown. Wigman's treatment of soldiers' deaths and mourning choric groups was received with consternation as *passé*. It was deeply disappointing. Even the varied day devoted to performances from foreign groups could not lift the spirits of the Congress participants.

Ausdruckstanz as theatre performance seemed to be without vision. Had the ten years of intense excitement pioneered by Laban and Wigman burned out? Their towering personalities seemed to have dwarfed the very thing they hoped to awaken – individual creativity. Free movement there was. Choreography abounded. The old grammar, the codes, the conventions attacked, broken and re-assembled to their own taste by Laban and Wigman had become the new grammar, codes and conventions. Nobody was breaking them. The only progressive element was the plan for the High School, which was presented to the public and offered hope. With their proposed mixed curriculum they should have had a chance of educating rather than training, from which courage to start a post-*Ausdruckstanz* era might have arisen. But economic and political events would intervene.

This follow-my-leader state of affairs contrasted with the lone road plied by Oskar Schlemmer. His performances with the Bauhaus Theatre during the previous season, in Dessau and Frankfurt, offered innovative theatre in what he regarded, according to his diary entries, as a post-expressionist, post-New Objectivity style. Oskar Bie, from his standpoint as a ballet expert, could not understand why the public were so enthusiastic with the primitive, misconstrued comicalness of the strutting movers. The equally conservative Artur Michel simply asked, 'What is this?' Schlemmer mused over the shift in style of the portrayal of man in art from the futurists' insistence on the portrayal of man's energy, the expressionists' on essence and never appearance, through the Neue Sächlichkeit preference for realism, to a present interest, his own interest, in man as a beautiful art object. The balance of abstraction, proportion and law on the one hand and nature, emotion and idea on the other, would always be present, he wrote. His work embraced form and eschewed politics. 'You cannot persuade Paul Klee to be George Grosz,' he remarked, implying that the Bauhaus directives to Klee to be more political were a wasted effort. In an entry in May 1929, Schlemmer recorded his love of simplicity and of starting and remaining with the basic things that a body does. 'Walking is a grave event,' he wrote, let alone leaping and dancing. He had been invited to participate in the Munich Congress but had had to turn it down. Indeed for the whole year he worked not as a dance person but as a visual designer, culminating in the decor and costumes for Schoenberg's *Die Glückliche Hand* in Berlin, a production concurrent with the ailing Congress. The contrast of Schlemmer's mechanised idealism of man, leading almost to a negation of the body, with the corporeality of the movement choirs could hardly be missed, but the evidence suggests that the *Ausdruckstänzer* paid little attention to Schlemmer. Schlemmer also recorded the increasing impact of reactionary pressures from German culture in general on all avant-garde artists, the Bauhaus in particular. While Laban's way of working was leading him to the State Opera at Unter den Linden, Schlemmer's was about to face implacable opposition.

Laban himself was not at a point of despair nor at a low creative point, whatever Schlee's views of German dance in general might have been. He had two extremely challenging projects ahead: Bayreuth, in which he was already engaged, and Unter den Linden. The task at Bayreuth was the 'Bacchanale' in *Tannhäuser* (Paris version), again, plus the movement in *Götterdämmerung* and *Parsifal*. His collaborators were to be Siegfried Wagner as director of the whole festival, and Arturo Toscanini as its musical director. He organised his own dancers combining the ex-Choreographisches Institut dancers, the *Kammertänzer* and Jooss's Essen group. Jooss was billed as his choreographic collaborator.

For Laban, Bayreuth was the high point of his artistic career, 'a time of unclouded joy and inspiration'. Always an ardent admirer of Richard Wagner, he wrote in *A Life for Dance* that he saw in Wagner's music and writings 'his tremendous way of thinking in terms of movement'. Indeed, 'he was also a decisive influence on the art of movement'. He developed a close working rapport with Siegfried Wagner who 'supported my endeavours in the most touching and sympathetic manner.' Siegfried sat in on every dance rehearsal, noting the moves in his score.

1930 was a year of upheaval at Bayreuth, for during the season, before the performances had begun, Siegfried died, thus creating a hiatus in the season's direction, and, more problematically, a hiatus in the family succession. Richard Wagner's widow Cosima had previously been responsible for the aesthetic of the productions from the beginning of the century, working from the family court, Wahnfried. On her death her son Siegfried, described as rather unprepossessing, took over her responsibilities and became an active artistic director of the productions. More significantly, he inherited a stronghold of nationalistic fervour, expressed in the Festival, in the operas themselves and in the political leanings of the Wagner dynasty. Frederick Spotts, in his history of Bayreuth, expresses the atmosphere under Cosima and her historian son-in-law Houston Stewart Chamberlain as 'nationalism gone berserk', with the focus on 'German culture' generated by Wagner and his writings, 'the regeneration of the German soul' being the call. Chamberlain had married into the family and brought his racist and anti-Semitic writings with him, turning Bayreuth's passive nationalism into 'an aggressive, crusading force'. Wahnfried and the Wagner theatre together were 'a holy place of the German soul', 'a centre of artistic religion', 'a psychic spa'. Such was the fervour and awe with which all things Wagnerian were viewed. Siegfried's widow Winifred was an active right-winger who supported Hitler long before he came to power (he stayed at Wahnfried regularly throughout the 1920s). Siegfried pursued advances in the modernisation of the productions while living in an atmosphere of intense conservatism at home. But in 1930, in the middle of the season, on Siegfried's death, Winifred took it upon herself to take over the leadership of the Festival, bringing with her its Nazification. From 1931 Bayreuth became more and more a personal theatre of Hitler's, and from 1933 more or less the court theatre of the Third Reich president.

The 1930 season started for Laban, Jooss and their dancers with every promise of success, working closely with the world-famous conductor Arturo Toscanini, assisted by Karl Elmendorff from the Munich State Opera and Kurt Söhnlein, who designed the *Tannhäuser* scenery around which the 'Bacchanale' would take place. With the exhilaration of working in such surroundings and with such high-profile fellow artists, they rehearsed in their usual Labanite way, often outside, creating a Venusberg of tremendous vigour. The response of the press to the 9 August premiere was, as usual, conflicting. Ernest Newman regarded the whole *Tannhäuser* production as daring, especially the appointment of 'the avant-garde choreographer Rudolf von Laban . . . The Bacchanale caught for once the spirit of the marvellous score.' But Alfred Einstein disagreed: 'Bayreuth lacks the courage either to stick to the conventional or to mount something truly original.' They had created, he blasted, 'a stylistic monster'. On balance, the press were more in favour than not. From the dancers' point of view it was a great success, and the whole cast of singers and production team were stimulated by the vigour and abandon of the 'Bacchanale'. In any case, Laban was asked to return for the next season. Quite how much Jooss helped him with the choreography is open to dispute, but the history of Laban's choreographic career shows that from 1924 onwards he had always had Bereska as a rehearsal assistant and to some extent must have come to rely on her. In 1930 she was not there and Jooss himself took the view that his collaborative role had been considerable. Possibly Laban's audacity and insight into things Wagnerian, tempered by Jooss's increasing compositional skills, were the magic ingredients.

The ensuing developments at Bayreuth could not have passed Laban's notice. Winifred had to replace her dead husband, and she did so with Heinz Tietjen. He was about to become Laban's superior through Tietjen's job as Intendant of the Prussian State Theatres, Unter den Linden, the Kroll Theatre in Berlin, the Wiesbaden, Kassel and Hanover theatres. Laban's post covered the same theatres, but for movement and choreography only. Tietjen was regarded by Winifred, though not by everyone, as 'the most important impresario in Germany'. He had both conducting and directing skills, but was generally distrusted by both the conservatives and the avant-garde. He clearly had the ability to walk the tightrope of public opinion and political intrigue, for his own politics were liberal and yet he managed to remain in place, if not in favour, throughout the Nazi period. From Laban's point of view he had a model in Tietjen of how to function at Unter den Linden when he took up his post on 1 September, and later indeed on how to survive after the 1933 takeover by the Nazis. But their relationship deteriorated, as we shall see.

Personally, Laban started a new lifestyle on 1 September, for he had to give up his practice of 'living over the shop'. Since his Paris days he had always had his headquarters at, in, or over his studio. Until 1919 when he left his second wife he had two abodes, his domestic one with wife and children and his professional one. From 1920 'home' had been a room associated with his work space, and latterly that had been at Gillstrasse. Now he had to vacate that as the Choreographisches Institut moved to Essen, subsumed into the Central School under Jooss. Susanne Ivers came with him to Unter den Linden as the first ever resident notator. His erst-while student Jutta Klamt took over Gillstrasse for her school. Laban no longer had a headquarters for his own research and work, but rather occupied the office of movement director and ballet-master in the Opera House. The archive materials that he had at Gillstrasse needed a home. Plauen was the answer, and so it was that Marie Luise Lieschke's home became Laban's depository. For the next six years he had to find his own accommodation, with difficulty and displeasure, often changing addresses. Possibly, as gossip will have it, the addresses belonged to women friends, but that is not easy to verify. He went regularly to Essen for masterclasses and examinations, but stayed in a hotel there.

The duties at Unter den Linden were complex. They included the stand-ard tasks of a ballet-master in a major house, that is, the creative challenge of choreographing for new opera productions, personal responsibility for the opera ballet including the daily class for the *corps* and soloists, for their standard of dancing and reliability in rehearsal and performance, for run-ning the opera ballet school for children aged seven to sixteen, and for the student group, including auditions, examinations and liaison with parents. Laban was also expected to mount dance evenings with the company, indeed all eyes were turned to what he might produce with the most prestigious ballet company in Germany. While much of this was standard work, it was not standard for Laban. He had always had other people to run his schools, to check on his dancers, and latterly to give class. Ballet was not his medium. He was also used to having a choreographic assistant. Here he had none of this support, except Susanne Ivers as notator, but she was no replacement for Bereska. Additionally, he was commencing this challenge in Berlin, the capital city of Prussia, at a time when the political power of that state was already threatened by the National Socialists, three years before Hitler dominated Germany as a whole. Berlin itself was used to the Brownshirts of the SA (Sturmabteilung), the Nazi equivalent of the communists' Freikorps with which Laban had been only too familiar in Stuttgart and Hamburg. The street Unter den Linden, leading to the Brandenburg Gate and the Reichstag, was the political highway of the city down which marched any group of people who wished to demonstrate, or were coerced into so doing. The opera employees could not miss any social or political gestures, for these took place right there outside their 'front door'. This atmosphere, together with the reactionary pressure generally on avant-garde art and the unrest generated by rising urban unemployment, formed the context for the next four years of Laban's artistic life.

His work at the Opera began with his usual vigour. For the regular house magazine, *Blätter der Staatsoper*, that contained details of and background information on every forthcoming production, he contributed 'On the creative foundation of dance works' and proceeded to show what he meant through choreographing a tumultuous version of the *Polovtsian Dances* that end the second act of Borodin's *Prince Igor*. At the premiere of 11 October 1930 he received favourable responses from Max Marschalk in the *Vossische Zeitung* and from Oskar Bie in the *Berliner Borsen Courier*, although Bie saw Laban's strength as being in the ensemble choreography rather than the virtuoso solos that Bie regarded as *de rigueur*. The critics' eagle eye was on this performance, Laban's debut in the post. Alfred Einstein remarked on the applause which set the public's approval on Laban's position (he could hardly have ignored it) but he put it down partly to the magnificence of the symphonic music. Susanne Ivers notated the dances, the first dance score of its kind. While this must have seemed an epoch-making development, the practical value of such a score was never put to the test. As an archival record it remains evidence of a kind not found for other incidental dances in the opera repertoire.

The season continued with a one-act comic opera, *Die Zierpuppen*, for which a seventeenth-century country dance and sarabande were wanted; but Gounod's *Margarete* (*Faust*) in November, for which Laban created the *Walpurgisnacht Bacchanale*, was his next real opportunity. Edwin Neruda's review remarked on the comments that the conventional establishment might make, while the public hailed it enthusiastically. Bie on the other hand, looking for virtuosity, found it boring, while Alfred Einstein, always a stinging critic of Laban's work, found it without the least stimulus: where were the witches? Where were the womanly qualities? Only in Daisy Spies and Dorothea Albu; not in the choreography. Laban himself remarked in *A Life for Dance* that battling with the opera establishment was a permanent feature of his work in mainstream German theatres. His wish to shift concepts and practices was always resisted. Whether his choreographic talent for *Margarete* was as weak as his critics suggested, or whether their expectations were as hidebound as he suggested, is open to debate. That he was up against opposition is not in doubt. How he coped with it was, and is, the interest.

At the end of November he had his first opportunity to contribute to a dance evening, at the Kroll Opera in the Platz der Republik given for the Lawn Tennis Club 'Rot-Weiss'. He re-choreographed *Jeux*, the dance poem created by Nijinsky to Debussy's score, a trio for two women and a man in tennis gear. The event did not attract critical reports. The Kroll was in its last season, a victim of the financial debts accrued by the Prussian State Theatres. Already regarded as an expensive and expendable Berlin opera house by the state financiers, there being four others, the diminishing income caused by the devastating slump had to be balanced by economies. Performance excellence was of no interest to the money men. Under Otto Klemperer's musical direction and with innovative designers like László Moholy-Nagy outstanding modern work had been included in the repertory – inadequate reason to forestall its closure. The Völksbühne theatre association, with its block bookings for the season and therefore a voice in programming, would more likely have resisted closure had there been less moderns in the proposed season: Paul Hindemith, Kurt Weill, Leoš Janáček. The Kroll's demise brought the inevitable threat of imminent financial stringency nearer to the major houses.

Also at the Kroll, in December, the Charpentier opera *Louise*, a melodic swinging antidote to the reverence for Wagner, was well received. Laban's ballroom dances were apparently kept in the appropriate style. More to his taste was his opportunity for the *Silvesterspuk*, a New Year's Eve informal performance, for which *Abschied von der Bar* (Farewell from the Bar) and *Sextor* were directed by him, along with a short comic opera, *Spiel und Ernst* (Play and Earnest). Here he could use his gift for irony and caricature, which he did in both the movement and the costume designs.

Concurrently he reorganised the ballet school. Whether this move emerged from his views on children's dance, on the kind of dance he wished to include in opera, or because he was directed to make changes, is not clear. Although the documents read as if the idea were his, financial cuts in 1930–31 were instituted everywhere. The carefully prepared rationale for change was dated 1 November 1930. In it he proposed categorically that the present children's school, which included academic schoolwork, should be closed as soon as possible, the necessary dance classes being given on four to six afternoons per week. The whole organisation of the people concerned with the school and its curriculum should be reviewed urgently. He gave several reasons, strongly criticising present methods, amongst which was the necessary shift from an emphasis on training, acrobatics and technique to one on art. He showed how his proposals would be economically advantageous, no doubt an essential point. He went on to look at the increased responsibility to be given to parents for the general education of their children, the opera retaining only responsibility for the essential dance classes. He looked at how this would work from the youngest child up to those ready to become *corps* dancers or soloists. The draft was sent to the General Intendant, Tietjen.

That Laban would have found a traditional ballet education for children ethically deplorable and aesthetically inadequate almost goes without saying. That he would have immediately succeeded in completely revamping such an entrenched tradition without the pressure from above is questionable. Did the need for financial cuts enable him to choose this means of economy over others he might have made, or was this means suggested to him as a ruse by the state authorities, already Nazi-dominated, who wished to bring in more controls, possibly with a racial ingredient, in order to pursue their cultural revolution? Was he a visionary innovator or was this the first of several instances in which he was an unwitting pawn? The outcome was that by March 1931 the suggested new arrangements were in place. There is nothing in the documentation to suggest anything other than school economies. Needless to say, parents responded in alarm. Laban was involved in getting the 'dismissed' children into ordinary schools for their morning lessons, the correspondence continuing into 1932.

This was not the only economic/aesthetic decision to be made by Laban. The *Sozialistische Monatshefte* for July 1931 reported that the soloists of the State Opera had been given notice by the Intendant. Laban, through his plan to choreograph entirely through an ensemble, was stated as the instigator of this loss of work. It had been put to the soloists in March and announced in May by Laban in *Singchor und Tanz*. The dancers retaliated through an open letter to Laban in the press arguing their case, signed by Rudolf Kölling, Jens Keith, Daisy Spies, Dorothea Albu, and Eugenie Nikolaieva. What alarmed the Opera administration was the formation of a

Ballettkollectiv by six of the soloists through which they managed to obtain good performing possibilities, the words 'Performances by Soloists of the State Opera' used as publicity. Court injunctions followed. They managed to keep together for at least a season.

Further suggestions appeared in the press that Laban's aesthetic and choreographic preferences were not the only reasons for the soloists' dismissal. Plenty of instances exist in the routine reports submitted by Laban after each performance to the effect that a soloist was late, too late to put on make up, did not turn up for rehearsal, and so on. Possibly the discipline was lax, later correspondence suggesting that Laban inherited that state of affairs from Max Terpis. Or were the dancers choosing the means of poor workmanship to get at a choreographer who did not enjoy virtuosity, who found a star system not to his ethical taste? Or was it partly a strategy by the administration, with the closure of the Kroll as the indisputable reason given for the need for a reduction in personnel, as was suggested by Joseph Lewitan in *Der Tanz*, Laban being the scapegoat? Whatever the underlying power-play, Laban was to become master of an ensemble and able to work in his accustomed manner, depriving the virtuosity- and personality-starved critics of their titillation – but not until the 1931–32 season.

The 1930–31 season continued with one work in February requiring new choreography, Strauss's *Eine Nacht in Venedig*. It proved to be highly successful, Bie commenting on the skilful way in which Laban intermixed soloist and ensemble, how he used characterisation and had composed a very funny 'Pigeon's Dance'. 'A feast for the eyes,' was Einstein's view.

It was Willi Godlewski in *Singchor und Tanz* who opened the discussion on the relation of ballet and expressive dance. This relationship, on the face of it an aesthetic one, was to become a political issue as nationalism became a more prominent part of cultural life, not only through the National Socialists but also through von Papen's National Centre Party. German dance, the dance of the German people – Wigman's dance, Palucca's dance, Günther's, Kreutzberg's, Laban's dance – became more and more a symbol of German superiority in this art form, and contrasted with ballet which was regarded as an importation. In April Wigman played to acclaim at the Berliner Theater, in May Harald Kreutzberg and Yvonne Georgi guested at Unter den Linden in a stylish programme with *Train Bleu* and *Planeten*. But at the City Opera Lizzie Maudrik was successfully mounting balletic work; at Munich Kröller was doing the same, as were some other city houses. Diaghilev's Ballets Russes' visit to Berlin in 1929 was recalled as very French, foreign. Was ballet a suitable dance form for Germany?

That was the question which was about to become important. This discussion, only just beginning, was complicated by the very problem that Schlee had commented upon, namely had *Ausdruckstanz* (or German Dance) had its day? Werner Suhr continued the discussion in *Der Tanz* in May with 'Dance and the Present Day', a review of Wigman's work. Schlee notwithstanding, there were plenty of people for whom Wigman was still the 'goddess' of dance, transcending nationalist issues through her sheer brilliance as a performer.

May and June 1931 were extremely busy months for Laban. He masterminded a mixed evening of the one act-comic opera *Spiel und Ernst* with a *Carnivalistische Tanzsuite* and rehearsed the dances for the operetta *Zigeunerbaron* (The Gipsy Baron). Here Laban drew on his childhood repertoire of czardas, to much applause. Concurrently preliminary rehearsals for the Bayreuth performances of *Tannhäuser* took place in the Schauspielhaus around the corner from the opera house, in Gendarmenmarkt. This time he had no Jooss to help him, but with many of the same dancers joining him they reassembled the 'Bacchanale' together. At the beginning of July they all left the city for the joys of the Wagner Festival and the 21 July opening night.

Under Winifred Wagner's hand the atmosphere leading up to the Festival was embattled, orchestrated by the mutual dislike of the world-renowned Arturo Toscanini and European-renowned Wilhelm Furtwängler. Both were notoriously vain and temperamentally dogmatic, Toscanini regarding the score as inviolate while Furtwängler saw it as open to interpretation. While there was still one season to go before the total Nazification of Bayreuth, Winifred's open involvement with Hitler and his associates gave the Festival an unmistakable flavour. The 'Bacchanale' was not so enthusiastically received; possibly the spirit of the first creation proved elusive in reconstruction. No summer school was held despite the euphoria of the previous year, with the exception of a notation course. Laban took off for a month in Austria where he had been booked to teach a course in Dance Art at the Austro-American Conservatoire of Music, Art and Theatre situated at the resort of Mondsee.

With the knowledge that his one-year contract with the Prussian State Theatres had been extended for a further three – possibly even as a condition of that – Laban applied in August for German nationality. Had the veneration of the German soul at Bayreuth encouraged him to embrace all things German? Was obtaining a German passport a shrewd guess at what might be necessary in the future? As Schlemmer wrote of this period in his diary, 'In these times even contracts that seemed safe can be threatened.'

9

The Nazification of Culture

Berlin, 1931–1934

Throughout the 1930–31 season, despite his main focus being essentially on his practical job as an employee in Berlin, Laban continued to write, to teach and to examine in his schools, to lecture and to champion both amateur dance and literate dance. His independent and entrepreneurial spirit continued to function. The education of the public at large in dance, as well as dancers' professional education through the hoped for High School, remained a burning interest. He ran a small Laban Tanzstudio in Berlin for occasional Kammertanz works, partly in order to have demonstrators other than the opera soloists for his lectures. He had not been without his own, or his and Bereska's, small company ever since he began his career. He needed to continue that outlet to cater for the iconoclastic side of his creativity. He had begun work on his autobiography, which, although not published until 1935, gave him a chance to look back at his childhood and his whole career in movement. In it he makes little reference to his days at Unter den Linden, or to the problematic time under the Nazis, which suggests that he had already written much of it by 1932–33.

His loyal circle continued their special responsibilities on their own, with vigour. As examples, Martin Gleisner had written in May on 'The Child and the Dance' in *Die Jugendbühne,* Albrecht Knust had published in *Schrifttanz* a coherent account of the orthographic rules of Laban's notation. Through the Hamburger Tanzschreibstube, which he continued to run with Azra Laban, Knust had prepared 'Proposals for the Writing of Group Movements'. Movement choirs being the most active users of notated scores, Knust's developments for the notating of structurally choreographed group movement, canons in time and in space for example, were a necessary addition. His ideas facilitated the expression of group movement on paper rather than having to write down the movement of each individual member of the group. They also influenced choreography for amateurs through showing possible group forms that could be used to temper the group feeling associated with amateur expressive dance. The composi-tions of Knust's student Lola Rogge, whose work was to play a significant part in the dance celebrations of the Olympic Games of 1936, showed the influence of his organised and systematic approach to bodies in space and time. A Movement Choir festival in Hamburg during the summer was a further example of Labanite activity. The choirs from Hamburg under their lead dancer Veith, those from Berlin under Gleisner, and from Mannheim under Harry Pierenkämper had shared together in the dancing of a notated work, while also performing their own dances. The Frankfurt choir under Bodmer and Müller had performed *Hymnus der Arbeit* (An Anthem on Work), a section from Laban's *Alltag und Fest*, as a summer celebration, also using the notation score.

The continued success of his movement choirs and the necessary devel-opment by Knust of the notation were, on the one hand, welcome news to Laban. On the other, they were indicative of how endeavours he had started were becoming less and less under his own control. Knust wrote to Laban about the notation development, rightly asking Laban's opinion on whether these developments, and new writing signs, could become part of the established system. Laban immediately saw the danger for the future of his notation, which he envisaged as universal, of the introduction of signs to the system because of any specialist needs. Where might that lead? What other specialist needs might appear? He demurred for some time but finally agreed to Knust's request. But for him it was a realisation that his 'child', long sought for, was no longer solely his own but was now in the general domain of dance and dancers.

While Fritz Klingenbeck explored the problems of notating ballroom dancing, writing in *Der Tanz*, Dussia Bereska established her modest Laban school in a largely unresponsive Paris, and the ubiquitous Labanschulen continued to teach their amateur, professional and children's classes. Laban-inspired work was certainly being pursued energetically both near and far. The Dresden-based Wigman School celebrated its tenth anniver-sary, and the dance magazines, both national and international, noted it with issues and articles devoted to her work. Special performances were given. The celebrations in Berlin constituted a clear recognition of her artistry and especially of her central role in German dance.

As soon as the autumn season began in September 1931, the full effect of the economic slump was felt by everyone. Until the spring of 1931 no one had believed that the recession would last: it was regarded as a short-term response to international difficulties. By the summer there were still no signs of a recovery. The seriousness of the repercussions of the lack of

foreign investment on the economy as a whole became unavoidably obvious as unemployment escalated and firms collapsed. The closing of publicly funded institutions began, arts institutions being a favoured target.
Some of the first to go were the Art Schools. The one in Breslau, where
Schlemmer worked, the Köningsberg and Cassel schools, and the Folkwang
Art School at Essen were all affected. The Folkwang dance department
remained open under Jooss, but with a severely cut budget. Gertrud Snell
lost her job, Sigurd Leeder taking over the teaching of notation. Bereska
offered Snell a limited opportunity as an assistant in Paris, where the
impact of the recession was less violent. The dance magazines felt the
financial squeeze. Despite an appeal for readers, *Schrifttanz* published its
final edition in October 1931. So collapsed the first attempt at an academic
dance journal. *Der Tanz* took its place, deciding on a more general editorial
policy, and included the responsibility for publishing the proceedings of the
Deutsche Gesellschaft für Schrifttanz set up in 1928 and administered by
Lieschke. Dance scholarship, promoted in *Schrifttanz* through the encouragement of erudite articles on a wider spectrum of dance topics, was dealt a
blow, but dance literacy through notation still kept a voice. Indeed, an
exhibition entitled 'Tanzschrift – Schrifttanz' was mounted for the autumn,
touring to Essen and Mannheim, which included scores illustrated by photographs from the two well-known art photographers Charlotte Rudolph of
Dresden and Robertson of Berlin.

Before the opera season began, the Laban Tanzstudio's Kammertanz
group under the leadership of Annemarie Dunkel and Edgar Frank, both
Choreographisches Institut dancers, took a tour of small works to Kiel and
Wiesbaden, so enabling Laban to retain a small independent art-making
voice. Robst, still working from time to time with Bereska from Paris,
danced with them. Ilse Loesch and four young dancers completed the
company. In the meantime Laban began rehearsals for new productions,
Weber's *Oberon* for 2 October and Wolf-Ferrari's *Die Schalkhafte Witwe*
(The Cunning Widow) for 20 October, which had had its world premiere in
Rome six months before.

Bruno Walter guest-conducted the Weber, a brief appearance at Unter
den Linden much applauded, and Aravantinos, a regular designer, provided the admired atmospheric decor. Bie approved of Laban's ballet for
knights, elves, gnomes and fairy creatures, while Einstein congratulated
him on finding a way beyond the description of fairyland to suggest youth,
merriment and spirituality. His ensemble method was felt to be well suited
to this scenario. The Wolf-Ferrari reviews made no mention of the third-act
dances, given to the second rank of performers, and in any case of little

consequence to the piece as a whole. Leo Blech, the resident conductor, was much applauded. All in all, the season began well.

The contrast between these productions for a frock-coated and well-heeled audience with Martin Gleisner's *Rotes Lied*, a production for the fortieth anniversary of the Berlin district of the Deutschen Arbeiter Sänger-bund (German Workers' Guild of Singers), could hardly have been greater. Five hundred schoolchildren, five hundred youths and two thousand sing-ers, mostly men, sang, spoke and moved with the theme of the brotherhood of the battling workers, their history, their present struggles and their will for the future. The venue was a football field with forty thousand festival participants in all. Such a gathering as this was an example of the strange alliance between members of two extreme political parties. The Commu-nists had strong representation in the local organisations and local govern-ment, but so too did the National Socialists. Both spoke out against capital-ism and elitism, both had militant worker members. Laban's ideas were concurrently presented – his dance for all on a football pitch, his innovative theatre work on a prestigious stage.

December brought an opportunity for two dance evenings at the Schillertheater, in Berlin-Charlottenburg. These could have been Laban's showcase for new choreography, but he chose to present excerpts from the *Zigeunerbaron* and *Prince Igor* and a repetition of *Carnivalistische Tanz-suite* with its *Frauentanz*, *Männertanz*, *Humoresken* and *Spanische Tänze*. Working with the opera-ballet ensemble, without soloists, he could not produce satirical comments like *Die Grünen Clowns* or *Nacht*, nor abstract dance poems like *Der Schwingende Tempel*. He had neither the will nor the skill to utilise the ballet technique of his dancers for his own vision.

Laban made a conspicuous flop of another opportunity. He was given the sole responsibility for the production of Sidney Jones's *Die Geisha* to be the New Year's Eve production. The reviewer's suggestion that the less said about it the better sums up his gaff. He misjudged the stylishness that an operetta of this kind required. At the Opera, 1931 ended for him on this weakened note.

Economies at Unter den Linden began again in January 1932 with notice to Susanne Ivers that her appointment would cease in July. She was one of several marginal employees at the opera to go. Her practical useful-ness on a daily basis could not be argued for, although her archiving position and her notation teaching in the ballet school could. Her depar-ture at the end of the season would be a blow to Laban's visions of literate dance for the theatre as well as a slight prestige blow, for having a notator at his side in every rehearsal carried a small cachet. Productions continued with Bizet's *Carmen*, for which dances were required for 13 February. Apparently Laban made no impression with his ensemble. It is no wonder that Artur Michel, in the *Vossische Zeitung*, asked who should represent Germany in the forthcoming International Choreographic Competition in Paris. The ballet of Unter den Linden was the natural candidate as the company of the leading house, but Michel implied that with no soloists it could not be chosen. Would Wigman be a better choice? On the same day Oskar Bie criticised Laban for doing nothing significant at the State Opera.

The extraordinary atmosphere in which all these people worked cannot be imagined. Localised Nazi terror was daily becoming more formidable, more tolerated, more sinister in terms of the censorship of plays and books. Obstruction of the lawful expression of opinion and disruption of theatre and film performances was becoming commonplace. While Unter den Linden itself was not a target, art museums had whole modern collections closed and museum directors were sacked, Hildebrand Gurlett at Zwickau being one. The Bauhaus was threatened with closure altogether, and a concert of Hindemith's music was forbidden by the local Nazi-dominated council. Historian John Willett tells us that any means to hand, from letting off stink bombs to unleashing quantities of white mice in mid-performance, were used to combat 'Eastern-Bolshevistic-Judaic-Marxist art'. Anything modern was a target, anything foreign, anything Jewish. This type of hooligan behaviour, once occasional, shifted to being the norm. People were beginning to decide where they stood, some too frightened to object let alone to intervene, while others decided to join in.

In this atmosphere Laban was required to arrange dances for the Berlin Frühjahrmodewochen (Spring Fashion Week), in early March. One can imagine his tongue in cheek as the opera-ballet danced an oriental fantasy *Fischfang am Jangtsekiang* in performances shared with the designer Hans Vaterland, celebrating the influence of eastern design on fashion. At the Opera, movement for *La Traviata* was next, for 9 March. Nothing of note was commented on in the press reviews. It would seem that Laban was losing a taste for ballet and theatre, fashion and fantasy, in a time of such portentous upheavals. Schlemmer wrote in his diary, 'Berlin is gradually fading away, tired of theatre, tired of people.'

The Prussian State elections for the Landtag took place in April. The result was a massive increase in the vote for the Nazis, a loss for the Socialists and the Communists. From that moment on the Nazification of Prussia, with Berlin at its heart, accelerated openly and legally. The election for the Presidency, also in April, was won by Hindenburg with Hitler on his heels, the communist Ernst Thälmann nowhere in the race. This result gave people a slight breathing space in which to contemplate what horrors might follow if the Nazis gained power over the whole country.

The opera season ended with the repertoire offering Laban little opportunity. Verdi's *Sizilianische Vesper* was given in June, in which there was a ballet in the fourth scene that Verdi provided with 'dolled up and flashy music'. Only one critic noted it, regarding the whole thing, both music and dance, as 'kitschy'. Laban left Berlin thankfully, for Paris, there to visit Bereska's school and the newly opened Archives Internationales de la Danse started in April by Rolf de Maré.

The most significant part of his Paris stay was the July International Choreographic Competition, to which he was invited as one of the fourteen jury members. Rolf de Maré asked him to contribute an article for the competition programme. He decided on 'La Danse dans l'Opéra', illustrating it with his own work at Unter den Linden. Held at the Théâtre des Champs-Elysées, this high-profile competition proved momentous for German dance and for Laban. Kurt Jooss's resounding success with *The Green Table* was not expected. He was known, but this ballet, with its politically sensitive theme, created with choreographic skill and executed by the Folkwangbühne of Essen to perfection, took the first prize. Laban was overjoyed even to tears for his student, but also humbled, for he recognised that Jooss had surpassed him as a choreographer. Jooss had achieved with *The Green Table* what Laban had sought to do with his political works, *Gaukelei* particularly. Jooss's embrace of the step patterns of classical ballet while retaining the eukinetic that he had learnt from Laban had achieved the post-expressionist style looked for by Schlee two years before at the Munich Congress. The triumph altered Jooss's life, for he was offered a tour immediately and was soon able to form the Ballets Jooss as an independent major touring company. Naturally there was a spin-off for Laban, as Jooss's teacher and erstwhile collaborator, and, in Paris, for Bereska. Her school, 'Méthode Rudolf von Laban, Maître de Ballet de l'Opéra de Berlin,' added '(Professeur de Kurt Jooss)' after the success of the competition, and she achieved more enrolments into her professional courses.

Other significant artists were successful too. Rosalia Chladek, with dancers from the Hellerau Laxenburg school, won the second prize with a highly acclaimed work, *Contrastes*, and Dorothée Günther's group from Munich won the third prize with *Miniatures*. Oskar Schlemmer had been expected to take a prize but the performance of his *Triadic Ballet* was hampered by disasters with the music, the score parts not arriving on time, and with problems in finding a black dance carpet essential for the lighting and colour aspect of his choreography. In the event he came a disappointing sixth.

The competition attracted many overseas dancers to Paris, including Americans. Bereska had advertised a six-week international summer school to take place at Napoule commencing immediately after the competition. Kurt Graf, an Unter den Linden dancer, and Robert Robst were her experienced assistants. Laban was advertised as giving private lessons. While Mary Wigman made her second American tour, American students came to Europe to study German dance and to learn Laban's notation and choreology.

Concurrent with this successful and artistic summer school the political power struggles in Germany took a particularly sinister turn. Franz Von Papen, put in as Chancellor by President Hindenburg, and using the emergency powers voted in by Hindenburg's cabinet, set about eliminating opposition to his proposals for change. By dissolving the elected Prussian government by decree he in effect put an end to any pretence of democracy, his action precipitating the end of the Weimar Republic as it moved inexorably closer to a legally created authoritarian mode of government. Still unable to get agreement, he dissolved the Reichstag by the same means, further opening up a route towards dictatorship that Hitler was only too ready to manipulate. Such was the volatile situation in Berlin when Laban returned there in September, after a brief stay with his faithful and supportive friends, Frau Marie Luise Lieschke and her husband, in Plauen.

Routine ballet-master business kept Laban mainly in Berlin at the start of the season. The first fresh work he had to make was the incidental dances for Mozart's *Idomeneo* given on 12 November. They were hardly noticed, attracting one line, if any, in the reviews, and one adjective: 'inconsequential'. They were in any case interwoven into the production.

He was not well. Letters suggest that his recurrent depression was taking a hold. His habitual financial difficulties haunted him, as letters to Zurich show. Herr Gams was pressing him for the completion of the repayment of the loans still outstanding from their agreements dating from 1921 when all the royalties from *Die Welt des Tänzers* went to him; but he was still owed substantial sums for supporting Laban, Laban's mother and sister, Maja and the five children during 'the nightmare years' in wartime Zurich. Laban could not comply. Any money he had over and above essentials was always spent on repaying debts from previous writing and research. On a personal level he was very much alone in Berlin. That he missed Bereska's daily support and the apprentice hubbub of the Choreographisches Institut was clear to see. His choreographic duties seemed to be performed in a perfunctory mood. In contrast, Wigman danced successfully at the Bachsaal, and Palucca appeared to be on the way to becoming the darling of Berlin. Jooss toured *The Green Table* with his newly established independent company. Their independence made an unwelcome contrast in Laban's mind with his own employee state. Their undaunted pioneering spirit that seemed to be coping positively with the recession, with the unemployment, with the political militarism, put his own poorly performed duty to make incidental dances to Mozart in an unfortunate light.

A further aggravation occurred through the formation of the Deutscher Körperbildungsverband, an organisation of teachers which united dance schools with rhythmic gymnastic schools. The battle with the physical training, physical education, body culture people would not go away. Indeed under the Nazis it would intensify. The body culture people would never understand that dance was an art, an expression of the soul, the body being a means, not an end. However often, however succinctly, however well said and well demonstrated, the effort to explain was wasted. Dance had nothing significant in common with rhythmic gymnastics, though unfortunately plenty in common of little consequence. They could be watched as similar but never experienced as similar. Therein lay a problem that would haunt Laban's work till his death. Because the Körperbildungsverband had a solid power base, with both male and female membership, linked with male-dominated sport, the far less well organised female-dominated dance people were easily swept into joining with their stronger counterpart. Laban tossed these things aside, but they dug into his deepest hopes for the renewal of dance as an art for all. He taught a series of lectures in the Sport and Physical Education department at Humboldt University, just over the road from Unter den Linden, during this season. Even if movement teachers dented some of his hopes, he was able to present at university level what he really believed in. But he knew that talking about dance, and dancing, were two different kinds of knowing.

The year ended with Laban contributing to the obligatory Christmas festive production. That year it was held at the Schauspielhaus am Gendarmenmarkt, just round the corner from Unter den Linden, and was Kalisch's operetta *100,000 Thaler* (100,000 Quid). All he had to provide was a women's quintet to Strauss's *Tritsch-Tratsch*.

The infamous date of 30 January 1933, the day on which the Weimar experiment in democracy finally collapsed, the day on which, by stealth and by political bungling on the part of his opponents, Adolf Hitler became Chancellor of Germany, was celebrated on the streets of Berlin by a mammoth torchlight procession down Unter den Linden and through the Brandenburg Gate. Brownshirts and the army paraded in front of an applauding public whose arms, raised in the now familiar salute, expressed their belief in the tyrant whom their impotent government had allowed to be put in a place of extreme power.

Almost immediately Hitler's right-hand man, the scheming Hermann Göring, was made Interior Minister of Prussia, in command of the most crucial force, the police of Berlin. He set about removing from positions of power anyone thought to be leftish or liberal and replaced them by members of the Nazi party, mostly by the SA or SS officers. The installation of these people in key positions within institutions of education, culture, industry and local government paralysed any kind of opposition almost before anyone had considered it. The State Opera was not excluded. Laban found new people about the building interested in everything that went on, in everything that was said, in every decision made and endeavour undertaken. The 'Heil Hitler' greeting became obligatory, and Laban had to give it.

On 6 February the first indications of serious changes arrived in the form of an order to reduce the number of children in the State Opera Ballet School. While this was effected as a necessary economy in the dire financial stresses of the ever-increasing recession, it also hid the first round of directives towards ideological and racial discrimination. The evidence is that by July 1933 it was common knowledge that all Jewish dancers, both children and adult, had ceased to be engaged. The majority of the children were dismissed, whatever their backgrounds, forty-five out of a possible fifty-four. Parents wrote appealing for their daughters' reinstatement, some pleading that although they were not Aryan their child had been given solos and must therefore be talented. Others wrote that they were party members, that their child was a Hitler Youth member, that the child's mother was a teacher for Kraft durch Freude (the Nazi leisure organisation). None of these protestations made the slightest difference. Laban was given the authority to re-engage a small number of 'artistically talented' young dancers, both from the Unter der Linden school and from others, such as the Stadt Oper Ballett Schule, in order to have sufficient child dancers and *Eleven* for productions at the minimum cost. It goes without saying that no Jewish child was amongst this group, but there is not a shred of evidence to suggest that Laban gave preferential treatment to the children of party members. By 1934, any complaints by the parents of young people not engaged had their replies vetted by Josef Goebbels' office.

The next to go were members of the opera in general: singers and *corps de ballet*, orchestral players and administrators were not reappointed for

173

the next season, the reason given by the General Intendant quite blatantly as 'nicht arisch' (not Aryan). One letter came into Laban's department, passed on by the General Intendant's office, from an actress who wished to watch the newly introduced Laban-based movement classes. She knew that as a Jewess she could not participate, nor, she wrote, did she wish to watch with any hope of employment, but simply out of interest in the innovative approach. Several initials and remarks frame the letter. Laban's were indicative of the powerlessness of anyone in the organisation to go against the racial directives. He did not say she could not come; he said that he had no power to support her application because she was 'nicht arisch' and returned it to the General Intendant, Tietjen. The lack of trust, internally, was typical of all organisations. No one knew who was an informer.

From time to time Laban slipped away to Plauen to breathe a fresher air than that of the overwhelmingly Nazified Berlin. No doubt he also discussed with Lieschke what could be done in the extraordinary circumstances in which they all found themselves. One might ask, why did Laban not protest? Why did he not leave his job rather than participate in these outrageous purges? Why did he not leave the country, emigrate there and then? Unlike countless other artists, Schlemmer for example, he did not lose his job, his work was not hounded down as Kandinsky's was or Brecht's, he was not accused of 'Bolshevism', or communism, as Martin Gleisner was; he had no Jewish forebears himself as did the editor of *Der Tanz* Joseph Lewitan, and he was not at this point accused of any misdemeanours, either ideological or racial. For many liberals, the awfulness was seen as so irrational, so bizarre, that it could surely not last.

But remaining aloof was impossible. One week after Laban returned from a break in Plauen, on 27 February, the Reichstag was burned down, ostensibly by a communist arsonist. The Reichstag was just down the road from the Opera, and Laban and his colleagues must have been only too aware of it. William Shirer, in *The Rise and Fall of the Third Reich*, recounts the drama of it, the intrigue which caused it, the advantage reaped by Hitler because of it. The following day, apart from widespread and noisy arrests, Hitler persuaded the failing President Hindenburg to sign a decree suspending the seven sections of the constitution which guaranteed individual and civil liberties, and adding restrictions curbing the right to free expression of opinion, freedom of the press, and the right of assembly.

House arrests and confiscation of property were introduced all in the name of 'the protection of the people and the state' from 'communist acts of violence'. This decree put anyone who overtly criticised the regime in danger of arrest. One way to survive, since combining confrontation with retaining a job was now not an option, was to lie low or carry on as if nothing were amiss, cock a furtive snook at the planted infiltrators, and avoid participation in the Hitler salute if possible. This, according to Gertrud Snell, was what Laban did. She had left Bereska's Paris school immediately on hearing of Hitler's accession to power. 'It seemed the only possible thing to do in light of such a catastrophe,' she vouchsafed years later. Goebbels, through his efficient propaganda machinery, fuelled fear of communist plans to burn down every major German building, all untrue. The nation was becoming brainwashed into believing that terror was the only way to overcome 'the enemies of all true Germans'.

In this atmosphere Wagner's *Rienzi* was given a new production at the State Opera on 11 March, Laban creating the Lucretia pantomime in the third act. Included by the dramaturge Dr Julius Kapp in place of the more customary *ballett* in this new realisation of *Rienzi*, the pantomime was highly successful, albeit a small part of the production. It was mostly well received, but Alfred Einstein was grudging to Laban to the end; it was his last opportunity to review opera before his departure from the *Berliner Tageblatt*, to be replaced by a racially and ideologically correct reviewer. Two days later art and politics combined. The Opera House was taken over for the pomp of the state commemoration of war dead. Attending were Hitler, Hindenburg, von Papen and Göring, flanked by rows of SA, SS and army troopers. The chorus and orchestra of the opera company provided the music.

The season continued with the Berlin festival, for which Laban had some minor roles to play, but on 10 May a more significant action took place. A torchlight procession of thousands of students stopped opposite the University, and faced the square alongside the Opera House. A monumental pile of books had been collected there. It was transformed into a bonfire as the students threw their torches onto it. By the end of that terrible night, twenty thousand books had been consumed. Thomas Mann, Stefan Zweig, Albert Einstein, H. G. Wells, Havelock Ellis, Sigmund Freud, André Gide, Emile Zola, Marcel Proust – all went up in flames. According to a student proclamation, 'any book which acts subversively on our future or strikes at the root of German thought, the German home, and the driving forces of our people' was worthy only of destruction. This event was no spontaneous youthful demonstration: it was organised by Dr Goebbels, the new Minister for Propaganda and Enlightenment, who attended, watched the conflagration, and spoke to the students of 'the burning of an old era whose flames light up a new order'. To get to his place of work at the Opera House, Laban walked through this square daily. He must have seen its sordid aftermath. The sheer terror that the burning spectacle must have aroused can hardly be imagined. Simultaneously, the sense of militant exultation in the perpetrators gave them encouragement for further deeds of vandalism.

Beside this, Laban's current internal fight to have the rank and pay of soloist excluded from the ballet company seems puny. It was, in any case, disallowed. The democratic ensemble that he had achieved the year before was overthrown. Elitism returned. By June the dismissals of children and non-Aryan performers was complete for that year. He left for Warsaw, to be jury member of the International Dance Competition there. By July, Conrad Nebe had replaced Lewitan in *Der Tanz*. This kind of authoritarianism was getting closer and closer to Laban, for *Der Tanz* was the official mouthpiece for the German Association for Schrifttanz. Would his notation books be on the list of forbidden reading? Ill, Laban returned from Warsaw as soon as he could, to Lieschke and Bereska in Plauen. August was spent in Bavaria, at Tegernsee, at a spa. He wrote, in another letter to Gams on financial matters, that he was under Dr Geiss there. His incipient physical and mental ill-health, especially troublesome in difficult times, had surfaced yet again.

Still not recovered, Laban returned for the new season, the last with his present contract, which would expire on 31 August 1934. He must have had mixed feelings. Part of him would have been ready to fight for dance, as he had always done. He had, after all, been through many political traumas in Zurich and Stuttgart; he had fought opera house opera-ballet battles once before, in Mannheim; he had survived hardships, disappointments, penury, and risen again to fight on. This present trauma, although worse than most, although as yet not on the scale of the 1914–18 war, could yet, he may have thought, be survived, even be turned into a support for dance. Part of him would have presented the proud face of the ballet-master of the most prestigious house in Germany while privately loathing the whole set-up. The fact that he had 'made it' must have boosted his morale more than anything else; the gibes of his youth by his family that 'Rudi' was going to be an artist and then, horror of horrors, a dancer, were vindicated. Their attitude had long since changed to one of admiration. Laban must have wished that his father could have lived to see where he was, at the top of his artistic tree, just as his father had been at the top of his military tree. Another part of him must have been deeply concerned with what his options might be at the end of the year when his contract expired. Would he be offered a further three years at the Opera? If not, would he be able to pick up where he had left off in the freelance entrepreneurial world that had always been his way of life until his present post?

Which of these would best serve the dance? Who would decide, himself or his Nazi employers?

What cannot have failed to confuse his thinking was the apparent pro-Nazi stance of the Lieschkes. It seems a mystery that Marie Luise Lieschke could be a Party member and yet at the same time support Laban's work wholeheartedly. It was she who kept his notation association going while he was at Unter den Linden, she who housed his archives, she who promoted his movement choir ideas and his fight for literate dance. Gertrud Snell's view was that Lieschke's attitude was nothing but a front. It was her way of helping Laban to keep his outside work going. But a crucial letter of 1937 between Laban and Lieschke shows her unshakeable belief in the Party and its ability to save German culture. They must have discussed this, but no document vouchsafes what passed between them except her visitors' book which records his sojourns at Plauen, with and without Bereska. One other name occurs here more than once, although not simultaneously with Laban's visits: Winifred Wagner, the overt Nazi.

Laban returned in September 1933 to Berlin for a new production of Bizet's *Carmen* for which he created ensemble dances. They were much admired by the new reviewer of the *Berlin Tageblatt*, Karl Westermeyer, and appreciated also, he wrote, by the audience. The production was apparently lavish, with two dozen horses on stage in the procession that followed the *ballett*. No signs here of financial stringency. At almost the same time, Kurt Jooss and his company secretly fled the country, tipped off that his arrest was imminent for retaining Jewish company members. His anti-war ballet *The Green Table*, as well as *Big City*, his comment on urban life, were in any case irritants in the face of the regime's re-armament programmes. The Central Laban School in Essen, at which the Laban Diploma examinations for all the Laban schools were organised, found itself without its day-to-day leadership, for Jooss was its director. Just what would happen and what action should be taken was unclear. It seems that Laban and the teachers decided to await events.

By the end of September the media world knew what Dr Goebbels had in mind for them as the Reichskulturkammer (RKK) was by then fully working. William Shirer describes the work of the RKK as 'the regimentation of culture on a scale which no modern Western nation had ever experienced'. He goes on: 'No one who lived in Germany in the thirties, and who cared about such matters, can ever forget the sickening decline of the cultural standards of a people who had had such high hopes for so long a time.' Membership of one of the seven Chambers – for the Press, Radio, Theatre, Fine Arts, Music, Literature and Film – was obligatory in order to work within any of these fields. Goebbels had the power to withhold membership for 'political unreliability' and through this means to deprive a person of the means of earning a living. Anyone overtly lukewarm to National Socialist concepts and practices would qualify for his attention. The purpose of the RKK was to 'guide and organise', a euphemism for highjacking the arts and the professions to give voice to Nazi propaganda.

Laban was silent on his response to 'Dr G's' plans. It has to be remembered that he had been fighting for years for the government, whether at local or national level, to support dance institutions, especially a High School. While music and art schools had long been political pawns, they had nevertheless had the recognition that government patronage can provide. One can surmise that Laban could see a chance for a supported High School for Dance. He had been given no indication that his work was seen as degenerate; indeed he saw it as humanist and apolitical. He also admired much of German philosophical and literary culture. It would seem, by staying, that he thought that he could make something of the RKK's interferences.

At the Opera everyone was subject to the Reichsmusikkammer. Choice of repertoire was subject to Goebbels' scrutiny, performances of works by Jewish composers being forbidden. Mendelssohn and Mahler were out, so too were Schoenberg and Hindemith threatened. Naturally all performers and opera employees were vetted. Laban was in a far easier position than the conductors, the programme planners, the opera employee selectors, all led by Tietjen. These people had to confront the straitjacket being applied by Goebbels. Laban had only to go along with it; and he did.

Still unwell during October and November, Laban undertook a small lecture tour from Plauen in early December speaking on 'The Spirit of the New Dance', one state opera dancer demonstrating for him. What he said is not recorded, but he must have taken into account the dictum of the Reichsfachschaft Deutscher Tanzlehrer, the Nazi organisation for dance teachers, working under the title Neue Deutsche Tanz. Over the summer of 1933 all local newspapers had carried details of the social dances that were considered degenerate and therefore disallowed, like the Foxtrot, the Tango and the Charleston, and those that were considered good German dances, Waltzes, the Rheinlander, Bechfelsschrittler, Marches, the Gallop and the new Friedrichshainer – in other words, only dances such as people's grandmothers had performed, plus those community dances that were newly created and directed to be danced. *Der Schwung von Gestern und der Schritte von Heute* was the call: yesterday's swinging energy and today's steps. The New Dance that Laban lectured on would not have been the

Neue Tanz of 1921, but surely must have been that of the RKK. The only other topical discussion he could have used was that raised on German theatre dance by Fritz Böhme who, as an acknowledged supporter of the regime, was in a dilemma as to whether it was ideologically correct to regard ballet as German, with its foreign associations and origins. The German dance of Laban and Wigman was agreed on as German and therefore without doubt ideologically clean (although one wonders that no one worried about its founder being Hungarian). Of what was Nazi theatre dance to consist? Böhme was treading carefully. To lecture on the New Dance as Laban did in Plauen and Chemnitz, and remain employed, he must have discussed the party line on dance.

Would he have objected to the promotion of old-fashioned community dances? Remembering his eclecticism, it seems likely that he would not. He loved the tango. Composer Adda Heynssen had written several for him, and he would certainly have deplored its dismissal; but he was not a pure modernist. He valued folk traditions, along with satire, the grotesque, the comic, the new, the creative . . . all of them.

The man behind this new state-organised folk dance-based curriculum for dance teachers was one of Laban's age-old rivals, Dr Rudolf Bode, a keen physical culture and sport enthusiast with an influential school in Munich and a strong following throughout the Weimar years. Conservative to the hilt, a Party member since the early twenties, he had been appointed by the RKK to oversee physical training and had highjacked amateur dance as part of his brief. At this point, while his job was in the Opera, Laban could do nothing about it, but in the next few years the two men would lock horns as Laban attempted a rescue operation. No wonder Laban felt ill, for he could see his years of persistent effort to promote creative dance for all in danger of being undermined by his arch-rivals, the physical training fraternity.

For the time being, Laban-based amateur dance was flourishing un-scathed. It was regarded as German, and its curriculum was not molested. Knust and the Hamburg choirs continued their creation of new choric works and performed at regional festivals, as did groups in Lubeck and Nuremberg, and a few young groups surfaced as freshly successful. One such was the group run by two staunch Labanites, Jenny Gertz and Ilse Loesch, who offered 'choric work' in Halle, where they had set up a Haus der Tänzer (Dancers' House). Knust also continued to get published articles on dance literacy, discussing topical worries about whether notation killed the flow of movement or not, and on how dances could be circulated and made known to a wider public through the written score.

1933 ended with the traditional Silvester (New Year's Eve) festive performances, for which the Opera put on *Donna Diana*. The new Nazi newspaper, the *Völkische Beobachter*, strongly approved of the ballet as eye-
catching and as putting the production into the first rank. Laban went on to
remount the 'Walpurgisnacht Bacchanale' in Gounod's *Margarete* for early
February and created the fairy dances for Weber's *Oberon* for early April.
These bread-and-butter choreographic jobs gave him little scope and
offered little challenge.

His major problem arose from another quarter, created by the invitation
from Mr and Mrs Elmhirst, of Dartington Hall, England, to provide a refuge
for the Ballets Jooss and for the performer department of the Essen Laban
School. However much Laban must have been relieved that Jooss and his
company were safe and able to continue working, his own school was
decimated. Twenty-three of the performer students and several faculty
members left for Dartington, including Sigurd Leeder and Lisa Ullmann,
setting up the Jooss/Leeder School by the beginning of April 1934 in
premises built for them by the Elmhirsts. The questions to be tackled by
Laban were who could lead the Central School, and would the City of
Essen continue to support it with half its faculty and students gone? In the
event, Knust was persuaded to fill the gap, taking up the post on 1 April,
the young Lola Rogge taking over his leadership of the Hamburg Movement Choirs. To bolster Knust, who was known only as a notator and
teacher/choreographer for amateurs, Laban signed a contract with Essen
stating that he would give so much time regularly to the school, in person.
He immediately set about forestalling concerns about standards by preparing a 'Lecture and Dance Evening' to be given in the Folkwang Museum on
28 March with soloists and students, entitling it 'New Dance in a New Era'.
He prepared his speech while commuting to and fro to Berlin, there rehearsing the 'Bacchanale' from *Tannhäuser* with a fresh cast for a 2 May
performance.

Two weeks later Goebbels announced the establishment, by the Theatre
Law, of the Reichstheaterkammer, to which dance and dancers became
subject. He did this during the Berlin Festival Week, also outlining National
Socialist policy for the arts in a speech at the Volksbühne. The Festival
performance at the State Opera was Wagner's *Meistersinger*, Wagner becoming daily a symbol of Nazi art. Laban arranged the movement.

While keeping a personal hand on the Essen school, he had somehow to
fit in serving as a jury member for the Vienna International Dance Competition, organised by Rolf de Maré, which culminated in its final round on 5
June. He was certainly rushed, but he could not have missed the plethora

of blackshirts on every corner in Vienna. He then had to come back to Berlin to complete rehearsals for his last production of the season at Unter den Linden, Bizet's *Die Perlenfischer*. The dances for the fisherwomen and the dancing girls were a 'decisive high moment', judging by the audience applause. He had managed to complete his commitments at the Opera with a well-received production.

The end of his contract as choreographer was celebrated by a matinée on 1 July. It was a grand affair attended by Goebbels, Göring and Hitler himself. The international standing in which Laban was held was reflected in this line-up of top political/artistic dignitaries. According to an anecdote years later, reported in the Magazine of the Laban Guild: 'He sat at the right side of the head of state. After a lively conversation His Highness said to Laban: "I never thought that dancers were such intelligent people."

"Isn't it astonishing how prejudiced people are," replied Laban. "I had the same misconception concerning heads of nations."'

At the time of the anecdote no reader realised that this was a description of 1 July 1934, 'His Highness' being in fact the Führer. How true the details are is hard to guess, but in essence it sums up the situation: that Laban was regarded as a valuable, international figure to be used rather than abused by the regime and that Laban was prepared to live on the edge of his luck, audacity being his line of defence.

What cannot be ignored are the activities of Hitler the day before, for 30 June 1934 went down in Nazi history as the purge of the SA, the brownshirt storm troopers, and the murder of their leader, Röhm, Hitler's ally of some fourteen years and, as Shirer describes him, co-designer of the Nazi terror and degradation. He was shot point blank for treason, at Hitler's personal instigation, in a hotel on the shores of the Tegernsee near Munich (where Laban had taken his summer spa cure), together with countless officers and men of the SA, along with other political figures whom Hitler wished out of the way. Göring and Goebbels participated in other parts of Germany on the same quest, on the same night. There is no suggestion that Laban knew what had gone on, for it was not announced until two weeks later. What the reader needs to grasp is Laban's closeness to the villainy, the danger that lurked for him and anyone else regarded by the regime as disposable, and the rapidity of the change of face that the Nazi leaders were able to assume within one twenty-four-hour span. Laban slipped into a morass of false and unrealistic hopes, retaining a futile misconception that he could win these people over to his ideas for dance art. How could liberty of the individual's bodily expression be swallowed by such monsters? By 1 July 1934 he had not grasped the situation, or would not face it.

Laban's own comment on the cessation of his employment at the Opera, made years later when he was established in England, was that he was dismissed by Göring; but this remark is not quite accurate. It is more likely – for Laban's contract ran its course – that no new three-year contract for him was proposed, but that Lizzie Maudrik, the ballet choreographer of the Berlin City Opera, was preferred by the RKK, reflecting a taste for ballet's star system over Laban's ensemble German dance style. Göring could have been party to it, for he was influential. Maudrik was installed on 1 August, bringing with her two soloists as the core of the reintroduction of a star system. What became immediately apparent was that 'Dr G' and his Propaganda Ministry had other proposals to put to Laban.

10

Survival

Berlin, 1934–1937

That Laban always regarded the promotion of dance as a battle against a varying array of antagonists is evident throughout his career. He had fought personal battles against penury, against ill health, against ridicule from the establishment, including his own family, against stereotypical ideologies on sexual freedom, over the nature of success, and over the ever-present fashion to reject nonconformist ideas and practices. He had fought professional battles over the acceptance of a notation system for dance and the whole concept of dance as a literate art, over the value of individual movement vocabularies as well as received movement vocabularies, over the place of men in dance, over the renewal of the role of theatre in a modern society, over the unsuitability of mainstream theatre buildings for dance audiences and performers, over sponsorship for a High School for dance, over the essential role of movement expression and the arts of movement, for the well-being of human culture, and more. That September 1934 offered another battle was par for the course, as far as he saw it. It was one that he could not possibly win, but that prospect may never have crossed his mind, for the man was an optimist with a belief in his own mission.

It could be argued, and surely has been, that Laban knew well enough what sort of people his employers were, how his international reputation would be used to promote not dance but Nazi dogma, and that he should have emigrated like the majority of modern artists, including many of his acquaintances. Where he might have gone is pure speculation. To his sister Renée in Geneva? To his sister Melanie in Budapest? To Bereska in Paris? Suggestions have been made that he should have declined to work as a government employee; but this is a non-argument, for to work as a dance person at all, whether as a teacher or choreographer or performer, everyone was subject to the RKK. Unsupervised and unprescribed work was no longer a possibility. Oskar Schlemmer tried to stay and keep a low profile rather than emigrate. He survived wretchedly until 1943, with his creativity atrophied, but already in 1939 he wrote, 'I cannot overcome my doubts and worries . . . compromising daily voluntarily and involuntarily with the state of affairs . . . I am concerned about the long range psychic effects of such anguish.' Laban was to experience the same anguish but not until the inevitable psychological and physical effects of a fall from Nazi favour caught up with him in 1937. He could have decided to collaborate fully. To do so he would have joined the Nazi Party, which he never did. He would have had to renege on all his principles of individual freedom of expression, which he never did. Instead, he compromised.

One aspect of the regime's dictates for dance that coincided with Laban's own was the emphasis on community and the central place of movement activity in the life of the common man and woman. The arch conservative Rudolf Bode had charge of what kind of movement that might be, and Laban relished the idea of finding an opportunity to challenge him and secure the art of movement and expression through movement, instead of Bode's choice of massed physical training. Kraft durch Freude (Strength through Joy) was the imposed organisation for amateur recreation for which all dance teachers were agents. So too were all leaders of physical culture, outdoor recreation, sport, camping and so on. Not to join the organisation resulted in loss of the permit to teach. Laban schools automatically became subject to Kraft durch Freude curricula and dictates. Laban movement choirs continued to function under the same umbrella but the equal position of men and woman within them changed. Nazi ideology saw male dancers as folk dancers, so that the position of male choir members became difficult. They began to withdraw, pushing the function of Laban-based movement choirs awry, for the role of movement choirs was always intended as the spiritual aspect of the dance of modern urban 'folk', essentially for both sexes. With the men taken away, the choirs were not only emasculated in artistic form but also in function. They took on the look of healthy activity for young women. What Laban had to do was to ensure that their leaders retained their ethos as groups of radical performers fighting for freedom of corporate and corporeal expression.

The day after Laban's farewell matinée at the Opera House, *Eine Nacht in Venedig* was performed again as part of a Kraft durch Freude mission, responsibility for the dances being Laban's. That performance completed his contract there, and he left for Essen to run the summer school, presiding over the examinations for the students, especially those gaining the sought-after, and difficult to gain, Laban Diploma. He taught the four-week course personally, with Knust as his right-hand man. Embedded in it was a

Chorische Tagung (Choric Meeting) run by Marie Luise Lieschke. While the school, which was professional, could run its own curriculum almost unaltered, provided no student was Jewish and that no teacher was communist or offered 'degenerate' art, the community dance meeting was vulnerable to Kraft durch Freude dogma. Everyone was expected on all occasions to give the Nazi salute and greet each other with 'Heil Hitler', but community dancers were also expected to give some reverence to the Nazi flag, the swastika, just as did the Boy Scouts, Girl Guides and Hitler Youth. Laban created a choric work on the A-Scale, with swing and eukinetic content, and he taught a course on choric dance and music plus one on choric dance and words for which it would have been easy to use his standard well-tried content. He also taught one on what the content of a choric work might be. There he would have touched on difficulties, for content is essentially political. Spiritual content was what he had to cover and the question would be: what kind of spirit? The Nazi spirit? Or the Rosicrucian-inspired spirit of tolerance, communion and collaboration that he had always evoked in his choirs? *Fight and Liberation*, a choric dance title that he used in his Zurich school and for his Hamburg choir, and later at the Art of Movement Studio in Manchester, was a favoured topic. Did he use it in Essen in 1934? He would have been on safer ground to stick to formal content, to encircling, to pathways, to leading and following, to linear and clump-like group forms, and the like. And yet formal content is political too. His choirs did not have rows of unison movers or regimented formations, but loose groups of mutually responsible individuals.

It was Knust who had the overtly problematic task of creating a piece entitled *Consecration of the Flag*. He used his knowledge and skill with group forms to create a 'rhythmic dynamic heroic' dance, according to the report written by Lieschke. Everyone joined in the other Knust works, the unproblematic and often danced *Feierliche Kanon und Spiel* (Celebratory Canon and Play) and *Festlicher Marsch* (Festive March). Fritz Böhme, the academic member of the course faculty, also played safe while speaking on the choric dance. He kept to history and concentrated on the dance of Old China and Ancient Greece.

Laban cannot have missed the news from Vienna of the assassination by Hitler's men of the Austrian Chancellor Dollfuss on 24 July. Described euphemistically as a resignation, the truth was apparent to all after a reign of terror for several months by the Austrian Nazi supporters. Even while Laban had sat on the jury of the Viennese Dance Competition in June the riots and murders were taking place around them. As the dancers danced, so the dictator murdered. But Vienna was the city of Laban's erstwhile family home. It was here that he had learnt his first lessons in art and theatre craft. The regime's tyrannical methods were infiltrating the very domain of his childhood roots.

Just when Laban was offered the directorship of the Deutsche Tanzbühne by Goebbels is not known. How long he had to think about it, and what alternatives were on offer, if any, are not documented. To commence on 1 September, directly after the completion of his contract with the State Opera, he was given a six-month provisional contract, with the legal status of his employment left vague, to lead what had been a professional dance association recently taken over by the Propaganda Ministry. Laban's brief was to organise performances of artistic dance works, choreographing them where necessary, and to promote young German dancers, especially those who were out of work because of the recession. Such a strategy stood in line with other government department methods for overcoming high unemployment. How Laban was to accomplish this remained unstated. It was up to him to find a way. He was given an office in Potsdamerstrasse and immediately he offered jobs to two faithful former assistants, Susanne Ivers and Gertrud Snell.

The appointment offered him the opportunity he needed to pursue his mission for dance from a sponsored position. It also offered the RKK the opportunity to use his name and skills for their own ploys, especially to give the international theatre world the impression of support for modern dance and thereby attract foreign companies to Germany. The next three years saw a battle of wills between men promoting two disparate ideologies, conducted with guile by both Laban and the Ministry officials.

In the world of Berlin music, Wilhelm Furtwängler was engaged in a similar duel. The renowned conductor Carl Ebert had resigned from the State Opera, Bruno Walter had left, Kurt Weill's music had been dubbed degenerate, Schoenberg and Franz Schreker were dismissed, Arturo Toscanini refused to conduct at Bayreuth. Hindemith was the composer defended by Furtwängler but Furtwängler did not keep up his stance for long. Richard Strauss, Rudolf Wagner-Regeny, Carl Orff, and lesser-known composers Werner Egk and Paul Hoeffer sought favour. Laban must have considered his own position in relation to the attitudes and strategies of these people, all known to him, some as close colleagues, especially as Ebert and Wagner-Regeny.

The first major event Laban organised, acting under the dictates of the RKK, was the Dance Festival held in December 1934 at the Volksbühne in Berlin. It reflected an eclectic choice of style, and was performed by leading soloists and groups, predominantly from the Wigman studio. There were appearances by the internationally well-known Harald Kreutzberg, Yvonne Georgi with a small company, and a group under Mary Wigman. Also performing were groups led by Dorothée Günther, well known after her success in the Paris competition of 1932, and by Valerie Kratina, the group of Jutta Klamt, and the ballet pair from the State Opera, Alexander von Swaine and Alice Uhlen. Gret Palucca was the popular solo dancer well known to Berlin audiences. Laban presented *Dornröschen* (The Sleeping Beauty) with the State Opera ballet, creating the costumes and set also, a remounting of the production he had done two years previously, in co-operation with the present opera choreographer Lizzie Maudrik. Maudrik also produced a traditional ballet, *Puppenfee* (The Fairy Doll). The Festival had the usual mixed press. While Fritz Zielisch was ecstatic in the national-istic press, reporting tumultuous applause, Joseph Lewitan, now writing for the *Dancing Times* of London, was as usual uncomplimentary to the Ger-man dance. He found Palucca lacking in spark, thought Georgi's work was provincial, while Wigman's was hurriedly thrown together. Neither Kreutz-berg nor the Klamt group could he deride, although they were dancing in a style he disliked. Günther's work he admired, especially the young dancer Maja Lex. Best of all for him, expectedly, were the ballet pair. A handsome book compiled by Laban was published to accompany the Festival in which he gave a historical overview of German dance, Palucca, Wigman and Günther also contributing articles. An exhibition of 'Dance in Art' held concurrently at the Prinzessinnenpalais depicted what could be seen as ideologically correct images of dancers in painting, drawings and sculpture. There would have been no Wigman *Hexentanz* photographs nor Laban *Der Grünen Clowns* figures here. The gala on 13 December was attended by Goebbels, whose office kept a close eye on every detail of 'their' festival. Apparently it passed muster: no one lost his job because of it.

By now it was clear that unlike most visual artists, musicians and writers, the dance world had decided not to emigrate but to stay in Ger-many. Two different groups were apparent: those who embraced the politi-cal regime and those who simply wanted to survive. The former were mostly administrators, Burger, Cunz, Ebrecht, Niedecken-Gebhardt and, one must add, Lieschke. The latter were mostly dance artists, though not entirely. Dorothée Günther used the Hitler Youth from this time as percus-sion players for the music of her partner, Carl Orff. Klamt was Party ori-ented, working with her chosen unhappy mix of gymnastics and dance, a Bode/Laban mish-mash. Wigman was a survivor, but there is no doubt that her bitterness towards and jealousy of Laban had increased with his accept-ance of the Deutsche Tanzbühne job. That, on top of his gaining the Unter den Linden post when she was tipped for it, was indeed hard for her to stomach. Studying her work at that time was Yat Malmgren, a young Swedish actor/dancer. He picked up the sour partisanship of the Wigmanites. Laban's work was simply dismissed by them on principle. The problem for Wigman was that in those troubled times she needed Laban's support but resented her dependence.

After the efforts of the Dance Festival, the Tanzbühne team turned to the next assignment. In January 1935 their office moved to better accommodation in Konstanzstrasse and the teaching staff expanded, Marianne Vogelsang being taken on as a teacher. She could be seen as an audacious choice by Laban for, although young and not yet well known, she was a committed socialist, a fact known to Laban but not to the authorities, according to Gertrud Snell. The building was described enthusiastically by a visiting academic, Dr Johannes Günther, and reported in the official press, as 'A House for Dance', with classes, rehearsals, administrative activities, notating, costume-making all going on. It seemed much as it had been in the Choreographisches Institut. The difference was that Laban was no longer experimenting with provocative artistic ideas regardless of personal expense, effort and audience fury, but rather following an extremely vague outline from the Ministry, to unstated rules, with some anxiety over the RKK's views. That is how he described his uncertain situation to Lieschke in a letter in April.

He kept his hand on the Central School in Essen, run for day-to-day purposes by Knust, and for publicity's sake gave a student *cum* teacher performance at the Volksbühne in February. He needed to attract students of high calibre to take the place of those who had gone with Jooss and Leeder to Dartington Hall. The programme reads as thoroughly conventional. Quite how the RKK saw the continuation of these out-of-hours activities is not known. What is sure is that they were noted, monitored and stored to be used against the man if the need arose. In March he spent some time in Essen on the examinations for the Laban Diploma. These were always undertaken by Laban personally, and anyone who gained the Diploma, including several people who were later crucial pioneers in the USA and in Britain, vouchsafed that it was a gruelling and learning experience involving skills, knowledge and creativity.

In Paris, Bereska promoted Laban's work through lecture-demonstrations at the premises of Archives Internationales de la Danse under the patronage of Rolf de Maré. Laban's curriculum vitae of this period, written several years later, records that he lectured in Paris, too, at this time. Bereska was as successful as any of the modern dance people in France, but the French never had an alternative dance scene of any dimension. There was ballet, there had been Diaghilev, and that was that. Whatever Laban did, it was on a small scale, and the French did not take to his notation nor to anything German.

At the Deutsche Tanzbühne all eyes were set on preparations for 1936, centred on Berlin, the host city of the next Olympic Games. Hitler, having refused to contemplate such an event in his Reich in 1933, calling them 'an invention of Jews and freemasons', eventually saw the Olympics as a golden opportunity to promote his ideals and himself as Führer to an international audience. Once he had changed heart he took the organisation and finances out of the hands of sportsmen, making it an immense project of the Reich itself on a grandiose scale. He personally intervened in the plans for the new stadium, ensuring that it would be the most magnificent stadium ever built. What greater opportunity would there be to hoodwink the world into believing that Germany was a wonderful place under National Socialism? It was he who wanted an open-air theatre on the site, for had not the original Olympians (whom he declared to have been Aryans) been both outstanding athletes and outstanding artists? Germany must have the opportunity to show evidence of her cultural achievements and abilities. An ideal bowl-shaped site in the adjacent Murellen Valley was shown to him. A Greek theatre must be built, dedicated to one of the great National Socialist poets, Dietrich Eckart. As the building programme of the Olympic complex began the heroic scale of the site caused great excitement, with its mammoth arena, Olympic bell tower, and parade ground for 250,000 people. The theatre was described as the jewel of the project, with a pine-covered hillside acting as a backdrop to the stage.

While sport was the excuse, the arts were to play their part in international relations. An elaborate programme of theatre performances, art exhibitions, concerts, plays, operas and dance events was planned by the RKK, together with filming the whole Games and their preparation, plus media coverage of all events. Laban and his team attended a meeting on 27 March 1935 at which the three large projects envisaged by the RKK were discussed. An international dance competition was to be hosted and Laban was to invite all the best known choreographers to enter. A dance festival was to be held for folk dancers from all over the world; Laban was to organise it. The new open air theatre would be opened by a performance of German dance, masterminded by Laban under Goebbels' guidance.

These events formed the main occupation for Laban for the next year. He was artistic director of each event, Snell acting as secretary and executive, with Ivers as her assistant. Extra staff were taken on. Richard Thum, who had been a dancer in Laban's *Titan* in 1927, joined the team. Some time during the spring of 1935 Knust left Essen to open the Berlin Schriftstelle in the Deutsche Tanzbühne building. It was decided that he should notate the dances for the opening of the Dietrich Eckart Theatre along with other day-to-day notating briefs. Adolf Ebrecht was the Party member allotted to the team. There was nothing for him to do, according to Snell, except to ensure that the Nazi salute was given at all occasions and that nothing subversive was uttered in the office.

The question of the opening ceremony of the Olympic Games themselves in the stadium was also discussed by the RKK. That a dance element was wanted seemed likely, and that Laban should undertake it seemed appropriate. But the Games themselves were a sporting event, and two other men were prominent in the planning: Carl Diem, who masterminded the entire Games, and Rudolf Bode, both strong supporters of the regime. Concurrent with these deliberations, Laban and Bode engaged in the anticipated power battle over who should direct dance strategy under the RKK. The Kampfbund für Deutsche Kultur (League for the Struggle of German Culture), an established organisation with a division for movement and dance, was headed by Bode. He also headed the official teachers' association and, as has been said, had been instrumental in laying down the curriculum for both gymnastic and dance teachers. He was no dancer. His gymnastic system, popular and successful in the 1920s, focused on the body. He had no interest in a body–mind concept, let alone a spiritual dimension to corporeality. Correspondence between his organisation and Laban's reveals his attempt to get Goebbels to back his domination of dance by subsuming it officially into his movement domain. But Goebbels did not concur. Eventually Laban managed to extricate amateur dance out of body education and into theatre, taking it into the Reichstheaterkammer (RTK) where Bode had no foothold. Laban argued his case succinctly. Amateur movement choirs performed art works. Their dances were about feeling and had deeply spiritual themes, he wrote. The letters give some insight into the jockeying by the lower ranks of the Party members, such as Bode, for recognition by the authorities, as well as security of employment. No doubt 'Dr G' noted the struggle.

This battle did nothing for Laban's position *vis-à-vis* the opening of the Olympic Games. Was he ever actually asked to do it? No correspondence has been found to confirm this one way or another. If he had been asked, would he have undertaken it? His distancing of himself from all things sportive suggests that he would not. In any case, he had plenty to do to fulfil the three assignments allotted to him as well as continuing the day-today full-time running of the classes at Konstanzstrasse. Snell was in charge of the teaching and of organising the rehearsals for the unemployed dancers who formed the main bulk of participants. Ivers administered short tours for dancers to show their work. It was a rewarding procedure giving hope and experience to young talented people.

Martha Graham's rebuff of the Tanzbühne's invitation to participate in the choreographic competition is well documented in the *Dance Observer*. She was not alone. Laban had some difficulty in getting acceptances, for the vast number of emigrés had taken with them their stories of the Nazi use of the arts for propaganda purposes. Many overseas dance people would have none of it. Equally, the sporting community had scruples about attending Games hosted by a country which overtly did not offer equal opportunity to all athletes. By 1935 Jewish athletes were not welcome in sports facilities, and had no chance to prepare for selection for the German teams. But despite these obvious violations, visiting Olympic officials returned home sufficiently satisfied to advise their countrymen to participate.

While the preparations for 1936 occupied much of Laban's own time, his erstwhile students continued to promote his ideas in their own way. Knust pioneered the choreographing of a dance work on paper as a notated score, completing the work before meeting the performers. The incidental dances for the summer performances of Wagner's opera *Rienzi* at the open-air theatre in Zoppot were created by Knust in this spirit. How successful they were is not known, but the experiment was undertaken partially as a test of viability for the method of creating the piece for movement choir that Laban was making and Knust was writing for the Dietrich Eckart Theatre opening. No doubt Laban saw this opening as a very public demonstration not only of his belief in choric dance but also of the efficacy of his concept of literate dance. It could have appeared to him as a magnificent opportunity, and he certainly attacked the preparations in this spirit.

Knust's former student and talented choir leader Lola Rogge presented a choric work in Hamburg in June. She created *Die Amazonen* for women, the male members of the choir having left. Whether it was already decided that she would contribute to the Dietrich Eckart Theatre opening before creating this work, or after, it is hard to tell. The title alone demonstrates its content. It was of the ilk called for by the RKK, the glorification of healthy womanhood. Unwittingly the young woman had shifted the position of the Hamburg Choir towards the aesthetic of the regime. Most probably none of the participants was aware of the dangerous road on which this work embarked. After all, why not celebrate your own womanhood through dance?

191

The Jooss/Leeder School at Dartington held an August summer school, the equivalent to the four-week course that had always been run in Germany. The curriculum included Laban's choreutics and eukinetics as well as notation, along with Jooss and Leeder's development of a modern dance technique. The teachers were Jooss and Leeder, Lisa Ullmann, and for music, Fritz Cohen, the company's musical director.

The summer school of the Deutsche Tanzbühne, taking place after the Dartington one, took quite another form, a summer camp. It was held at Rangsdorf, some fifteen miles south of Berlin, with good transport from the city to enable working dancers to commute. With cheap holiday accommodation and a lake, it offered attractive places outside and in to work. About a hundred dancers attended, some Labanites, some new. Classes were held, choric dances were made, folk dances were taught. Concurrent with it Laban's autobiographical book *Ein Leben für den Tanz* (A Life for Dance) was published. No references at all were made in it to political issues, and no 'Heil Hitler' was written in the preface.

During the camp a new organisation was launched – the Reichsbund für Gemeinschaftstanz (State League for Community Dance). No doubt this was Laban's answer to Bode. Here he set up an artistically centred organisation for amateur dance in association with the RTK out of Bode's reach. Heading it was Marie Luise Lieschke who documented its aims and creation, following the RKK dictates to the word. Laban was prepared to go along with all that, provided dance for amateurs retained its artistic soul. He had won the Bode battle and that was sufficient for the time being. But it was too much for one of his staunch helpers, Fritz Klingenbeck. Believing that Laban had given up opposition to the regime, he left, distressed, to continue his own quiet opposition from Vienna.

Dr G, ever thorough, visited Rangsdorf. On his return to Berlin he wrote in his diary: 'Laban does his job well.'

Laban's presentation at the Dietrich Eckart Theatre would be the next test. Would he be able to present individual freedom through corporate corporeal expression? Lieschke herself is an enigma. Devoted to Laban's work, in no way amorously connected to him but a staunch personal friend, she was absolutely firm in her support of the Party. She believed that the Party and Laban could co-exist, even collaborate. She was proved wrong.

September and October 1935 saw more dictates from the RKK. The Fachschaft Bühne was set up, to oversee all matters of performance as the division of the RTK for the stage. Licences for all teachers of theatre skills and acting and some dancing were introduced through the RKK's Order No. 47, preceded by the inevitable examinations, appropriate curriculum and appropriate race being their content. Laban teachers such as Sylvia Bodmer would have been caught by this order, for, married to a Jewish doctor, her choices would have been to divorce him, to stop teaching, or to leave. They did indeed emigrate, to Britain.

The autumn task was to mount again a dance festival at the Volksbühne for November. It followed the format of the previous year with almost the same artists appearing, nine performances in all. The additions were theatre ballets from Cologne and Hamburg and movement choir performances from Hamburg (under Rogge) and Berlin (under Feist). The first half of each programme was given to young unknown dancers, in line with the brief dictated by the RKK to promote the talented unemployed. Whether the whole *pot pourri* made good theatre is unlikely, but it certainly reflected the dance culture of the moment. Also that autumn Aurel Milloss, choreographer at the Dusseldorf Opera, who had been a Choreographisches Institut student and was to go on to a distinguished career in the major European opera houses, produced an original version of Laban's *Gaukelei*, just as Jooss had done in Essen in 1930. It had an extremely topical scenario: the downfall of a tyrant. Milloss, a fellow Hungarian, would have enjoyed the dig at the authorities, but it was a risky form of play.

On 5 November 1935 Laban obtained German nationality, having put the whole process into action four years previously. His motivation for doing so remains a subject for speculation. To work in Germany as a foreigner was almost impossible, so he could have done it for safety reasons, but that would have been out of character. A letter to Lieschke from 1937 suggests that he was genuinely fond of German culture and had been content to associate himself with Germanness in 1931. As soon as he could, once in England, he tried to revert to Hungarian citizenship. But by that time he was 'ashamed to be German'.

The preparations for the August Olympics dominated the Tanzbühne from January 1936 onwards. The opening ceremony of the Games themselves was not Laban's responsibility. Dorothée Günther and Mary Wigman shared the honours with Gret Palucca, who would dance a solo. Laban's work for the opening of the Dietrich Eckart Theatre was ready for rehearsals. *Vom Tauwind und der Neuen Freude* (The Spring Wind and the New Joy) was its title. It was rehearsed by twenty-two movement choirs in separate cities all over Germany, each one a Laban movement choir trained in his method, all devoted to him and his ideals. He had assistants with whom he planned the mammoth task of getting over a thousand dancers ready and co-ordinated. Knust, who had written the score, was a key player. Lotte Müller, an ex-Tanzbühne Laban dancer, Grete and Harry

193

Pierenkämper from Mannheim, Lotte Wernicke, who also created her own work for the opening, and Heidi Woog, a long-time associate, were his helpers. They learnt the work through the score, deciding how to divide the parts between the twenty-two groups, and dispersed to teach the choirs their individual roles. Participants remember the process as inspiring, not only because of the theme of the piece – the thawing, warming winds of spring overcoming ice-bound winter, hardship giving way to fruitfulness, warmth and joyous celebration – but also the knowledge of being part of a huge and pioneering endeavour. Some choir members had never worked with Laban himself. He had god-like qualities for them, and this was their chance to experience his renowned charismatic personality.

Grete Wraage von Pustau, whose group from Nuremberg participated, saw it as a massive celebration of Laban's work – not the function that the RKK had in mind for the occasion. For them, the celebration should be for Hitler's leadership, the warm wind of National Socialism thawing the ice of Weimar confusion and deprivation, the fruitfulness of working for the state productively, the joy of community being the joy of German Aryan superiority. By the way in which Lieschke presented the work to the RKK, this is what they expected to get, so the rehearsals went on undisturbed.

On 20 April 1936 a further accolade was given to Laban. Announced by Hanns Niedecken-Gebhardt, by now a staunch Party member, Laban was appointed to direct a newly created organisation, the Meisterwerkstätten für Tanz (Master Workshops for Dance) as a division of the Deutsche Tanzbühne. His contract ran from 1 May 1936 to 31 March 1937. It is clear from this appointment that Laban was still in Goebbels' good books. Mary Wigman was incensed. She felt that Laban was in a position to recommend her for this particular job. It was the final straw for her in the already strained relationship between the two of them. Her diary of 15 May was the recipient of her feelings: 'There hovers the figure of Laban, juggling between his ideals, $^3/_4$ of which are already lost, and a wish to survive, and what one would call collaboration.'

Laban's staff were Ebrecht, the Party mole, Ivers and Thum, their new workplace being located in the Charlottenburg district of Berlin, at Königin Elisabeth Strasse 1, Austellungshalle. In addition, the administrative staff, hired especially for the dance surrounding the Olympiad, were Snell, and Fräuleinen Brice, Meyer and Massek, with contracts until the end of August 1936. Also in April the Fachschaft Tanz (Dance Department) of the RTK was officially inaugurated with August Burger as its leader and editor of its journal, completing the Nazification of dance literature. The first edition had an article by Gauleiter A. E. Frauenfeld, secretary general of the RTK, entirely in praise of Hitler. Burger's article explained how dancers, especially on artistic matters, were to be organised by the Party. In this first edition Lieschke, Snell and Ivers each wrote on the part of the department's work for which they were responsible. No mention was made of Laban, and he wrote no article himself. But in the second edition he contributed 'Master and Work in the Art of Dance' on the undertakings of the new organisation. Lotte Wernicke underlined Laban's view of amateur dance as art by writing on 'Choral dance as an artistic component of German Dance', implicitly underlining their independence from Bode.

The first of Laban's major undertakings for the Olympics was the celebratory week for amateurs, run by the Reichsbund für Gemeinschaftstanz on behalf of the RTK. During it, the *Tauwind* rehearsals, which involved putting the whole work together, took place in the magnificent new open-air theatre. Photographs show Niedecken-Gebhardt in attendance, with Laban's team of helpers on stage, Laban himself well up in the tiers of concrete seats getting a view of the whole architecture of the piece. The organisation was enormous. During the Prologue, to music composed for it by Carl Orff, the thousand participants emerged from the various entrances in a solemn promenade, impressive in itself for its sheer scale and mastery of space. The first *Reigen*, 'Kampf', had been rehearsed by the Pierenkämpers with the Mannheim, Heidelberg and Frankfurt choirs. Its theme was the struggle for space and for a territory. What better theme for a Nazi dance? But Laban treated it as a battle for each person to find relief from the daily regimentation of space by searching out a place in which to be an individual in a self-constructed small community. The second *Reigen*, 'Besinnung', had been worked by Lotte Wernicke with the Berlin choirs primarily, but involving all the participants. The theme was inward-looking, reflecting on inner feelings. The third *Reigen*, 'Freude', was joyous in mood. Knust and Lotte Müller had rehearsed it with groups from Kiel, Bremerhaven, Stuttgart, Erlangen, Hanover, Nuremberg, Brandenburg, and Braunschweig. Folk dance-like in character, movement into, within, and out of thirteen circles was the form. The fourth *Reigen*, 'Weihe', was a dedication, again a Nazi theme. But Laban did not have it as a dedication of the self to the State but to harmony between people and between people and nature. Heidi Woog had rehearsed it with groups from Mülheim am Ruhr, Essen, Ibbenburen, Cologne and Dusseldorf. The work had been composed with Beethoven's Ninth Symphony in mind, but since that very music had also been chosen to form the background to the opening ceremony in the stadium itself, new music had to be provided for *Tauwind*. Hans Claus Langer, whom Laban had known from their collaborations at the State Opera, wrote it, the Berlin Radio Orchestra and Choir performing it. Excerpts from Nietzsche's *Also Sprach Zarathustra*, a favourite Laban source from his early experimental days in Munich, were spoken by four actors.

For Laban this event was the epitome of all his beliefs in the strength and beauty of dance as art for all. Although the publicity could have been read as toeing the spirit of the party line, it could also have been read as conforming to Laban's idea of the spirit of community dance as art. He gave no indication that he was nervous about its reception. He appeared to believe that no one in his right senses could be anything other than moved and exhilarated by *Tauwind*.

Although the official opening of the Dietrich Eckart Theatre was not due until the night before the actual commencement of the Olympic Games, 20 June was the crowning end of the week for the dancers, with a dress rehearsal to a packed auditorium of invited spectators. Yat Malmgren's description captured the politics of the event. The 'invited' audience contained a substantial element of dragooned public. This was nothing new. Berliners were by now used to being told to attend this rally or that Party-controlled event. Not to comply was suicide. For *Tauwind*, the RTK were in evidence. At some point before the performance began a ripple of frozen excitement flowed through the crowd at the rumour that Hitler himself was to attend. Sure enough, regimented columns of blackshirts descended the aisles, stationing themselves at the end of each row of seats to be in full control of the masses present. With a further rustle, and heel clicking, Hitler and Goebbels, with their henchmen, took their places. All roared 'Heil Hitler', all saluted, all sang 'Deutschland über Alles', and the performance began. Helen Priest Rogers, an American visitor who had come over to study German dance and Laban's notation, was also there. She saw *Tauwind* preceded by Rogge's *Amazonen* and Lotte Wernicke's *Geburt der Arbeit* (The Product of Labour). She described it as a stunning evening.

Not so Hitler and Goebbels. Dr G's diary for 21 June records his response: 'Rehearsal of dance work; freely based on Nietzsche, a bad, contrived and affected piece. I forbid a great deal. It is so intellectual. I do not like it. That is because it is dressed up in our clothes and has nothing whatever to do with us.' This last remark says it all. Laban's artistic intent was seen for what it was and Goebbels had the power to inflict mortal damage. He acted quickly. The performance of *Tauwind* was forbidden and no press comments on it appeared. It was as if Laban's beloved work had never happened. But the booklet prepared beforehand, *Wir Tanzen*, and the programme have survived.

With this huge blow, Laban had nevertheless to carry on as if all were well. Indeed it is possible that he did not fully realise the severity of the treatment that was being prepared for him. The July International Dance Competition was held in the Theater am Horst Wessel Platz, the Volksbühne. The final night and prize-giving, on 27 July, was a glittering affair in the State Opera. As chairman of the organisation, Laban was given his instructions: a German group must win. He was appalled. He could have gone along with it, but decided to act independently. The documentation records how he sent Snell off frantically in a taxi to buy prizes for every competitor. His decision was that all should win equally. Wigman was dismayed, for her performance had received an enthusiastic ovation. Possibly unaware of Laban's dilemma, she blamed him again. Her diary records her anger that after all her efforts: 'The competition was a farce.'

Lewitan's review in the *Dancing Times* noted the unusual end of the competition, without prizes, and gave instead his own ranking of the participants. He also recognised that this affair could not be compared with the competition in Paris of 1932, nor to those of Warsaw in 1933 or Vienna in 1934, for some leading dance countries – America, England, France, Russia and Sweden – had sent no competitors. The soloists each presented a programme of some nine dances. The well-known Harald Kreutzberg he saw as the outstanding individual, with Mia Corak-Slawenska from Yugoslavia, with her clean technique and expressive talent, as second. The Polish dancer Zinta Buczynska he applauded because of her gripping expression studies with titles like *Worker* and *Child Without a Home*. Spanish, Polish and Italian competitors were praised, but Gret Palucca he found unmemorable. Of the groups, Dorothée Günther with Maja Lex were highly praised. The audience enthusiastically received Felix Parnell's Polish group, but it was too much of a variety piece for Lewitan. Lotte Wernicke gave her *Geburt der Arbeit*, a *Reigen* which gripped the audience. Wigman he found to be below her usual standard. Other competitors gave folk-dance related works, and the ballet offerings from various opera companies provided him with little interest.

After all the problems of getting the competitors together at all, the sheer labour for what was clearly a mediocre affair, and the shocking letdown after *Tauwind*, Laban was exhausted. All that remained for him was to tidy up the financial books of the competition and the festival. The documents show that every pfennig spent had to be accounted for and was questioned by the RTK auditors, including the extra presents and Snell's emergency taxi.

Wigman and Günther, on the other hand, had last-minute rehearsals in the stadium, the bulk of the preparations having taken place concurrently with the competition. Wigman's diary records the pressure of working with such large groups, the problems of slipping on the wet grass and the difficulty of fitting in private classes with visiting foreign students. The evening performance on 1 August after the official opening with the Olympic athletes was a spectacular show, 'Olympic Youth', with ten thousand boys and girls, Hitler Youth members, masterminded by Hanns Niedecken-Gebhardt. 'Truly a wonderful sight,' was Lewitan's opinion. Children in white dresses, youths carrying flags of all nations, girls in orange performing rhythmic ball and club gymnastics; Harald Kreutzberg and a soloist from the State Opera led a group of battling warriors, followed by a lament of eighty mourning women choreographed by Wigman. Lewitan found her theme inappropriate for a celebration of youth. Beethoven finished the evening as a background to dramatically lit processions. Such a show connected to the Olympics had never been seen before. Hitler's Games were truly spectacular.

The pomp and ceremony with which he painted the city is well described by the Olympics historian Hart-Davis. Bunting, flags, rows of cheering children, and thousands of arms in the Nazi salute had taken the place of 'Jews not welcome' notices. Hitler's motor cavalcade, down Unter den Linden, on up the decorated route to the triumphal entry of the stadium itself, was the beginning of a charade of international comradeship. Göring gave a spectacular reception in the State Opera for the visiting dignitaries, Lizzie Maudrik providing fifty dancers to waltz among the tables set up in the transformed auditorium. Goebbels excelled himself with his propaganda on German health of body and spirit.

It seems probable that Laban remained in Berlin for the Games, uncertain of what to anticipate. On 12 August his German passport was issued to him in Berlin. The retribution of the regime began to impinge on him, and on his group soon afterwards. Knust was the first to suffer. His Tanzschreibstube, flourishing with classes for visiting foreigners, was in an office and small studio. He was allotted a smaller studio. He was locked out of his office. Then his room was moved to the basement. Finally he was given a shoe-cleaning cupboard as his work space. He apologised to his students and slipped out of Berlin, to lie low in Munich.

Laban left Berlin too, ostensibly for a rest at Gundelsheim, near Heilbron. But the authorities followed him. He was investigated by the police and filled out the required forms. His Aryan ancestry was proved by the provision of documents showing the non-Jewish blood of his parents and grandparents. He provided details of his finances which showed that he owed considerable sums of money. But the crucial disclosure was his reply to the question as to whether he was or had ever been a freemason. He stated what they already knew, namely that he had been a member of the OTO (Ordo Templi Orientis) between 1917 and 1918 and that he was assigned the rank of Grand Master. He agreed that he was not a member of the Nazi Party.

The authorities were searching for a means to obliterate Laban without inflicting hardship too overtly to such an international figure. Laban's self disclosures contained what they needed. A translation from an internal news bulletin from the Propaganda Ministry puts the position: 'Freemasons who resigned their membership before 30 January 1933 and who joined the National Socialist Party, or who worked for it before that date, will not suffer disadvantage.' For all others, even if they had resigned before 30 January 1933, the following euphemism was offered: 'Individual treatment would be meted out.' The OTO was explicitly named as a banned organisation. Laban and all those associated with him were now in mortal danger.

Following up the police report, the RKK demanded an investigation of Laban by the Gestapo. The reply came that they had papers on him already and could find nothing political against him, gratuitously informing the RKK of the woman with whom Laban had been living at 12/13 Karlsbad, Berlin W35, information which Laban had not divulged. Correspondence continued between the RKK and the RTK and Propaganda Ministry over who was ultimately responsible for the Deutsche Tanzbühne and Meisterwerkstätten. Someone was going to have to deal with Laban himself and no one seemed to want to take the responsibility.

Snell and her two clerical assistants had their jobs terminated on 31 August. Susanne Ivers was the next to go. Informed that the Deutsche Tanzbühne and the Meisterwerkstätten were to be reorganised from 30 October, and despite the fact that she had claimed to be a Party member and one-time Kraft durch Freude teacher, she was relieved of her duties by 10 September. Richard Thum left on 31 October. Ebrecht brought in new ideologically correct staff to take their place.

Laban, now ill, withdrew to Plauen to the Lieschke's, his place of solace in times of stress. He remained there during October and November. On the back of a letter from the Propaganda Ministry dated 2 December can be found a note agreed between Laban and Department VI, headed by Herr Cunz: 'Laban resigns 1.11.36 as leader of the Meisterwerkstätten für Tanz and makes himself available only for special occasions as an expert.' He was to be paid a minimal amount until the expiry of his contract on 31 March 1937. The note goes on: 'No further agreement is envisaged. Dept VI closes the matter.' It is clear that discussion had taken place. The only possible way Laban could have continued after the OTO membership was known was by becoming a full supporter of the Party. He would not do so. Until the end of March he would have barely enough to live on and after that no means whatever of earning. He was crudely booted out of Berlin. In any case he had no home of his own there, or indeed anywhere.

It was Jo Meisenbach, for the second time, who came to his aid. Meisenbach – who, the reader will recall, had an interest in Laban's choreutic drawings and models, and shared his fascination with crystalline forms – had a good friend in a remarkable teacher, Andreas Dück. Meisenbach, whose birthday coincided with Laban's on 16 December, suggested that Laban accompany him to a birthday celebration arranged to take place at Lichtenfels in Bavaria with Dück's family. The plan was to see the quite extraordinarily beautiful drawings and paintings that the children of Seubeldorfer primary school had created under the guidance of their teacher. Dück was equally fascinated with crystalline forms, with abstract shapes and colours that reflected the magical state of the soul. Through his inspired teaching the children seemed to become aware of what Laban would always call 'the land of silence'. The meeting of Laban and Dück was an immediate success. The two men found much of intense mutual interest, so much so that instead of going on to Garmisch-Partenkirchen as he had first intended, Laban accepted the Dücks' proposition that he should stay in the neighbourhood so that they could work together on crystallogical matters. So it was that Laban resided at the cloister of Schloss Banz, a mile away from the little town of Lichtenfels, eking out a meagre existence in the company of a strict and spartan religious order. A time of crisis for him, he turned as usual to his crystals, his Rosicrucian belief, and found solace in coloured drawings, repeating again and again the same imaginative designs of man the mover in harmony with the cosmos, expressed through the interweaving of human bodies with icosahedral and dodecahedral forms.

Over the winter months the two men shared their deepest spiritual thoughts, in a time of such aridity in Germany. Laban visited the little school, shared movement play with the children and on many an evening sat together with the cloister's community of guests speaking about 'these things'. Dück maintained that Laban made a lasting impression on his listeners with his 'magical' personality.

By February 1937 the frugality and cold of the Schloss had affected Laban's health. Frau Dück took him in. While recovering, he made up his mind that emigration was the only future open to him. How to achieve it was an incredibly difficult problem. How to survive in the meantime with no home and no money was an immediate hardship. He decided to make a brief visit to Munich to his divorced wife, Maja, to tell her of his plan, and arranged with his publisher that the royalties from *Ein Leben für den Tanz* should be sent to her. In April, he went to Plauen. The visitors' book contains a despairing caricature of himself engulfed in his own archive with the caption 'Sonnenuntergang' (the sun is going down). From then on he tried to find a way of getting out of Germany, which meant that he had to have enough money to travel somewhere and a host of some sort to support him. But where?

In the meantime the new Meisterwerkstätten staff were announced on 1 May. Fritz Böhme would teach History, Gustav Fischer Klamt was responsible for Racial and Heredity Studies, Tamara Rauser would teach Ballet. Max Terpis was booked for Theatre Dance and Lotte Wernicke for amateurs. Laban could well have seen this reshuffle as a sickening distortion of his visionary plan for a High School for dance education.

Rolf de Maré was the means by which there seemed to be a possibility of Laban getting out. Paris was hosting a World Exhibition and the Archives Internationales de la Danse planned to mount a pavilion on 'La Danse Populaire d'Europe' and to contribute to a Congress on 'Le Science de l'Art'. De Maré managed to locate Laban at Frankfurt-am-Main in mid-July, where he was in contact with Lotte Müller. Knowing his critical situation, she had invited him to teach a summer course at her school, as had his ex-students in Hamburg. But the authorities thought otherwise. The schools were investigated and informed that if they employed Laban they would lose their Kraft durch Freude licences. They had no option but to concur, for the alternative meant that they could never teach again. These courses were Laban's only hope of earning his bread. By now he was unwell, undernourished, depressed and near desperate. He pursued the contact with de Maré who requested the resumé of a speech that Laban might make if he could be invited to take part in the Congress.

On 7 August 1937 Laban left Germany for good, receiving an invitation at the last moment from the Ministry for Foreign Affairs which enabled him to cross the border. He found himself swept immediately into the inner circle of the international congress participants on the aesthetics section of the Science of the Arts Congress. Exhausted and in shock, Laban attended Paul Valéry's opening address on 8 August and attended a reception at the Archives Internationales de la Danse building, hosted by Rolf de Maré and Pierre Tugal. A concert of new music and a lecture/performance at the Grand Amphitheatre of the Sorbonne by Serge Lifar and his 'friends from the opera' preceded Laban's contribution. Laban spoke on 'la nouvelle science de danse' discussing 'the way to the aesthetic in dance'. It must have been a challenging ordeal for he was ill, and yet conscious of the need, and of his own ability, to make his mark in that august group. The Congress ended with a gala at the Opéra on 13 August, and Laban found himself thereafter on his own in Paris, no longer a paid-for guest, with no plan.

He was in touch with Bereska, but did not stay with her. She was in any case by now an alcoholic, her school closed or closing, for no Frenchman wanted German dance by 1937. She was about to leave for Belgrade where a promise of some future had been offered. Laban gave his address to Lieschke as care of Frau Frances Bartha, Paris 16, Avenue Hoche 8. Where he actually stayed is not known, except that it was a very poor lodging place.

News reached him from Lieschke that a smear campaign had been launched in the German press designed to ensure that he could never return. On 3 September he wrote to her a bitter, despondent letter full of rage, indignation and disbelief. 'Who is the swine?' he asked, who had written these slurs, lies and innuendos. He searched in his mind for who would want to annihilate his reputation. He was accused of being an aristocrat and a debtor, both qualities that he had been accused of before. But for the first time someone was accusing him of being a homosexual – what he called 'the 175 affair', referring to the offence which carried imprisonment in a concentration camp. Such an accusation he found particularly bizarre and hateful. In his mind he traced the rumour back to the ballet department of the Berlin State Opera, where he had studiously refused to tolerate such practices which he presumed, he wrote, might have been problematic in his predecessor's time but not in his. He had never discussed the subject with Tietjen nor given it any thought while he was there, but he named Julian Algo as a possible source. Some dancers could be hostile on this account, he thought, but he could not understand why Tietjen would lie. Had he really accused Laban, or was it actually the regime, using Tietjen's name? Could it be Cunz? In her letter, Lieschke had defended the regime. If it were not the regime, he replied, it was an individual, who must be found and stopped – not for himself, Laban wrote, but to save German dance. His movement choirs, his space harmony studies had been decried as 'stinking of freemasonry'. The prevention of the summer courses at his pupils' schools stemmed from the same poisoned source. The liar must be found, for the future of 'our dance' was in jeopardy, he wrote. In the letter, almost incoherent in his distress, he realised that it was not just the regime that was putrid but ordinary German people too, for the way that they joined in the denunciations, the lies, the filth. 'For the first time, I am ashamed of being German,' he concluded. This was his last communication with Germany.

His problem now was how to be allowed to stay in France. He was back in the familiar catch-22 situation of an inability to earn in a city where, to stay, he must be seen to have sufficient means of support. He had only the remnants of the ten Marks with which he entered the country and some small change from selling some of the gifts that he had been given at the Congress. He began the wearisome game of applying for short-term permits to stay for two weeks at a time. His health started to disintegrate, physically and mentally. Another ex-pupil, Frances Perret, helped to look after him in whatever way she could. On 4 November he made an application to the Paris authorities for an identity card, giving his address then as 59 Boulevard de Courcelles, Paris 16e. A lonely and destitute figure, he holed up in a cheap room, to survive the winter, or not.

11

The Will to Rekindle

Dartington, Newtown and Manchester, 1938–1945

Laban was able to enter Britain on the strength of a personal invitation from his ex-pupil Kurt Jooss. There was no official position to come to, no red carpet. The man who emerged from the boat onto the quayside at Southampton on a cold 6 February in 1938, looked a sorry sight; but not an unfamiliar one. Refugees, fleeing from the violent harassment on the Continent, were arriving in Britain with increasing regularity, telling of friends who had disappeared into 'camps for their own protection'. The immigration authorities received them all with caution and placed severe restrictions on their freedom. Laban, with virtually no possessions, a tired, emaciated and despondent sixty-year-old man, was allowed to stay in the country for six weeks on condition that he did not undertake work, paid or unpaid. How familiar this must have felt to him. The repetition of his permit problems in Switzerland in 1914–17, again in Germany in 1919 and 1920, and more recently in Paris, must have brought home to him his situation, an unwelcome no one in no-man's-land.

On arrival at Dartington Hall, near Totnes in Devon, he was taken in by Jooss, Aino Siimola his wife, and Anna their eight-year-old daughter, to recover in their home. The house had been newly built for them by Leonard and Dorothy Elmhirst, the wealthy philanthropic visionary owners of the Dartington estate.

Laban was incapacitated. His ever-weak digestion was crippled by his lack of nourishment in Paris. His fragile mental state tipped over into acute depression through the traumas of his changed circumstances and his loss of identity and purpose. The photographs of the period show him haggard. He turned to what he always did in times of trouble, *meine Sache*, his choreutic models and drawing, his sacred geometry, to find solace and strength from his Rosicrucian-based wisdom of crystals. Jooss supported him as well as he could, but he had the school and the company as his prime concerns.

Laban had to assess where he was, who constituted the circle into which he had been propelled. What was Dartington? Dorothy Elmhirst, from the prominent wealthy, socially and artistically active Whitney family from New England, herself imaginative, caring and far-seeing, had married Leonard Elmhirst, a Briton with an intense interest in rural culture. Educated at Cornel Universities with a focus on theology and agriculture, he had met by chance the poet Rabindranath Tagore, who commissioned him to develop an institute for Rural Reconstruction in India where rural poverty was extreme. Inspired by these experiences, Leonard had proposed a unique rural development in Devon, based around the battered remnants of a medieval hall house. Experiments in community living, in agriculture and local industry, arts and culture, made Dartington Hall and its estate a centre for exploring new ways of combating the encroachment of modernity on rural traditions. This was no Monte Verità, but some of the same spiritual and educational values and courageous hopes abounded, though without the excesses of Oedenkoven's commune. Throughout the 1930s, artists had been welcomed to Dartington. Architects, painters, potters, weavers, theatre producers, sculptors, landscape gardeners, musicians and dancers could all be found. With the expansion of Nazism, Dartington became host to fleeing individuals who made up a dynamic cultural community of incredible talent. No wonder, then, that Jooss, his company and his school with Sigurd Leeder, had been offered a safe base from which to make works and train young dancers when Germany became impossible.

The Jooss/Leeder School, operating in purpose-built studios, the open-air theatre and the small Barn Theatre, might have seemed a natural institution in which Laban might find a niche. But would it have been? After all, Jooss had moved on from the Tanzbühne days in Hamburg. With Leeder, he had embraced aspects of ballet and developed the Jooss/Leeder technique. The curriculum read as typically Labanite, with choreutics, eukinetics and script (that is notation) on the timetable, but the classes were of another order to those of the Choreographisches Institut. Sigurd Leeder was a teacher of genius, according to accounts from his pupils. Eukinetic and choreutic scales were turned by him into exquisite studies, and the School went about its work around the Ballets Jooss, by now a famous international touring company. Leeder had been cautious of inviting Laban to Dartington. He only supported the idea when the Elmhirsts understood that he would brook no interference, let alone contribution, from Laban. In any case, Laban had no wish to teach there. What motivation he had, and that was almost non-existent for quite twelve months, focused on the broader issues of his vision of dance for all, of dance as a means to spiritual health, not an end in itself. It was choreosophy, not choreography, that lurked in his demoralised being, as he toyed with his models in an atelier loaned to him by the Elmhirsts in the courtyard of the Hall.

Also at the Jooss/Leeder School was the young teacher Lisa Ullmann. It was she who had passed through Paris some time in the autumn of 1937, on holiday. While there she had found Laban. Appalled at his destitution, but with no means there and then to alleviate his plight, she had discussed the problem urgently on her return to Dartington. Jooss's personal invitation, and probably the purchase of Laban's ticket, was the result. Ullmann had arrived in Britain with the Essen school in 1934. She had by now established a role for herself in the community. Personally, she had become attached to Richard, Dorothy Elmhirst's son by her first marriage, but about the time that Laban arrived, Louise Soelberg, an American dancer in the Ballets Jooss, had caught Richard's eye. In the school and company Ullmann was not of great significance, for in the eyes of the dancers, no one could compare with Sigurd Leeder. Her training, in Lotte Wedekind's Labanschule, plus two years at the Choreographisches Institut, had given her broad-based skills, including notation, work for amateurs and children as well as body training for theatre dancers. By September 1935 she had already experimented with movement choir work for amateurs, largely shop girls from Plymouth, through Workers' Educational Association classes. She had done well and been encouraged to make the classes regular and to continue the next year. By 1938 her weekly classes were in their fourth year and she was gaining a clearer idea of dance as a means of recreation and education. So it was that in April 1938 she journeyed to Paris to an International Congress at which dance as a method of education was to be considered. No doubt the initial work of Laban and his disciples contributed to the Congress's quest.

Ullmann was not a lone pioneer in Britain; far from it. Throughout the 1930s dance renewal was burgeoning. Enthusiasts of the English folk song and dance flourished, with Douglas Kennedy taking the lead on the founding work of Cecil Sharp. The Imperial Society of Teachers of Dancing enlarged their range of styles to include Greek Dancing, under the guidance of Ruby Ginner. Many similar rhythmic practices to those of Dalcroze were expounded, with the revival of ancient Greek dances as one source material. Laban and Wigman's work was known. The *Dancing Times,* with a wide readership, had published regular reports on dance in Germany. Annie Boalth, Laban-trained in Germany, had emigrated to Britain in the early 1930s, finding a successful role for herself teaching movement for dancers and actors, while Anny Fligg, similarly German-trained, was known as a German dance teacher of amateurs. Mary Wigman's appearance in London in 1928 had been hailed as 'an event of outstanding importance', and the Viennese *Ausdruckstänzerin* Gertrud Bodenwieser had impressed with her group in 1929. Several British dance schools had introduced German dance experimentally into their own curricula by 1930, but the *Dancing Times* reported that 'these ultra modern methods have not made good', and that Michel Fokine rather than Laban was favoured in theatre dance. Writing in 1936, Jeanette Rutherston concluded that German dance had influenced choreography for the *corps de ballet*, who were no longer 'a vague accompaniment to dress the stage' but an essential part of the dance, and that German ideas were being used more and more by teachers in regular school and recreational classes.

The physical training sorority at Bedford Physical Training College under the far-sighted leadership of the principal, Margaret Stansfield, had for ten years pioneered connections with the new dance occurring on the Continent. She had taken the initiative in 1930 to second their teacher of Greek Dancing, Freda Colwill, to Vienna to study with Bodenwieser. She returned fired with new ideas for the teaching of dance to her gymnastic orientated students. Leslie Burrowes, Wigman-trained, who became the most well known promoter in Britain of European dancing, opened her dance studio in London in 1932. An accomplished performer, she was hired that year to teach at a dance summer school in Buxton. Several physical training people participated. One, Joan Goodrich, from Bedford, was inspired by Burrowes' work. Goodrich was given leave of absence and financial help from Margaret Stansfield, as she felt she must study with Wigman. She trained at Dresden for the best part of a year, returning to begin a highly influential role in bringing German dance to British teachers. Already in October 1932, at the Twelfth Ling Physical Education Association Conference, Freda Colwill had taught 'Central European Dancing', as the Laban/Wigman/Jooss/Bodenwieser work was to become known. The previously unshakeable hold of set dance forms was being questioned. That the German way might offer an alternative, or a supplement, was being discussed in other colleges, but at Bedford it was acted upon. Students were encouraged by Stansfield to include dance in their teaching practice in schools, and the gifted ones found posts where they could introduce the new dance.

The women's physical training colleges at this time, as Lorna Wilson remembered, were run on similar lines to girls' boarding schools. Propriety and discipline reigned, both personal and academic. The students were drawn largely from the British public school system – that is, from private girls' boarding and day schools – and on qualifying went back into them to teach. Goodrich adjusted her passion for Wigman to this environment.

Students came down the gymnasium in threes, with a Wigman-style dynamic in contrast to their former Greek lyric/pyrrhic styles. Group dances, modelled on Wigman's ensemble work, were composed for the end-of-year demonstrations, *Enigma Variations*, *Everyman*, *Episodes*. Wilson recalled her task as a solo figure of Peace in one, given music to interpret, an idea to go on, with the movement to be improvised from her own intuition. The mix of freedom, movement knowledge and acceptance of individuality that Laban's work was to give these young women would be a revelation.

Diana Jordan, although originally from the Bedford college, had decided to devote her energies to education in the arts, and especially in dance. A sensitive teacher with vision and a deep-rooted interest in the arts, she too had taken courses with Wigman. She established a place for herself early on by publishing *The Dance as Education* in 1938, the first book in Britain to put such a concept forward. She emphasised that dance should be recognised as one of the arts in education and not a branch of physical education, because movement, its means of communication, proceeded from emotions, ideas and from actions that could not be put into words. She named qualities that she valued in dance as education: individuality, freedom, sensitivity to rhythm and to the laws of movement. The development of moral qualities gave a rationale for dance for children: awareness, judgement, tolerance, courage, initiative, self-discipline. No mention is made of her knowledge of German dance, indeed the American John Martin is the dance person quoted; but to promote German ideas in 1938 would not have been popular.

All these women, talented and pioneering, fuelled a hunger for something better for children than copying given movements. Even some German *Körperkultur* teachers had felt the same longing. A few using the methods of Bode, Mensendieck and Loheland had found their way, with difficulty, into dance in their own country in the 1920s. In Britain in the 1930s the educational climate was far more conducive to change. John Dewey's educational work, focusing as it did on learning by doing, and Froebel's work on creativity in the kindergarten, were just two streams of thought on schooling that found resonance in the culture of a Britain that was opening up to a recognition of the worth of each individual, in contrast with the authoritarian tendencies of Germany. John Macmurray's *Reason and Emotion*, published in 1935, discussed the topics in the forefront of educational debate in Britain at the time. Teachers of child-centred education were wrestling with the very issues Laban had addressed in Germany – reason/emotion, tradition/modernity. In this climate it was the combination of Goodrich and Jordan that would prove invaluable to Laban as he began to grope for a renewal of purpose. He had survived Nazism, but could he find the will to enter another battlefield?

For the first weeks of his stay in Britain Laban's own horizon was limited to Jooss's house. By 25 April he was given permission by the Home Office to stay for a further six months. He could not remain indefinitely as Jooss's personal guest and was given a room in The Barton on the Dartington estate. So it was that Lisa Ullmann, returning from Paris, saw Laban, her erstwhile hero, her mentor from Berlin days, struggling with ill health and despair. She was at a loose end personally, and this must have contributed to her decision to commit herself to help this man to find his equilibrium and to regain his strength and vision. Throughout the summer she nurtured him, she fed him, she talked with him, she encouraged him. In fact, she probably saved his life.

In the autumn a further six-month permit was issued to him. He began to think, indeed he had to think, of the future. He must work, he must earn; neither was permitted, but somehow he had to become independent of the modest charity offered him by the Elmhirsts. But how? Where? Would he be allowed to stay in Britain? Could he start an institution for movement at Dartington? Did he have the strength? Dorothy Elmhirst was particularly supportive and keen to broadcast his philosophy and method to British listeners. To that end she encouraged him to write, to capture for the English language reader his crucial ideas. With almost no notes to which to refer, he attempted to encapsulate his life's work. These half-English, half-German scribbles eventually became the beginnings of his book *Choreutics*, not published until 1966, after his death.

One can find letters dated December 1938 between his eldest daughter Johanna, now in New York under the name of Juana de Laban, and Dorothy Elmhirst. Juana had espoused her father's work and was researching the possibility of opening a Laban Institute in New York, the equivalent of the Choreographisches Institut. She needed funds and suggested that if she could get someone to sponsor him, her father should come to New York and together they could run a centre. She had herself entered with a regular immigration quota visa. Laban did not dissuade Juana from pursuing the idea, although he had not enjoyed his New York experience of 1926 at all.

In August Suzanne Perrottet travelled to Totnes. In her interviews with Giorgio Wolfenberger she says only that she came on impulse. She stayed with Jooss. Photographs suggest a rivalry between her and Ullmann, each for quite different reasons claiming rights of possession over Laban. He apparently shared with her the reconstructed drawings of his *Sache*. They must have discussed the possibility of a Christmas course in Switzerland, for on 12 December Laban left Dover for Geneva. Her notes (she was a copious note-taker) on the course exist, but there is no mention of it in *Ein Bewegtes Leben*, Wolfenberger's biography of Perrottet, which suggests that it was not an event to be remembered. One can imagine that Laban was far too disabled to teach with any verve or purpose. He visited his sister Renée, a resident of Geneva, before returning. He had accepted an invitation to visit the school of his erstwhile student Lea Daan in Antwerp, *en route* to Switzerland. Was he looking to see if Belgium might be a place to work? His Alien's Card records that he returned to Dover on 15 January 1939 and that in March he received a further permit to stay in Britain, but only for three more months.

Yat Malmgren, by the late thirties a budding Swedish recitalist, related that during the summer he was invited by Jooss to come to Dartington with the possibility of joining the company. Somewhat reluctantly he attempted to learn the Jooss/Leeder style while simultaneously rehearsing his solo programme. He was observed by Ullmann. She brought him to Laban, convinced that Laban would be interested in his approach to dance. For Malmgren this was a significant moment, an encounter with the great man himself. He visited Laban again, fascinated by the space models and drawings in his workroom, but before long the war intervened and he sailed for America. It was sufficient contact for Malmgren to feel able to call on Laban again, in fifteen years' time, as we will see.

Throughout 1938 and 1939 the belligerent activities of Hitler intensified. From the Austrian Anschluss, the invasion of the German-speaking Sudetenland region of Czechoslovakia, the Jewish pogroms, especially Krystallnacht (Night of the Broken Glass), his expansionist moves and racial intimidation increased in ferocity. War became ever nearer. Britain was forced to be more open-minded in accepting her proportion of the accelerating numbers of desperate refugees. On the strength of this shift in policy, Laban was given permission in July to stay in Britain 'for an unlimited duration' and allowed to 'engage in his profession of lecturer and writer on ballet dancing'.

This freedom was short-lived. On the outbreak of war on 3 September 1939, all aliens had to report to the police, where categorisation for future internment took place. By mid-October it became clear that Laban would be exempted from internment on the grounds of his ill health. Ullmann was allowed to continue her teaching. Overnight, as it were, the status of her family in Berlin, and her brother in the German army, changed from being one of supportive friends to official enemies.

The Jooss/Leeder school was in chaos. Foreign students dispersed im-

55. The Dietrich Eckart Freilichtbühne with the Olympic Tower under construction in the background. (Allsport/Hulton Getty.)

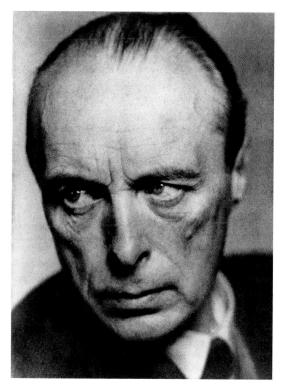

56. Laban, photo taken on his visit to Lea Daan's school in Antwerp, 1938. (Laban Collection.)

57. Laban in his work room at The Barton, Dartington Hall, 1939. (Laban Collection.)

58. Laban with Lisa Ullmann, c. 1939. (Laban Collection.)

59. Lisa Ullmann and Laban, with Joan Goodrich and Diana Jordan, at Rock House, Newtown, at their first holiday course, summer 1941. (Laban Collection.)

60. Movement choir at the Modern Dance Holiday Course at Moreton Hall, 1942. Betty Meredith Jones in dark trousers. (Laban Collection, gift of Lorna Wilson.)

61. Modern Dance Holiday Course, Sheffield, January 1945. (Laban Collection.)

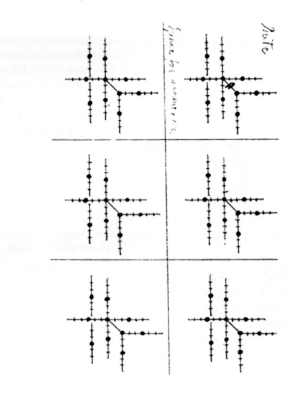

62. Effort graphs developed by Laban for Paton Lawrence & Co., 1942. (Warren Lamb Collection, National Resource Centre for Dance.)

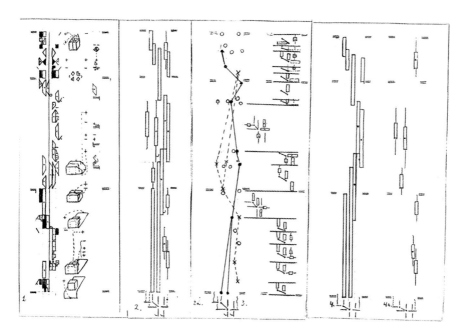

63. Notation and linear effort graphs for the analysis of the manual processes in wrapping Mars Bars, 1942. (Warren Lamb Collection, National Resources Centre for Dance.)

64. Exercises in Laban/Lawrence Industrial Rhythm, demonstrated by the first students of the Art of Movement Studio, Manchester, 1947. (Photo by Roland Watkins.)

65. Class at the Art of Movement Studio, Manchester. From left, Mary Elding, Valerie Preston, Warren Lamb, with Lisa Ullmann, 1947. (Photo by Roland Watkins.)

66. Geraldine Stephenson demonstrating choreutics in the icosahedron, 1947. (Photo by Roland Watkins.)

67. Art of Movement Studio students in an open-air class in the garden of Myfanwy Dewey, 1948. (Laban Collection.)

68. Sylvia Bodmer's Young Dancers Group. Maureen Myers, Ronnie Curran, Cecilia Bagley, 1948.(Laban collection, gift of Enid Platt from Sylvia Bodmer's estate.)

69. Men's creative movement course held for Devonshire's Emergency Teacher Training, led by Joan Russell, August 1950. (Laban Collection, gift from Joan Russell's estate.)

70. Modern Dance Holiday Course class, with observation, held at Dartington Hall, 1952. In front of group: Bill Carpenter, Michael Leonard, Irmgard Bartenieff. (Photo by Photo Reportage, Laban Collection.)

71. Laban at the Modern Dance Holiday Course at Dartington Hall, 1952. Margaret Bodmer with Veronica Tyndale-Biscoe behind. (Photo by Photo Reportage, Laban Collection.)

72. Group work at the Modern Dance Holiday Course, Dartington Hall, 1952. (Photo by Photo Reportage, Laban Collection.)

73. Modern educational dance with first-year girls in a Lancashire secondary school, late 1940s. (Laban Collection, from Myfanwy Dewey's estate.)

74. Movement at a primary school in Manchester, c. 1950. (Laban Collection.)

75. The Saltarium of the Art of Movement Studio at Addlestone, 1955. (Photo by Colin Westwood, Laban Collection, gift from Lisa Ullmann's estate.)

76. Laban at Addlestone, 1957. (Laban Collection.)

DRAWINGS BY LABAN

It is often difficult to ascertain the date of Laban's space drawings because he repeated almost the same form on more than one occasion. Most are coloured, but the originals of this small selection drawn at Dartington Hall in 1938-1939 are all in black and white.

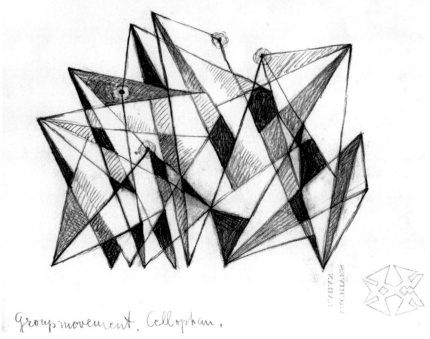

Group movement. Cellophan.

77 (above and below). Group movement seen as spatial form. (Laban Archive, National Resource Centre for Dance.)

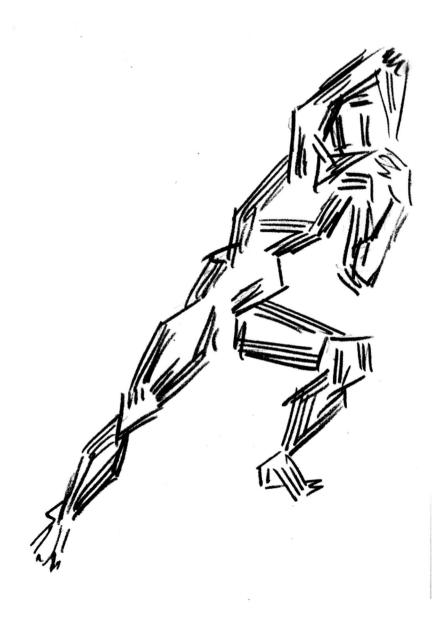

78. Labile figure of a man. (Laban Archive.)

79 (above and below). Stable figure in a dodecahedral form. (Laban Archive, National Resource Centre for Dance.)

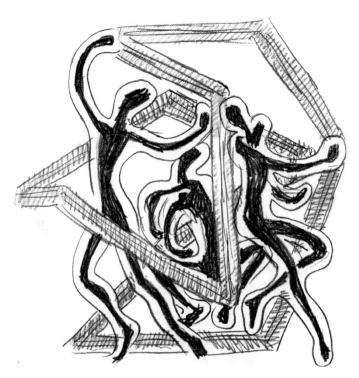

80. A three-ring harmonic form danced by three figures within an icosahedral framework. (Laban Archive, National Resource Centre for Dance.)

81. Group of six dancers oriented in an equator, a space harmony form, surrounded by a twelve-ring of alternating labile transversals with stable peripherals. (Laban Archive, National Resource Centre for Dance.)

82 (above and below). Dancers converging and diverging in spatial counterpoint. (Laban Archive, National Resource Centre for Dance.)

mediately, the remnants moving into smaller premises on the estate. The company continued to function, and Jooss choreographed *A Spring Tale* and *Chronica* for the season. The dancers departed for a New York tour in December, Jooss remaining to attend to the school.

Devon and Cornwall became host to scores of children evacuated from big cities and industrial sites in the expectation of immediate bombardment by German aircraft. As fighting raged in France and Belgium, the anticipated aerial onslaught never came, the autumn being dubbed 'the phoney war'. Dartington continued its cultural activities over the winter of 1939–40 for the community gathered there. Laban, billed as 'Mr R. de Laban', agreed to give a series of seven lectures on the 'history of dance and its significance in education from the psychological and physiological point of view: Fridays at 8 p.m. from January 26th.'

Also continuing unabated was the pioneering work in dance of Joan Goodrich. She could be found promoting 'Central European Dance' at Loughborough Summer School in August 1939, assisted by Joan Donaldson. In addition to her regular teaching at Bedford Physical Training College she taught dance in the Easter holidays, under the auspices of the Ling Physical Education Association's refresher courses. She received a mixed response, but enough women were impressed by her work to strengthen the foothold of Laban-based dance in Britain, months before he taught anything himself.

The devastating defeat of the Allied troops in France in June 1940, their astounding retreat from the beaches of Dunkirk in the armada of little boats, left Britain open to invasion from the victorious and much better equipped German forces. Defiance was the call from Winston Churchill, and defence of the realm. Vulnerable coastal areas became the subject of special treatment, in the expectation of the imminent arrival of the enemy's fleet and armies. Dartington found itself in the midst of those parts of Devon designated a Protected Area, from which all aliens had to be removed forthwith. Ullmann was obliged to leave, as well as Laban. They had nowhere to go, like countless others rapidly moved out of the coastal regions of Britain. Neither Laban nor Ullmann had any money to pay for a bed, if they could find one. The Elmhirsts supported as many of their homeless community as possible and Laban and Ullmann were recipients of their generosity on a personal level, for they were offered space in their Mayfair flat in London. With virtually no luggage beyond the obligatory gas masks, the two travelled to Upper Brook Street on 18 June. The Jooss/ Leeder School found itself with no teachers, for in the same exodus Jooss was interned in the Isle of Man, as was Leeder, and Hein Heckroth, Jooss's designer, was one of the luckless aliens 'deported to the Dominions', in this case to Canada.

Dorothy Elmhirst, on Laban's behalf, turned her attention to investigating if there might after all be an opening for his work in America. After trying several contacts there seemed hope at the 'New School of Social Research', an institution in New York based on a topic much beloved by both Elmhirsts. Could Laban's ideas on movement, education, dance and community find a role there? But before long came the negative answer that the qualifications required for entry into America would be difficult to fulfil, for neither Laban nor Ullmann would be accepted under the quota of qualified teachers; and while Laban could qualify as an 'eminent scholar', Ullmann could not. If they wished to work together, America was out of the question.

In London, Ullmann made contact with Leslie Burrowes and taught for two weeks in her Chelsea studio. Among the pupils were Margaret Dunn, later to become a leading educationist, and Mary Skeaping, later to become ballet-mistress of Sadler's Wells Ballet. Ullmann's work was received with enthusiasm and she booked a studio in Baker Street for further daily classes. Laban was still ill enough to require a doctor's attention. Dr Hanns Cohn prescribed for him a rigorous diet for severe stomach problems. Staying in the flat, Laban continued writing *Choreutics* and talking at length to Dorothy. She was so optimistic that, in retrospect, he saw these weeks as a turning point in his recovery. He dared to hope again.

The Battle of Britain, a war in the air, raged throughout August 1940 as drove after drove of German fighters and bombers battled over southern England for supremacy of the skies. London was not the prime target. The German air force was attempting to destroy the planes of Fighter Command both in air battles and by bombing them as they stood on the ground on the emergency air strips surrounding the capital. The savagery of the fighting, the loss of life amongst pilots, the nearness of defeat, brought the trauma of war close to everyone. Apparently through error, one German pilot dropped his bomb load on London. The retaliation was swift. Berlin was immediately heavily bombed. For Ullmann this was a terrible day, for her mother was a Berliner. Before too many days had passed, the East End of London was attacked, set on fire by thousands of incendiaries, followed the next day by high-explosive bombs. The Blitz had begun. It became imperative that everyone who could do so should leave the capital.

Somehow it was arranged that Laban and Ullmann should seek refuge in an insignificant rural Welsh location, Newtown in Montgomeryshire. There Ullmann searched the town ('no one wants aliens'), full to the brim already with evacuees, eventually, and desperately, finding three single spaces, for herself, Laban and, at Dorothy Elmhirst's request, for Mimi the Jooss's family maid, in the Elephant and Castle Hotel. October was a fraught month. The remaining few students of the Jooss/Leeder School were encouraged by Dorothy to move to Newtown to be taught by Ullmann. They would have none of it, preferring to stay together in the hope that Sigurd Leeder would be released from internment and teach them again. In November Jooss and Leeder were freed, moving to Cambridge in the hope of finding some possibilities of working there. But the Ballets Jooss, now in South America, needed Jooss with them to make fresh repertoire to provide them with an adequate programme to continue touring. They could not get across the Atlantic to Jooss, nor he to them. Before long they had no option but to disband.

Laban simply kept on writing throughout the moves, sending chapters of *Choreutics* to Dorothy Elmhirst for safe keeping as they were written, Chapters X and XI by October. He had to report to the police his every move and was not permitted to leave Newtown overnight, nor 'to possess a bicycle or maps'. Ullmann now found herself in difficulty in respect of earning money, for having lost her employment with the Jooss/Leeder school she had automatically lost her work permit. A cheque to her for £20, presumably a month's allowance, can be found from Dorothy Elmhirst to cover the hotel bill. Ullmann showed her tenacity by contacting the local secondary school. Schools everywhere were in a chaotic situation, with their male staff called up into the forces, many of the female teachers also shifting into the forces or into the land army as agricultural workers, or into war work in the newly created munitions factories. Towns were either devoid of children, all having been evacuated to the country, or, like Newtown, saturated with an influx of urban children billeted on the community without their parents. Miss Cutting, the headmistress, took up Ullmann's offer to teach in the school, unpaid, and agreed in return to help Laban with his English writing.

News of Laban and Ullmann's whereabouts reached the British pioneers of dance teaching. During the summer the leading figures in the training of women teachers had already met at the office of the Physical Education Association to discuss the growing phenomenon of 'Central European Dance'. Goodrich, Jordan (now organiser for Worcestershire County Council), His Majesty's Inspectors Penny and Hammonds, Phyllis Spafford representing the Ling Physical Education Association, and Douglas Kennedy, had put their heads together. The result was, despite the interference of war, a plan for a large gathering of interested educationists at Reading

University, to take place during the Christmas holidays and to be master-minded by Diana Jordan. Ullmann was invited to teach practical classes and Laban to give a lecture. Ullmann had no permit to work. Through the intervention of the Elmhirsts, it was granted and Ullmann launched into the beginning of what would become her outstandingly successful mission to bring Laban's ideas and methods to British teachers.

Noteworthy is a brief exchange of letters at this time triggered by Jooss and Leeder's return for four days to Dartington to collect their belongings. There they were castigated by Dorothy for not having made more use of Laban in the school. Having thought about the profound discussions she had had with Laban at Upper Brook Street, and having read letters from him in which he outlined his last speech in Berlin given before the perform-ance of *Tauwind*, she was struck by his depth of understanding of the same problem that she and Leonard addressed, namely, community, the arts and harmony between people. Jooss, alarmed at having upset his benefactor (he was still receiving an allowance from the Elmhirsts), besought Laban to put things right for him. Laban did so, by blaming himself as 'idle' in a self-deprecating letter. Asked by Dorothy what he thought of the school, he declined to interfere but did comment that the notation had been refined in a manner not to his taste, referring presumably to the innovations made by Leeder to accommodate the stylistic intentions of the Jooss/Leeder tech-nique. The slight unease between the parties, understandable and of no apparent significance, actually hid a growing preference on the Elmhirst's part for Laban's way of looking at dance and coping with difficulties over that of Jooss or Leeder. Notes in the Dartington records can be found of Laban and Ullmann's ability to free themselves from financial dependence on the Elmhirsts and on the Elmhirsts' advisers, insisting that Jooss should be encouraged to make more effort to do the same. In the years to come this preference sharpened, affecting the manner of the Elmhirsts' continuing and considerable support of dance. Entangled in the same correspondence, Laban told Dorothy that he had started a second book, on his notation, perhaps nudged into it by Dorothy's inquiry.

In the Christmas vacation, with the Blitz in full spate, teachers gathered at Reading with difficulty. Ullmann taught and gave a lecture on Laban's behalf, since he was restricted by the Aliens Order and denied permission to leave Newtown. The Laban Archive reveals the beginning of a highly significant trend in the collaboration between Laban and his younger col-league. She became his spokeswoman. Text after text can be found in Laban's hand of notes for lectures to be delivered by her. Her neatly written full texts from which she read lie beside them. The developing relationship between these two was a remarkable one. They were mentor and disciple, he with an international liberal outlook, she with a Germanic and somewhat authoritarian view of life not far from the surface. He told her what to say and teach, while she nurtured him, looked after his domestic needs, and learned. Her talents lay firstly in finding contacts and avenues for his work, with profound diligence, and secondly in leading training classes for teachers, superbly. The weak link in this otherwise efficient way of working was apparent to Laban from the beginning but possibly not to her, and perhaps not to the public absorbing her classes: that she worked entirely from received knowledge. The detail of the material that he supplied for her classes is quite remarkable. He never did such a thing for anyone else. In Germany, Wigman, Gleisner, Bereska and Knust were all set free to find their own ways. The later British colleagues and apprentices, of which Diana Jordan, Jean Newlove, Geraldine Stephenson, Marion North, Warren Lamb, Joan Russell and myself are examples, were all set off to make individual interpretations and developments of what each had experienced and understood of Laban's concepts and methods. Ullmann, in contrast, saw herself as the only one who really understood him, the only true protector of his ideas, a self-view that crystallised on his death but that started here in Newtown through an accident of fate.

This special relationship came about because of weaknesses as well as strengths on both sides. His poor health, his negligible English and his travel restrictions were balanced by her difficulty in appreciating British culture, traditions and behaviour, her lack of academic appreciation of current educational philosophy, and her own authoritarian education. Her devotion to Laban, which shifted from protective to possessive, was both an asset and a stumbling block. But on the positive side, their combined gifts, together with his charisma, were to become formidable.

1940 ended with one positive note for them both, for they found a much better place to live – Rock House, just outside Newtown in the hamlet of Llanllwchaiarn, with rooms in a large ex-school/farmhouse with grounds. Rock House became a base for nearly two years from which a gruelling hand-to-mouth existence was operated. Ullmann, not even permitted at that time to own a bicycle, had her own two feet as her only means of keeping in touch with the wider world.

The Ling Physical Education Association used their considerable organising experience to host two conferences in April 1941, the first at Bedford Physical Training College, during which Central European Dance was taught by Betty Meredith-Jones. The second was a landmark conference devoted entirely to 'Modern Dance', held at St Margaret's School, Bushey, at which the leading figures taught: Laban, Ullmann, Louise Soelberg, Diana Jordan, Joan Goodrich, and Douglas Kennedy. Goodrich, the course organiser, had gathered together a remarkable group of participants, people in responsible positions within teacher training as well as educational organisers in the field and keen practitioners. Members of His Majesty's Inspectorate were invited to visit. She could hardly have collected a more influential group. Plans for the promotion of Laban's ideas in British schools were discussed, supported by practical classes. Laban and Ullmann made a very strong impression. Lorna Wilson recalled Laban standing on the stage unrolling a strip of notation and Ullmann reading it apparently spontaneously. Muriel Cuthbertson, a much sought after improvising pianist, accompanied her. It was a magical experience which made a great impact on the conference members. The matter of the name for this kind of work was raised. 'Central European' or 'modern' were thought to be misleading, 'modern' at that time referring to dance in musical comedy or ballroom dancing. Although no conclusions were reached, everyone went away with the firm belief and determination that this work, whatever it might be called, should be available to British children.

What Laban had failed to achieve in Germany, namely dance for all children in the general education system, seemed possible in Britain. Whereas he had been highly successful through privately run Laban schools in Germany, here support was coming from the most influential centres. A substantial stir in the teaching training methods and in courses for serving teachers was the inevitable result of the spearheading work of Goodrich, Jordan and their collaborators. Laban was especially drawn to Diana Jordan, recognising in her a fellow artist, a spiritually aware person, as he vouchsafed in a letter to her.

Ullmann found herself in demand. By June 1941 she told Dorothy Elmhirst that she was teaching at St Gabriel's College, now evacuated from London to Darlington in the north of England, giving classes at Welshpool and at Aberystwyth University, and on the lawn at Rock House. Her travel difficulties from rural Newtown can hardly be imagined, but by June she was at least permitted to own a bicycle.

Thoughts of starting a training centre were mooted. Laban's models ranged from the one room at Oetenbachgasse in which he had started in Zurich to the well-positioned Berlin Choreographisches Institut or even the envisaged High School. Anything was possible. The participants at Bushey had suggested an unambitious centre in the first place with a goal to enable people 'to gain knowledge of the work'. In the event Ullmann opened a 'centre' at Rock House, with one pupil, Betty Meredith-Jones. Laban had started in Stuttgart in 1920 with one pupil, so such individual treatment was not strange to him. He knew well that revolutions may start from small beginnings.

Meredith-Jones was at that time looking for ways of introducing freer movement into her recreational classes. Housed in a caravan in the Rock House grounds, by the river Wye, she cycled with Ullmann daily to the church hall in Newtown for three hours of practical work, spending the evenings with Laban on theory. It was an utterly life-enhancing experience for her, leading to a lifetime of work in movement. Veronica Sherborne was similarly propelled into an innovative movement career. As Veronica Tyndale-Biscoe, a student at Bedford, she kept a diary of her training. For 8 July 1941 she jotted 'doubtful' of her first encounter with Ullmann there. By 11 July the entry on the course read, 'I've loved every minute of it. Life is really worth living during weeks such as this.' The power of their teaching was prodigious.

In August, a three-week Modern Dance Holiday course was offered, using the church hall and the Rock House lawn. The training pattern of Germany reappeared, for here, as there, holiday courses offered a popular if incomplete way of learning. Ullmann taught three hours of choreutics in the morning and three of eukinetics in the afternoon, plus an early morning body training. The dynamics of her teaching was 'terrific', her impact 'electric'. She taught something that was seen as relevant to adult life, not exercises for children, to which physical education people were accustomed. She enthused, she enlightened. The whole event was different from anything these young women had ever experienced before.

The Rock House course was the first in which Laban had been involved for longer than a few days. According to one participant, Barbara Cox, he sat on the floor, pointed at the seven students, demanding 'Dance!' In alphabetical order they did, one at a time. Laban's English was 'appalling'. As a figure, he was bizarre, a haggard, monosyllabic evaluator, not of exercises but of freely created movement. The critique was not of a task being right or wrong but on a quite personal level, about possibilities for that individual. His strangeness, plus Ullmann's protection of him, put him in a position one-removed from the student, somehow special.

Jordan, Goodrich and Ullmann decided that an organisation devoted to running such courses should be inaugurated, no doubt to free them of dependence on the Physical Education Association. Modern Dance Holiday Courses came into being, to play a crucial role for ten or more years. 'Diana [Jordan] was the real educationist amongst us,' was Ullmann's view. Joan Goodrich was described as 'a very fine dancer, rhythmic, elegant and full of verve, with a glowing quality'. With Ullmann, the three made quite a team.

Throughout the autumn Ullmann ploughed ahead with her mission, through the increasing opportunities in the teacher training domain. In the meantime Laban had been contacted by Frederick Lawrence, a management consultant concerned with work efficiency in industry, their correspondence having started through Lawrence's professional contact with the Elmhirsts for their Rural Industries projects. Lawrence was impressed by Laban's fresh views on movement analysis and his ability to notate work patterns on paper. He saw it as a possible solution to the ineffectiveness of the present methods that relied on film and verbal description. In December 1941, Lawrence wrote to Christopher Martin, the Elmhirst administrator, that he hoped to collaborate with Laban on 'joint efforts' and that thereby Laban could earn and cease to need an allowance. Laban was enthusiastic. His interest in craftsmanship and occupational rhythms was long standing, starting with his observations in childhood, continuing in his connections with the Werkbund in Munich and his beloved procession of crafts and guilds in Vienna in 1929. Here, he divulged to Dorothy Elmhirst, was his opportunity 'to further some social intentions' that he had been harbouring and to contribute to 'the national defence' of his adoptive country. Lawrence was a man, and Laban enjoyed male thinking and male company; indeed he needed it to counterbalance the female world of dance education.

Britain in 1941 was in the throes of an all-out war effort. Everyone was engaged in work of some kind towards 'beating the Hun'. All were besought to maximise every opportunity to increase production, from building one more Spitfire aircraft, to knitting one more pair of oiled wool socks for the Navy, to squeezing one more evacuee into the spare room, to 'digging for victory' by turning the tennis court into a vegetable patch and a chicken run. Everyone had a role to play, and women found themselves confronted by unimagined employment challenges. The use of Work Study Methods, so-called time-and-motion study, introduced from America through the ideas of F. W. Taylor, increased in most industries to address the demands of wartime output and to find ways of enabling women to undertake tasks in heavy industries, hitherto a male domain. Laban was in the right place at the right time. Ever curious and ever a pragmatist, he found an absorbing challenge through his collaborations with Lawrence. Paton Lawrence & Co. were located in the industrial city of Manchester. Being in the category of alien person permitted to engage in 'industry or agriculture', Laban was allowed to travel there without special dispensation. The first problem he tackled with Lawrence was at Tyresoles Ltd, in which women were having to undertake heavy lifting jobs usually done by men. Laban introduced the use of momentum. Through swinging movements of the whole body the women were able to achieve what the men had done through leverage in the arms. The two men discussed rhythm and the need for swing (the inadequate translation of *Schwung*) in women's work. But 'swing' was a difficult word to introduce into industry because of its connotations with popular music and dancing. 'Lilt' became the agreed term for what he introduced to replace brute force. And his method worked. Soon he was employed as 'Adviser to Paton Lawrence & Co., 90 Deansgate, Manchester', once more an independent pioneering and earning man. But still unwell.

1942 began with a January Modern Dance Holiday Course at Moreton Hall, Oswestry, a school that took seriously the place of the arts in education. The now familiar team of three 'together with Mr von Laban himself' taught 'technique and group work'. What is remembered by Elma Casson and Lorna Wilson is his teaching of the *Polovtsian Dances* from Borodin's *Prince Igor*. His stimulating direction of them all in his adaptation of his original choreography for the Berlin Opera Ballet's professional dancers was quite dramatic and memorable. What a different experience from triple runs in threes down the gymnasium! Additionally, Dr Carl Vogel, a Czech refugee, joined them to work with sculpture, and Dr C. E. Salt with poetry. Did Laban have his 'Tanz, Ton, Wort, Plastik' school in mind? The question as to whether Modern Dance was a technique or not was discussed, Laban showing, apparently to satisfaction, how its technique dealt with the basis of movement rather than consisting of a series of technical movements.

The problem of closely associating dance with physical education, well known to Laban in Germany and vigorously fought by him there, was already surfacing. Holiday course members not from a physical education background, of which Barbara Cox, a lecturer in education, was an example, were alarmed by the number of gymnasts on the course and the quality of their artistry, or rather, as Cox saw it, their lack of it. There were indeed exceptions, but a problematic situation for Laban's work as art was brewing. It has to be remembered that Ullmann was not trained as a choreographer, nor had she made works, nor had she been a performing member of a company although she was closely associated with the Ballets Jooss. Her strength lay in the Labanite creative way of training the dancer but not in interpreting roles or in providing dances that had something to say to an audience. Significant gesture to Ullmann meant a universal gesture, based on movement's fundamental principles of the inherent harmony in shape and dynamics, not one of comment or satire, comedy or pathos. Laban, of course, was a choreographer, a theatre man, but inexperienced physical education teachers were not his accustomed material. The Tanzbühne dancers, the *Kammertänzerinnen*, the opera dancers, were all theatre-oriented young people with dramatic courage, and, in Berlin at least, a first-class technique. With these, he had made all manner of successful works. Apparently, he stayed one place removed from Ullmann's pupils, just as he had done from his Labanschulen pupils in Germany. It was only the students of the Choreographisches Institut, that is, potential professionals, who had really interested him, the schools being a means of livelihood. Was Modern Dance in British education to be an art form or not? The question would have to be raised. At this point, 1942, he did not introduce work with a theatrical bite at all. He proposed that Ullmann should teach the amateur movement choir material, which she did. Goodrich's experiences in Dresden learned through the dramatic expression of Wigman she passed on to dance-oriented Bedford students from 1935 onwards. Elizabeth Swallow and Mary Baron are examples of many who by now were teaching dance as art in secondary schools, creating dance dramas and movement choirs for the whole school. I was one of Baron's passionate schoolgirl *Ausdruckstänzerinnen*. The Wigman/Goodrich/Baron line was no British version of *Körperkultur*, but nearer the style of the Tanzbühne Laban.

Ullmann's work throughout the spring continued apace with success, despite the bombing and the increased austerity of the war. The costly Battle of the Atlantic between the German U-boats and convoys bringing essential supplies, oil, food and raw materials to Britain was at its most bitter, increasing the shortness of supply of all commodities. A packet of biscuits was an untold luxury, a lemon or an onion a rarity to be queued for, a banana an occasional ration available only for children. Ullmann continued. She taught regularly at Chelsea Physical Training College, evacuated from London to Borth in Wales, and visited Bedford Physical Training College, Laban advising her what to teach. The emerging call was for 'dance as a means of education of the whole person'. While educationists were more and more supportive, the ordinary person in the street was bemused. The local newspaper at Newtown could make little of her response to an interview question, that she taught universal movement forms with cosmic significance.

Laban was wrestling with his passport problems. His acquired German nationality was obnoxious to him. He applied to revert to Hungarian citizenship but was refused, his birthplace no longer being in that country, and so started a lengthy campaign to gain Czechoslovak papers. Success would have enabled him to shift from the status of alien to one of ally. But it was not so easy, with far too many applicants in the queue. He had to continue with 'German' firmly on his identification documents. The correspondence shows that he had entirely lost touch with his children, except Juana, being unable to give their whereabouts or professions.

Meanwhile, the Tyresoles project continued, Ullmann assisting. It developed into experiments towards the design of a training method for the women workers: 'Lilt in Labour'. They tried out exercises with wooden mallets designed to develop swing in the whole body, co-operation and a sense of rhythm. The *Tyresoles Laban/Lawrence Training Manual* was the first of many company-specific manuals written to enable the instructors from the factory floor to lead purpose-designed classes with their work force. Laban still had severe restrictions on his freedom to travel. His Aliens Card was peppered with police stamps to verify that he had arrived in Manchester, or in Totnes, to work for a day with Lawrence, and had again returned to Newtown. Special permission had to be sought by Lawrence for Laban to return to Totnes for a protracted period to develop the method 'Laban/Lawrence Industrial Rhythm', *in situ* with the Rural Industries on the Dartington estate. He got the permit, just as nearby Exeter was being pounded in the Blitz.

Once there, he set up a workforce training programme with Ullmann over June and July 1942, Betty Meredith-Jones acting as assistant. The Dartington Hall Sawmills and Green Crops were the departments studied. Hand planting cabbages, lifting potatoes, pruning fruit trees, thinning beetroot, filling sacks with peas, picking cherries needed both the movement and visual stresses and strains to be considered. Laban designed job-specific 'operational exercises' to increase efficiency. A group of women selected as trainers were taught the material to pass on to their peers, under the supervision of Winsome Bartlett whom the Estate appointed as Women's Welfare Officer.

The idea of movement training for operators was not unfamiliar. Because women, hitherto mostly housewives, were the predominant labour force, some sort of training was essential, not only to develop the kind of physical strength they would need but also to develop precision in detailed work, to cope with monotonous repetition, to observe industrial secrecy and to work as part of a team. The idea of 'lilt in labour' was not disassociated from 'workers' playtime' or 'music while you work' played onto the factory floor on the wireless, in that it promoted a sense of rhythm and lightened the step in a long day shift, or even longer night shift. The brochure promised that it would 'bring that swing and lilt in labour, which makes efficiency a pleasure'.

Laban urgently needed to relocate himself, finding a home in remote Wales extremely inconvenient as the opportunities and duties from Paton Lawrence increased. The question was, to where? Manchester presented an obvious choice, London being an unlikely second, but his recent contact with Gilbert and Irene Champernowne, through the Elmhirsts, complicated the choice. They had set up, in May, the Withymead Centre for Psychotherapy and Art Therapy, Laban being asked to advise on the use of dance and movement there. This appealed to him as another challenge. Withymead, near Exeter, not far from Totnes, was an attractive possibility but too far from the industrial heartlands of Britain. Finally, on 17 September 1942, Laban and Ullmann took possession of a flat at 131 Palatine Road, West Didsbury, a southern well-to-do part of Manchester.

They had already discovered that Sylvia Bodmer lived in the same district of Manchester, as the wife of a doctor with an established practice. Bodmer, of Swiss origin, a highly intelligent and educated woman, had trained with Laban at Gleschendorf and Hamburg, becoming a soloist with the Tanzbühne Laban in the pioneering twenties. She was delighted to meet up with him again and he shared her delight. She brought with her a wide experience of groupwork, having run the Frankfurt Movement Choirs in association with the city opera for some ten years. She was able to contribute to the theatrical and artistic side of dance, an excellent complement to Ullmann's strength as a trainer. Bodmer was also an amateur mathematician, able to discuss with Laban whatever complex choreutic problems occupied him at the time. She soon became one of the team. In fact she was a teaching member of the second Modern Dance Holiday Course at Moreton Hall, held just before the move to Palatine Road. Also invited to the Moreton Hall course was Lawrence, who talked of the connection of movement as art with movement in industry, so offering a broader view of Laban's work and culture in general than had hitherto been provided on a dance or physical education holiday course.

No. 131 Palatine Road offered more possibilities to Laban and Ullmann. They gave private classes there in the basement, and could travel far more readily from such a metropolitan centre. The Paton Lawrence connection offered Laban work with W. C. Holmes & Co. Ltd from October 1942 that continued until 1946. A foundry in Huddersfield, with both heavy and light parts to the production line, Holmes & Co. brought him, over the years, into the problems of piecework and bonus calculations, key issues likely to trigger industrial unrest. He designed, with Lawrence, a measuring test for speed, skill, attitude and reliability, appropriate for each part of the assembly line, and concentrated on getting each worker into a part of the line for which he or she was compatible in terms of effort and for which the bonus could most easily be earned.

He started with Hoover Ltd in November, training their time-and-motion men in Laban/Lawrence Industrial Rhythm, and with St Olave's Curing and Preserving Co. Ltd. His whole industrial endeavours were consolidated by the publication of the booklet *Laban/Lawrence Industrial Rhythm* in which Laban's beliefs on movement and work were put forward, tempered by Lawrence's knowledge on how to express ideas to management. He sent a signed copy to Miss Cutting, in appreciation of her attentions to his English.

A young trainee, Jean Newlove, began her apprenticeship with Laban, following in the tradition of those before her. Instead of being sent to finish off choreography, as the young Jooss had been, or to start a movement choir as had Gleisner, or like Knust to develop the notation, or Loeszer to be a dancing partner, Newlove was despatched, on occasion, to Dartington Rural Industries to sort out problems there and to keep Winsome Bartlett appraised of the developments in Industrial Rhythm. Like all Laban's apprentices, she did whatever was needed at that moment, and learned as she went. Working with Laban on a one-to-one basis over several years, as Newlove did, and as Wigman had done before her, had the result one would now expect: it set her off on an extensive career in the area of the arts of movement for which she had a gift – movement in theatre.

From Laban's intense study at this time two strands of analysis emerged: the patterns of the job to be done and the habitual patterns of the worker's personal behaviour. For the first strand, the stopwatch had been the main equipment for time-and-motion study experts, who advised the elimination of all extraneous movement other than that essential to the task itself. The ever tighter movement patterns thus achieved should have led to ever faster operations and so to greater output per person per shift. But it did not. It led to stress and fatigue, error, to unnecessarily long 'toilet breaks', and to absenteeism. What Laban suggested instead was revolutionary.

It was concepts of harmony that he applied. If the job required a downward pressure then he introduced, somewhere in the movement phrase, an upward movement and released pressure, as a preparation or as a recovery. If a twist to the left were necessary, one to the right should be added. Bigger movements, not smaller, were advocated; more rather than less. His ideas on eukinetics, developed in Germany as *Antrieb*, or the inner impulse, he refined as a theory and practice of *effort*. Quicker, stronger, more direct movements, prioritised by traditional time-and-motion engineers, he discarded. Instead, moving with all varieties of quickness and slowness, strength and lightness, directness and indirectness, free and controlled flow were seen by him to be essential to enable a human being to survive the rigours of the intense industrial war effort. While each operation might take seven per cent longer, the operator would be able to sustain work throughout the shift so that at the end of the day output was increased and the worker would feel less like a robot and more like a whole person.

For the second strand, the workers' personal behaviour, effort analysis was again used to observe the unique patterns of each operative, and compared as compatible or incompatible with the job to be done – an approach never attempted by time-and-motion people because they did not have the means to reveal the choreutic and eukinetic content of movement, nor to see the connection between job effort and behaviour effort. Laban/ Lawrence Industrial Rhythm discussed the misplacement of workers as inhumane. Evaluations like clumsy, weak, slow were adjectives that evidenced poor selection methods, not worker inadequacies. Manual and clerical workers, as well as management could be assessed and placed in a compatible work situation where it was believed that job satisfaction might replace frustration and stress.

To make these leaps in management practice Laban had to adapt his recording methods. His dance notation was no help as it stood, for small arm movements with tools and materials on a conveyor belt at chest height were a different proposition from large, full-bodied dance. He had never had a graphic means for eukinetics beyond words, which were quite inadequate for this degree of refinement. The surviving documents show how he experimented with several written means, coming up with operation graphs that an engineer could follow. Bodmer's papers brim with signs and symbols that she tried out with him. These became, by 1947, his simplified version, the effort graph, as published in his book *Effort*.

Independently of Laban's own research, his influence was growing slowly and steadily in the educational field. In Germany, expansion had always been coloured by his own involvement, his own electric personality, or through a Tanzbühne dancer or a qualified Choreographisches Institut graduate. In Britain growth occurred without his personal touch. Dance Clubs associated with his name were springing up with no direct input. One in Doncaster, excellent in its own way, was an offshoot of the teacher training college there; one in Birmingham was led by Lilla Bauer, an ex-Jooss dancer. The problem of dilution, or interpretation, of his radical ideas by partially trained people was already in place by 1942, as well as the beginnings of what was to become disaffection between those encountering Laban's ideas via Ullmann and others meeting them through a Wigman or a Jooss/Leeder artist. People devoted to dance as a means of education and those inspired to work in dance as art did not always see eye to eye.

Before 1942 ended, Elsie Palmer, organiser of physical education for the county borough of Manchester, had arranged weekly evening classes advertised as a 'Recreative Course in Modern Dance' for her teachers, in Central Manchester. She did not hesitate to employ Ullmann on a regular basis. Palmer's role in developing dance in Manchester schools, and later throughout Lancashire, was crucial. Starting as a self-styled 'games girl' working first in community centres during the depression years and later as a school's organiser, she had observed the revolution of the 1930s in child-centred classroom teaching. She was struck by the discrepancy between the behaviour of interested self-motivated children there, and their teacher-motivated, tolerating behaviour in the physical education class. She was well on the way to finding a revolutionary method for her teachers when she discovered modern dance at the holiday course at Moreton Hall. By January 1943 she had a year-long twice-weekly course set up, now titled 'Modern Educational Dance', for which forty-five teachers enrolled. They proved a loyal and inspired group, Palmer joining in every session.

The third Modern Dance Holiday Course, held at Moreton Hall in the Christmas vacation of 1942–43, was attended by over fifty participants. Now divided into three groups, elementary, intermediate and advanced, they took part in four practical classes a day, ending with notation from Laban himself. A new ingredient to the course was a demonstration class with children given by Ullmann and what was reported as 'a brilliant lecture' by Laban on 'the origins of dance from the centres of ancient culture'. He wanted to locate dance education in dance history as a whole, to give people a sense of where they were in an ongoing process of change. Also, for them, it placed Laban as one man in a tradition of spasmodically arising radical thinkers, Noverre and Fokine being his immediate predecessors. Bodmer's notes reveal that he also planned with her a dance-drama for her to rehearse. Dramatic tension was the key. 'Damnation and Revolt', 'Possessiveness and Greed', 'Condemnation', 'Distrust and Jealousy', 'Scepticism and Heartlessness', 'Ambition and Desire' were the titles of episodes. Details of the movement elements to be used for each expression neatly display her tutored preparation.

1943 was a year of consolidation for Laban's industrial employment. He worked for Mars Confectionery on how best to wrap chocolate bars, at Dunlop improving work for women, at J. Lyons on food production, in addition to his regular Industrial Rhythm clients. The correspondence shows that the Ministry of Supply had to approve a German national giving advice on sensitive war work such as the design and manufacture of rubber tyres for military vehicles at the huge but secret complex of Fort Dunlop in Birmingham.

Laban continued to prepare with Ullmann what she should teach. A course in Birmingham given in March 1943 was typical. His notes include what content he advised for children aged six, ten and twelve years old, including special work for boys. That he had never personally taught children was apparently not an issue with the course participants. Nor, in all probability, did they know. Ullmann gave a course of fifteen classes at Hendon, with Laban's detailed notes for teaching 'exercises 1 to 56', over eight weeks. She read a speech for him at a conference on 'The Contribution of Physical Education to the Education of Man'. It was his content, her delivery. Why did he not give it himself? Because, after internment began for aliens, he was put into the category of those only allowed to work in industry or agriculture. He had to get special permission, which was not easily granted, every time he needed to do anything else. To get his work heard he had to have a spokesperson. Ullmann was willing to be it.

Articles on Laban's educational work began to appear by 1943. Bronwen Lloyd Williams, headmistress of Moreton Hall School, wrote in the *Journal of Physical Education* on twentieth-century pioneers of dance, listing Laban with Wigman, Jooss, Bodenwieser, Duncan, St Denis, Shawn, Graham, Humphrey and Weidman. For her, Laban's position was amongst fellow dance artists, not theorists or educationists. She also put her view that his radical research on workers and work in industry offered an insight into what true education of the person through movement might be. In her position of leadership, she had to decide what should be taught to her pupils under the heading of physical education, and she could no longer ignore the changes to the established curriculum that knowledge of his work made imperative.

It was during 1943 that a third avenue of exploration – drama – opened for Laban. John English invited him to adjudicate amateur drama performances at the Highbury Little Theatre in July and to teach the actors. Laban agreed with enthusiasm, although he had to go through the rigmarole of getting consent to be away from Manchester for one night. So began a fruitful use of his theatrical talents in *Wort* rather than *Tanz*. At last he could use his sense of comedy, satire, pathos and caricature, and here he could work with men as performers as well as with women.

The momentum of educational work continued and increased. He and

Ullmann were both in demand. His reputation grew, controversially. Many teachers in favour of his new ideas were considered 'over the top' in their enthusiasm. This evolution was not going to be a quiet one but a well-refereed revolution. The main opposition came from men in physical education, who saw competition as uppermost and creativity as a side issue. More generally it was impossible for some teachers who had not themselves tried to create in movement to conceive of the value of a school hall full of children doing their own thing, with apparently no discipline. The yardstick of excellence in physical education was about to be shifted. Where regimented unison, quick response to commands and good imitation had been the criteria, another radically different set of values was to be put in place, operating concurrently, or in some instances replacing them.

In one opportunity, in May, Laban had the challenge to present his ideas in contrast to other popular dance methods, of which Ruby Ginner's revival of ancient Greek dance forms was one, Madge Atkinson's Natural Movement was another. Ullmann read his script. In July she taught at Sheffield, with material straight out of his 1926 book *Choreographie*. Crystals, their use as spatial orientation in space and as structures of universal significance to the human state were studied, ballet's *port de bras* being taken as the starting point for Laban's dimensional A and B scales in space. Again and again, he located his work in relation to that of others, but so often his students failed to follow suit, so isolating his work as an independent phenomenon.

The report of the summer school, the fourth Modern Dance Holiday Course at Moreton Hall, shows that 'physical, mental and inspirational approaches' were taken by individual teachers and brought together in group work. Laban taught movement observation and 'gave the students the understanding, and feeling, for the dance as a whole'. His notes show what he covered. The primary quality of modern dance he stated as joyous and refreshing; it should aim to form right movement habits and engender a co-operative spirit. The development of a sense of rhythm, by which he meant effort rhythm, should play a fundamental part in dance teaching. The shapes arising from rhythm should be sought, as should the vitalising function of stopping and action, or stillness and stir, as well as the contrast of contracting with releasing, of stance with stepping out. Inner rhythm could be switched on and skills of observation learned by dancing in this way. The universality lay in the knowledge that all nature followed these same fundamentals, as man had throughout his existence. The letters I T Y X and the figures 1 2 3 and 4 he gave as fundamental symbols captured in our written languages and built into our movement language as expressed in dance. (Taken into movement, the letters are fundamental body positions, and the numbers are the straight number 1, the twisting number 2, the curved number 3, and the angular number 4.)

The course seems to have been an important one for the future of dance education. Distinction was deliberately made between educational and recreational dance. Lawrence spoke, Vogel and Salt contributed, and Lilla Bauer with her Jooss artistry and Ilse Laredo, a Wigman dancer, gave a recital. The breadth offered by this course could not be missed. It is remembered as inspirational.

On a technical point, the motion factors were given by Laban as 'energy, space, flow and speed', later to be settled as weight, space, flow and time. Ergonomic language seems to have been the influence at this point. He changed his mind several times on these technical terms, not wanting to settle on any one. But in the end, in 1947, he did – one might say unwisely, for it closed a concept that needed to stay open, for words appropriate for effort in industry, in theatre, in therapy and in the school hall are not identical.

At this time, the Withymead Centre for Psychotherapy through the arts was in correspondence with him, kindling his interest in developing his observation of an individual's effort profile. Effort observation was already a workable tool for assessment, but he looked at it anew as an instrument towards designing treatment through therapeutic intervention. He had no opportunity to travel to Withymead so he tried out his personality assessment methods on Sylvia Bodmer and Diana Jordan at Moreton Hall. He chose people he knew well and regarded as colleagues.

An effort profile was, indeed still is, a highly personal profile. It seeks to reveal how a person deals with the world through his or her effort behaviour, which is largely made up of unconscious effort choices. At the fourth Modern Dance Holiday Course Laban chose two thoroughly grounded individuals as guinea pigs; someone less secure might find the effort profile too much of a self-revelation, both fascinating and disturbing. People are drawn to self-knowledge and understanding. For the untutored, something like an effort profile was as mysterious as a horoscope. Am I like that? Will I respond like that? Is that the real me? These questions could easily be followed by: how does he know? The immense skill of Laban's eye, built up over at least forty years of looking at movement, gave him techniques simply not available to other people, certainly not to people with only a few months' summer schooling behind them. He appeared to be able to see into another person in a way nobody else could. Bodmer and Jordan knew him too well to do anything other than take an interest on a professional level; but would everyone? 'Mystique' is a word used of the aura that some people saw around Laban. His acute and apparently mysterious observation skills were one reason for it. Mary Wigman had not called him 'the magician' for nothing.

Notes for this summer school show how strenuously Laban advised Ullmann to go beyond 'moving' into 'dancing'. Group work should be more than moving together, he urged. He wrote the words 'atmosphere' and 'collective life' beside the plans for a group dance. 'The shell of awkwardness' of students needed to be shed. They must be led into the exhilaration 'of the inner rhythm'. He did not mention the 'land of silence', but that is where he wanted to lead them.

During 1943 the Manchester Dance Circle was formed, most members being teachers from the Greater Manchester area. Joining the classes were members of Joan Littlewood's Theatre Union, a highly proficient and radical amateur drama group. Creative movement formed part of their regular training, reflecting Littlewood's interest in Laban's work, and the Dance Circle offered a chance to study further. Sylvia Bodmer played a leading role in the Manchester Dance Circle from the beginning. While it was to become, after the war, a recreational group, in 1943 it was a platform for Ullmann's training classes, for Bodmer's movement choir works, and for Laban's lectures. It was definitely educative, informative and recreative. Over the next two years Laban spoke to members on 'Industrial Rhythm', 'Dance and Drama', 'History of Dance', 'The Source of Modern Dance'. Many members also attended Ullmann's weekly class for teachers organised by Elsie Palmer, the majority for the second year running. They were beginning to introduce dance into their schools, slowly, with Palmer's cautious and caring guidance. And what a success their partnership proved to be, for dance in Manchester schools and then Lancashire schools became legendary.

A talk given to the Doncaster Dance Club in the autumn of 1943 illustrates the typical content of similar talks that year. Ullmann gave it, as ever, from Laban's notes. Dance for children was the topic. She outlined its goals, struggling with the concept of body–mind unity for which English has, or had then, no established word. Phenomenology was not a well-known subject. Phenomenology of dance had as yet never been mentioned, but that was what Laban wanted to get across. Universality was again a theme, with quotations from Herbert Spencer, Plato, and Christ in a gnostic hymn. Laban's Rosicrucian beliefs were never far from the surface. Education was for him an education of the whole person, including the spirit.

Religious overtones could be found here, just as they had been in Zurich during the First World War. Twenty-five years made no difference.

Herbert Read's influential book *Education Through Art*, published in 1943, tackled issues central to Laban's tenet that dance was a means to education. Read knew nothing of Laban at the time of writing (1941, before Laban became established in Britain), but he regarded movement as central to education in general and to education through the arts in particular. He quoted Dalcroze, the most widely known movement/music pioneer, as the one person who dared to embrace Plato's call to give aesthetic education a central place in developing the child's appreciation of and dexterity in 'rhythm, harmony and grace'. By 1957 Laban was found sharing a platform with Read at a conference of the Society for Education Through the Arts, his practice recognised as one step nearer the Platonic ideal than that of Dalcroze. Read encompassed both Platonic values and Jungian psychology, as did Laban. Read's writing on children's art became standard reading for teachers in training, strengthening the already fertile ground for Laban's art of movement. Read warned that value given to logic and to rational thinking, so strong and well established in educational circles, countermanded the call for art and the aesthetic to be recognised as the way children comprehend the world. Laban knew the problem only too well from his struggles with the education elite in Germany, but in Britain, through the convincing voice of respected educationists like Read, Laban's way forward, supported by his colleagues, was more hopeful than ever before.

1944 and 1945 continued with a strengthening of movement in industry and movement in education, but no significant expansion was evident in movement as therapy or in drama. Classes for two or three pupils continued in the basement of 131 Palatine Road. Mary Elding, a Theatre Union member, recalls an occasion when Laban taught there. He gave a short task prepared individually, each dancer working in a corner of the small and dreary space. Each danced, and they learned to observe. He enabled them to see how exciting each person's individuality was. 'It was astounding. He opened one's eyes to creativity.'

These two years brought acute pressure for Laban and Ullmann to set up a full-time training institution. Their haphazard hand-to-mouth existence seemed incompatible with the depth of their developing influence on British education. People needed to be trained through a sustained course. Dartington was still thought of as a possible venue, as notes of discussions with Peter Cox on behalf of the Elmhirsts vouchsafe, but these ideas came to naught. Laban wanted an arts environment for his institution, definitely not a physical education one. Goldsmiths' College in London was considered, with Ullmann in mind, for the training of teachers within a physical education department. She was a guest teacher there in 1944. But Lilla Bauer was appointed and so closed that avenue. While Manchester seemed more and more likely to end up as the location, London was vigorously combed for possible accommodation. An agent searched for property in Chelsea, Hampstead and Gower Street, but he reported that London was overcrowded. As the war drew to an inevitable close, anyone wanting to start up an enterprise had to compete for the few available properties standing amidst the bombed sites.

Even to dream of a substantial institution was only possible through the generous offer of one of His Majesty's Inspectors of Schools, Myfanwy Dewey. Discreetly, she offered to give £9000 to £10,000 to a trust for the purpose of starting a College of Movement, informing the Board of Education of her offer. Dewey, a well-educated and cultured woman, was passionately taken with Laban's ideas on dance and movement as a means of education. She did much more than her position required of her to promote them, leading classes and demonstrations herself. A person of some private wealth, she became a benefactor on a personal level as well as a vigorous professional supporter. Her offer could not be taken up, but it kindled dreams. The College of Movement she had in mind seemed to be close in concept to the High School longed for by Laban and Wigman in 1929. Dewey engineered an invitation for Laban to a high-level residential conference run by Westmorland County Education Committee at Langdale, a quiet valley in the Lake District. It was entitled 'Human Relations in Society and Education'. John Trevelyan and John Macmurray, both influential academics, were prominent participants. Laban's speech on 'Movement in Work and the Arts and its Effect on Human Relationships' aroused much interest. This level of intellectual exchange on broad cultural topics was just what Laban needed. In the physical education/dance community he found so little stimulation. Their ideas, not new for him anyway, were mostly initiated by him. Here he was challenged. The College of Movement as discussed with Dewey needed faculty and support of the calibre and breadth of vision of this conference. Laban knew that he would never get the kind of vigorous institution he wanted if he allowed his work to be swamped by current specialist interests.

Documents show that he wanted a research institute to run alongside the College. He hoped for Ullmann and Jordan to join him on the faculty, Meredith-Jones and Newlove to be added as student assistants. He made a feasibility plan including detailed financial estimates and the risks to be taken by sponsors. He thought through the problem of educating different kinds of students in the same institution, grant-aided qualifying teachers with independent dancers and industrial students gaining quite different qualifications, if any. Would it be better to be independent or to settle for a host institution? These administrative problems filled a part of his mind while the other was on the stuff of movement itself, as always. He was, as he said, an artist and a researcher, not an administrator. How to balance incompatible needs and wishes was a familiar scenario to him. 1945 was no different from any other turning point in his big-dipper career.

12

Post-War Avenues

Manchester and Addlestone, 1945–1958

At last the war was over. VE Day (Victory in Europe), celebrated on 8 May 1945, opened up better prospects for establishing a school. The spirit of renewal pervaded the country, combined with the extreme austerity of the immediate post-war years. Laban had met both feelings before, in post-war Stuttgart. His dedication to spiritual regeneration, to co-operation between people, to the equality of all men, reflected the feel of the day. Post-war Britain was astir with fresh ideas, not least in the arts and in education. The General Election held in July 1945 resulted in a landslide victory for Labour on a platform of radical social change. Before long Britain was fully a welfare state, with National Insurance, National Health, National Assistance and major industries nationalised. The 1945 Education Act instructed teachers to educate children not only according to their age but also their individual abilities and aptitudes. Laban's work offered a direct expression of these passionately held hopes for the future by a war-weary electorate.

Scattered over the country, individuals enthusiastic for new ideas in education were appointed to positions of responsibility. Alec Clegg became Chief Education Officer for the West Riding of Yorkshire County Council, to begin the first post-war education year. He immediately contacted Laban with a plea for help for teachers of dance in his area. This north-easterly part of Britain was to become a fine example of what inspired teaching could achieve, influenced by Laban's philosophy of the role of the movement arts in child-centred education. Having appointed Diana Jordan as a colleague in Worcestershire, Clegg knew her qualities. Before long she was on his staff again, spearheading the dance programme, but not before she had started the Midlands Dance Group for people in Birmingham and Worcester. She immediately inaugurated the West Riding Movement Study Group, where people danced but also learned, considered and discussed. West Riding was to become a centre of excellence for the arts in education,

233

matching, but quite different from, the excellence of the school work in physical education and dance in Lancashire inspired by Elsie Palmer.

Many of Joan Goodrich's ex-Bedford students were now well established in teaching posts in both schools and colleges, influential at grass roots level. Joan Donaldson pioneered dance at the Liverpool specialist physical education college. Lorna Wilson, having taught at the general college of Bishop Otter, Chichester, had begun the task of introducing dance to Dartford Physical Education College students. The mood in the colleges had changed. The war had altered for ever the pre-war staid atmosphere and restraining practices. The influence of the American troops posted all over Britain with their distinct culture was infectious. Their relaxed way of moving, their informality, their be-bopping, their jazz, acted as an incentive to the English young ladies of the specialist Physical Education Colleges to 'undo their stays' and show the world that they were ready for something new. The moment was right for an explosion of expression of self in movement. But the old guard was not so sure.

At the same time, Basic Movement began to appear as a subject. People were appointed to teach Basic Movement in the teacher training colleges for primary-aged children as well as in the specialist physical education colleges in preparation to teach secondary-aged girls. Basic Movement was seen as a Laban-based solution for gymnastics teachers for what should be taught in place of Swedish drill to satisfy the current educational focus on learning by discovery. It was thought that fundamental skills and dexterity could be taught to beginners through discovery. But Laban's belief in movement as the expression of spiritual values was absent. His lectures on his work in industry may have contributed to the experiments in Basic Movement. He distinguished between job effort and individual effort, objective and subjective, functional and expressive, but also showed how related they were through effort. While expressive movement clearly led to dance and drama, functional movement led to sport and apparatus work in the gymnasium. Was there a form of movement neither truly expressive nor truly functional that could be regarded as 'basic'? Elma Casson regrets that this trial and error period of applying Laban's movement themes to gymnastics occurred in such a public arena. Inspectors and peers had access to the teaching experiments long before she and her co-experimenter Mary Fraser had sorted out what they wanted to sort out. Laban, aware of the attempts being made, asked Casson to tell him what she thought gymnastics was about so that he could advise her how to approach the problem. She recalls unhappily that at that point she was not able to answer. He appears to have allowed the muddle to run its course. Elsie Palmer, reflecting ten years later, described how a child in a physical education lesson had responded to a 'basic' movement task with dramatic movement, a possible response but a misplaced one from the teacher's viewpoint. Such was the confusion created by enthusiasm and premature exposure. Lorna Wilson suggests that Basic Movement was an idealistic but unrealistic dream.

As 1945 continued and the Modern Dance Holiday Courses and short weekend courses ran, the fruitful relationship between Laban and the British Drama League began. A course in Bournemouth, in which a 'Dance Fantasy' was created, succeeded beyond expectations. Notes show how Laban planned it all, he and Ullmann sharing the teaching. The appreciative letter from Frances Mackenzie of the British Drama League show that his talent for mimicry had had a chance to blossom. His understanding of dramatic tension and performers' intent had been fantastic indeed.

In the autumn of 1945 Laban worked at the Manchester Ship Canal. His task focused on the loading and unloading techniques, the co-operation of ships' gangs with crane drivers and shore gangs. He needed to identify the unloading cycle of different cargoes and the places where 'the flow of the dock work' broke down. The foundry of Sykes and Harrison & Co. employed him concurrently. During the year he advised the Royal Air Force on parachute jumping. These assignments earned him sufficient fees to live on, modestly, as well as giving him enjoyment that his skills were usefully employed. He and Lawrence were busy writing a text on their collaboration and its findings. It was marketed first as 'The New Motion Study' but eventually was published, in 1947, as *Effort*. They built up a small establishment, the Management Training Institute in Manchester, where young men and women could learn to use the Laban/Lawrence Industrial Rhythm tests and to design purpose-built Lilt in Labour exercise programmes for particular firms. Management associations started to invite Laban to speak to them, so he found himself having to explain his methods to engineers and shop floor stewards.

By the end of 1946 his industrial work took on another layer. While in the employ of Barlows Ltd, engaged in finding efficient and humane ways to pack large bales, he expanded his job efforts from an exclusively blue collar domain to the clerical and executive ranks of the firm. He was developing from the Lilt in Labour concept, which was entirely for manual workers, to the idea that personality as expressed in effort could be assessed for management as well. The Laban/Lawrence Test set itself out to 'be an original technique of observation and analysis of a candidate's behaviour during an interview'. The purpose was to recruit and create 'contented and efficient staff'. The test identified overt capacities, latent capacities – that is, capacities that could be trained – and lacking capacities. Lacking capacity was not seen as necessarily detrimental for teamwork amongst executives, and could be useful. What one lacked another should have in order to create a balanced team. The terms 'attention, intention, decision and precision' were applied not only to manual jobs but for planning, selling and managing a product. The link with Jung's concepts of psychological types and psychic functions was very close. Although Laban did not acknowledge Jung at this time, he undoubtedly used his psychological research as a starting point, or rather an ending point for explaining his own empirical and insightful observations.

Effort was published by John Macdonald. Written with Lawrence for the industrial market, the text aimed to present a rationale for a fresh approach to time-and-motion study. The term 'war effort' had been in regular use for the duration of the war. It was a concept that Laban described as a 'collective effort' made in response to a common political and economic goal. Effort by individuals of which it comprised 'was often forgotten', he wrote, in contrast to 'the fascination with the struggle for technical mastery of the environment.' His consistent concern for the imbalance between interest in Man and in the Machine came to the surface again in *Effort*.

He stated that 'a person's efforts are visible in the rhythm of his bodily motion', underlining that he saw rhythm as the core of individual effort. In the book he explained systematically the rich variety of movement qualities and flux. He and Lawrence tackled the problem by looking at the appropriateness of the body's exertions to the task to be undertaken. If an object to be deposited was delicate, then light, controlled exertion would be effective; swinging a heavy object required strong, freely flowing actions. Inappropriate effort would result in ineffectual work. (Note their difficulty in finding a word for 'effort'/'exertion'; neither was adequate, but verbal language had nothing better to offer them.) The appropriate path in space, in terms of straight and curved, together with the right proportions of speed in terms of quick and slow instances in the action's rhythm, were further essential ingredients of efficient performance. The book proposed eight basic combinations of 'WST exertions' (weight/space/time exertions) as prototypes against which a sense for the effort varieties and proportions might be developed in the mover and the observer. The variable weight/space/time units suggested by Laban and Lawrence would have made sense to the time-and-motion study engineers, for whom space and time were always considerations. Weight was a new factor completing the basic WST triad, controlling flow being a supplementary element introduced by them.

Laban discussed transitions from one exertion to another and the finesse of exertion qualities through examples around each prototype. Awareness of the bodily feeling of these differences could be taught to give the trainee a sense of the choices available to him – to speed up or slow down, to restrain or free up, to straighten or to curve, to strengthen or to weaken. He illustrated his points with examples from the work place and through a specially devised notation system, the effort graph. The technical discussions in the book are copious and detailed. They make hard reading, for Laban and Lawrence were attempting to do what they themselves stated as impossible: to describe in words the ephemeral qualities of movement. The smell of a rose cannot be described, nor the taste of good wine, nor can the dynamic flux of human movement; and yet they had to try.

'Rhythm speaks to us independently of the task to which it applies,' Laban continued, implying that rhythm is read by an observer as meaningful and reacted to, for example with excitement or depression or calmness. Assessment of our own and our neighbour's effort rhythms lead to 'peaceful intercourse', he wrote, picking up the post-war desire for reconciliation between people on a national level and within industrial relations.

He included both manual and mental exertions in his discussion, so giving his research relevance to both shop floor and management, a politically helpful line to take in a period of post-war industrial trials of strength. 'There is no insuperable gap,' he asserted, 'between the efforts of a workman and those of an administrator.' Both reflection and mental control are effortful. Attending, intending and deciding, all management tasks, take effort and are observable in 'shadow moves'; that is, in subtle changes of weight, space and time in bodily postures and gestures as well as facial expression. The examples he gave of finesse in mental exertions were variants of prototypes. For finesse of attention he mentioned 'surprised, suspicious, enquiring, frightened or sullen' as possible colourings, each visible in shadow moves in WST. He showed the effort connection thus: in the manual workforce operational efforts are predominant and individual shadow moves subsidiary, while in management shadow moves predominate and operational efforts, such as filing, letter-writing, telephoning, are subsidiary.

He concluded the book with a heartfelt statement: 'The inhibition of the freedom of movement and its degradation to a means of production only is a grave error which results in ill health, mental and bodily discord and misery, and thus also in a disturbance of work.' Through art-making in movement this degradation could be reversed, or at least counteracted.

In the meantime, and overlapping with his writing of *Effort*, the decision

237

to launch a school of some sort was so urgent that choices had to be made. It was to be Ullmann's institution, not Laban's. So it was that on 25 December 1945 Ullmann and Lawrence took possession jointly of the first floor of 183–185 Oxford Road, at the All Saints crossroads in Manchester, on a five-year lease. The premises were by no means ideal, comprising a largish room with windows down one side looking onto the main thorough-fare, a smaller studio, an office, a cramped changing space and a dilapi-dated shower area, all over the top of a printing works. This, then, was the Art of Movement Studio, the first British equivalent of a *Bewegungskunst-schule*. It opened with four students in January 1946.

But Laban was not content with this expedient solution. He corre-sponded with Kenneth Barnes of the Royal Academy of Dramatic Art to discuss a centre in London as the Stage Branch of the Manchester institu-tion. He was well aware that he could no longer work in the area of professional dance and dance theatre. His successes with the British Drama League, his January adjudications on the productions of the Metropolitan Vickers Dramatic Association, in the Old Trafford district of Manchester, filled him with the hope that he might find a firm opening for that side of his nature. For the moment nothing came of a London venue, but he had a goal.

The Modern Dance Holiday Course at Sheffield, held in the Christmas school holidays of 1945–46, is still remembered with delight. For Geraldine Stephenson, still a student at Bedford, it was 'just stunning – it knocked me over.' The magic lay in the swishing and swirling groups and Laban's dextrous melding of masses of dancing bodies into one pulsing, breathing unit. The teaching team experimented in co-operative teaching. Laban taught a theme on 'dance drama' in which conflicts and dramatic resolu-tion featured. Ullmann's theme on 'choral dance' entailed creating group work on the harmony of form. Jordan's work on 'community dance' was on response, human relationship and the festive spirit, while Meredith-Jones's theme on 'dance of work' related to folk dance material based on occupational rhythms. Effort training was the central topic of the course; each teacher took ten minutes of the class on a pair of effort opposites and moved on to repeat the material with another group of participants. Dance composition was taught partly by dancing together and partly by watching other people dance together, still related to effort. Every class included 'movement observation', and the chosen dance theme of the teacher was central to each class. 'Observation' sounds clini-cal, but under Laban it was thrilling, an appreciation unfolding from the unique creativity of each individual as the capacity to observe deepened, a positive and eye-opening experience.

It was at Sheffield that Ullmann suggested the formation of a formal organisation to act as a forum for all the people now interested and engaged in Laban's work. The idea was greeted with enthusiasm and a sense that belonging together would strengthen the pioneer mood and safeguard standards. So the Laban Art of Movement Guild was born. During the spring of 1946, 'sitting amongst a carpet of bluebells in Miss Ullmann's garden', its constitution was discussed with Palmer, Lawrence and leading Manchester people. They set ambitious aims: 'to establish the status of teachers and practitioners of the Art of Movement', 'to publish', and 'to inspire research', in the areas of education, industry and art. Laban became the Guild's Life President.

The August Holiday Course, held at Bishop Otter College, near Chichester, was a success, well-attended and participated in with enthusiasm and a sense of pioneering purpose. Bodmer's notes record that Laban undertook personality profiles of his colleagues, Joan Goodrich, Lilla Bauer and Bodmer herself. The language of interpretation is more florid than before, and suggests that he might have combined personality profiles with consulting the oracle of the *I Ching* (The Book of Changes). That Laban threw coins for reading in the *I Ching*, is no secret. It was a knowledge from his youth that he used from time to time, partly for relaxation and partly for confirmation. (I vividly recall Laban, Ullmann and myself tossing the coins one evening in 1953. My reading came out with the title 'youthful folly', which at the time seemed highly appropriate. I cannot recall the other titles exactly, but in essence they came to 'wisdom' for Laban and 'motherliness' for Ullmann.) Bodmer's notes give the descriptive words for Joan Goodrich as tolerance, frolicsome, liveliness, jocundity, triumph, hopeful. Lilla Bauer's include warmth, exuberance, agitation, rapture, fervency, pathos, and lyricism. Sylvia Bodmer's include wildness, turbulent, heroic, solemn, intoxicated, introspection. These suggest rather more than the customary language of the effort-derived profile. They probably ended up as the themes for dramatic dance plays based on their personalities.

Concern was expressed after this Chichester course that Laban was regarded with awe to a degree that was worrisome to some participants. Admiration for his skills and vision was one thing; adoration of him as a charismatic personality was another. This admiration had been with him all his life. He was very attractive, not only in his younger days, as Mary Wigman's diaries remind us, but also in his sixties. His nature, his acceptance of people on their own terms, his sensuous face, his delicate hands, his expressive body, his penetrating eye-contact, could be disarming. Ullmann's original protection of him developed into a distinct attempt to keep other women at bay. The roving eye of his German days was almost dormant, but as he increased in health, mentally and physically, his eye did fall on compatible spirits. He was, after all, almost the only man amongst a large group of unattached women, many of whom were inspired by him. It was not surprising that for some their admiration took on a personal colour.

The season of 1946–47 was economically difficult for everyone. Bread rationing was introduced on top of all the other food restrictions. Coal was almost unobtainable. The winter was abysmally harsh. Manchester froze, and so did the Art of Movement Studio, with its one gas fire. By September fourteen students were enrolled, an international assortment of people, varied in their aspirations and their ages, but many with performance and theatre as their goal. Several students from the Continent had waited all the war to train with Laban. Nobody had any money; frugality was the rule for students and teachers alike. Although the timetable gave training, choreutics, eukinetics, industrial rhythm and notation as the subjects taught, the perception of what was learned was on quite another level. Hettie Loman put it thus: 'Here was a system with a difference. No [other] studio could offer to its students the fundamentals of life as shown in movement.' She emphasised that anyone who looked at movement as only a physical act was missing the point. She was learning about her own creativity through movement experiences. Other people could be helped 'to break down the barriers which divide themselves from their inner creative powers.' Mary Elding saw what was offered as a mixture of idealism and wholeness that seemed an answer to the world's woes. In every class their was a relevance to life in general, to people, to community. Such awakened creative power was volatile. The grubby and inadequate studios sweated with vital energy. That was the student mood of 183–185 Oxford Road. Laban's involvement behind the scenes was intense. He laid down the curriculum. Up front, he appeared from time to time to lead a session (one could not call it teaching) on the history of dance, or on industrial work, while Ullmann trained the fourteen students and Bodmer created group works of spiritual and social significance.

For Laban, regular work in amateur drama increased over the next few years: a Drama Festival in Birmingham was one such engagement, a British Drama League course in York was another. More significant was his meeting with Esmé Church. She was directing a newly opened theatre school connected with the Bradford Civic Playhouse. She wrote in October 1946 to ask if Laban would be interested in co-operating on a children's theatre production. He would. From January 1947 he juggled his industrial commitments in order to be able to teach and produce at Bradford 'on Tuesdays and Fridays'. 'It is so tempting to resume my artistic work,' he wrote to Church. So began a most enjoyable period of theatre collaborations. They were punctuated by his absences through ill health. He was never free from his stomach disorder, and his distressing deprivations in 1936 and 1937 eventually caused a heart condition that, from time to time, he was unable to ignore. But these afforded an opportunity for another of his apprentices, Geraldine Stephenson: she taught as his deputy, in this way beginning a successful career using movement in theatre and television.

Preparations for participation in the first post-war International Choreographic Competition, to be held in Copenhagen in the summer of 1947, took on a major role in the curriculum. *The Forest: A Cycle of Life* was the title of the work created for Copenhagen, choreographed by Bodmer and Ullmann. The scenario was as complex as in Laban's earlier works *Gaukelei* and *Die Geblendeten*. It had political overtones and a spiritual subtext. Laban apparently had nothing to do with it and did not come to the competition itself, but judging by his guidance of Ullmann's work, he probably talked with her about her parts of the piece. Looking back on it, it had a 1930s style to it, exacerbated by post-war restrictions. Clothes rationing was at its most stringent, the only materials available for costumes being parachute silk, net, and ex-army long-john underwear. Ingenuity, however creative, could not overcome the limitations. As dancers, the cast was drawn from utter beginners – like myself, a sixteen-year-old novice with two terms' training – plus men from amateur drama, together with thoroughly expert dancers and actors. The performers' variety repeated Laban's Tanzbühne taste for casting of 1923 in Hamburg. Music was specially composed by Eric Hudes and an ambitious lighting design was devised by Benedict Ellis.

The work was not well received in Copenhagen. Compared with the thoroughly professional troupe of the winner, Jean Weidt, with his dreamlike and macabre work *La Cellule*, or Ivo Cramér, another winner, with his telling piece on Christ, *The Message*, both impeccably presented with dancers who had managed to work during the war, *The Forest* was an amateur contender that bungled its lighting on the night, the reddish terrors of the 'Nightmare' coinciding with the calm movement of 'Dawn'. It was not alone: A. V. Coton, writing in the *Dancing Times*, reported that most contenders were not worthy of mention.

While the international standing of Ullmann and Bodmer was dented by this event, the pre-performance presentations in Manchester for teachers and the Manchester Dance Circle were received with acclaim. As an example of group work of a kind accessible to schools and college students, it was a thoroughly useful piece of work. Used as publicity for the Art of Movement Studio and for Laban's own work, three demonstrations were spaced over the year, usually started with a talk by Laban, and illustrated by the students, dressed in red tunics. Short studies followed and excerpts from *The Forest* ended the evening. It attracted teachers to apply to the Art of Movement Studio, but not prospective dancers.

Reports on a course in London's Baron's Court district in May 1947 illustrate the progress and the problems of the educational work for teachers. Laban had written *Modern Educational Dance*, with the help of Veronica Tyndale-Biscoe, and was in the throes of editing the book, it being essential that a text for teachers should be available. In it he proposed sixteen basic movement themes as a skeleton for a dance-in-education curriculum. At this course, the themes were taught together with Laban's rationale for presenting them. Participants were asked for comments. Those from Sally Archbutt, at that time a beginner schoolteacher with Central European Dance in her training, and from Belinda Quirey, a practising dance historian from the dance establishment, still exist. Their reports give insight into the responses to Laban's proposals from dance people adhering to contrasting perspectives.

Archbutt's response was critical of the amount taught, the sense of panic engendered by sixteen 'lumps' of information landing on her in one week; but overall she saw how these themes might organise the practical knowledge that she had already learned in college into a kind of plan to cover several years' work with youngsters. Quirey on the other hand was copious and detailed in her criticism. While Laban gave broad sweeps of introduction on the history of dance as it related to society at large and led up to his proposals, Quirey's detailed knowledge of dance steps of the various periods covered filled her with annoyance at Laban's over-broad brushstrokes on history. She had difficulty in seeing the shape of the wood for the errors in the trees, as she saw it. She looked at each theme from the view point of academic dance. Why, she asked, should children 'play with their fingers and toes', as Laban suggested in his first theme ('Awareness of the Body'), when they could be learning essentials like positioning? Her major criticism was for the other participants, who of course were mostly primary school teachers. How could such people, who had no idea how to control a foot, let alone find their balance, become teachers of dance? The teaching methods through improvisation, though enjoyed by Archbutt, were a nightmare for Quirey, not only to practice, but in terms of purpose.

The sight of untrained bodies dancing, so difficult for Quirey, was to be a huge stumbling block to the acceptance of Laban's educational work. For people schooled to look for placement, for footwork, for alignment, for control, for beauty, the sight of children and adults apparently cavorting in ugly, uncontrolled, self-indulgent, sentimental movement was extremely difficult to stomach. The inner view – dancing experienced from within – was not an approach that the dance schools or the Imperial Society of the Teachers of Dancing appeared to consider. Not that Laban's work was all 'cavorting' – far from it; but even so its aesthetic was as highly problematic for the ballet-trained person as the unnatural rigour and artificiality of ballet was for the young radical modern dancer. Antipathy to Laban's work can be found in most issues of the *Dancing Times*.

It can be argued that whether Laban's exposition on dance history was accurate or not is irrelevant. The striking point is that in devising *Modern Educational Dance* he found it essential to connect it to social life and especially to the working habits of contemporary people living in a time of industrial revolution. Existing dance forms, social dance and ballet, musical comedy and vestigial folk dance were not 'the movement-expression of industrial man'. Finding an appropriate form for this fired him to create his modern dance. The future happiness of children depended on having and retaining a rich movement life in contrast with the limited repetitive work patterns that would dominate their adult lives. Skilful step dances, unlike liberated creative movement of the whole body/soul, could not serve this purpose.

The universality of the movement forms that he proposed was the rationale given for his choice. Theories in cognitive psychology on how people perceive the world, and in motor learning on how skills are acquired, suggest that Laban's idea to teach basic forms, or archetypal forms, or 'universal forms' as he called them, was absolutely right. He recommended creating variation on prototypical spatial forms and rhythms, with each prototype experienced fully, corporeally and with intent. He set about designing sixteen progressive themes in a curriculum from infant through junior to secondary-aged children. Veronica Tyndale-Biscoe was his helper, and no doubt he discussed it all with Goodrich and Jordan.

Current research in motor learning suggests that Laban was on target by proposing play, refinement and creation as broad teaching strategies. Piaget's research on children's learning supports the view that Laban comprehended how children experience the world, shifting as they develop from concrete to abstract conceptualisation of the body, space and time.

Laban divided the movement themes into groups of four, organising them as a spiral curriculum. The main headings touched upon in the spiral were the body, effort, space, and relationships to others. Gradually, from the simplest theme, 'awareness of the body' and its parts, the themes guided teachers in the way to introduce and build up experiences of eukinetic and choreutic forms, performed alone, with a partner and in groups. The sixteenth theme was 'concerned with the expressive qualities or moods of movements'. Substantial dance sequences and whole dance works were included here, both lyrical and dramatic. He suggested broad categories of dance, such as he had used in Hamburg, as being appropriate for top seniors. 'Cultivation of artistic taste and discrimination' he included in his final discussion on the purpose of the themes.

The book continued with an exposition on effort and his findings in his industrial research, showing its relevance to teaching, and a chapter on spatial orientation and harmony. Observation of movement was the final topic discussed, in which he included the influence that movement experiences have on the child's mind. 'Movement is a means of education' was the strong message.

Ullmann applied for naturalisation papers late in 1946 but was told that she would have to wait for four years because of the backlog. Laban received his Certificate of Identity in the summer of 1947, which, although he was still classified as an alien, opened up his mobility and freedom to work. Their personal situation in the rather staid British educational world was not an easy one. An inevitable question, with its innuendo was: were they living together, or 'living together'? Would it be easier if their relationship was formalised? Laban was evasive. He had no wish to promote the idea that he had an intimate relationship with Ullmann, nor to get himself mixed up in any conventional arrangement. He told her that they could not marry because he was already married to Maja. But he failed to add that he had been divorced since 1926. Ullmann was very keen to get the Art of Movement Studio recognised by the Ministry of Education, as correspondence with His Majesty's Staff Inspector E. R. Clarke shows. With that official recognition teachers could be seconded on salary, or on a grant to study there. She had to soldier on in a rather uncomfortably unconventional situation while trying to get her somewhat shaky institution conventionalised.

This longing for safety and a settled lifestyle was commented upon by Joan Littlewood, the iconoclastic director of Theatre Workshop, in her autobiography. She took the view that Ullmann, 'Laban's companion and protector', distrusted the interest and time spent by Laban with Littlewood, Ewan McColl and their politically volatile theatre company. Laban relished their discussions, enjoying both the artistic and social debates generated by the company's aims and performances. Ullmann was nervous of anything political, having experienced it only too closely in Germany. Littlewood believes that Ullmann steered Laban away from theatre and theatre people into the safe haven of education, gradually but deliberately. He allowed it to happen. Was he just too tired, at sixty-nine, to battle spiritually with the pulls of his conflicting interests? He needed Ullmann, he wanted to support her, although her laudable devotion to his work was not necessarily in areas that really interested him. His apprentice Jean Newlove soon became the movement trainer of Theatre Workshop, beginning a successful independent international career using her Laban knowledge in theatre.

In July, Laban and Ullmann travelled to Interlaken to teach on the first post-war modern dance summer school in Switzerland. Harald Kreutzberg joined them on the teaching staff. It was not an easy time, for those who had remained in Germany and those who had emigrated had to come to terms with their different experiences of the war, their various political affiliations and struggles. Jooss was still in England, failing to convince the British Arts Council to keep his Ballets Jooss from folding in the extreme austerity of the post-war economy. Wigman was still in Germany. It was not until 1949 that these big names of the second generation of German dancers met together for the third summer school, without Laban. Perrottet remembered the 1947 course primarily for the novel ideas of Laban's industrial work, an unusual topic for a dance summer school. Modern technique, much admired through the classes of Leeder, Kreutzberg, Rosalia Chladek and Hans Zullig, were what the Swiss dancers expected. Effort studies were not really to their liking. Just as Wigman had difficulties establishing herself again after the war, so too did Laban, difficulties compounded by age, by changes in taste, and by the Continent having moved on in a different way from Britain.

While Ullmann visited Liverpool weekly in the autumn of 1947 to teach at I. M. Marsh Physical Training College for Women, Laban started at Carnegie Physical Training College for Men, a tough assignment and not one to his taste. A day course for movement at the Durham County Drama Association and another at the Bishop Auckland Little Theatre Club were much more his line, as was his continuing collaboration with Esmé Church at Bradford. With her he produced scenes from J. B. Priestley's *Johnson over Jordan* as the performance to open their season. The necessary travelling in unheated trains was not helpful to Laban's health. He was ill again in October, having to send deputies to take his classes.

January 1948 saw Ullmann in a second round of discussions, this time with Ruth Foster, who had taken over from E. R. Clarke, in the attempt to get recognition by the Ministry of Education for the Art of Movement Studio as a Further Education College. It failed again, no decisions having been made on just which training schools to support officially: the educational ballet branch of the Royal Academy of Dancing, the Greek Dancing School, or only modern dance?

The battle between modern dance and ballet, familiar in pre-war Germany, was just as eagerly fought in Britain in the immediate post-war years. Two outstanding pioneers in ballet, Ninette de Valois and Marie Rambert, were determined to re-establish British ballet as a major theatrical force. To found a prestigious national performing company, although expensive in a time of dire austerity, was the aim. Germany was doing the same, their opera houses being some of the first buildings to rise from the catastrophic devastation of their cities. Ballet, and opera, became symbols of recovery. In Britain this spilled over into education. Naturally, there existed strong anti-German sympathies. Who wanted German ideas or German culture in Britain? For a while it looked, understandably, as if the rather shaky educational ideas of the ballet world might attract those elements of the educational hierarchy who valued discipline.

In 1948 Laban had further opportunities in industry, this time at Pilkington's Tile Works in St Helen's, commencing in March. As usual he took along young inexperienced apprentices to help him – this time myself, soon joined by a more mature student, Warren Lamb. Laban's gift for recognising the talents of individuals was right on target with Lamb, who went on to a career that developed from his initiation into industry and management at Pilkington's. My usefulness was limited primarily to teaching Lamb how to write down his observations in effort graphs and notation. We were a sufficiently useful team to find ourselves taking on the observation and recording of operatives at Pilkington's on behalf of Paton Lawrence, while Laban took the train to Bradford, to teach for Esmé Church. In April Laban was critically ill with typhoid; Lamb and I continued, and he sent another apprentice, Geraldine Stephenson, to Bradford. Church wrote to 'Uncle Laban' that she was doing well in his long absence.

Correspondence began between Laban and Ann Hutchinson, writing from New York, on the development that had taken place in the notation during the war and in the immediate post-war years. Hutchinson, a student at the Jooss/Leeder School at Dartington, had started the Dance Notation Bureau soon after her arrival in New York when the war in Europe began. Meeting up with other Laban-trained emigrées Irmgard Bartenieff and Els Grelinger, together with Helen Priest Rogers who had studied with Knust in Berlin, they pooled their knowledge and resources to begin the serious work of developing the profession of notator for the American dance world.

By 1947, after laudable drive and publicity, the choreographers Jerome Robbins, Doris Humphrey and Antony Tudor had asked them to notate their works. Hutchinson, in consultation with her colleagues, needed to adjust the notation to suit the needs of American modern dance and ballet, just as Knust had needed to do in 1932 in order to write the group work of the movement choirs. She wrote to Laban requesting some rule clarification and changes. While the questions were crucial to her, Laban was not really interested, his mind being on effort. He passed the letter to his notation apprentice of the moment with the demand, 'You answer it, Val.' Needless to say I could not possibly do so, with my elementary knowledge. It was right and proper that he should interest himself in the American problem. Communication in sign form had been forbidden during the war for fear that the notation, and similar coded messages, might have carried information useful to the enemy. The inability to share had caused profound differences of attitude and needs in the notation centres in New York, Germany and Britain. The understanding of the movement of the torso and the chest through Humphrey and Graham techniques differed fundamentally from each other, and from the free use of the torso resulting from arm movements that sufficed in the works written by Knust, and in the expressionist dance practised in Manchester, let alone the torso–hip moves found in the Jooss/Leeder technique.

One example of the problem: what should a forward direction sign in the third column of the notation staff indicate? Hutchinson wanted it to mean a tilt forward of the chest, while for Knust and Laban it meant an arm-with-upper-part-of-the-body reach forward. Either could be argued as logically possible, but the Laban/Knust version had been in place since 1928. Could these two views accommodate each other? Did Laban's prior rule have to take precedence, did Hutchinson's professional need have priority? Hutchinson wanted another change, to use the term 'Labanotation' while 'Kinetography Laban' remained the European title. Laban admitted that he found the suggested name for the system not at all to his taste and that her developments violated the basic rules of his system, but he had to admit that he used an adapted version himself for the industrial work. He knew that the notation was no longer truly his own, but everyone's. Hutchinson found some of Knust's writing unusable in her circumstances. In the case of these two notators this was a classic confrontation of an unstoppable force meeting an immoveable object. Sparks would fly between New York and Essen, where Knust worked, for some years to come. At this point Laban corresponded with Hutchinson, but not very helpfully, and she was understandably not pleased. He turned his attention to his new symbol system, the effort graph, while I, as the student teacher of notation at the Art of Movement Studio, simply taught both ways of writing and referred to the notation by both names.

At this time, Ullmann and Laban moved into a semi-detached house with a small garden, at 8 Neston Avenue, somewhat nearer to the Art of Movement Studio. With them came Ullmann's mother, staying with her to recover from the stress of a war spent in Berlin and the sadness of losing her son in the last days of the war. Ullmann acquired a very second-hand car through the generosity of Myfanwy Dewey, which enabled her to travel more easily to her Lancashire evening classes several times a week, taking a teaching apprentice with her as demonstrator. At the Art of Movement Studio various apprentices began to supplement the supposedly regular timetable. Geraldine Stephenson taught anatomy and music appreciation, I taught notation, Cecelia Bagley gave composition workshops in the evening, and Mary Elding taught drama. It was the Choreographisches Institut all over again, plus industrial work, drama, and forays into schools and theatres, activity from 9 a.m. to 10 p.m., a veritable all-absorbing whirligig.

The Laban Art of Movement Guild flourished, gaining more members, holding its first Conference in April 1948, at Buckingham Gate in London, but without Laban and Ullmann – a great shock to everyone and a deep disappointment. Both children's work and therapy featured. An ambitious but short-lived magazine, *Movement*, was floated by the Guild. Was it intended to be the British equivalent of *Schrifttanz*? Its very broad aim – 'to treat the arts and all aspects of life from the standpoint of Movement' – was accomplished through wide-ranging articles, written both by people who held a central role in the Laban circle and by others who were peripheral. John Trevelyan wrote advocating movement education in schools. The problems of getting anything going in this difficult period are exemplified by Trevelyan, who had by now been sent abroad, as director of the British Families Education Services, British Zone, Germany, catering for the children of servicemen in the occupational forces. Paper was scarce, resources were put into war damage reparations, people were required to undertake national service in the forces, and no one had any money. *Movement* folded after two issues, the vision that went into it unmatched by the practical realities of life in 1948.

It is noticeable that by this time, 'Movement' had been given a capital 'M' in writings about theoretical and practical movement undertakings stemming from Laban. In speaking about the work, the word 'movement' took on a subtext, especially in the educational world, where, if you said you taught movement, it meant 'Movement'. But also in the Paton Lawrence circle, Laban's philosophy of life, expressed by his ideas on human movement, became capitalised. For those people engaged in promoting Movement – the Guild, the Dance Circles, the Elmhirsts, the physical education sorority, even the thoroughly down-to-earth Lawrence – the word took on almost hushed overtones. And the sense of concerted endeavour to promote harmony amongst people, and between people and the environment, was infectious and exhilarating. The Gleschendorf fervour was reincarnated at holiday courses, the Choreographisches Institut's spirit of disregarding difficulties was present at the Art of Movement Studio. Laban's ideas set people free to hope and to create, just as they had set Mary Wigman free at Ascona. Laban's posthumous article 'Light–Darkness' discussed 'enlightenment' and 'the ecstasies found through creative movement'. The insight into what seemed like awesome truths through the participatory experience of choreutics and eukinetics caused one to pause, hold still, and take stock.

Bodmer's choreographic talent took flight, too. She created chamber works for four Art of Movement Studio dancers, forming them into the Young Dancers' Group. Was it the (very different) British version of the Kammertanzbühne Laban, Bodmer taking the role that Bereska had had in the 1920s? Here the tours were to small theatres, schools and community centres, not mainstream theatres, Bodmer's interest being to reach a wide audience. From time to time the Young Dancers Group illustrated lectures by Laban, just as Katabü members had done in Germany. In the 1948 season they followed him to Leeds Training College. Laban showed interest in the group but was only marginally involved. In a letter in response to Gleisner's wartime contact with him, Laban had written, 'I don't know much about dancing now. My interest for research is prevailing.' More and more, drama was his art medium, or rather his research medium, rather than dance. He, now with Stephenson not Ullmann, led a summer school at York for the British Drama League, teaching movement for actors. Together they created a dance-mime for performance. At the same time Ullmann taught a Ministry of Education course for teachers of infants at Chichester.

After a brief recovery with Ullmann in Wales at Capel Curig their hectic programme continued at Dartington for the Modern Dance Holiday Course summer school. Laban, Ullmann, Bodmer and Goodrich taught as before, but they were joined by a new contact, Arthur Stone, a brilliant headmaster skilled in educational drama. As well as movement and dance, art activities and drama became part of the curriculum. Influential visitors came from the Ministry of Education. Soon after, the Art of Movement Studio was asked to run a supplementary course of one year's duration for teachers, intended for those who had had a two-year training or the Emergency One-Year Teacher Training for people coming out of the forces. Students fees would be paid, plus some living costs. Ullmann, with a sigh of relief, had obtained what she needed, some measure of security, and possibly some respite from endless travelling to teachers' courses. The teachers might now come to her.

The 1948–49 season continued the pattern already set up, Laban concentrating on his own affairs and Ullmann on hers, under his guidance. He lectured to Manchester University students on his methods in industry, assisted by apprentice Warren Lamb. With Esmé Church, he produced *The Shawl* and then *The Twelve Months*, a full-length play with movement and music, with the Bradford Civic Theatre School students. The characters in it were reminiscent of *Ritterballett*: 'robust peasants, aristocratic elegant court couples and superhuman beings'. Pathos and humour resulted. He created his first production with the Art of Movement Studio students, a movement version of *The Magic Flute*, with music composed by Adda Heynssen who, having composed for dance in the 1930s in Germany, had rejoined the Laban circle. Here again was a re-emergence of an earlier method, the one he used for his tour of Wagner characters with Gertrud Loeszer in 1926; that is, opera themes as dance with no music or freshly written music.

The Art of Movement Studio's autumn 1948 open day was notable. Hettie Loman, an actress turned choreographer, had started to make works. Sharp duos and quartets had come easily to her, but for this occasion she made her first group piece, *Scarecrows*, a vicious dark and athletic work with menacing crow-like images to Stravinsky's *Rite of Spring*. Ullmann's opening speech, written for her in Laban's hand, included reference to dance as art for the first time.

A course at Dartington Hall on 'the teacher and the arts', run by the County of Devon in January 1949, was an outstanding event in which Laban and Ullmann both taught dance, collaborating daily with Imogen Holst on singing, Clifford and Rosemary Ellis, Dorothy Elmhirst, Leonard Bennett and Peter Cox on painting and playreading. Puppet theatre and concerts by the Amadeus Quartet completed what was described as a delicious six days.

Throughout the season there were so many demands for Laban and Ullmann that the more senior Art of Movement Studio students were despatched to teach in their place. Elding found herself in rural centres in Lincolnshire teaching movement for drama, while Lamb deputised for

Laban in the East Riding of Yorkshire and the University of Hull. Stephenson was sent to teach effort in speech and movement for actors at Ormesby and Wolverhampton. The British Drama League work, which Laban undertook himself with assistants, increased, attracting large numbers of actors and teachers of drama. The course at Dartington in March 1949 is remembered as a watershed, participants departing to introduce Laban methods into theatre schools. Significant, and gratifying for Laban, was the number of men involved. In August the British Drama League held a two-week holiday course at Dartington again, Laban sharing it with Esmé Church, and a second one, this time in Matlock, two weeks in early September, Annie Boalth joining Laban and Ullmann. Sandwiched between these two was the Modern Dance Holiday Course, on which Ullmann taught as usual, Laban contributing a few classes in the effort observation course taught by Lamb. Such a condensed programme was killing; but, as the poor attendance on the Easter Laban Guild course in London had shown, people would only come if 'Lisa and Laban' were teaching. Without the respite of a holiday, the next season for the Art of Movement Studio started immediately after Matlock, with a new course for teachers in addition.

On 15 December 1949 Laban's seventieth birthday was celebrated with as much ingenuity as rationing and cold weather would permit. Theatre Workshop serenaded him at home with songs written by Ewan McColl in his inimitable folk song style, while in the evening as many friends as could be fitted into 183 Oxford Road joined in a typically anarchic jamboree. He was moved by gifts and messages from his former students in Germany, many of whom had emigrated. The monumental scores of the three-act ballet *Teufel im Dorf*, choreographed by Pina and Pia Mlakar in Munich and notated there by Knust, was a very special present, the first full score of its kind. Rolf de Maré sent this message: 'The whole of this century the art of dance has been inspired by your ideas, never has one man meant so much to an art, for such a long time, as you have to dance.' On behalf of the Archives Internationales de la Danse he sent a *plaquette d'honneur*. German newspaper cuttings marking the birthday of 'The Master' were read, Aurel Milloss, international choreographer, being quoted as saying, 'Laban is the greatest stimulus in the history of dance.'

The evening was a strange mix, reflecting Laban's transnational status. Ullmann led a Polonaise, Bodmer danced a 'Ritual of Homage', folk songs from Bratislava were sung together with a *Ländler* and a *sevillanas*. The students danced a frolic 'To Laban's Birthday', Ullmann taking the part of the wizard Alaban. Laban and Ewan McColl improvised a zany theme straight out of Laban's Munich Fasching celebrations originally made for

Score of *Teufel im Dorf* (The Devil in the Village), ballet by Pina and Pia Mlakar for the Ballet of the Munich Opera House, written by Albrecht Knust in 1942 and presented to Laban for his seventieth birthday, 1949.

the medical fraternity there. Lawrence gave an oration of suitable seriousness and magnitude. Austerity food and drink abounded and merriment
was as high as it had been in the decorated premises of the Choreographisches Institut in Berlin after the 1928 Congress and the tumultuous success of the notation there. The *Dancing Times* noted his birthday without
enthusiasm.

Attempts to locate Laban's erstwhile students to celebrate his birthday
showed just how difficult life was in post-war Germany. His daughter Azra
lived in the Russian Zone, her brother Arpad in the American Zone, as did
his ex-wife Maja, still in Munich, while Hamburg was in the British Zone.
People were divided from one another, lost, dead or emigrated to unknown
places. Laban managed to make contact with Albrecht Knust and Jo Meisenbach, and 'Snellchen' came to England by 1950. Some, like Fritz Klingenbeck, were reluctant to make contact because of Laban's employment by
Goebbels, while Herta Feist held back because of her own close contact
with the Nazis. In a sense, anyone who had not stayed and gone through
the horrors of the war in Germany had difficulty in re-establishing contact
with people who had remained. Although Jooss went back to Essen in
1951, it was hard. As a British dancer at the Folkwangschule there in 1952,
I was left severely alone by fellow students.

Laban's text for *The Mastery of Movement on the Stage* was completed
and published in 1950, his work at the Bradford Civic Theatre School being
the final inspiration. John Macdonald, of the publishing house Macdonald
& Evans, proved a staunch supporter and wise editor. With this book Laban
stated clearly his current interest in movement as theatre, making, with
Effort and *Modern Educational Dance*, a remarkable trilogy. The first edition contained chapters on movement and the body, and variations of
elementary movements. The whole progressive sequence of 305 exercises
followed Knust's way of introducing movement through kinetography. No
doubt advised that to include so much material written in an unfamiliar
notation system was of no help to actors, he decided on a compromise by
devising a strange alternative made up of letters signifying body parts with
signs used in writing and mathematics to indicate action. (The second
edition, edited by Ullmann after his death, resorts to words. In the fourth
edition of 1980 she was able to have the exercises written in Labanotation,
a measure of the time it took for his notation to become a recognised and
read system.) He went on to chapters on the significance of movement
in acting, and the roots of mime, relating effort to characterisation and
situational conflict. The last chapters concentrate on group work and suggestions for group plays. The book constitutes a statement of Laban's

theory of expressive movement, as clearly put as he was able to at that time. Ullmann's editions add developments from the last eight years of his life on the work he continued to undertake in voice and movement in drama.

Laban's focus on movement as therapy was beginning. Dr Rolf Kosterlitz, a psychotherapist, had become interested in Laban's work in industry, and lectured at the Laban Guild Conference on the stress caused by having to undertake tasks for which a person could be constitutionally unsuited. He emphasised the innovations that the collaborations of a psychotherapist and a movement trainer could make in the realm of psychological disorder. Chloe Gardner, one of several occupational therapists interested in Laban's ideas, wrote about her work in a mental hospital, showing how effort analysis could guide treatment in a mental health institution. She pioneered the diagnostic usefulness of effort observation, its use in the design of appropriate occupational therapies and in the inclusion of creative movement therapies as a treatment mode. From America, Irmgard Bartenieff wrote of her success in using Laban's work, learned in Germany, in physiotherapy, and how it expanded into therapy of the whole person. Her work was beginning to have a following. Beatrice Loeb, a *Kammertänzerin* in Rome with Bereska and devotee of Laban's work, demonstrated her concepts of occupational therapy in the home through the practice of creative craft-making of all sorts.

Laban first met Irene Champernowne, a psychotherapist and leader of the Withymead Centre in Countess Wear, Exeter, in March 1949 at a conference in London on music and art therapy. He spoke on 'The Remedial Value of the Art of Movement' and Champernowne immediately booked him for three autumn visits, one for ten days' duration. A strong centre for therapy through the arts was her aim, and although she had corresponded with Laban it was not until this personal meeting that she realised the potential for his method, seeing how it could help in the expansion at Withymead from painting, clay and music therapy into a more broadly-based and co-ordinated method. What started as a private clinic had become a company in 1945. It was later further strengthened by being established as a Trust 'to foster education and treatment of psychological sickness', with Leonard Elmhirst, his son-in-law Maurice Ash, and John Trevelyan acting as Trustees.

In December 1949 a brainstorming meeting had been held at Withymead in which the educationist John Trevelyan, the Jungian psychiatrist Dr Culver Barker, Irene and Gilbert Champernowne, and the current art therapists thrashed out the necessary knowledge and financial support required to establish a credible arts therapy method to enhance the current some-what *ad hoc* situation. Laban's participation was requested. As ever, Laban introduced an apprentice, in this case Veronica Tyndale-Biscoe. While her work lay fundamentally in teacher training, at this point she could supple-ment the time that Laban could give to Withymead.

The need to train movement therapists was addressed by deciding that Dennis Hill, an erstwhile patient at Withymead, should attend for three years at the Art of Movement Studio and take personal classes with Laban while there. In the autumn of 1950 he began. The archives record his somewhat chequered career and illustrate a new type of student attend-ing the Studio. The difficulties some encountered and the problems their dancer/teacher co-students had in accommodating their needs can be found in reports.

Hill gave an account of teaching at a school for 'backward children' and in a child guidance clinic and mental hospital. Letters from the Champer-nownes show that they were concerned that aspiring therapists attending the Art of Movement Studio courses might be given a false impression that they were qualified to practice, a concern shared by Laban. The Withymead connection focused Laban's mind on the relationship between his work and that of Jung. His industrial experiments had drawn on that relationship but the responsibility for treating mentally disturbed patients required him to research more deeply into personality, stress and intervention tech-niques. Until his death this was the new area that he pursued with rigorous concentration, balanced by his love for movement in theatre, his interest in movement in industry, and his support for movement in education. The practical placements for Hill show the connections that Laban was develop-ing in the domain of mental health. Hill returned to Withymead after two years in Manchester, and, supported by Tyndale-Biscoe, taught there for a while as the representative of Laban's work.

All these interests had their frustrations. Laban's archive contains a heartfelt doodle entitled 'The 3 Hard-Boiled Ones' (The H-B Os). These, he noted as the industrialist, the educationist and the therapist of the me-chanical and traditional type, each of whom had specific inhibitions. And there was a fourth, the hard-boiled theatricalist, in ballet. He drew a free-hand diagram contrasting Action, as he envisioned it, with Counteraction as he encountered it. For him, movement action was in the service of Industry, through welfare and efficiency, while the Hard-Boiled One coun-teracted by looking for profit and being content with routine. In education, movement promoted a balance between things physical and mental while the 'H-B O' was a disciplinarian with traditional values. In therapy, his proponents sought rehabilitation but were counteracted by supporters of physiosomatic medicine. As for artists, showmanship, theatrical business and the routines of the 'H-B Os' were forces counter to true theatrical performance. He did not leave it there. The doodle continued on to thoughts about the misguided public who were led away from the 'central principles of life' as practised in Movement. He named workmen, consumers, parents, teachers, patients, practitioners, audiences and producers who were misled into collapse, muddle, degeneration and unhappiness. He must have been feeling very low that day.

Laban's own involvement in drama increased during 1950 with regular monthly weekend courses in London. At the same time the theatrical aspect of the Art of Movement Studio crystallised through the choreographic successes of Hettie Loman. Having gained her diploma in 1948 she remained as a graduate assistant-*cum*-teacher. Dances which had Laban's political drive and humour appeared through her artistry and in a style which, although expressionist, was up to date in theme and treatment. *Streets Without End* was her most ambitious work in 1949. It had elements of Jooss's *Big City* but instead of taking class distinction as its theme it looked broadly at the tapestry of city deprivations and hopes. *Pleasure Spent*, a duo on teenage jive, *Once I Had Laughter* on a concentration camp theme, *Born of Desire* a duo for a childless couple, and *Masquerade of the Heart* on memories of wedding-day treachery, were some of her dances. I played the Crippled Child in this work, and Loman could not get the movement she wanted from me. Laban took three sheets of paper, put one between my knees, one between my elbow and ribs, and one between my foot and the floor. 'Now dance,' he said. That did the trick.

During 1950 Loman and six dancers – Ronnie Curran, Lamb, Archbutt, Joan Carrington, Meg Tudor-Williams and myself – formed British Dance Theatre. The public found our work 'very serious', commenting on our expertise in a new style. To a ballet audience, Loman's programming was heavy and with unfamiliar grotesque qualities. She paid no attention to traditional aesthetic values. The Art of Movement Studio could not support a group. No sponsor with dollars materialised as one had done to support the Tanzbühne Laban in Hamburg. After touring in the north, the company moved to London. A television performance from the BBC's Alexandra Palace in December gave the company a start.

The theatrical training at the Art of Movement Studio had already started a down turn, through the influx of teachers as students. Throughout 1949 the original dance theatre oriented students, expressionist dancers as political through dance as Theatre Workshop, had become alarmed by the shift in emphasis in both what was taught and who their new student colleagues were. By 1950 the shift was even stronger. There was a growing opinion that any aspiring modern dancer would find inadequate training at 183 Oxford Road and be well advised to audition for Sigurd Leeder's school in London. One, Stella Maude, had already done so. Leeder had failed to gain recognition from the Ministry of Education – a bone of jealous contention with Ullmann – but his school was well recognised by the professional dance world in London, as his presence in the *Dancing Times* shows.

Laban decided to try again for a theatre training institution in London, as the stage branch of the Art of Movement Studio. In the spring of 1950 he and Ullmann gave a series of intensively prepared dance-drama Saturdays at the YWCA in London, and continued to do so in 1951, assisted by Stephenson. They were highly successful. London was the place to be, for 1951 was the year of the Festival of Britain, the celebration planned by the Labour government to lift flagging post-war spirits. The South Bank was the site, the Festival Hall the newly built concert hall there, the Dome of Discovery and the Skylon symbolising future hopes and scientific invention. People flocked for their first colourful experience in many a long year. Laban had hoped to have a modern dance group to perform there, but British Dance Theatre had taken the Art of Movement Studio's best dancers, and somehow no others could be found.

At about the same time the Laban Art of Movement Guild formed a London Group, offering a programme with and for movement artists. Ernst Berk, choreographer and dancer, demonstrated, Litz Pisk gave a session on her movement training at the Old Vic Theatre School, recitals and concerts were arranged. Laban pushed forward with the plans for a London-based mime school, with Ullmann as director and himself as main guest lecturer. At the same time British Dance Theatre, from the company's studio in Westbourne Grove, independently advertised their own training classes. Somewhat acrid letters passed between Loman and Oxford Road at this time. Again, nothing came of Laban's plan for a stage branch, while British Dance Theatre managed to keep its poverty-line existence going, settling for a strained relationship with Manchester. A letter from Ullmann to an American friend stated that they did have 'a graduate company touring successfully' – all was not industry and education – but in truth she wanted nothing to do with it. Ullmann's difficulty in accommodating success in her graduates contrasted with Laban's expectation of it. Rivalry with younger colleagues who, as she saw it, might jeopardise her position in the Laban circle, was to surface as the years went on, and had already started here.

These frustrations notwithstanding, Laban's overall influence grew. Setting a seal on his place as a force in British culture was an invitation to be the subject of the prestigious 'Profile' article in the Sunday *Observer* in July 1951. The article itself was unimpressive; it was being there at all that mattered, a recognition usually reserved for an establishment figure. There is a certain irony here: in a profile from 1929 he was hailed as the spiritual leader of German dance; here he was congratulated as a key figure in British industry. Such is fate, such is opportunity.

Several booklets on his work had been published, and continued to be published, through the Laban Art of Movement Guild. They were mostly written by Laban, with dextrous corrections from Marjorie Bergin, the Guild's editor, much admired and trusted by Laban. *The Art of Movement in Education, Industry and on the Stage* (although it contained very little on stage dance) came out in 1950. Two years later a second edition appeared, now entitled *The Art of Movement in Education, Work and Recreation*, with additional sections on recreational and therapeutic movement work. The texts were a heavy read, understandable to the initiated but difficult for the general public, particularly because of the writing style. German sentence structure still came readily to Laban, as did the penchant in that language for multiple words. The delicious experience of moving described in words sounds either metaphysical or trite; to avoid the latter he went for the former. His way of expressing things spilled over into the writing style of other colleagues and apprentices. Also appearing in 1950 was a special edition of *The New Era in Home and School* devoted to his work, underscoring the increased interest in his views.

One course deserves note. In the summer of 1950, coinciding with the Modern Dance Holiday Course at Dartington Hall, was a drama course given by the American University Theater, led by Arch Lauterer with Nadine Miles. Laban and Ullmann taught movement classes daily. As John Hodgson put it, the movement work they offered became the highlight of the course, spilling over into voice work and productions. A dance-drama based on Prometheus was rehearsed, surely a version of Laban's 1922 Tanzbühne work. This version had music written for it by Imogen Holst. Laban also worked on a topical political piece 'with barbed wire'. The experience for the students of a production with this combined talent was stunning. *The Mastery of Movement on the Stage* was published during the course, and auditions held for the Art of Movement Studio were well subscribed.

With Ullmann so much absorbed and in demand in the educational world, Laban returned to his earlier collaborator, Sylvia Bodmer, for his movement researches. As a mathematician, she had always taken readily to choreutics. Now Laban was penetrating further into his beloved subject, looking for the correlation of shape and dynamic rhythms, and the nexus between psychology and choreutics. Bodmer's notebooks overflow with diagrams in both his and her writing. The steeple, the arc, the round and the double bend were scrutinised in their regular, expanded and contracted forms. Her comprehension of harmonic principles, and the function of the scaffolding provided by platonic solids in relation to the psyche and to the structure of the body, must have warmed his heart. Bodmer was able not only to write about it, simply and coherently, but also to choreograph studies which, like those of Sigurd Leeder, were mini-artworks. Here, in this subject, was a true colleague for him. He had 'discovered' new choreutic scales which he called the 'mixed seven rings', and in so doing penetrated further into the kinetic coherence of three-dimensional space. He decided that he should reorganise choreutic materials, starting with the Primary Scale, and numbering its arrival points from 1 to 12. His Christmas card to Bodmer, complete with an effort graph decorated with holly and Santa Claus astride an icosahedron, showed his new concept.

He and Ullmann continued their gruelling programme of holiday courses, for Ullmann in addition to her full-time commitments at the Art of Movement Studio. For Laban it surrounded his industrial assignments, his writing, and his drama productions. They were both expected at the Guild courses, at the Modern Dance Holiday Courses, at the Studio's own Christmas and Easter courses, at the London weekend courses, and others. People came to be taught by them personally. Their teaching, described as 'nectar', was on another level than anyone else's. They did not teach on the 1951 summertime Modern Dance Holiday Course, but slipped away to Saundersfoot to rest, draw and recharge. The report in the Guild's News Sheet illustrates the response: 'It was a great disappointment to find that Mr Laban and Miss Ullmann were not at the course.'

Irene Champernowne wrote asking Laban to work at Withymead to get movement therapy fully established there. His reply was telling: he would like to, but could not afford to unless paid properly, because 'I have to work so hard to make a living.' Withymead's poor financial state meant that his therapy work had to be covered by younger people, Dennis Hill and Veronica Tyndale-Biscoe. Warren Lamb too was useful in the therapy field. He, with Joan Carrington, led a course on personal effort assessment for a group of psychiatrists brought together by Dr Culver Barker of Withymead. Lamb used his observation skills of individual effort patterns and Laban's theory of the link between behaviour patterns and Jung's psychic functions for the assessment. Lamb, although useful as an employee of Lawrence's, was beginning to be engaged for assessment assignments in his own right. He took off for America, undertaking a tour of the Chapters of the American Institute of Industrial Engineers, lecturing on Laban/Lawrence methods. This behaviour was a trifle too independent for both Lawrence and Laban. For a while, relations with Lamb were strained. While Laban delighted in the success of apprentices – indeed, was utterly dependent on their success – he had to retain some control, for financial reasons if no other. But as ever he empowered people by his apprentice method and they worked independently with confidence.

The August 1952 Modern Dance Holiday Course at Dartington Hall warrants mention for its clear division between a curriculum for physical education teachers, which featured 'Basic Movement' taught by Elma Casson and Margaret Dunn, and one for dancers in which *The Swinging Cathedral* (Laban's *Der Schwingende Tempel* of 1922) was reconstructed by him with Ullmann's help. In addition, a special dance course was offered for men. On it were two people about to become influential: Bill Elmhirst, Dorothy and Leonard's youngest son, and Bill Carpenter. Both were interested in the therapeutic and spiritual side of movement. Laban took to Carpenter. The two men were able to discuss matters easily, and before long Carpenter became one of the Laban circle, helping him to write on his researches into movement and personality. Bill Elmhirst, a profoundly spiritual young man, was taken with Laban's desire to leave Manchester for the south. The premises at Oxford Road, already supplemented by various halls around the city, were quite inadequate for the student numbers now enrolling for the teachers' one-year courses. A serious search began for a place where the whole gamut of Laban's activities could take place.

In the spring of 1953, Bill Elmhirst found an estate in Surrey, a former school. It included large rooms, living accommodation, various huts and some sixteen acres of neglected land. Laban was unable to see it: he was yet again extremely ill in hospital. With outstanding generosity, Bill bought the estate for Laban and his work. As Laban gradually recovered, recuperating in the Lake District, arrangements to move south were finalised. Three young teachers were to come too: Geraldine Stephenson, already established as a solo performer and producer of dance-drama, and two newly appointed teachers, Marion North, teacher-trained and a gifted apprentice for effort work, and myself, returning from a period in the theatre and at the Folkwangschule in Essen working with Jooss and Knust. We made a varied trio. Together we shifted south in July, to Woburn Hill, Addlestone. Bill Carpenter had paved the way, overseeing the plumbing, the insurance, the chimney sweep, the jungle in the garden, while Ullmann battled with the Ministry of Education and the Ministry of Supply to get the new premises approved, while also giving a 'Farewell Demonstration' to the good friends of Manchester.

Laban was entranced with the new site. He saw immediately what could be done with it: an open-air theatre here, a lecture space there, a lawn for dancing. A modern-day Ascona lay at the back of his mind, and indeed the next season's schooling included gardening, fruit picking, jam-making and rose pruning, a new experience for teachers and students alike. The association with Dartington, kept up since 1938, was now closer than ever, Dartington's Rural Industries supplying furniture for the new buildings. Bill Elmhirst became a student, with others from Withymead. Bill Carpenter brought his caravan and lived on the site. Just about everything had to be done on a shoestring to get the premises ready for the September academic year. One building, a wooden chalet, was to become student accommodation. It was as yet unfurnished, uncarpeted, uncurtained and filthy. Dartington cloth arrived by the roll, and I recall making a great many curtains on a sewing machine borrowed from my mother. We all cleaned the schoolboy debris from the classroom floors, painted the walls, with Ullmann cooking and Laban encouraging. In between stitching and scrubbing we drove to Ashridge, some forty miles away, to the Modern Dance Holiday Course, Stephenson to teach the more advanced dance students and acting, North to aid Dunn with basic movement and primary school work. Laban, Ullmann and I came as occasional visitors, returning to Addlestone to stitch.

Addlestone was an uninspiring commuter village on a branch railway line, a mile from Weybridge, a typical small, well-off Surrey town. The business of setting up a local network of interested people and potential supporters began with an open day in November 1953. Laban left Ullmann to lead the day and rehearse the demonstration with the new intake of students plus the few who had stayed on from Manchester. Stephenson gave a solo recital drawn from the dances she had created and performed over the last two years. The Surrey public were not as open as the Mancunians, parochial and suburban rather than metropolitan (the Art of Movement was first thought to refer to a new type of removal firm!).

Laban, buoyed up by the rural environment of Addlestone, played a distinctive part in the teaching side of the Studio's 1953–54 course. He laid down how the sixteen basic movement themes, as written rather vaguely in *Modern Educational Dance*, should be made more concrete in order to be taught by the 'school teachers' on the supplementary course and thence by teachers generally. The 'trainers of teachers', as he called the college lecturers on the special course, gave critiques of these teaching endeavours, and should also understand the theoretical physical/mental basis of the themes, he wrote. Laban sat in on these experiments, as did North and I, learning as we went along. He also rewrote the prospectus, including in it work on 'movement disturbances and corrective training' as part of the curriculum, in line with his own present focus on therapy. The number of students enrolling who had been patients at Withymead reflected the contact that he maintained with the Champernownes. Ullmann taught the Guild's Refresher Course for corporate members, with Bodmer, while Laban concentrated on working with Carpenter on the research for a new book on the psychology of movement. But he did observe and advise on a Drama Weekend Course in the West Riding where Diana Jordan and Arthur Stone undertook the practical classes.

The relationship between the Laban Art of Movement Guild and the Art of Movement Studio was not entirely satisfactory. When the Guild first began, before the Studio started, it encompassed all aspects and levels of Laban's work. As soon as the Studio opened, the professional training side was located there, inevitably; and yet the Guild organised itself as if it were a professional status-giving institution, with corporate and associate members. Later, membership was subdivided until a hierarchy of some delicacy existed, with Graduate Members, who had their own professional courses, Sectional Members with specialisms in art, education or industry, and finally Fellows, the gods of gods. The problem lay in the simple but unacknowledged fact that one year at the Art of Movement Studio, or any number of holiday courses, was not long enough to acquire the essential skills to enable people to engage in dance as a career. Those of us lucky enough to have been in at the beginning had at least three years of Laban teaching, years in which we performed, toured and learned what dance art encompassed. The Guild's hierarchy was an attempt to alert people to the level of knowledge that individual members had, or could have. Its courses were an attempt to provide knowledge and to contribute to the building up of a thoroughly trained British base for Laban's work.

In February 1954, for the first time, the Art of Movement Studio hosted the Guild's Annual Conference, as a residential weekend, bringing the two organisations closer. Laban gave the formal Laban Lecture on 'Art of Movement'. The fact that Laban and Ullmann lived there brought people even closer to them, so that the feeling of a movement family around Laban was strengthened. The inclination for people to imagine that they had a personal relationship with Laban, rather than simply a working relationship, was resisted by Ullmann. The door to their apartment was understandably very firmly shut. On many occasions access to Laban, whose whole domain was in their apartment, was barred, with Ullmann as the keeper of the keys. An in-house joke was to call the draught-excluding drapes at the end of their corridor 'The Iron Curtain', a term much in the news as a metaphor for the impenetrable divide between the USSR and the West. Laban was in any case fully occupied working with Carpenter on the new book, provisionally entitled *Movement Psychology*. From time to time he escaped to work quietly in the summer house in the gardens.

April and May were busy months for him. An Easter course in West Riding was organised by Jordan for German teachers of art, physical education and music, both men and women, Laban being engaged to introduce them to dance as a means of education. He led another vacation course at Addlestone on dance for men, assisted by Ullmann and Graeme Bentham. He gave time to ensuring, if he could, that men succeeded in dance. With the Hamburg men's group, Feist's male dancers, and his own Choreographisches Institut men in mind, he devised and taught a course to make British men feel confident in expressive movement. Dance-dramas, B-scale studies in space, daring effort sequences and group work were the themes. In May he was again at West Riding for a course on dance and dance accompaniment. How to handle music was a problem for all teachers. Adda Heynssen had produced records and sheet music of piano pieces for dance, but many teachers had no pianist and only a wind-up gramophone that wore out records in no time at all.

Yat Malmgren joined the teaching staff, part-time, for the summer term. He had found himself unexpectedly without work, and so contacted Laban, who was delighted to have the opportunity to propose the employment of a man, especially one with whose work he had instinctively felt at home at their brief meetings at Dartington in 1939. Malmgren taught technique classes that offered the students a distinctly different way of dealing with bodily discipline.

Bill Carpenter's death in June 1954 was a fearful blow to Laban. The man had seemed to understand Laban's ideas, and, being an excellent linguist as well as knowledgeable in psychology, had been able to help Laban to express his concepts in a readable manner. The book they were writing was incomplete, and indeed has as yet never been published. Seriously concerned with what to do with the unfinished text, he thrust parts of it into the hands of a surprised Malmgren. The trust Laban had in his abilities was unexpected. Malmgren read the text, and as his comprehension grew so did his view that the contents were of profound significance for actors. Laban seems to have judged that of all the people around him at that time, Malmgren was the one to take his mature work forward on character analysis for the acting profession. Malmgren stayed on the teaching staff for a further year, but a combination of financial stringency and Ullmann's lack of ease with his methods led to his departure in July 1955, taking with him the energy and determination to follow up his new insights.

Leonard Elmhirst, always a profound supporter of Laban's far-reaching ideas on the fundamental role of movement in the spiritual and physical health of the human race, was concerned for the future. He took the initiative to suggest and achieve the formation of a Trust designed to protect and promote Laban's research while simultaneously safeguarding the generosity of his son Bill. The Laban Art of Movement Centre was thus inaugurated, in October 1954, including the Art of Movement Studio in its jurisdiction, so giving Laban, at last, a status for his research. In exchange for the freehold of the Addlestone site, Laban and Ullmann contracted to give their services, their books and papers, and the Art of Movement Studio, to the Trust. Whether they really absorbed what they had undertaken, namely to give up their personal independence in return for property, is debatable. Laban had never done such a thing before.

An unwelcome subtext could not be hidden: that however excellent Ullmann might be at teaching, she was not thought to be the person to interpret and project Laban's profound insights for the public. Without Carpenter, Leonard Elmhirst saw that the breadth of the wisdom emanating from Laban in his last years of mature thought was in danger of being swamped rather than supported by Ullmann's institution, concentrating as it did almost exclusively on teachers. Leonard's brother Pom, with Lawrence and Joan Goodrich, became Trustees and were joined shortly afterwards by the educationist Christian Schiller. The records of the Trustees show that Ruth Foster, an educationist with a special interest in drama as well as dance, was approached to join Ullmann. She would be expected to broaden the scope of the Art of Movement Studio and to encourage inclusion of other arts in the curriculum. As an experienced and gifted speaker with extensive command of the English language, she was judged by the Trustees to be a valuable person who could present Laban's mature thought to a broad spectrum of professional people. But she declined. It would have been difficult for anyone to join the Laban/Ullmann domain. He might have welcomed it, but she would have experienced it as an intrusion. Foster apparently found the atmosphere at Addlestone too claustrophobic for her taste.

In October Laban's contribution to the world of work was given establishment recognition when he was featured as Man of the Month in *Scope: The Magazine for Industry*. It carried a substantial article on his innovations, especially on the relation of the worker's profile to the work to be done. In the same month he joined Diana Jordan again in Yorkshire, there to advise rather than teach. The five days were reported as a resounding success and as a source of delight to him.

The last four years of Laban's life were relatively calm, punctuated by increasing episodes of ill health. His seventy-fifth birthday was planned as a celebration with gifts and dancing at the Toynbee Hall Theatre in London. British Dance Theatre dedicated Loman's new work *Catch Me a Hay Ride* to him. Heynssen had written the music score for it and I had notated it. Stephenson contributed solos, and Martin Browne of the British Drama League addressed the audience. Laban was not there, but again in hospital. By February 1955 he was well enough to give another Laban Lecture at the Guild's Annual Conference. The title, 'The Three R's of Art of Movement Practice' (recreation, research, rehabilitation) enabled him to talk about recreation as creative group dancing. 'To make a personal and communal statement *in movement* about that which inspires and occupies us is surely something entirely independent from all other forms of incentives,' he said. The autonomy of dance, the uniqueness of the danced statement, was what he wanted to convey. Today we forget that these ideas were not understood. On research, he emphasised future investigation of personal and collective expression, knowing that he could only glimpse what future generations might uncover, believing and hoping that he had contributed. Today these investigations have developed into the disciplines of choreology and ethnochoreology, and influenced anthropology, sociology and more. Rehabilitation, the third R, he described as in its infancy, referring to the gradual recognition of organic therapies. The curative effects of dance could be experienced in festive dance activity and in dance as an art therapy, dance therapy as a fully professional occupation being his unstated vision.

In his research time spent at Addlestone, Laban worked with his last apprentice, Marion North. His insights collated with Carpenter were directed to personality assessment and career advice. This centred on effort observation techniques, 'for which North had a remarkable gift', he wrote to Gleisner in America. He remained in touch professionally with Esmé Church, with Paton Lawrence, and with Withymead. Jordan's work at Wooley so attracted him that he wrote to her expressing his spiritual affinity with her and his willingness to advise there again, which he did.

After contributing to a summer course on the arts in general at Hereford and going on to their own summer course at Ashridge, Ullmann started the

1955–56 season by adding evening classes in London to her already full-time job as principal and administrator, as well as right-hand woman professionally and domestically for Laban. No wonder then, that the Trustees responded to her requests for more help – though not always in the way she wanted. Their concern was for her overtaxing schedule, but also for her reluctance to delegate and to co-operate with them. In their turn, they seemed unable to appreciate that Laban's way of functioning had always been highly individual, highly self-motivated, self-justified, pragmatic, visionary; on paper it might appear impractical, but it was (mostly) thoroughly feasible. The financial uncertainties were worrying to the business minds of Trustees (though quite normal for Laban and Ullmann), so plans were suggested to bring together under one umbrella the various Laban enterprises – the Guild, the Modern Dance Holiday Courses, the various groups affiliated to the Guild, the notation enterprises, Laban's industrial work, the personality assessment research, and so on. No doubt it appealed in principle to Laban, but such diverse activities undertaken by people with distinct aims, talents and interests did not bring the parties together at all readily. They experienced little in common, although they knew that there was a common thread: movement. The motivation to amalgamate was just not there. Nor did Diana Jordan, a woman with an independent turn of mind, see any purpose in relinquishing her leadership of the Modern Dance Holiday Courses to a central bureaucracy with Ullmann as its main executive. Unfortunately, Ullmann's attraction as a superb teacher was diminished by her reputation as a possessive protector of the man himself.

Laban continued to appear from time to time at courses, notably in West Riding, spoke at conferences, gave the Laban Lecture annually for the Guild and was polite to visitors from abroad who came to see his centre and 'the great man himself'. He completed one more book, *The Principles of Dance and Movement Notation*, begun some ten years earlier. He did not want to spend time on it, but in order to gain a copyright on his own system, in the light of the imminent publication in America of a Labanotation textbook by Ann Hutchinson, he had to publish it. So, with me to assist with the technical illustrations, he finished it, to be published by Macdonald & Evans in 1956.

Laban's last choric dance work was a Saltata (the dance equivalent to a cantata) performed in March 1955 at Wembley Stadium in a Festival of Movement and Dance organised by the Central Council for Physical Recreation. Bizet's *L'Arlésienne Suite* was chosen as the music, and, with support from Ullmann, he devised a festive work for high, medium and low dancers. The Art of Movement Studio students formed the core of the cast, with others joining the many rehearsals in London. The mood was alternately joyous, solemnly calm and vigorously forthright. It was good to perform, but unadventurous. This was no *Titan* of 1927, no *Faust* of 1922, no *Tauwind in der Neuen Freude* of 1936. Nevertheless, beside the other performers, who were mostly of the *Körperkultur* sort, the Women's League of Health and Beauty being one such group, choric movement as art was clearly visible in this harmonious work.

In the summer of 1955, a new large architect-designed space for dance was opened adjoining the studios at Addlestone. A gift from Beatrice Loeb, of the Rome Kammertanz of 1924–25, it was named the Saltarium. A Saltata was created and performed in celebration, and this new space greatly enhanced the facilities, as student numbers increased. Even this increase was not sufficient to provide enough income for the Addlestone enterprise to be profit-making. Without weekend, evening and holiday teaching, Ullmann and Laban would have had a very bare living. They and the young faculty had earned considerably less for two years than the maintenance grants from the Ministry given to their students.

Laban was well enough to be present throughout the Modern Dance Holiday Course at Ashridge in August. He taught effort leading to characterisation and dance drama. Jordan, Ullmann and North gave complementary courses. Choral dancing on the lawns in Ashridge's sublime and baronial surroundings satisfied one side of Laban's nature-loving personality. He was still well enough to contribute to the October refresher course for Corporate Members (by now called Professional Members). At Brighton, twenty-three dedicated dancers shared the 'nectar' of Laban, Ullmann and Bodmer, the Central European trio. Ullmann trained them, Bodmer engaged them in group sensitivity, and Laban, 'in his liveliest manner', inspired them, Adda Heynssen completing the quartet with her music.

The 1955–56 season included four Saturdays at the YWCA in central London on 'choral dance plays', created, rehearsed and informally performed, Laban and Ullmann leading them. The push towards establishing a firm Laban culture in London, as there had been (and still was) in Manchester, Lancashire and Yorkshire, was as strong as ever. Over the next years, evening classes in London, three times a week, were the norm, North sharing the burden with Ullmann.

The feeling that his life was coming to a close led to increased activity by Laban to get his researches and his acute movement observation skills passed on to capable apprentices. Warren Lamb and Marion North were working with John Armistead on the Laban/Lawrence Test. Laban started, with North, a correspondence course on movement observation, and a

267

twelve-week course on 'the psychological implications of movement'. He and North started a Youth Advice Bureau based on each individual's 'movement portrait'. He collaborated with Mr Burman of Paton Lawrence on patenting and marketing a collapsible icosahedron to facilitate understanding of his choreutic work. It all seemed somewhat frantic and fractured, but in reality his insights into the psychological ingredients of movement, on which he was working with Carpenter when the latter died and on which he continued to work with North, formed a core of new knowledge with which he experimented, to the end. *Effort and Recovery*, the final title of this work, remained unfinished. Other half-finished documents abound from this period.

Some of Laban's long-lost children visited him. Perrottet's son Allar established an apparently happy rapport with his father, but shortly after returning to Switzerland, where he had professional problems in his career as a theatre designer, he committed suicide. Laban was profoundly affected by his death. For the first time in his life he experienced extreme guilt when contemplating his gross and life-long neglect of his children. Allar had resented it; little Dussia never forgave either parent. While Laban was ill in the summer of 1957, his youngest son Roland came. For the first time his begotten children and his movement children met each other, with a suspicion of rivalry.

The Trustees were troubled. What would happen when he died? Who would carry on his broad ideas? Would Ullmann manage to teach and to administer what was now a larger concern, with greater overheads, higher costs and not much more income? They proposed an advisory committee for strategic planning to complement the existing management committee. For Laban, the thought of being directed, encouraged, supported and organised by two layers of committees must have created a mixture of annoyance, amusement and fatigue. Laban was not comfortable with finding himself an employee in his last years. His free spirit had to take flight in walks in the gardens, while the student teachers danced their choreutics and dance-drama on the lawn under the tutelage of the younger generation. Leonard Elmhirst, Lawrence and Goodrich understood his vision pretty well, but Pom Elmhirst struggled to comprehend. Christian Schiller, an educationist of repute, was brought in as an extra Trustee, but he proved impatient with the idiosyncrasies of the Laban set-up. For Ullmann, doubly anxious about the evident down-turn in Laban's health and about her own future, and with her difficulty in coming to terms with the successes of her younger colleagues and the methods of her Trustees, this was not an easy time.

As Laban's influence grew world-wide, the man's energies were ebbing, his ill health finally overcoming his will. He did give the opening inspirational talk, on rhythm, to the incoming students for the 1957–58 season, introducing them to 'creation day', the traditional baptism of fire whereby, having just arrived, and knowing neither fellow students nor teachers, everyone created something and performed it for the rest. He saw the appointment as administrator of an educationist, George Cruikshank, to take the burden from Ullmann. He was aware that at an international gathering in Germany approval had been given for his notation to be adopted as the universal tool for dance research, especially in folk dance. He gave his last Laban Lecture in February 1958, on 'The World of Rhythm and Harmony'. It was simply an exposition on his beloved land of silence and his appreciation of Plato's quest. One of his last assignments was to give a speech at the Conference of the Joint Council for Education through Art, Ullmann and North speaking too. Movement, he said, concerns the whole person; not mere motion, but movement is the great integrator, with all its spiritual implications.

Laban died on 1 July 1958. His funeral service in Weybridge Parish Church was bizarre. Neither he nor the majority of the packed and distraught congregation were churchgoers. To the dancers, teachers, therapists, actors and collaborators, traditional words seemed utterly inappropriate for his life. He was buried in an inconspicuous grave in the cemetery at Weybridge. Eventually a stone was placed. It reads: 'Rudolf Laban', and above his name, 'A Life for Dance'.

Laban's apprentices and collaborators struggled with the inevitable traumas that follow the death of a person of genius. His range was so enormous that no single person could begin to encompass all of it. Today his concepts are alive and well, adapted, pruned and developed to accommodate the needs and demands of the twenty-first century.

13

No End

Although Laban was in Britain for the last twenty years of his life, and in this book I have concentrated on his immediate surroundings, his work had already taken root elsewhere during his lifetime. The last forty years since his death have shown that the many branches to his core ideas have become established parts of the international heritage of the movement arts. It is not an exaggeration to claim that evidence of his ideas working well can be found as far afield as Japan, China, New Zealand, Canada and the United States, South Africa, Brazil, Chile, as well as east and west Europe and elsewhere, with wide acknowledgement of his contribution. To document this posthumous expansion adequately would require another book. All that can be included here is a glimpse of the activities and influence of some of his foremost and close students and colleagues through whom the expansion of his work has proceeded.

Because his focus shifted throughout his life as opportunities offered themselves and interests erupted, people who worked with him in 1913, 1921, 1936, 1942, 1949 or 1953, for example, encountered his perspectives and priorities of that moment. All developed whatever Laban had given them, so that now we can trace his initiating ideas in dance theatre, dance scholarship, dance therapy, choreology, ethnochoreology, dance literacy, dance as recreation, drama, movement profiling and dance education. The breadth of influence of one man is astounding.

Mary Wigman, his earliest and foremost colleague in dance theatre, retained her pre-eminence as the outstanding modern dancer of Germany in the 1920s and 1930s. She has a place in every history book. Her post-war teaching kept European Modern Dance alive and she gave inspirational training to dancers and dance teachers who have permeated European dance. Numbers of her pre-war students and members of her ensemble emigrated, especially to the United States, where she was famous through her tours. Their work could be found in small companies and schools from the 1930s onwards across the country, giving America a European dimension to the explosion in modern dance associated with Martha Graham,

Doris Humphrey and Charles Weidman. Wigman people filtered into the university campuses as the dance departments began to be an accepted part of American college life. Her influence on American dance is immense.

The most renowned Wigman follower in America was Hanya Holm whose teaching and choreographing in New York put her into the same category as the other great pioneers of American modern dance. Her teaching retained the emphasis on space and dynamics and kinetic studies while other pioneers developed their own style of dance technique. Through her adaptation of Wigman's Laban-inspired method, Holm's influence is unequalled as a teacher who enabled dancers to find their own voice, as Laban did in his day.

Kurt Jooss returned to Essen in 1951, to direct the Folkwangschule dance department and to re-establish a dance company. He continued to choreograph. The works that have remained in the international repertory are those notated in Labanotation. Today his daughter Anna Markard re-stages these on the major ballet companies, so keeping German modern dance ballets before an international public. The revolution of *Tanztheater* emerged from Pina Bausch's hand, her first training being at the Folkwang-schule in Jooss's time there. Her debt to Laban's dance theatre is visible.

Albrecht Knust returned to the Folkwangschule in Essen after the war, there to continue his scholarly work safeguarding and developing Laban's notation as Kinetography Laban. He trained thoroughly a small number of notators who have gone on to pioneer the use of notation as a research tool in dance, especially in folk dance, ethnology, ethnochoreology and anthropology. His influence is felt especially in Europe, including eastern European countries. His leadership, with Ann Hutchinson, of the research side of the International Council of Kinetography Laban (ICKL), generated discussion on issues of analysis and orthography of the notation. The ICKL continues as the active forum for debate on dance literacy through notation.

Ann Hutchinson's personal influence on the development and promotion of Laban's notation, at first in New York and later in London, has been profound. The Dance Notation Bureau, which she opened with others in the 1940s, operates as the busy hub of new careers in dance of notator, reconstructor and dance director. The Bureau's extension at Ohio State University has led to the inclusion of Labanotation in postgraduate work and in the training of professional reconstructors. Hutchinson's book *Labanotation* is the internationally read textbook. She has trained notators and been part of the modernisation of notation technology as well as showing how dance literacy as a whole, so close to Laban's heart, is a modern tool for dance research. She contributed to the setting up of the

Labanotation Institute at Guildford in England. Hutchinson has had to cope with the Benesh notation organisation being, as it were, on her doorstep in London and rightly successful within the ballet world. After an early period of jostling for position, a situation of co-existence has settled, the present generation of notation students enjoying a choice.

Lisa Ullmann, for whom Laban's death was a personal tragedy, continued as Principal of the Art of Movement Studio at Addlestone until 1972, leading the training there of teachers of modern educational dance. She saw the expansion of his educational work into the majority of primary schools and countless secondary schools in Britain. She became a focal point for visitors interested in his work and oversaw the posthumous publication of *Choreutics* and new editions and translations of his earlier books. She published his drawings in *A Vision of Dynamic Space* and took upon herself the task of collating Laban's papers. Lisa Ullmann continued as a loyal ambassador for Laban's work throughout her life, travelling internationally.

Irmgard Bartenieff, a Laban Diploma graduate who emigrated to America, took her understanding of Laban's therapeutic and notation work with her. She pioneered bodily therapy based on her Laban heritage and opened the Laban/Bartenieff Institute in New York, initially as a complementary institution to the Dance Notation Bureau. There her vision, combined with that of others, is used to train people in movement analysis centred on Laban's experiential effort and space work. Trainees from that institution have fanned out all over America and into Europe.

Until the 1970s modern educational dance became integrated into the British state education system, being taught in most primary schools and a proportion of secondary schools. At that point an uncomfortable transition took place, accommodating modern educational dance to the importation of American modern dance. Laban's modern educational dance was exported especially to Canada, Australia and South Africa, through residencies and summer courses given by outstanding teachers with Laban training from the Art of Movement Studio. From these short courses the work spread. Wherever child-based education was valued Laban's educational work has flourished. As soon as subject-centred work became politically correct his creative emphasis gave way in favour of educating children in dance as a body of knowledge to be learned rather than a means to individual growth. Thereby his notation and analytical methods became more prominent within education than his experiential work. Although the educational climate in Britain shifted during the end of Ullmann's period of influence, this shift did not occur simultaneously in other countries, so that while interest in Laban's educational work waned in Britain it waxed elsewhere. This see-saw situation continues, in politically motivated rises and falls.

Laban's work can be found in drama schools in unexpected places; São Paulo in Brazil for example, Durban in South Africa. Yat Malmgren's system of character analysis based on Laban's text has been taught by him to generations of theatre students at the Drama Centre, while Jean Newlove trains actors at the East 15 Centre, both in London. Many well known actors thank their Laban-based training, Bernard Hepton and Sean Connery among them. Being dependent on the initiative of individuals, no one method developed in detail on a par with that in dance education. Now Laban movement work for actors is usually combined with the methods of other renowned theatre men, Laban's effort theories being a perfect complement to Stanislavsky's and Grotowski's recommendations.

Movement and dance therapy, centred on Laban's understanding of the correlation of Jungian psychology with an individual's effort behaviour, is now established on both sides of the Atlantic. Researchers have developed related models with other psychological bases and together initiated the profession of movement and dance therapist. Diagnosis is achieved through movement observation and interpretation and a movement programme is introduced as treatment alongside other arts therapies and conventional methods.

Dance morphology has been made possible through Laban's pioneering work. Studies in the phenomenology of dance have confirmed his insights into the pre-reflective nature of movement experience, proprioceptive studies have furthered his initial focus on awareness of the body, cognitive psychology studies have evaluated his choreutic understanding, confirming his advice on mapping spatial experience. Wherever dance studies require a detailed look at the movement material, Laban's methods are still regarded as invaluable, and are capable of being integrated into interdisciplinary dance research. While the sociology of dance and dance politics contribute methods of looking at dance from an outsider's point of view, in order to reach a scholarly level of the insider's view of dance some aspects of Laban's work are almost always essential. Choreology, the scholarly study of the movement of dance, initiated by Laban, has been expanded to encompass a multi-perspective of dance as a whole event which includes aural, visual and kinetic study of the performer, the sound or music and the space and time in which the dance takes place.

The Art of Movement Studio became subsumed into the Laban Centre for Movement and Dance when Marion North took over its directorship on

Lisa Ullmann's retirement in 1972. She shifted the emphasis from education only to Laban's earlier fascination with dance theatre at the cutting edge and gradually expanded the Centre into the international training institution that it is now, integrating practical and academic excellence. It offers courses in choreology, design and music for dance, dance politics and sociology, dance history and dance literacy. With its specialist dance library to complement the main focus on dance as theatre, the breadth of the High School for Dance devised by Laban and Wigman in 1929 but never achieved in his lifetime, is being realised. The Centre's dancers, choreographers, scholars, notators and teachers are now found across the globe.

North's own published work on personality assessment through effort observation is widely used by movement and dance therapists today. Warren Lamb's contact with Laban enabled him to transform the Laban/Lawrence Industrial Rhythm into Action Profiling. Lamb has focused on the selection of management teams through observation of candidates' movement preferences, but Action Profiling is used by other people wherever the dynamics of social interaction are the focus in behavioural studies. The work of these two apprentices has carried forward the focus of Laban's last years. He said to theatre director Joan Littlewood who congratulated him on his inspiring introduction of effort, 'It is only just beginning.' That is how it has proved to be.

While a young teacher my apprenticeship led me to expand Laban's writing on modern educational dance into a practical handbook for teachers, still used. It led me to expand his notation to cope with improvisation through introducing Motif Writing, now part of the system. I found that his choreutic practice, which I received as movement scales, was capable of transformation into ways of using space for post-modern choreographers. On behalf of the Laban Centre for Movement and Dance I curated the Laban Collection, quantities of documents on the man's life and work prior to 1945 collected from all over Europe. It is now a publicly accessible resource for scholars. Inspired by the master choreographer Aurel Milloss, I returned to Laban's desire for the establishment of choreology not only as a science of folk dance, which was already well established, but of theatre dance. To do so entailed looking at how other artist/researchers deal with time, energy, space, and kinetic flow – Merce Cunningham for example, George Balanchine, Pina Bausch, William Forsythe. Today's choreological studies based on his insights moves forward into coping with the theory of digital dance and video dance, and the border crossing of contemporary choreographers towards neighbouring art forms.

Countless individuals who encountered Laban directly – far too many to name – went on to successful careers in the movement arts and sciences, or simply found their lives radically enhanced. Now people trained by the second, third and fourth generations of Laban-based teachers continue the dissemination of whatever part of his heritage appeals to their gifts and functions in their domain. From time to time a person returns to Laban's texts, searches them deeply for the richness of content that lies beneath the somewhat awkward writing style. Three examples working internationally have to suffice. South African Rosemary Brandt applies her understanding of Labananalysis to the teaching of ballet. The Dutchman Ruud Vermey applies choreological concepts to his training of champions in Latin-American sport dance. The third is American, the renowned choreographer William Forsythe. He has transformed and expanded Laban's choreutics according to his own aesthetic and iconoclasm to find a unique way of creating new movement.

In a BBC radio broadcast in 1997 a concerted view was voiced that Laban was a genius. Working in movement, the most ephemeral of media, it is easy for his genius to become invisible. The evidence of his influence is not amenable to the usual publicity treatment, the prestigious coffee-table book or the appealing film. It is contained in the dancing of generations of young people for whom movement is an enthralling medium, one freed and opened out by his humane insights. There are plenty of people all over the globe who intend to carry on addressing the crucial questions that he raised on how to provide for the innate need for people to use their bodies expressively through art. He used the phrase 'the desert of dancelessness' for cultures that ignore that need. It seems that wherever his message is heard the desert starts to bloom.

Glossary

Bewegungschöre. Movement choir. A similar concept to a singing choir or a speech choir: a group of amateur men and women learning and participating in an artistic work, sometimes coming together with another choir to perform the work together. Dance works created for movement choirs were choric works designed to be danced by trained amateurs for their own enjoyment, with spiritual or uplifting content of some sort. Occasionally soloists danced particular roles with them, and sometimes the choir acted as the moving chorus in a local opera production. Just as singing choirs join together to sing at Christmas or Easter and used to join to sing at wedding celebrations and harvest festivals, so choric works were created to celebrate local events and seasonal changes, the solstice or dawn, strictly never associated with any religious denomination.

Bund. Best translated as guild. It is an organisation of like-minded people bonded together through pursuance of a common cause, possibly with some promise of affiliation given on joining.

Choreographie. The literal translation is dance writing, that is, dance notating; and that is how Laban used it. Today, as 'choreography', it stands for making new dances or composing a new work.

Choreographisches Institut. Literally, an institution for dance writing. Laban deliberately used this term to mean both the notating of dances on paper and the composing of new dance works. It might more appropriately have been called the Choreologisches Institut, for it was the logic of dance that was researched there in practice and in written form. However, Laban took the view that choreological knowledge was needed and used by choreographers in the construction and editing of their works. Hence the use of the open-ended adjective 'choreographisches'.

Choreology. The science of dance, or the logic of dance; the study of the

276

hidden rules in movement that make it expressive and functional rather than arbitrary and nonsensical. Originally choreology encompassed eukinetics, choreutics, kinetography and choreosophy. Today it has developed to include the perspectives on movement and on dance offered by other artist/researchers since Laban's death.

Choreosophy. Literally, the study of dance wisdom. The history of dance from pre-history to today reveals the consistent role of dance in culture, taking social, theatrical and religious forms. The wisdom lies in understanding these manifestations, including their magic, and their significance for human well-being.

Choreutics. The study of the spatial forms of movement. A term coined by Laban alongside eukinetics to elevate this study into a subject essential for the development of dance. Choreutics is a multilayered subject. On the surface it consists in spatial exercises or scales, comparable to musical scales, performed as everyday bodily training. These are organised in and around the octahedron, the cube and the icosahedron. The first produces stable movement scales in the cardinal directions; the cube orientation produces off-balance labile scales, all diagonal; the icosahedron produces scales which balance stability and lability. It was these that Laban developed as his working system of space harmony (*Raumlehre*). He had in his mind Arnold Schoenberg's *Harmonielehre*, the description of his new atonal system of musical harmony. Hidden in choreutics is Laban's knowledge of the wisdom of crystals, the secrets of mathematics present since pre-history, used by the ancient Egyptians and described in the Hellenic period by Plato and Plotinus.

Effort. The dynamic rhythm of a person's movement. In personal effort this is created by preferences in how that person responds to the world; that is, how he or she behaves. Such patterns are unique to each individual, and seen in the differences of timing, of weight use, of spatial patterning and flow that a person exhibits. In job effort this is the dynamic rhythm required for a particular task, either a manual task or an administrative one, again seen in use of time, weight, space and flow. Effort developed in connection with Laban's work in industry, and went on to be used in drama, in dance, in personality assessment and in movement therapy.

Eukinetics. The study of the rhythm and dynamics of movement. A term coined by Laban at the beginning of his career to elevate this study from a general interest in rhythm to a subject essential to the development of the domain of dance. Laban wished to show the world that another way to look at the rhythm of movement through its own grammar existed quite distinct from Dalcroze's Eurhythmics, whose grammar was that of music. Eukinetics led to Laban's discovery of effort and the four motion factors that underlie it.

Gymnastik. The literal translation as gymnastics is confusing since it conjures pictures of gymnasts vaulting over boxes and horses, swinging on ropes and parallel bars and so on. That is understood by *Turnen. Gymnastik* consisted of free-standing exercises in unison, sometimes with hand-held balls or ribbons, usually in time with counts or music and executed according to commands.

Kammertanzbühne. Chamber dance theatre. A small group creating and touring programmes of small-scale works, comparable to a chamber music ensemble.

Kinetography. The method for writing movement on paper. Laban's term for his movement and dance notation coined to distinguish it from *Choreographie*, the name for Feuillet's method of 1700. Now more usually known as Labanotation.

Körperkultur. Physical culture. Systems of body movement designed for health (*Hygiene*), beauty (*Schönheit*), strength (*Kraft*), and joy (*Freude*) associated with particular names, Bode, Mensendieck, Loheland; some for women only, some for both men and women. The equivalents today are aerobics, callisthenics, and so on.

Reigen. Literally, a round dance, used commonly in the Middle Ages to describe stepping dances in a ring, possibly holding hands, enjoyed by ordinary people as well as imagined to be dances of angels in heaven. The well-known friezes of the Dance of Death are in *Reigen* form. In Laban's time the term was in common use for a dance for amateurs, ensemble in construction, that had some spiritual content, participatory and possibly celebratory in nature.

Scales. Part of choreutics. Scales are the movement sequences organised on logical bases and used in the dancer's training by Laban schools. *Schwungskalen* or swinging scales are logical sequences danced with momentum and swing so that one movement follows another in three-dimensional variants of swinging to and fro. The logic lies in organising what movement follows another by balancing the directions aimed for and passed through during each swing according to the harmonic balance of the three symmetries in movement: up with down, open with across, backwards with forwards. The A and B scales are sequences of twelve movements, symmetric transformations of each other located in the icosahedron. These scales took some time to crystallise since they were derived from what Laban observed to be the patterns made by people in expressive gesture. They are archetypal in that they are formed as ideal whole body versions of gesture. The A-scale Laban took as having female characteristics, since it was an archetype of the defence movements, especially those found in fencing; while the B-scale was the archetype of attacking movement in fencing and so seen as masculine.

Tanzbühne. Literally, dance-stage or dance-theatre, a term used variously. The Tanzbühne in Hamburg and Berlin was a support organisation, a kind of club, that made block bookings for members for the season. The Tanzbühne Laban was Laban's performing company giving a season of dance works at a known theatre venue and then touring. The Deutsche Tanzbühne was a country-wide support organisation hijacked by the National Socialists. Their purpose was to facilitate the dissemination of Nazi dictums on dance practice and to put on dance performances which promoted Nazi propaganda such as caring for unemployed dancers, rejecting the avant garde, promoting German dancers as the best, and insisting on racial correctness. Laban was appointed Director of the Deutsche Tanzbühne.

Writings by Rudolf Laban

BOOKS

Laban, Rudolf von, *Die Welt des Tänzers* (The Dancer's World), Walter Seifert Verlag, Stuttgart, 1920; 3rd edition, 1926.

Laban, Rudolf von, *Choreographie: Erstes Heft* (Choreography: First Volume), Eugen Diederichs, Jena, 1926.

Laban, Rudolf von, *Gymnastik und Tanz* (Gymnastics and Dance), Gerhard Stalling Verlag, Oldenburg, 1926.

Laban, Rudolf von, *Des Kindes Gymnastik und Tanz* (Gymnastics and Dance for the Child), Gerhard Stalling Verlag, Oldenburg, 1926.

Laban, Rudolf von, *Schrifttanz: Methodik, Orthographie, Erläuterungen* (Written Dance: Methodology, Orthography, Explanations), Universal-Edition, Vienna, 1928; English and French editions, 1930.

Laban, Rudolf von, *Schrifttanz – Kleine Tänze mit Vorübungen* (Written Dance – Short Dances with Preliminary Exercises), Universal-Edition, Vienna, 1930 (text in German, English and French).

Laban, Rudolf von, *Ein Leben für den Tanz*, Carl Reissner Verlag, Dresden, 1935; (trans. 1975 as *A Life for Dance*, see below).

Laban, Rudolf & Lawrence, F.C., *Laban Lawrence Industrial Rhythm/and Lilt in Labour*, Paton Lawrence & Co., Manchester, 1942.

Laban, Rudolf and Lawrence, F.C., *Effort*, Macdonald & Evans, London, 1947.

Laban, Rudolf, *Modern Educational Dance*, Macdonald & Evans, London, 1948.

Laban, Rudolf, *Mastery of Movement on the Stage*, Macdonald & Evans, London, 1950; 2nd edition revised by Ullmann, Lisa, *The Mastery of Movement*, ibid., 1960; 4th edition revised and enlarged by Ullmann, Lisa, *The Mastery of Movement*, ibid., 1980.

Laban, Rudolf, *Principles of Dance and Movement Notation*, Macdonald & Evans, London, 1956.

Laban, Rudolf (ed. Ullmann, Lisa), *Choreutics*, Macdonald & Evans, London, 1966.

Laban, Rudolf (compiled by Ullmann, Lisa), *A Vision of Dynamic Space*, Falmer Press in association with Laban Archives, London, 1984.

ARTICLES

Laban, Rudolf von, 'Symbole des Tanzes und Tanz als Symbol' (Symbols of dance and dance as symbol), *Die Tat* (December 1919) pp. 669–675.

Laban, Rudolf von, 'Kultische Bildung im Feste' (Religious education in festival), *Die Tat* (June 1920) pp. 161–168.

Laban, Rudolf von, 'Die Bewegungskunst und das neue Theater' (The art of movement and the new theatre), *Die Fahne* (January 1921) pp. 14–19.

Laban, Rudolf von, 'Eurhythmie und Rakorhythmie in Kunst und Erziehung' (Eurhythmy and "Rakorhythmie" in art and education), *Die Tat* (May 1921) pp. 137–139.

Laban, Rudolf von, 'Der moderne Tanz' (The modern dance), *Die Tat* (February 1922).

Laban, Rudolf von, 'Festwille und Festkultur' (Desire for festival and culture of festival), *Die Tat* (February 1922) pp. 846–848.

Laban, Rudolf von, 'Aus einem Gespräch über das Tanztheater' (From a discussion about dance theatre), *Die Tat* (December 1922) pp. 676–680.

Laban, Rudolf von, 'Die Erneuerung in der Bewegungsregie des Theaters' (Renewal in the directing of movement in the theatre), *Hamburger Anzeiger* 19 May 1923.

Laban, Rudolf von, 'Tanzformen' (Dance forms), *Die Rampe* (magazine of the Deutsches Schauspielhaus, Hamburg) (Season 1924/25, 1 November).

Laban, Rudolf von, 'Vom Geist des Tanzes' (The spirit of dance), *Die Rampe* (magazine of the Deutsches Schauspielhaus, Hamburg) (Season 1924/25, 1 November).

Laban, Rudolf von, 'Der Tanz und die neue Generation' (Dance and the new generation), *Die Freude* (September 1925) pp. 398–402.

Laban, Rudolf von, 'Der Tanz als Eigenkunst' (Dance as an art in itself), *Zeitschrift für Äesthetik und Allgemeine Kunstwissenschaft* (1925) pp. 356–364.

Laban, Rudolf von, *Choreographische Abende* (Choreographic evenings) (booklet, 1925).

Laban, Rudolf von, 'Tanztheater und Tanztempel' (Dance theatre and dance temple), *Die Schönheit* (Heft 1, 1926) pp. 42–48.

Laban, Rudolf von, 'Das Tanztheater' (The dance theatre), *Die Schönheit* (Heft 1, 1926, *Appendix*) pp. 3–4.

Laban, Rudolf von, 'Plagiat in Tanz und Gymnastik' (Plagiarism in dance and gymnastics), *Die Schönheit* (Heft 2, 1926, *Appendix*) pp. 19–20.

Laban, Rudolf von, 'Vom Sinn der Bewegungschöre' (The idea of movement choirs), *Die Schönheit* (Heft 2, 1926) pp. 84–91.

Laban, Rudolf von, 'Geist und Form des Tanzes' (Spirit and form of dance), *Der Tanz* (November 1927) pp. 2–5.

Laban, Rudolf von, 'Das tänzerische Kunstwerk/oder: Wie es leiben und leben sollte' (The dance art work/ or: how it should be to a T), *Die Tat* (November 1927) pp. 588–591.

Laban, Rudolf von, 'Tanztheater und Bewegungschor' (Dance theatre and movement choir), in Gentges, Ignaz (ed.) *Tanz und Reigen* (Dance and 'Reigen') (Bühnenvolksbundverlag, Berlin, 1927) pp. 72–79.

Laban, Rudolf von, 'Vortragsbezeichnungen und Bewegungsbegriffe' (Performance expressions and movement terms), in Stefan, Paul (ed.), *Tanz in dieser Zeit* (Dance at this time) (Universal-Edition, Vienna, 1927) pp. 25–28.

Laban, Rudolf von, 'Choreographie und Theater' (Choreography and theatre), *Der Scheinwerfer* (March 1928) p 22.

Laban, Rudolf von, 'Tanzschrift und Schrifttanz' (Dance notation and written dance), *Schrifttanz*, (June 1928).

Laban, Rudolf von, with Skoronel, Vera, 'Zwei äusserungen zum II. Deutschen Tänzerkongress' (Two comments on the 2nd German Dancers' Congress), *West-Woche* (Düsseldorf) (June 1928) pp. 10–11.

Laban, Rudolf von, 'Grundprinzipien der Bewegungsschrift' (Basic principles of movement notation), *Schrifttanz* (July 1928) pp. 4–5.

Laban, Rudolf von, 'Tanzkomposition und Schrifttanz' (Dance composition and written dance), *Schrifttanz* (October 1928) pp. 19–20.

Laban, Rudolf von, 'Die Entwicklung der Bewegungsschrift Laban' (The development of the Laban movement notation), *Schrifttanz* (October 1928) pp. 27–30.

Laban, Rudolf von, 'Vom Tanzinhalt' (The content of dance), *Der Tanz* (November 1928) pp. 2–3.

Laban, Rudolf von, 'Das chorische Kunstwerk' (The choral art work), *Singchor und Tanz* (Heft 12, 1928) pp. 160–161.

Laban, Rudolf von, 'Das tänzerische Kunstwerk' (The dance art work), *Die Tat* (November 1927) pp. 588–591.

Laban, Rudolf von, 'Vom Tanzinhalt: Studien über die Pole des Tanzkunstwerkes' (The content of dance: studies concerning the poles of the dance art work), *Der Tanz* (Heft I, 1928) pp. 2–3.

Laban, Rudolf von, 'Grundprinzipien der Bewegungsschrift' (Basic principles of movement notation), *Schrifttanz* (October 1928) pp. 4–5.

Laban, Rudolf von, 'Tanzkomposition und Schrifttanz' (Dance composition and written dance), *Schrifttanz* (October 1928) pp. 19–20.

Laban, Rudolf von, 'Die Entwicklung der Bewegungsschrift Laban' (The development of the Laban movement notation), *Schrifttanz* (October 1928) pp. 27–30.

Laban, Rudolf von, 'Choreographie und Theater' (Choreography and theatre), *Der Scheinwerfer* (Heft 11/12, 1928) p 22.

Laban, Rudolf von, 'An die deutsche Tänzerschaft' (To the German dance community), *Der Sturm* (No. 19, 1928/29) pp. 258–260.

Laban, Rudolf von, 'Die Erneuerung in der Bewegungsregie des Theaters' (Renewal in the directing of movement in the theatre), *Singchor und Tanz* (15 January 1929) pp. 18–19.

Laban, Rudolf von, 'Probleme des Tanzes' (Problems of dance), *Schrifttanz* (January 1929) p 19.

Laban, Rudolf von, 'Rhythmus der Jugend 1929' (Rhythm of youth 1929), in Booklet *Jubilaeumswoche des Nationaltheaters* (Jubilee week of the National-theater [Mannheim]) (June 1929) pp. 21–22.

Laban, Rudolf von, 'Über die tänzerischen Berufe' (The dance professions), *Der Tanz* (December 1929) pp. 2–4.

Laban, Rudolf von, 'Das Choreographische Institut Laban' (The Laban Choreo-graphic Institute), in Freund, Liesel (ed.) *Monographien der Ausbildungsschulen für Tanz und tänzerische Körperbildung Band I Berlin* (Monographs of the train-ing schools for dance and for body training for dance Vol. I Berlin) (Leo Alter-thum Verlag, Berlin, 1929) pp. 11–14.

Laban, Rudolf von, 'Aufgaben und Möglichkeiten der Tanzschrift' (Aims and possi-bilities of dance notation), *Jahrbuch des Tanzes 1929* pp. 196–198.

Laban, Rudolf von, 'Vom Sinn der Bewegungschöre' (The idea of movement choirs), *Schrifttanz* (June 1930) pp. 25–26.

Laban, Rudolf von, 'Anna Pawlowa', *Schrifttanz* (June 1930) pp. 8–9.

Laban, Rudolf von, 'Vom Geist des Tanzes' (The spirit of dance), *Singchor und Tanz* (15 June 1930) pp. 179–180.

Laban, Rudolf von, 'Sinn der Leientanzfeier' (The idea of an amateur dance festi-val), *Tanzgemeinschaft* (No. 3, 1930) p. 5.

Laban, Rudolf von, 'Das Tanztheater' (Dance theatre), *Das Prisma* (Vereinigten Stadttheater Duisburg-Bochum) (Heft 14, 1930–31) pp. 133–136.

Laban, Rudolf von, 'Neue Tanzkunst' (The new art of dance), *Magdeburger Tages-zeitung* (8 December 1934).

Laban, Rudolf von, 'Die deutsche Tanzbühne', *Deutsche Tanzfestspiele 1934 unter Förderung der Reichskulturkammer* (Carl Reissner Verlag, Dresden, 1934) pp. 3–7.

Laban, Rudolf von, 'Deutsche Tanz' (German dance), *Singchor und Tanz* (1934).

Laban, Rudolf von, 'Meister und Werk in der Tanzkunst' (Master and work in the art of dance), *Deutsche Tanz-Zeitschrift* (May 1936) pp. 1–4.

Laban, Rudolf von, 'Entstehung und Entwicklung des Gemeinschaftstanzes' (Origin and development of community dance), *Die Westmark* (August 1936) pp. 608–609.

Laban, Rudolf von, 'Die deutsche Tanzbühne', in *Die tänzerische Situation unserer Zeit* (The dance situation of our time) (Carl Reissner Verlag, Dresden, 1936) pp. 3–7.

Laban, Rudolf 'The President's Address at the AGM of the LAMG' (27 August 1947) (on the breadth of his vision of the art of movement), *LAMG News Sheet* No. 1 (January 1948).

Laban, Rudolf, message of good wishes to first issue, in *Movement* (Summer 1948) p. 3.

Laban, Rudolf, 'What has led you to study movement? (answered by R. Laban)', *LAMG News Sheet* (No. 7, September 1951).

Laban, Rudolf, 'The Key to the Space Harmony of Movement' distributed by Laban on his 70th birthday, December 1949.

Laban, Rudolf, 'Presidential Address at the AGM of the LAMG' (1952) (on Art, Education, and Work), *LAMG News Sheet* (No. 8, March 1952).

Laban, Rudolf, 'The Art of Movement in the School' (given at the Annual Guild Conference 1952), *LAMG News Sheet* (No. 8, March 1952).

Laban, Rudolf, 'The Work of the Art of Movement Studio', *Journal of Physical Education* (Vol. 46, No. 137, 1954) pp. 22-30.

Laban, Rudolf, 'A Letter to Guild Members', *LAMG Magazine* (No. 12, March 1954) pp. 5-9.

Laban, Rudolf, 'The Art of Movement' (The Laban Lecture, 1954) (reported by his secretary D. Bond) (primarily on choreosophic concerns), in *LAMG News Sheet* (No. 12, March 1954) p 22.

Laban, Rudolf, 'Foreword by Rudolf Laban' in Hutchinson, Ann, *Labanotation* (Theater Arts, New York, 2nd edition, 1970) pp. xiii-xvi, (written by Laban in 1954).

Laban, Rudolf, 'Letter to Guild Members', *LAMG Magazine* (No. 14, March 1955) pp. 4-9.

Laban, Rudolf, 'The Three R's of the Art of Movement Practice' (The Laban Lecture 1955), *LAMG Magazine* (No. 14, March 1955).

Laban, Rudolf, 'From Rudolf Laban's Early Writings' (English translations of notes made by Laban which later formed the basis of *Ein Leben für den Tanz* (1935)), *LAMG Magazine* (No. 15, October 1955).

Laban, Rudolf, 'Movement' (The Laban Lecture 1956), *LAMG Magazine* (No. 16, March 1956).

Laban, Rudolf, 'Vorwort' (Foreword) in Knust, Albrecht, *Abriss der Kinetographie Laban* (Outline of Kinetography Laban) (Das Tanzarchiv Verlag, Essen, 1956) pp. ix-xi.

Laban, Rudolf, 'Movement, an Art and a Philosophy' (The Laban Lecture 1957), *LAMG Magazine* (No. 18, March 1957).

Laban, Rudolf, 'Education through the Arts', *LAMG Magazine* (No. 19, November 1957) p. 4.

Laban, Rudolf, 'The Objective Observation of Subjective Movement and Action' (Lecture given at the International Congress of Physical Education for Women), *LAMG Magazine* (No. 19, November 1957).

Laban, Rudolf, 'The World of Rhythm and Harmony' (The Laban Lecture 1958), *LAMG Magazine* (No. 20, March 1958) p. 6.

PUBLISHED POSTHUMOUSLY

Laban, Rudolf, 'Movement as an Integrator, i) Movement Concerns the Whole Man' (talk given on behalf of LAMG. at Whitsun Conference 1958 held at National

Film Theatre by the Joint Council for Education through Art), *LAMG Magazine* (No. 21, November 1958).

Laban, Rudolf, (a collection of his writings, as a tribute): 'The Importance of Dancing' (The Laban Lecture); 'The Educational and Therapeutic Value of Dance'; 'Meaning'; 'Dance and Symbol'; 'The Aesthetic Approach to the Art of Dancing'; 'Dance as a Discipline'; 'The Rhythm of Living Energy'; all in *LAMG Magazine* (No. 22, May 1959).

Laban, Rudolf, 'The Rhythm and Effort of Recovery. Part I', *LAMG Magazine* (No. 23, November 1959).

Laban, Rudolf, 'The Rhythm and Effort of Recovery. Part II', *LAMG Magazine* (No. 24, May 1960).

Laban, Rudolf, 'Light – Darkness', *LAMG Magazine* (No. 25, November 1960).

Laban, Rudolf, 'Dance in General', *LAMG Magazine* (No. 26, May 1961).

Laban, Rudolf, 'Extract from an Address held by Mr Laban on a meeting for Community Dance in 1936', *LAMG Magazine* (No. 52, May 1974).

Laban, Rudolf (trans. and ed. Ullmann, Lisa), *A Life for Dance* (Macdonald & Evans, London, 1975) (see *Ein Leben für den Tanz*, 1935).

Gleisner, Martin, 'Conversations between Laban and myself', *LAMG Magazine* (No. 65, November 1980).

Laban, Rudolf, 'Man Agog', *LAMG Magazine* (No. 67, November 1981).

Laban, Rudolf, 'Notes on Movement Therapy', *LAMG Magazine* (No. 71, November 1983).

Bibliography

Akademie der Kunst der DDR, *Positionen zur Vergangenheit und Gegenwart des modernen Tanzes: Laban, Wigman, Palucca, etc.*, Berlin, Akademie der Kunst, 1982.

Bartenieff, Irmgard, *Body Movement*, New York, Gordon & Breach, 1980.

Bennett, John G., *Gurdjieff: Making a New World*, London, Turnstone Books, 1976.

Benton, Tim, & Benton, Charlotte, *Form and Function: A Source Book for the History of Architecture and Design 1890–1939*, London, Crosby Lockwood Staples, 1975.

Berliner Staatsoper, *200 Years Jubilee Book*, Berlin, M. Hesses Verlag, 1942.

Blavatsky, Helena P., *Key to Theosophy*, 1889.

Bode, Rudolf, *Ausdrucksgymnastik*, Munich, C.H. Beck, 1926.

Brandenburg, Hans, *Der Moderne Tanz*, 3rd edition, Munich, G. Müller, 1921.

Calder, Angus, *The People's War: Britain 1939–1945*, London, Pimlico Edition, 1992.

Campbell, Joan, *The German Werkbund: The Politics of Reform in the Applied Arts*, Princeton, NJ, Princeton University Press, 1978.

Coton, A.V., *The New Ballet: Kurt Jooss and his Work*, London, Dennis Dobson, 1946.

Dell, Cecily, *A Primer for Movement Description*, New York, Dance Notation Bureau, 1970.

Deutschen Gesellschaft für Schrifttanz, *Schrifttanz, Eine Vierteljahresschrift*, Vienna, Universal Edition, 1928–1931, Neudruck, Hildesheim, Georg Olms Verlag, 1991.

Dohrn, Wolf, *Die Aufgabe der Bildungsanstalt Jaques-Dalcroze*, Hellerau, 1912.

Evans, Richard J. (ed.), *Society and Politics in Wilhelmine Germany*, London, Croom Helm, 1978.

Fletcher, Sheila, *Women First: The Female Tradition in English Physical Education 1880–1980*, London and Dover, NH, Athlone Press, 1984.

Foster, John, *The Influence of Rudolph Laban*, London, Lepus Books, 1977.

Fuchs, Georg, *Die Revolution des Theaters; Ergebnisse aus dem Münchener Künstlertheater*, Munich and Leipzig, Georg Müller, 1909.

Gasser, Manuel, *München um 1900*, Munich, Wilhelm Heyne Verlag, 1977.

Ginner, Ruby, *The Revived Greek Dance*, London, Methuen, 1933.

Gleisner, Martin, *Tanz für Alle*, Leipzig, Hesse & Becker Verlag, 1928.

Gosling, Nigel, *Paris 1900–1914: The Miraculous Years*, London, Wiedenfeld & Nicholson, 1978.

Green, Martin, *Mountain of Truth: The Counterculture Begins 1900–1920*, Hanover NH, University Press of New England, 1986.

Günther, Helmut, *Rudolf Laban in Stuttgart, 1920*, unpublished, 1980.

Hart-Davis, Duff, *Hitler's Games: The 1936 Olympics*, London, Century Hutchinson, 1986.

Hodgson, John, & Preston-Dunlop, Valerie, *Rudolf Laban: An Introduction to his Work and Influence*, Plymouth, Northcote House, 1990.

Huelsenbeck, Richard, *Dada Almanach*, Berlin, Erich Reiss Verlag, 1920.

Hutchinson, Ann, *Labanotation*, New York, New Directions, 1954; 3rd edition, New York, Theatre Arts Books, 1977.

Hutchinson, Ann, *Your Move: A New Approach to the Study of Movement and Dance*, London, Gordon & Breach, 1983.

Jaques-Dalcroze, Emile, trans. Rubinstein H.F., *Rhythm, Music and Education*, London, Chatto & Windus, 1921.

Jordan, Diana, *The Dance as Education*, London, Oxford University Press, 1938.

Journal of Physical Education, especially 1933–1970.

Jung, C.G., trans. Hull, R.F.C. *Four Archetypes: Mother, Rebirth, Spirit, Trickster*, London, Routledge, 1972.

Kandinsky, Wassily, trans. Sadler, M.T.H., *Concerning the Spiritual in Art*, New York, Dover Publications, 1977.

Knust, Albrecht, *Dictionary of Kinetography Laban*, Plymouth, Macdonald & Evans, 1979.

Koegler, Horst, 'In the Shadow of the Swastika: Dance in Germany 1929–1936', *Dance Perspectives* 57, (Spring 1974).

Konig, Peter-R, *Das OTO-Phänomen*, Munich, Arbeitsgemeinschaft für Religions- und Weltanschauungsfragen, 1994.

Laban Art of Movement Guild Magazine, especially Nos. 1–29, 1947–1962.

Lamb, Warren, *Posture and Gesture: An Introduction to the Study of Physical Behaviour*, London, Duckworth, 1965.

Lamb, Warren, *Body Code: The Meaning in Movement*, London, Routledge & Kegan Paul, 1979.

Lämmel, Rudolf, *Der Moderne Tanz*, Berlin, Oestergaard Verlag, 1927.

Lange, Roderyk, *The Nature of Dance: An Anthropological Perspective*, London, Macdonald & Evans, 1975.

Lenman, Robin, 'Politics and Culture: The State and the Avant-Garde in Munich 1886–1914,' in Evans, Richard J. (ed.), *Society and Politics in Wilhelmine Germany*, London, Croom Helm, 1978.

Lucie-Smith, Edward, *Symbolist Art*, London, Thames & Hudson, 1972.

Main Currents in Modern Thought, Vol. 31, No. 1., September 1974, (issue on Laban).

Maletic, Vera, *Body Space Expression*, Berlin, Mouton de Gruyter, 1987.

287

Marchev, Robin P., *Wahrheitssucher und Schwindler: Aus der Chronik der Loge Libertas et Fraternitas (bis 1919)*, unpublished, 1990.

Marwick, Arthur, *The Home Front: The British and the Second World War*, London, Thames & Hudson, 1976.

Meltzer, Annabelle, *Latest Rage the Big Drum: Dada and Surrealist Performance*, Ann Arbor MI, UMI Research Press, 1976.

Ministry of Education, *Moving and Growing*, London, HM Stationery Office, 1953.

Morgan, Kenneth O., *The People's Peace: British History 1945–1990*, Oxford, Oxford University Press, 1990.

Morison, Ruth, *Educational Gymnastics*, Liverpool, I.M. Marsh College, 1956.

Müller, Hedwig: *Leben und Werk der Grossen Tänzerin*, Wenheim, Quadriga, 1986.

Müller, Hedwig & Stöckemann, Patricia, '. . . *jeder Mensch ist ein Tänzer'*, Giessen, Anabas-Verlag, 1993.

The New Era in Home and School, May 1959, (issue on Laban).

Newlove, Jean, *Laban for Actors and Dancers,* London, Nick Hern Books, 1993.

North, Marion, *Personality Assessment through Movement*, London, Macdonald & Evans, 1972.

North, Marion, *Movement Education*, London, Maurice Temple Smith, 1973.

Obersaucher-Schüller, G. (ed.), *Ausdruckstanz*, Wilhelmshaven, Florian Noetzel Verlag, 1992.

Open University, *Europe 1900–1914: The Reaction to Historicism and Art Nouveau*, Milton Keynes, Open University Press, 1975.

Pachter, Henry, 'Expressionism and Café Culture', in Bronner, S.E. & Kellner, D., *Passion and Rebellion: The Expressionist Heritage*, New York, Columbia University Press, 1988.

Pagé, Suzanne, & Billeter, Erika, *Sophie Taeuber*, Paris, Musée d'Art Moderne de la Ville de Paris, 1990.

Palmer, Elsie, *Mind and Body: A New Humanism*, Laban Art of Movement Guild, 1958.

Petermann, Kurt, *Tanz Bibliographie*, Munich, KG Saur, 1981.

Peukert, Detlev J.K., trans. Deveson, R., *The Weimar Republic*, London, Penguin, 1991.

Preston-Dunlop, Valerie, *A Handbook for Modern Educational Dance*, London, Macdonald & Evans, 1963; 2nd edition published as *Handbook for Dance in Education*, 1980.

Preston-Dunlop, Valerie, *Readers in Kinetography Series A and B*, London, Macdonald & Evans, 1966/67.

Preston-Dunlop, Valerie, *Practical Kinetography Laban*, London, Macdonald & Evans, 1969.

Preston-Dunlop, Valerie, *Point of Departure: The Dancer's Space,* Sevenoaks, Dunlop, 1984.

Preston-Dunlop, Valerie, 'Laban and the Nazis: towards an understanding of Rudolf Laban and the Third Reich', *Dance Theatre Journal*, Vol. 6 Nos. 2 & 3, 1988.

Preston-Dunlop, Valerie, 'Rudolf Laban: the seminal years in Munich 1910–14', *Dance Theatre Journal*, Vol. 7, Nos. 3 & 4, 1989.

Preston-Dunlop, Valerie, *Laban, Schoenberg and Kandinsky 1899–1938,* in *Danse Tracée,* Paris, Actes Sud, 1990.

Preston-Dunlop, Valerie, 'Laban in Zurich 1914–19: the nightmare years', *Dance Theatre Journal*, Vol. 10, No. 3, 1993.

Preston-Dunlop, Valerie, & Lahusen, Susanne (eds), *Schrifttanz, A View of German Dance in the Weimar Republic*, London, Dance Books 1990.

Read, Herbert, *Education Through Art,* 3rd edition, London, Faber, 1958.

Richter, Hans, *Dada Art and Anti-Art*, New York, Oxford University Press, 1965.

Russell, Joan, *Modern Dance in Education,* London, Macdonald & Evans, 1958.

Schlemmer, Tut (ed.), trans. Krishna Winston, *The Letters and Diaries of Oskar Schlemmer*, Evanston, Northwestern University Press, 1972.

Segel, Harold B., *Turn-of-the-Century Cabaret*, New York, Columbia University Press, 1987.

Sherborne, Veronica, *Developmental Movement for Children*, Cambridge, Cambridge University Press, 1990.

Shirer, William L., *The Rise and Fall of the Third Reich*, New York, Fawcett Crest, 1950.

Sorrell, Walter, *Dance in Its Time*, Garden City, NY, Anchor Press/Doubleday, 1981.

Sorrell, Walter, *Mary Wigman Ein Vermächtnis*, Wilhelmshaven, Florian Noetzel Verlag, 1986.

Sorrell, Walter (ed.), *The Mary Wigman Book*, Middleton, Conn., Wesleyan University Press, 1975.

Spotts, Frederick, *Bayreuth: The History of the Wagner Festival*, Cambridge, Yale University Press, 1994.

Stahl, E.L., *Das Mannheimer Nationaletheater: Ein Jahrhundert Deutscher Theater Kultur im Reich*, Mannheim, Benshermer Verlag, 1929.

Steiner, Rudolf, trans. Hahn, G., *An Introduction to Eurythmy (1913–1924)*, New York, Anthroposophic Press, 1984.

Stuck-Jugendstil Verein, *Herman Obrist: Wegbereiter der Moderne,* Munich, Stuck-Jugendstil Verein, 1968.

Szeemann, Harald, *Monte Verità, Berg der Wahrheit,* Civitanova Marche und Tegna, 1980.

Taylor, A.J.P., *English History 1914–1945*, Oxford, Oxford University Press, 1992.

Thornton, Sam, *A Movement Perspective of Rudolf Laban*, London, Macdonald & Evans, 1971.

Thornton, Susanne (ed.), *Studio 25*, Addlestone Art of Movement Studio, 1971.

Tzara, Tristan, trans. Wright, Barbara, *Seven Dada Manifestos and Lampesteries*, London, John Calder, 1977.

Varnedoe, Kirk, *Vienna 1900, Art, Architecture and Design*, New York, Museum of Modern Art, 1986.

Washton Long, Rose-Carol, *Kandinsky: The Development of an Abstract Style*, Ox-

289

ford, Clarendon Press, 1980.

Weiss, Peg, *Kandinsky in Munich, The Formative Jugendstil Years,* Princeton, NJ, Princeton University Press, 1979.

Wiles, John, & Garrard, Alan, *Leap to Life,* London, Chatto & Windus, 1957.

Willett, John, *The New Sobriety, 1917–1933,* London, Thames & Hudson, 1978.

Winther, F.H., *Körperbildung als Kunst und Pflicht,* München, Delphin-Verlag, 1919.

Wolfenberger, Giorgio J., *Suzanne Perrottet: Ein Bewegtes Leben,* Bern, Benteli Verlag, 1989.

Index

compiled by Frederick Smyth

The name of Rudolf Laban appears on almost every page of the text. To avoid an overloading of the sections under his name many references to him have been placed under other relevant headings.

The subjects of movement – which became Laban's art medium from about 1912 – and notation – interwoven with most of his activities and researches from early years – also receive frequent mention. Their indexation has, for practical purposes, had to be generally restricted to the more significant references.

Bold figures (123) indicate the more important references; italic figures (45) denote illustrations or their captions.

Aachen, Stadttheater, 106
Abraham, Karl, psychoanalyst, 15, 50
Abramowicz, Ruth, dancer, 147
action profiling, 274
Adenauer, Konrad, Mayor (1914) of Cologne, 34
Albrecht-Dürer-Verein, of artists and crafts-men, 53–4
Albu, Dorothea, dancer, 161–3; *53*
Algo, Julian, dancer, 62, 71, 74, 83, 149, 202
Amadeus String Quartet, 250
amateur dance, 58, 92, 98, 254–5, 179
Ambor, Cilly, dancer, 147
American University Theater, 258
Ancient and Mystical Order, Rosae Crucis, 11
Angiolini, Gasparo, dancer and ballet-master, 113, 116
anthropology, 271
anthroposophy, 29
anti-semitism, 5, 51
Aravantinos, stage designer, 167
Archbutt, Sally, dancer and teacher, 242, 256
Archives Internationales de la Danse (1932), Paris, 111, 170, 188, 201, 251
Armistead, John, and movement in industry, 268
Arp, Hans, artist and Dadaist 43–5, 56
art nouveau, 7, 9
art of movement, *see* Bewegungskunst
[Laban] Art of Movement Centre (trust, 1954), Addlestone, 264
    trustees, 264, 266, 268
[Laban] Art of Movement Guild (1946), 239, 248, 251, 257, 262, 266
    conferences, 248, 254, 262, 265
    courses, 259, 262

[Laban] Art of Movement Studio
    Manchester (1945), 185, 238, 240–2, 244, 246, 248–51, 255–9; *64–5, 67*
    Addlestone (1953), 260–2, 264, 267, 272, 274; *75–6*
art therapy, 228, 254–5
Ascona, *see* summer schools
Ash, Maurice, Elmhirst's son-in-law, 254
Atkinson, Madge, dance teacher, 227
Auerbach, Lotte, dancer, 118
Ausdruckstanz, 57, 66, 127, 155–6, 164, 207, 220
Austro-American Conservatoire of Music, Mondsee, 164
Azbe, Anton, art teacher, 7

Bad Mergentheim, Kurhalle, 126
Bagley, Cecelia, student and teacher, 248; *68*
Balanchine, George, dancer, choreographer and director, 274
Ball, Hugo, poet and Dadaist, 43–5; *17*
Ballets Jooss, 170, 172, 177, 180, 205–6, 213, 219, 245
Ballets Russes, 18, 163
Barker, Dr Culver, of Withymead, 254, 259
Barlows Ltd, 235
Barmel, dancer, 46
Barnes, Kenneth, Royal Academy of Dramatic Art, 238
Baron, Mary, dance teacher, 220
Bartlett, Winsome, welfare officer, 221, 223
Bartenieff, Irmgard, dancer and teacher, 246, 254, 272; *70*
basic movement, as a subject, 234–5, 260
Bastor, Willi, critic, 114
Bauer, Lilla, dancer and teacher, 224, 228,

230, 239
Bauhaus, 73, 89, 144, 156, 169
Bauhaus Theatre Department, 117, 156
Bausch, Pina, dancer and director, 129, 271, 274
Bayreuth, Festival Opera House, 152; *52*; *see also* Wagner
Bayreuth, Wagner Festival, *see* Wagner
Becker, Dr, Prussian Minister for Culture, 143, 152
Beckman, Grete, dancer, 94–5
Bedford Physical Training College, 207–8, 211, 215, 220
Beethoven, Ludwig van, 126, 198
  Septet in F major, 128
  Symphony No. 9 in D minor ('Choral'), 195, 198
behaviour patterns, 102–3
Behrens, Peter, architect, 27
Belensson, Raja, dancer, 94
Bell, Edith, dancer, 147
Benda, Dr Emanuel, lawyer, 76, 82
Benesh notation, 272
Bennett, John, writer, 29
Bennett, Leonard, lecturer, 250
Bentham, Graeme, dance teacher, 263
Bereska, Dussia [Olga Feldt], dancer, choreo-grapher and teacher, 83, 90, 96, 112, 121–2, 132, 215; *18, 22, 27, 34–5, 39, 41*
  her child, 'Little Dussia', 48, 96, **111**, 118, 135, 268
  at Bad Mergentheim, 131
  at Burg Lauenstein, 150
  at Gleschendorf, 74
  in Hamburg, 84–7, 90–1, 92, 112–14
  in Italy, 142
  in Mannheim, 69–70
  at Monte Verità, 47–8
  in Munich, 56
  in Nuremberg, 57, 59
  in Paris, 153, 183, 188, 202
  at Plauen, 153
  in Rome, 94
  in Scheveningen, 141
  in Stuttgart, 61
  in Zurich, 52
  touring, 92, 115
  and the Katabü, 123, 128, 134–5, 137, 150
  and the Laban Schools: Paris, 166–7, 170, 175; Rome, 94, 98, **108**
  Laban's colleague, **47–8**, 71, 76, 158, 165, 171, 176–7
  Laban's lover, 47–8, 76, 135
  her comedy, *Interpunktion*, 113
  her solo dances, **84–5**
Bergeest, Karl, dancer, 83, 88, 93–4, 98, 106
Bergin, Marjorie, editor, 258
Berk, Ernst, dancer and choreographer, 257
Berlin Dance Festivals: (1934) **186–7**; (1935) **193**

Berlin Schriftstelle (1935), 190
Berlin theatres
  Berliner Theater, 163
  City Opera (Städtische Oper), 163, 182; ballet school, 173
  Dietrich Eckart Theatre (Freihlichtbühne), 189–90, 191–3, 196; *54–5*
  Kroll Opera House, 158, **161**
  Neuen Theater am Zoo, 124
  Philharmonie, 91
  Schauspielhaus, 172
  Schillertheater, 168
  State Opera House (Staatsoper), 77, 144, 157, 159, 163, **173–4**, 175–6, 181, 195–7; ballet school, 161–2, 173
  Theater am Horst Wessel Platz (Volks-bühne), 123, 130, 197
Berner, Gretl, dancer, 112
Bernstein, A., theatrical agent, 73
Betz, Irma Otte (New York), 119
Bewegungschor, Der (1928), 135
Bewegungschöre (movement choirs), defined, **276**
Bewegungskunst (art of movement)
  Laban's school, Zurich, 39–40
  Laban's vision, 100
  Manchester (1945), 238
Bewegungsschrift, 133
Bie, Oskar, ballet historian and critic, 130, 156, 160, 163, 167, 169
Bienz, Oskar, dancer, 48
Birmingham Dance Club, 224
Bittner, Julius, composer, 147
Bizet, Georges
  Carmen, opera, 168–9, 177
  Die Perlenfischer, opera, 181
  L'Arlésienne, suite, 266
Blaue Reiter, art movements group, 34
Blavatsky, Helena, *Key to Theosophy* (1889), 19
Blech, Leo, conductor, 168
Boalth, Annie, teacher of movement, 206, 251
Bode, Rudolf, theorist, 21, 99, 104, 179, 187, 192, 208
  and 'Kraft durch Freude', 184
  at the Olympic Games (1936), 190
  Ausdrucks-Gymnastik (3rd ed., 1926), 99–100
Bodenwieser, Gertrud, dancer, choreo-grapher and teacher, 207, 226
Bodmer, Margaret, dancer, 77
Bodmer, Sylvia, dancer, choreographer and teacher, 74, 89, 241; *15, 22*
  at Frankfurt, 94, 96, 108, 149, 166, 222
  works in England, 192–3, **222**, 224, 228–9, 262, 267
  at Manchester, 229, 240, 249, 251
  movement research, **258–9**
  recollections, 75, 225, 239

The Forest (with Ullmann, 1947) 241–2
Böhme, Fritz, dance teacher and critic, 81, 118, 151, 179, 185, 201
reviews *Don Juan*, **114–15**, 155, 180, 186, 202
at Dance Congresses, 125, 130, 135–6, 155
Bomsdorff-Berger, Herbert von, theatre director, 48, 51
Borodin, Alexander, *Prince Igor*, opera, 160, 168, 219
Bradford Theatre School, 240–1, 250, 253
Bragaglia, Anton Giulio (Rome), 108
Brand, Max, composer, 146–8
Maschinist Hopkins, opera, 147
Brandenburg, Dora, wife of Hans, 27
Brandenburg, Hans, poet and novelist, 32, 34, 57, 130, 151
at Munich, 17–18, 26–7, 33, 118
and German theatre, 63, 73
and Laban, 57, 63–5, 68, 71, 93
and *Ritterballett*, 126
as a writer, 39, 42, 155
Der Moderne Tanz, 34; (2nd ed., 1917) 34; (3rd ed., 1921) 34, 64
Sieg des Opfers, poem for speech and movement (1914), 34–5
Brandt, Rosemary, ballet teacher, 275
Brecht, Bertolt, playwright, 130, 146
Breton, André, poet and critic, 89
British Dance Theatre (1950), 256–7, 265
British Drama League, 235, 238, 240, 249, 251, 265
Browne, Martin, of the British Drama League, 265
Buchholz, Dr Ludwig, Berlin Labanschule, 118, 125, 133, 135, 154
Buczynska, Zita, dancer, 197
Bund (guild), defined, 276
Burger, Albrecht, dancer, 60–1
Burger, August, administrator, 187, 194–5
Burrowes, Leslie, dance teacher, 207, 212

Cabaret Voltaire, Zurich, 43–6
Campbell, Jean, writer, 34
Carpenter, Bill, and the Addlestone Studio, 260–5, 268; *70*
Carrière, Eugene, on Isadora Duncan, 15
Carrington, Joan, dancer and teacher, 256, 259
Casson, Elma, teacher, 219, 234, 260
Central Council for Physical Recreation, Festival (1955), 267
'Central European Dancing', 207, 213, 215–16, 242, 267
Central School, *see* Laban, schools
Chamberlain, Houston Stewart, Wagner's son-in-law, 157
Champernowne, Gilbert and Irene, and psychotherapy, 222, 254–5, 259, 262
character analysis (Malmgren), 273

Charpentier, Gustave, *Louise*, opera, 161
Chesterton, G.K., *Magie*, 86
children's dance, 216, 225, 229
Chladek, Rosalia, dancer, choreographer and teacher, 155, 170, 245
Contrastes, 170
choral dance, 238
Choreographic Competitions, International
Paris (1932), 169, **170**, 197
Copenhagen (1947), **241**
choreographic method, Laban's, **83–4**
choreography (Choreographie), 118, 122, 126, 205; defined, 276
Choreographisches Institut, 205–6, 220, 224, 263; defined, 276
Wurzburg (1926), 83, 121–2, 126
Berlin (1927), 133–5, 141–3, 150, 216, 253; 39, *45–6*
Essen (1930), 159, 171, 206
choreology (Choreologie), 37, 118, 122, 126, 142, 270, 273–4; defined, **276–7**
choreosophy (Choreosophie), 122, 126, 205; defined, 277
choreutics, 70, 84, 205, 217, 240, 259, 268, 274–5; *38, 66*; defined, **277**
Chorische Bühne, 154
Chruchez, dancer, 46
Church, Esmé, theatre school director, 240–1, 245–6, 250–1, 265
Clarke, E.R., Ministry of Education, 244–5
Clegg, Alec, chief education officer, 233
Cohen, Fritz (Frederic), composer and director of the Jooss/Leeder School, 117, 192
Cohn, Dr Hanns, physician, 212
Colwill, Freda, dance teacher, 207
communism, 52, 82
community dance, 238
Confucius, Chinese philosopher, 102
Connery, Sean, actor, 273
Corak-Slawenska, Mia, dancer, 197
Corret, El, dancer, 74
Cosmic Circle, The, theosophists, 19
Coton, A.V., writer and critic, 241
Cox, Barbara, lecturer in education, 217, 219
Cox, Peter, and the Elmhirsts, 230, 250
Cramér, Ivo, dancer, choreographer and ballet director, *The Message* (1947), 241
Cruikshank, George, educationist, 269
Cunningham, Merce, dancer, choreographer, teacher and director, 274
Cunz, administrator, 187, 199, 202
Curran, Ronnie, dancer, 256; *68*
Cuthbertson, Muriel, pianist, 216

Daan, Lea, dancer and teacher, 210
Dadaism and Dadaists, **43–6**, 55, 63, 130; *17*
Dalcroze, Jaques, *see* Jaques-Dalcroze
Dalcroze Schools: Dresden-Hellerau, 22–3, 38; Vienna, 22
dance as art, 21

dance as education, **226–7**, 228, 231–2
dance as recreation, 269
dance clubs, 'Laban', 224
Dance Competitions, International
    Warsaw (1932), 176, 197
    Vienna (1934), 180–1, 185, 197
    Berlin (1936), 197
Dance Congresses
    Magdeburg (1927), 125–31, 134; *36, 38*
    Essen (1928), 133, **135–8**, 139; *45–6*
    Munich (1930), **153–4**, 170
dance drama, 226, 238, 260, 263
dance education, 270
dance literacy, 270
dance morphology, 273
dance movement profiling, 270
Dance Notation Bureau and Office, *see*
    Hamburg
Dance Notation Bureau (Hutchinson *et al.*,
    1940s), London, 271–2
dance of work, 238
dance philosophy, *see* choreology
dance scholarship, 270
dance symphony, 42; *see also* Laban, dance
    works
dance theatre, 50, 270
dance therapy, 270, 273
Dancing Times, The (London), 187, 197,
    206–7, 241, 243, 253, 257
Dartington Hall, 204–5, 211, 221, 230, 250–1,
    258, 260–1; *57, 70–2*
    see also Elmhirst, L. and D.; Jooss/Leeder
    School
Darwin, Charles, naturalist, 50
Davidge, Courtenay, journalist, 119–20
Debschitz, Wilhelm von, artist, 18, 21
Debussy, Claude, composer, 161
Delsarte, François, movement theoretician,
    14–15
Derp, Clothilde von, dancer, 45–6, *55*
Dervish dancers, 3
Desmond, Olga, and 'Rhythmographie', 59
Dessauer, Katrola, dance teacher, 150
Deutsche Bühne, support organisation, 76,
    80, 86
Deutsche Gesellschaft für Schrifttanz
    (1928), 133, 143, 153, 167, 176–7
Deutsche Gymnastiksbund (1926), 104
Deutsche Tanz Gemeinschaft (Wigman,
    1928), 136, 140, 143
Deutsche Tanzbühne, Berlin, 92, 186–9, 191,
    192–4, 199
Deutsche Werkbund, Cologne, 34, 53
Deutschen Arbeiter Sängerbund, Berlin, 168
Deutscher Körperbildungsverband, 172
Dewey, John, educationist, 208
Dewey, Myfanwy, schools inspector, 231,
    248; *67, 73*
Diaghilev Serge, ballet impresario, 18, 113,
    163, 189

Diederichs, Eugen, humanist, 61–3, 71, 73,
    109–10
Diem, Dr Carl, Olympic Games organiser
    (1936), 100, 190
Dollfuss, Engelbert, Austrian Chancellor, 185
Donaldson, Joan, dance teacher, 211, 234
Doncaster, Dance Club, 224, 229
Drama Centre, London, 273
Dück, Andreas, teacher, **200**
Duncan, Isadora, dancer, **15**, 26, 40–1, 46,
    67, 206, 226
Dunkel, Annemarie, dancer, 150, 167
Dunlop Rubber Co., 225
Dunn, Margaret, dancer and educationist,
    212, 260–1
Dürer, Albrecht, artist, 53
Durkheim, Émile, sociologist, 128
Düsseldorf
    City Opera, 149, 193
    Neussisches Theater, 142

East 15 Centre, London, 273
Easter Course, Berlin (1925), 111
Ebert, Carl, conductor, 189
Ebrecht, Adolf, administrator, 187, 190, 194,
    199
Eckart, Dietrich, poet, 189
Eckhardt, congress organiser, 154
economic turmoil, Germany, 166–7
Education through Art, Joint Council for,
    Conference (1958), 269
Education through the Arts, Society for, 230
Effner, Heinz, dancer, 128
effort, 223–4; defined, **277**
effort graphs (symbol system), 248; *62–3*
effort observation, 274
effort profile, 228
Egk, Werner, composer, 186
Einstein, Alfred, writer and critic, 158,
    160–1, 167, 175
Elding, Mary, dancer and teacher, 230, 240,
    248, 250; *65*
Ellis, Benedict, lighting designer, 241
Ellis, Clifford and Rosemary, lecturers, 250
Elmendorff, Karl, of Munich State Opera, 158
Elmhirst, Bill, son of Dorothy and Leonard,
    260–1
Elmhirst, Dorothy, 204–5, 209, 212–14, 216,
    218, 250
    her son, Richard, 206
Elmhirst, Leonard, 205, 254, 264, 268
Elmhirst, Leonard and Dorothy, of Darting-
    ton Hall, 180, 204–5, 209, 211–12, 214,
    218, 230, 249, 260
Elmhirst, Pom, Leonard's brother, 264, 268
Emergency Teacher Training, Devonshire
    (1950), 169
Emmel, Felix, writer, 136, 154
Endell, Auguste, artist, 8
English, John, and amateur drama, 226

294

Essen, Neue Tanzbühne der Stadt Bühnen, 136

Essen, Opernhaus, 152

eukinetics, 70, 84, 170, 185, 205, 217, 223–4, 240; defined, 277–8

Eurhythmie (Steiner), 29, 56

Eysler, Edith, dancer, 147

Fachschaft Bühne (1935), for stage oversight, 192

Fachschaft Tanz (1936), 194

Falke, Gertrud, dancer, 35

Falke, Ursula, dancer, 35, 134

Fauves, Les, group of artists, 9–10

Feist, Herta, dancer, teacher and amateur leader, 61, 67, 96, 99, 121, 253, 263
  at Berlin, 81, 103–4, 108–9, 111, 193; *24–6*
  as a performer, 114
  recollections, 71, 74–5, 91

Feldt, Olga, *see* Bereska, Dussia

Festzug der Gewerbe, Vienna (1929), **145–8**, 218; *48–9*

Feuillet, Raoul-Auger, *Chorégraphie* (1700), 133

Fischer, Hans, critic, 130

Flake, Otto, writer, 54

Fligg, Anny, dancer and teacher, 118, 206

folk dance, 178–9, 270

Fokine, Mikhail, dancer and choreographer, 207, 225

Forsythe, William, dancer, choreographer and director, 274–5

Foster, Ruth, educationist, 245–6, 264

Frank, Edgar, dancer, 67, 74, 83, 85, 94, 108, 117, 167; *22, 27*

Franz Ferdinand, Archduke of Austria (d. 1914), 35

Franz Josef, Emperor of Austria, 4–5, 35

Fraser, Mary, teacher, 234

Frauenfeld, A.E., Gauleiter, 194

freemasonry, 28, 53, 63, 72, 126, 145, 189
  and the Ordo Templi Orientis, 46–7, 199–200

Freie Tanz, 26, 55, 61, 108

Freie Tänzer und Tänzerinnen, 68

Freud, Sigmund, psychoanalyst, 5, 15, 50, 54, 122

Fricke, Martha, *see* Laban, Martha

Friedrich, Archduke of Austria, 5

Froebel, Friedrich, educationist, 208

Fuller, Loie, dance artist, 9

Furtwängler, Wilhelm, conductor, 164, 186

Gams, Laban's Swiss financier, 51, 66, 171, 176

Gardner, Chloe, occupational therapist, 254

Geiss, Dr (Tegernsee), 176

Gebhardt, Frau, Laban's pupil and admirer, 38–9

Geeret, Gisa, dancer, 146

George, Stefan, intellectual, 19

Georgi, Yvonne, dancer, 116, 136, 142, 163, 187

Gera, Reussisches Theater, 108–9

German dance, 157, 207

Gert, Valeska, dancer, 66, 132

Gertz, Jenny, teacher and choreographer, 94, 99, 105, 121, 149, 179

Giacometti, Augusto, artist, 45

Gindler Group, of gymnasts, 104

Ginner, Ruby, dance teacher, 206, 227

Gleisner, Martin, actor, dancer and choreographer, 96, 103, **108–10**, 148–9, 154–5, 174, 215
  as a dancer, 75, 81, 83, 108–9, 166
  corresponds with Laban, 249, 265
  as a writer, 151, 165
  Flammenden Zeit, choric work (1929), 149
  Rotes Lied (1931), 168
  book, *Tanz für Alle* (1928), 149

Gluck, Christoph Willibald, 113
  Orpheus und Euridice, opera, 124, 149, 155

Godlewski, Willi, critic, 163

Goebbels, Dr Josef, Propaganda Minister, 173, 175, 181, 198
  and the RKK, 177–8, 187
  and the RTK, 180–2
  and Laban, 181–2, 186, 189–90, 194, 253
  at *Tauwind*, **196**

Goethe, Johann Wolfgang von, poet and dramatist, 79–81, 99

Goldschmidt, Richard, pianist, 79–81

Goldschmitt, Bruno, mask-maker, 15

Goodrich, Joan, dance teacher, 207–8, 234, 243, 264, 268
  studies with Wigman, 207
  and Central European Dance, 211, 213
  and Modern Dance, 216–18, 220, 239, 249; *59*

Göring, Hermann, Prussian Minister, 173, 175, 181–2, 198

Gounod, Charles, *Margarete* (*Faust*), opera, 160–1, 180

Graf, Kurt, dancer, 171

Graham, Martha, dance pioneer, 120, 191, 226, 247, 270

Grelinger, Els, dance student, 246

Gropius, Walter, architect, 129, 144

Grosz, George, artist and Dadaist, 63, 153–4

Grotowski, Jerzy, stage director, 273

Grund, Gustav, critic, 106–7, 116

Guimard, Paul, architect, 9

Günther, Dorothée, dancer and choreographer, 170, 187, 193, 197, 206

Günther, Dr Johannes, academic, 188

Gurdjieff, George Ivanovitch, occultist, 12, 28

Gurlett, Hildebrand, museum director, 169

Gymnastik, 98, 103–4; defined, 278

Hamburg, theatres
  Conventgarten Theater, 77, 86
  Deutsches Schauspielhaus, 91, 98, 105
  Volksoper, 33
  Zoo Restaurant Theatre, 81, 91
Hamburg Tanzschreibstelle, 150
Hamburg Tanzschreibstube, 132, 165, 198
Handel, George Frideric, 113
harmony, 11, **21**, 223
Hart-Davis, Duff, writer, 198
Haslinde, Prussian civil servant, 143
Heartfield, John, painter and Dadaist, 63
Heckroth, Hein, artist and designer, 117,
  151, 211-12
Hennings, Emmy, diseuse and Dadaist, 43;
  17
Hepton, Bernard, actor, 273
Hertzka, Emil, of Universal Edition, 132-4
Heusheimer, Dr H., 132
Heusser, Hans, Dadaist, 56
Heynssen, Adda, composer, 179, 250, 263,
  265, 267
Highbury Little Theatre, London, 226
Hill, Dennis, movement student, *255*, 259
Hindemith, Paul, composer, 146, 161, 169,
  178, 186
Hindenburg, Paul von, German President,
  140, 169, 171, 174-5
Hitler, Adolf, 13
  a Wagnerian, 158, 164
  political moves, 169, 171-4, 181
  and the Olympic Games (1936), 189,
    194-6
  at the Berlin State Opera House, 175, 181
  and the Austrian Anschluss, 210
Hodgson, John, writer on dance, 258; *3, 8,*
  23, 28, 34, 36-7
Hoeffer, Paul, composer, 186
Hoffman-Hamisch, Wolfgang, radio
  interviewer, 152
Hoffmann, Reinhild, dance director, 129
holiday courses, *see* Easter, summer schools
Holm, Hanya, dancer, choreographer and
  teacher, 116, 271
Holmes, W.G., and Co., founders, 222
Holst, Frida, dancer and director, 149
Holst, Imogen, writer, composer and
  conductor, 250, 258
Homagk, Toni, dance teacher, 103
Hombrechtikon, Dance Farm at, 39-41
Hoover Ltd, 223
Horst, Louis, dance pioneer, 120
Howard, Walter, in discussion on dance, 130
Hudes, Eric, composer, 241
Huelsenbeck, Richard, Dadaist, 56
Humphrey, Doris, dancer, choreographer
  and teacher, 226, 247, 271
Hutchinson, Ann, and notation, 246-8, 266,
  271-2
  Labanotation (1970), 266, 271

Illing, Werner, *Aufbruch des Geistes*, choric
  work (1927), 130
Impekoven, Niddy, dancer, 46, 66-7, 108
Imperial Society of Teachers of Dancing,
  206, 243
impressionism/expressionism, experiments,
  23-4
industrial rhythm, 229-30, 240, 245; *see also*
  Laban/Lawrence Industrial Rhythm
International Congress, Paris (1938), 206
International Council of Kinetography
  Laban, 271
Ivers, Susanne, dancer and notator, 168,
  186, 191, 194-5, 199
  as a notator, 133, 151, 159-60, 168
  as a teacher, 150, 168

Jacobs, Arthur, educationist, 73
Janácek, Leos, composer, 161
Janco, George, Dadaist, 43, 45
Janco, Marcel, mask-maker and Dadaist,
  43-4, 56; *17*
Jaques-Dalcroze, Emil, theoretician, 15,
  21-2, 26, 132, 206, 229
Jawlensky, Alexei von, painter, 45
Johnson, William, historian, 5
Joint Council for Education through Art,
  Conference (1958), 269
Jones, Sidney, *The Geisha*, operetta, 168
Joos, Khadven, student, *see* Jooss, Kurt
Jooss, Anna, daughter of Kurt, 204
Jooss, Kurt, dancer, choreographer and
  director, 62, 66, 74, 96, 98, 136, 139,
  204, 206, 226; *20*
  his champions, 125, 144-5
  as a performer, 69-70, 85, 89, 107-8
  and *Gaukelei* (1930), 88, 149, 155
  as a writer, 90
  at Hamburg, 83
  at Munster, 93, 117
  at Bad Mergentheim, 131
  at Essen, 135-7, 150-2, 159, 167, 253, 260,
    271
  at Bayreuth (1930), 157-8
  at Dartington, 204, 209-10, 214, 245;
    interned and freed, 211, 213
  see also Ballets Jooss; Jooss/Leeder School
  his dance works
    Big City (1932), 177
    Chronica (1939), 211
    Drosselbart (1929), 152
    Green Table, The (1932), 170, 172, 177,
    Groteske, Herakles, Kaschemme, Larven
      (1925), 117
    Spring Tale, A (1939), 211
Jooss/Leeder School, 180, 188, 246-7
  at Dartington, 180, 192, 205-6, 210-11,
    213-14
Jordan, Diana, teacher, 208, 213, 215-17,
  233, 262-3 267; *59*

at Modern Holiday Dance Courses, 217,
238, 266
and Laban, 228, 231, 243, 245
The Dance as Education (1938), 208
Jugend (youth), 58
Jung, Carl Gustav, psychoanalyst, 50, 127,
230, 236, *255*, 259, 273
Junk, Walter, dancer, 53

Kabitz, Susanne, dancer, 133
Kahn, Erich Itor, composer, 129
Kalisch, *100,000 Thaler*, operetta, 172
Kallmeyer Group, of gymnasts, 104
Kammertanzbühne, defined, 278
Kammertanzbühne Laban (chamber dance
theatre, 'Katabü'), 86, 89, 91–3, **107–8**,
137, 220, 241
Laban/Bereska, 123–4, 134–5, 137
Bereska/Robst, 135, 150
Bereska (Balletto Laban, Italy, 1924), 94
Kampfbund für Deutsche Kultur, 190
Kandinsky, Wassily, artist, 7, 18, 34, 43, 56,
79, 174
Concerning the Spiritual in Art (1911), 19,
20–1
Kapp, Dr Julius, dramaturge, 175
Karjera, Maru, dancer, 147
Kasperltheater, 'Punch and Judy' show, 2,
115
'Katabü', *see* Kammertanzbühne Laban
Keith, Jens, dancer, 67, 74, 83, 94, 108, 117,
162
as a performer, 85, 89; *53*
Kennedy, Douglas, folk-music enthusiast,
206, 213, 216
kinetic empathy, 84
kinetography (Kinetographie), 133, 247, 253,
271
Kinetography Laban, International Council
of, 271
kinetoscope, 60
Klages, Ludwig, psychologist, *Künstlerische
Körperschulung*, 19, 99
Klamt, Gustav Fischer, teacher, 201
Klamt, Jutta, dancer and teacher, 136, 155,
159, 187
Klemperer, Otto, conductor, 146, 161
Klimt, Gustav, artist, 6, 9
Klingenbeck, Fritz, dancer, 123, 128, 131–3,
141, 145, 150, 166, 192, 253; *4–6*, *45*
Knust, Albrecht, dancer, notator, teacher
and choreographer, 74, 76, 109, 246,
253; *47*, *83*
at Hamburg, 82–3, 86, 92, 94–5, 98, 109,
151
at the Munich Festival (1929), 155
at Essen, 180, 184–5, 188, 260, 271
and the Olympic Games, 195
and notation, 131, 133–4, 141, 150–1,
165–6, 190–1, 247, 251, 252

and the score of *Tauwind*, 193
as a performer, 61, 87, 94–5, 112, 193
as a producer, 92
and Laban, 14–15, 58, 198, 215
Consecration of the Flag (1934), 185
Erwachen, 31
Feierliche Kanon und Spiel, 185
Festlicher Marsch, 185
Rienzi (Wagner), incidental dances, 191
Koch, Margot, dancer, 133
Kölling, Rudolf, dancer, 162; *53*
Körperkultur (physical culture), 21, 67–8, 72,
99, 121–2, 220; defined, 278
Kosterlitz, Dr Rolf, psychotherapist, 254
'Kraft durch Freude' (Strength through Joy),
184–5, 199, 201
Kratina, Valerie, dancer, 136, 187
Kraus, Gertrud, dancer, 146, 155
Kreibig, Manda von, dancer, 155
Krenek, Ernst, composer, 146–7, 155
Jonny Spielt Auf, opera, 146
Kreutzberg, Harald, dancer and choreo-
grapher, 116, 142, 163, 187, 197–8, 245
Krieg, Dr, Knust's friend, 82
Kröller, Heinrich, ballet-master and choreo-
grapher, 136–9, 154–5, 163
Mammon (Krenek), 155
Pagoden, 137
Kruscek, Maja, costume-maker, 44–6

Laban, Allar, Laban's son (by Suzanne
Perrottet, 1916), theatre designer, 41,
268
Laban, Arpad, Laban's son (1905), 15, 253
Laban, Azraela [Azra], Laban's daughter
(1902), 14, 141–2, 150–1, 165, 253; *6*
Laban, Etelke, Laban's daughter (1915), 17,
41
Laban, Georg, Laban's son (1914), 33
Laban, Johanna [Juana de Laban], Laban's
daughter (1910), 17, 209, 221
Laban, Maja (*née* Lederer), Laban's second
wife (m.1910), 30, 32, 35–41, 53–4, 58,
60, 253; *10*, *13–14*
recollections, 10, 14, 18
as a singer, 17, 29, 41
as a freemason, 48
and Perrottet, 23, 32
births of her children, 22, 33, 41
leaves Laban, 52
divorces him, 120–1, 244
receives royalties from his book, 201
Laban, Marie (*née* Bridling), Laban's mother,
1, 16, 35–8, 40–2, 51, 58, 120, 171; *1–2*
Laban, Martha (*née* Frick), Laban's first
wife (m.1900, d.1907), 7, 9–10, 14–15
Laban, Melanie, Laban's sister, 1, 42, 58, 63,
183
Laban, Renate, Laban's daughter (1912), 22
Laban, Renée, Laban's sister, 1, 35–7, 40,

120, 171, 183, 210
Laban, Roland, Laban's son (1917), 52, 268;
    43
Laban [de Varalja], [Field Marshal] Rudolf
    von, Laban's father, 1, 2, 4–5, 15; *1*

Laban, Rudolf Jean Baptiste Attila von
his life
    birth (1879) and childhood, **1–4**
    education, **4–6**
    military training, 6
    marriages: 1st, 7; 2nd, 17
    divorce, 120–1
    intimate relationships: Bereska, 47–8,
        76, 135; Perrottet, 7, 22–3, 30, 32, 41,
        48, 51–2, *13*; Ullmann, 244, 248,
        262–3
    financial problems: (1902–15), 14–15,
        17, 26, 33, 41; (1919–34), 53, 63, 66,
        171, 176
    financial aid, 51, 76, 133, 171
    nationality: Hungarian, 41, 58, 92;
        Czech, 56–8, 220–1; German, 164,
        193, 198, 220, 244
    pseudonym, Attila de Varalja, 14
    birthday celebrations: 50th, 151–2;
        70th, 251–2, *83*; 75th, 264
    depression, 15, 38, 51, 56, 204, 209
    injury (1926), 123–4
    ill-health: (1912–18), 18, 22, 26, 38, 40,
        51, 53–6; (1921–40), 70–1, 176, 178,
        99–202, 204, 209–10, 215; (1947–57),
        241, 245–6, 260, 265, 268
    death (1958), 269
    in photographs: (childhood to 1923),
        2–6, 8, 13–15, 19, 23, 27; (1925–36),
        32, 34– 5, 39, 41, 50–1, 53–4; (1938–
        49), *56–9, 71, 76, 83*
ideas and concepts
    'circular theatre for dance', 10, 50; *7*
    College of Movement, 231
    dance congresses, **124–5**, 130
    Festwille und Festkultur, **72–3**, 87
    Freie Tanz, 26, 55, 61, 108; for the
        young, 99
    High School for Dance, 141, 143, 156,
        178, 183, 216, 231, 238, 274
    'Labangarten' (for children), 39, 41
    notation, first forays, 14
    his Sache ('things'), 27, 204, 209
    Schwungskalen (training method), 31,
        49
    Tanz für Alle, 107, 151
influenced by
    art and artists, 6–9
    crystals, **53–6**, 200, 204, 227
    dervishes and sufis, 3, 8, 28–9
    freemasonry, 46–8, 51, 128, 199
    nature, **2–3**, 8, 29
    religions, 3, 6, 12

Rosicrucianism, 3, **10–12**, 24, 28–9, 32,
    120, 200, 204, 229; *5*
artistic leanings
    youthful talents, 2, 4
    early studies, **6–11**
    development and earning, **14**, 15, 17,
        23, 39
    architectural and space studies, 50; *77–
        82*
    drawings of harmony and movement
        sold, **53–6**
    choreology drawings, 123
    caricature, *10–11*
as a composer and pianist, 24, 46; *17*
as a dancer, 83, 85–6, 95, 97, 106–9, 113,
    120, 123, 128
and drama, 226, 235, 238, 240–1, 256;
    youthful talents, **2**, 3–5
and movement *(see also main index)*
    childhood leanings, 2–3
    becomes his art medium, 9, 20, **23–4**
    his 'Three Rs' (recreation, research,
        rehabilitation), 265
major appointments
    Bayreuth, guest choreographer (1930–
        31), 152, **157–8, 164**
    Berlin, Deutsche Tanzbühne, director
        (1934), 186–9, 191–4, 199
    Mannheim, guest choreographer (1921–
        22), 67–70
    Paton, Lawrence and Co., adviser
        (1941), 219, 222–3, 249, 265, 268
    Prussian State Theatres, Choreographer
        and Director of Movement, (1930–
        34), 77, 144, 157, 159, 163, **173–4**,
        175–6, 195–7; *53*
industrial assignments, 223, 225–6, 235,
    246, 259, 266
lectures
    'Dance in America', 120, 124
    'The Nature and Purpose of Dance',
        86–7
    'The Three Rs', **265**
    others, 76, 86–7, 94, 97, 142, 211, 266
dance works
    Agamemnons Tod (1924), **94–5**, 97–8,
        103, 109; *28*
    Balletto della Stella, Il (1923), 94
    Casanova (1923), *see Komödie*
    Dämmernden Rhythmen (recreated
        1925), 112
    Dancing Drumstick, The (sequence of
        dances, 1913), 31
    Don Juan (1925), **112–15**, 115–16, 120,
        123, 131, 142, 145, 149; *34*
    Erde, Die (projected), 3, 13, 24, 67
    Erste Epische Tanzfolge (dance sym-
        phony, 1921), 42, 69; *21–2*
    Fausts Erlösung (with Mönckeberg-
        Kollman, 1922), 77, **79–81**, 126, 267

Frei Tanz, Der (1914), 33
Gaukelei (dance drama, 1923), 25, 82, **88–90**, 113, 149, 155, 170, 193, 241; *27*
Geblendeten, Die (dance poem, 1921) 25, 69–70, 77, 80–1, 90–1, 103, 112–13, 241; *21; Schwingende Gewalten* (version for small group), 112–13
Grünen Clowns, Die (1928), 116, 137, 142, 168; *41*
Himmel und Erde (Oben und Unten) (1921), 69–70, 94
Ishtar's Journey into Hades (1913), **31–2**
Komödie (Casanova, 1923), 90, 123
Lichtwende (1923), 87–8, 109
Midsummer Night's Dream, A (Shakespeare, incidental dances, 1924), 98
Nacht (satire, 1927), 13, 126, **128–9**, 133, 155, 168; *36*
Narrenspiegel (1926), **115–16,** 123, 145; *35*
Orpheus und Euridice (Gluck, incidental dances, 1927), 124
Petits Riens, Les (Mozart, ballet, dance version, c.1924–25), 109
Prometheus (with Mönckeberg-Kollman, 1923), 91–2, 109, 258
Ritterballett (1927), **126–7**, 128, 131, 133– 5, 250; *37*
Sang an die Sonne (dance hymn, 1917), 47, 94
Schwingende Tempel, Der (dance symphony, 1922), 75, **77–9**, 80–2, 86, 95, 106, 120, 126, 168, 260
Spielmann, Der (dance drama, 1916), 42, 45
Tauwind und der Neuen Freude (1936), 193, **195–6,** 214, 267; *54*
Terpsichore (1925), 112–15
Titan (1927), 120, **126–8**, 133, 135, 155, 190, 267; *47*
Winter's Tale, A (Shakespeare, incidental dances, 1923), 91
Wunderblumen, Die (group dance work, 1917), 47
Saltata (last choric dance work, 1955), 266
solo dances, duos and trios, 85–6
choreography for operas and other works
Arlésienne, L' (Bizet), 266
Carmen (Bizet), 169, 177
Donna Diana (Resnicek), 180
Geisha, Die (Sidney Jones), 168
Götterdämmerung (Wagner), 157
Idomeneo (Mozart), 171–2
Jeux (Debussy), 161
Louise (Charpentier), 161
Margarete (Faust, Gounod), 160–1, 180
Meistersinger, Die (Wagner), 180
Nacht in Venedig, Eine (Strauss), 163, 184
Parsifal (Wagner), 157
Oberon (Weber), 167, 180
Perlenfischer, Die (Bizet), 181
Prince Igor (Borodin), 160, 168, 219
Rienzi (Wagner), 175
Schalkhafte Witwe, Die (Wolf-Ferrari), 167–8
Sizilianische Vesper (Verdi), 170
Tannhäuser (Wagner): (1921), 68–70, 103; (1930–31), 157–8, 164, 180: *52*
Traviata, La (Verdi), 169
Zierpuppen, Die, 160
Zigeunerbaron, Der (Strauss), 164, 168
producer and director of festivals, plays, etc.
Abschied von der Bar (1931), 161
Alltag und Fest (1929), 148; selection, *Hymnus der Arbeit* (1931), 166
Birth of the Dance in Hell, The (1914), 33
Carnivalistische Tanzsuite (1931), 164, 168
Dornröschen (1934), 187
Festzug der Gewerbe, Vienna (1929), **145–8**
Fischfang am Jangtsekiang (oriental fantasy, 1932), 169
In the Grove of Aesculapius (1914), 33
Magic Flute, The (music by Heynssen), 250
Mosaik (1922), 76
Phantastische Revue (1924), **105–6,** 128
Sextor (1931), 161
Shawl, The (with Esmé Church, 1948), 250
Spiel und Ernst (opera, 1931), 161, 164
Twelve Months, The (with Esmé Church, 1948), 250
books by Laban, referred to in the text
Art of Movement in Education, Industry and on the Stage, The (1950), 258
Choreographie (1926), 59, 64, 96, 109–10, 112, 227; *42, 44*
Choreutics (ed. Ullmann, 1966), 12, 209, 212–13, 272
Effort (with Lawrence, 1947), 224, **235–7,** 253, 268
Gymnastik und Tanz (1926), 96, **99–103,** 108, 121
Kindes Gymnastik und Tanz, Des (1926), 96, 98, **104–5,** 111, 121
Life for Dance, A (translation, 1975, of *Ein Leben für den Tanz*, 1935), 13–14, 33, 42, 67, 74, 87–8, 120, 127, 147–8, 157, 161, 192, 201
Mastery of Movement on the Stage, The (1950), 253, 258
Modern Educational Dance (with Tyndale-Biscoe, 1948), 15, 242–3,

253, 261, 274
Movement Psychology (with Carpenter, unfinished and unpublished), 263
Principles of Dance and Movement Notation, The (1956), 266
Tanzschrift: Methodik und Orthographie (1928), 143
Vision of Dynamic Space, A (compiled by Ullmann, 1984), 272
Welt der Tänzers, Die (1920), 25, 27, 49–51, 57, 59, **64–6**, 75, 87, 99, 101, 110, 171; *16, 18–19*

Laban Art of Movement Centre, Guild and Studios, *see* Art of Movement Centre, etc.
Laban/Bartenieff Institute, New York, 272
Laban Centre for Movement and Dance, 273–4
Laban diploma, 110–11
Laban Guild Conference, 254
Laban/Lawrence Industrial Rhythm, 218–19, **221–4**, 225–6, 250; *64*
  tests, 235, 267
'Laban' movement choirs, 95–7, 124, 184, 206, 220
  Altona, 155
  Berlin, 109, 114–15, 128, 130, *155*, 166, 193, 195; *26, 54*
  Berne, 95
  Budapest, 95, 103
  Essen, 115, 195
  Frankfurt, 148, 166, 195, 223
  Gera, 108–9, 128, 148, 155
  Halle, 155, 179
  Hamburg, 83, 87–8, 92–4, 103, 151, 179–80, 185, 191; *27, 31*
    Festivals: (1929), *47*; (1931), 167
    performances: (1923–6), 91, 97, 109, 112, 115–16; (1926–37), 124, 128, 133, 155, 166, 193
  Mannheim, 142, 155, 166, 195
  Jena, 110, 115, 148
  Lubeck, 95, 179
  Nuremberg, 179, 194–5
  Rome, 108
  Vienna, 95
  others, 195
'Laban' schools, 96, 110, 141, 166, 184, 216
  accreditation, 110–11
  Basle, 103
  Berlin, 8, 103, 118, 124, 141, 150, 160; *24*; Tanzstudio, 166, 168, 207
  Dartington Hall, 181
  Essen, 136–7, 149–51, 159, 167, 170, 177, 180–1, 188, 253, 260, 271
  Frankfurt, 94, 149
  Hamburg, ([Kammer]Tanzbühne Laban), 76, 86, 88, 90–3, 103, 107, 116, 141, 262
  London (Laban Centre for Movement and

Dance), 273–4
Munich, 27, 118–19; *9*
Munster, 94, 117, 138
New York (Laban Institute), 209
Paris, 150, 166, 171, 176, 203
Rome, 94, 112, 267
Trieste (Balletto Laban), 94, 112
Würzburg, 118, 123
Zurich, 103, 185; *16*
Labananalysis, 275
Labanbund (1926), 118, 120, 125–6
Labanotation, 247, 253, 266, 271–2
Labanotation Institute, Guildford, 272
Lamb, Warren, dancer and teacher, 215, 246, 250–1, 256; *62–3, 65*
  industrial assignments, 259–60, 267, 274
Landes, Heinz, dancer, 128
lands of adventure and silence, 8, 11
Langer, Hans Claus, composer, 195–6
Langwara, von, dancer, 46
Laredo, Ilse, dancer, 228
Latin-American Sport Dance, 275
Lautere, Arch, dance teacher, 258
Lawrence, Frederick, management consultant, 218–19, 221–3, 228, 235–9, 249, 260, 264, 268
Lederer, Maja, *see* Laban, Maja
Leeder, Sigurd, dancer and ballet-master, 84, 131, 211, 213–14, 245, 259; *20*
  and Jooss, 94, 96, 107, 117, 150
  and notation, 151, 167
  his school in London, 257
  see also Jooss/Leeder School
Leistikow, Gertrud, dancer and actress, 35
Lembke, Elso, dancer, 112
Lenin, Vladimir Ilyich, revolutionary, 44, 57, 60, 89
Lenman, Robin, historian, 17, 26
Leonard, arranger, 134
Leonard, Michael, dancer, *70*
Levinson, André, critic, 130
Lewitan, Joseph, editor and critic, 134, 163, 174, 176, 187, 197–8
Lex, Maja, dancer, 187, 197
Libertas et Fraternitas Lodge, Zurich, 48
Liebemann, Dr, psychologist, 130
Liebmann, Kurt, Congress speaker, 130
Lieschke, Dr Marie Luise, Laban's friend, 171, 174, 176, 185, 194–5, 199
  and the Laban Archive, 159
  financial support for Laban, 133, 142, 167
  letters from Laban, 188, 193, 202
  Nazi party member, 177, 187
  and the 1930 summer school, 153
  and the Reichsbund für Gemeinschaftstanz, 192
Lifar, Serge, dancer, choreographer and ballet-master, 201
'lilt in labour', 219, 221, 235
Ling Physical Education Association, 207,

211, 213, 215, 217
Linnebach, Adolf, stage techuician, 154
Liszt, Franz, 115
Littlewood, Joan, theatre director, 229, 244, 274
Loeb, Beatrice, dancer, 254, 267
Loesch, Ilse, dancer, 129, 167, 179
Loeszer, Gertrud [Ruth], dancer, 74, 83, 121, 129; *32, 34, 39*
    as a performer, 85, 90, 115, 128, 155
    as a teacher, 118, 122, 149
    and Laban, 96, 98, 106-8, 250
Loheland Körperkultur group, 68, 99, 104, 208
Loman, Hettie, actress, choreographer and teacher, 240, 250, 256-7
    Catch Me a Hay Ride (1954), 265
    Scarecrows (1948), 250
    Streets Without End (1949), 256
London, Toynbee Hall Theatre, 265
London, Wembley Stadium, 266
Lunacharsky, Anatoly, Russian commissar, 60
Lüth, Erich, writer, 90

McColl, Ewan, of Theatre Workshop, 244, 251
Macdonald, John, publisher, 236, 253
Macdonald & Evans, publishers, 253, 266
Mackenzie, Francis, British Drama League, 235
Macmurray, John, academic, 231
    Reason and Emotion (1935), 208
Madika-Szanto, dancer, 112
male dancers, masculinity, 83, 98, 103, 106, 109, 122, 184, 263; *27*
Maletic, Ana, dancer and teacher, 93-4
Malmgren, Yat, actor, dancer and teacher, 188, 196, 210, 263-4, 273
Management Training Institute, Manchester, 235
Manchester Dance Circle (1943), 229, 241
Mannheim, Nationaltheater, 25, 61, 142, 145, 148; *21*
Mannheim Opera, 68
Maré, Rolf de, ballet-director, 111, 170, 180, 188, 201, 251
Markard, Anna, Jooss's daughter, ballet-mistress, 271
Marschalk, Max, composer and critic, 160
Martin, Christopher, the Elmhirsts' adminis-trator, 218
Martin, John, critic and writer on dance, 208
Matisse, Henri, artist, 9-10
Maude, Stella, dancer, 257
Maudrik, Lizzie, dancer, choreographer and ballet-mistress, 163, 182, 187, 198
    Coppélia (Delibes), 155
    Puppenfee, 187
Mayer, Laban's personal agent, 119

Mayerova, Milca, dance teacher, 149
Mazzoni, Beatrice, dancer, 112; *39*
Medau Körperkultur group, 68, 99
Meisenbach, Grete, dance teacher, 149
Meisenbach, Jo [Johan Adam], dancer, 32, 53-4, 57, 99, 200, 253; *9, 14*
Meisterwerkstätten für Tanz (Master Work-shops for Dance, 1936), 194, 199, 201
Mempoteng, Mine, dancer, 74
Mensendieck, Bess, theorist, 21, 68, 99, 103-4, 208
Mentelberg, Ymelda Juliewna, dancer, 33
Menzler School, for 'Healthy and artistic gymnastics', 103
Merberle, Paul Alfred, exhibition administra-tor, 125
Meredith-Jones, Betty, dance teacher, 215-17, 221, 231, 238
Meumann, Max Alexander, critic, 8
Meyerbeer, Giacomo, *L'Africaine*, opera, 149
Michel, Artur, critic, **114,** 115, 156, 169
Michelle, Simone, dancer, x
Midlands Dance Group, 233
Milanovic, Vera, dancer, 93
Miles, Nadine, dance teacher, 258
Milloss, Aurel, choreographer, 85, 89, 134, 193, 251, 274
mime, 25
Miracolo, Giovanni, critic, 108
Mlakar, Pino and Pia, choreographers, *Teufel im Dorf*, 251, 252; *83*
Modern Dance Conference, Bushey (1941), 215-16
Modern Dance Holiday Courses: (1941-43), 217-19, 222, 225, **227-8**; *60*; (1945-55), 235, **238-9**, 249-51, 258-9, 260-1, 266-7; *61, 70-2*
Modern Educational Dance, 220, 225, 272; *73*
Modern Educational Dance Course (1943), 225
Moholy-Nagy, László, stage designer, 161
Mohr, Ernst, dancer, 42, 46
Moll, E.W., figurine-maker, 126
Moll, Ewald, Berlin privy-counsellor, 133
Mönckeberg-Kollman, Wilma, lecturer in choric speech, 79, 81, 91
Monte Verità, *see* summer schools
Moreau, Gustave, Symbolist painter, 5, 9-10
motif writing, 274
motion factors, 28, 228
Movement (short-lived magazine), 248
movement, **65-6, 99-104,** 248-9, 266, 269; *74*
    Bewegungskunst (the art of movement), 100-1, 104
    group movement, 165
movement action, 255
movement choir, 97-8
movement choir work for amateurs, 206

movement choirs, *see* Laban, movement choirs
movement choirs for children, 104–5
movement education, 248
Movement Notation and Movement Research, Institute for, Hamburg, 112, 117–18
movement observation, 227, 238
movement rhythm, 26
movement scales, 274
movement therapy, 254–5, 258–9, 273
Mozart, Wolfgang Amadeus, *Idomeneo*, 171–2
Muckermann, Friedrich, Jesuit priest, 154
Mulhausen, Schauspielhaus, 113
Müller, Alfred, *Rhythmische Gymnastik* (1926), 100
Müller, Lotte, dancer, 74
    at Frankfurt, 94, 108, 149, 166, 201
    at the Olympics (1936), 193, 195
Munich
    Artists' Theatre, 27
    Bavarian State Theatre, 155
    Opera House, 252
    Munich Werkbund, 27, 63, 218
music and art therapy, 254
musicless dance, 25
Myers, Maureen, dancer, *68*
Mylius, Adolf, Laban's uncle, 1–2

National Resource Centre for Dance, *62–3, 77–82*
National Socialism (Nazism), 169, 171–5, 177–8, 180–2, 185, 196
natural movement (Madge Atkinson's), 227
Nebe, Conrad, editor, 176
Neggo, Gerd, dancer, 74, 94
Neiger, Edgar, dancer, 112
Neruda, Edwin, critic, 160
Neue Sächlichkeit (New Objectivity), 97, 156
Neuer Weg, zu Kraft und Schönheit (UFA film), 120
Neurer, Dr, and the Essen Congress (1928), 135
New Dance, 153
New York, New School of Social Research, 212
New York Dance Notation Bureau, 246
Newlove, Jean, teacher, 215, 223, 231, 245, 273
Newman, Ernest, writer and critic, 158
Niedecken-Gebhardt, Hanns, theatre intendant, 94, 117, 125, 130, 144–5, 187, 194–5, 198
Nietzsche, Friedrich Wilhelm, philosopher, 54, 127, 131
    Also Sprach Zarathustra, 39, 196
Nijinsky, Vaslav Fomich, dancer and choreographer, *Jeux*, 162
Nikolaieva, Eugenie, dancer, 162; *53*

Nikolais, Paul, critic, 66
Nolde, Emil, painter, 29
Nolling, Motta, dancer, 112
North, Marion, writer and teacher, 215, 260–2, 265, 267–9, 273–4
notation, 240, 246–8, 252, 269; *42–4, 63*
    as Choreographie, **110**
    breakthrough (1927), **131–4**
    development, **150–1, 165–6,** 274
    in America (Hutchinson), 246–7, 266, 271–2
    see also kinetography, Labanotation, Tanzschrift
notation technology, 271
Noverre, Jean-Georges, dancer, choreographer and theorist, 95, 109, 116, 225
    Letters on Dancing and Ballet, 21
nudity, 121
Nurk, Helmi, dancer, 74

Obrist, Hermann, artist and craftsman, **7–9,** 18–19, 21, 27, 34
occupational rhythm, *see* industrial rhythm
Oedenkoven, Henri, and Monte Verità, 28–9, 205
Oesterreich, Laura, dancer, 35
Olbrich, Joseph Maria, architect, 9
Olympic Games, Berlin (1936), 166, **189–91,** 193, 195–6, 198; *54–5*
Ordo Templi Orientis (OTO), quasi-masonic society, 46–8, 51, 199–200
Orff, Carl, composer, 186–7, 195

pageant, *see* Festzug der Gewerbe
Palmer, Elsie, physical educationist, 225–6, 229, 234–5, 239
Palucca, Gret, dancer, 116, 136, 155, 172, 187, 193, 197
Pander-Gellmitz, Senta, dancer, 95
Papen, Franz von, Nazi politician, 163, 171, 175
Paris
    Écoles des Beaux Arts, 9–10
    International Congress (1938), 206
    Salon de Rose Croix, 10
    Théâtre des Champs-Elysées, 170
Parnell, Felix, dancer, 197
Paton Lawrence and Co., 218–19, 222, 246, 249, 265, 268; *62*
Paulin, Guadel, architect, 10, 14
Pavlova, Anna, dancer, 129
Péladan, Sar, aesthete, 11–12
percussion and voice, dancing to, 25
Perret, Frances, dancer, 203
Perrottet, Oliver, Suzanne's grandson, *14*
Perrottet, Suzanne, dancer and teacher, 24, 46, 53, 59, 99, 268; *10*
    as a musician, 44, 46, 59; *17*
    as a dancer, 42, 56
    at Munich, 32; *9*

in Switzerland, 39–41
at summer schools, 29, 35–6, 48, 150, 245; *14*
at Dartington, 209
correspondence with Laban, 7, 22, 26–7, 29
as Laban's mistress, 7, 22–3, 30, 32, 41, 48, 51–2; *13*
personality assessment, 266, 273
Peukert, Detlev J.K., historian, 139
phenomenology of dance, 229, 273
physical education, *see* Körperkultur
Piaget, Jean, psychologist, 243
Picabia, Francis, artist, 89
Pierenkämper, Grete and Harry, Mannheim movement choir, 148, 166, 193–5
Pilkington's Tile Works, 246
Piscator, Erwin, stage director and Dadaist, 63, 129, 146, 154
Pisk, Litz, movement teacher, 257
Plato, philosopher, 102
Platonic ideals, 230
Platonic bodies: icosahedron, 49, 125; octahedron, 49
Platt, Enid, dance teacher, *68*
Porembsky, Baroness, admirer of Laban's work, 38
Preston-Dunlop, Valerie, dancer, teacher and author, 215, 220, 241, 253, 260–2; *65*
  and British Dance Theatre, 256
  and notation, etc., 246–8, 265–6, 274
Priestley, J.B., *Johnson over Jordan*, play, 245
Proletarische Laiengruppe Leipzig, 155
psychoanalysis, 5, 15, 49–50, 63, 122
psychology, 5
psychotherapy, *see* Withymeade Centre
Puccini, Giacomo
  La Bohème, 5
  Der Mantel (*Il Tabarro*), 155

Quirey, Belinda, dance historian, 242

Rambert, Marie, ballet-director, 246
Rausch, Hans, dancer, 118
Rauser, Tamara, ballet teacher, 201
Read, Herbert, educationist, 230
  Education Through Art (1943), 230
Reading University, conference of educationists (1940–41), 213–14
recreative dance, 270
Reichsbund für Gemeinschafttanz (State League for Community Dance), 192, 195
Reichsfachschaft Deutscher Tanzlehrer (Neue Deutsche Tanz), Nazi organisation for dance teachers, 178
Reichskulturkammer (RKK), 177–8, 182, 188, 190, 192, 194, 199
Reichsmusikkammer, 178
Reichstheaterkammer (RTK, 1934), 180,

190, 192, 194–7, 199
Reigen, defined, 278
Reinhardt, Max, theatre director, 146
Reuss, Teodor, freemason, 46
rhythm 24, 26, 219
Rhythmik, 98
Richter, Hans, Dadaist, 44–5, 56
ritual, 8, 47, 63, 72
Robbins, Jerome, choreographer, 247
Robertson, dance photographer, 151, 167
Robst, Hermann [Robert], dancer and teacher, 112, 122, 135, 150, 171; *34–5, 39*
  performances, 113, 115, 128, 167
Rogers, Helen Priest, dancer, 196, 246
Rogge, Lola, dancer and choreographer, 134, 166, 180, 193; *30*
  Die Amazonen, 191, 196
Rome, Independi Theatre, 108
Roon, Ingeborg, dancer, 74, 85, 94, 108, 117
Rose Croix du Temple et du Graal, L'Ordre de la, 11
Rosicrucianism, 3, **10–12**, 13, 28, 31, 46, 63, 120, 185, 204, 229
Rouault, Georges, artist, 10
Rubinstein, Ida, dancer, 142
Ruckteschel, von, dancer, 46
Rudolph, Charlotte, art photographer, 167
Ruskaya, Jia, dancer, 108
Russell, Joan, writer on dance, 215; *69*
Rutherston, Jeannette, writer on dance, 207

Sacchetto, Rita, dancer, 18
Sacharoff, Alexander, dancer, 18, 45–6, 55, 67; *16*
St Denis, Ruth, dancer, choreographer and teacher, 226
St Olave's Curing and Preserving Co., 223
Salt, Dr C.E., poet, 219, 228
Samao, Betty Baaron, dancer, 29; *9, 14*
Satie, Erik, composer, 56
Sauer, Annie, dancer, 133
Sauerbeck, Emmi, dancer, 95
scales, defined, **278–9**
Scharf, Fritz, ballet-master, 60
Scheck, Gerda, dancer, 85, 94
Schilkowski, John, critic, 114
Schiller, Christian, educationist and trustee, 264, 268
Schiller, Johann Christoph Friedrich von, poet and dramatist, 99
Schlee, Alfred, dramaturge at Munster, 125, 132, 135, 153–4, 157, 164, 170
  as a musician, 130, 132, 146
  and notation, 132–3
  and *Schrifttanz*, 136, 142, 153
  and Universal Editions, 146–7
Schleglmuenig, Arthur, sculptor, 121
Schlemmer, Oskar, painter, dancer, designer and theorist, 129–30, 132, 142, 157,

167, 174, 183-4
at Magdeburg (1927), 125, 130
and the Bauhaus, 60-2, 89, 117, 156
his diary, 67, 129, 156, 164, 169, 184
Triadic Ballet, 117, 126, 170
Schmidt, Margarethe, dancer, 87, 95, 103
Schoenberg, Arnold, 21, 44, 46, 56, 178,
186; *17*
Die Glückliche Hand, opera, 156
Schönlank, Bruno, poet, 79
Der Gespaltene Mensch, choric work, 130
Schreker, Franz, composer, 186
Schrifttanz (periodical, 1928-32), 132-4,
136, 142-4, 151-3, 165, 167
Schulz-Dornburg, Rudolf, on 'Dance in
Opera', 154
Schwung, 219
Schwungskalen, Laban's training method,
31, 49
Science of the Arts Congress, Paris (1937),
201-2
Secession, Vienna, **6**
Seelig, Prussian Minister for Education, 143
Seidel, Ida, choreographer, 110
Seifert, publisher, 60, 75
Sendlein, Anna and Anton, Laban's aunt
and her husband, 1
Shakespeare, William, *A Winter's Tale*, 91
Sharp, Cecil, folk-music collector and editor,
206
Shawn, Ted, dancer and teacher, 226
Sherborne (*née* Tyndale-Biscoe), Veronica,
movement teacher, *see* Tyndale-Biscoe
Shirer, William, *The Rise and Fall of the
Third Reich* (1950), 174, 177, 181
Siimola, Aino (wife of Kurt Jooss), dancer,
94, 117, 204
Singchor und Tanz (journal), 149, 151, 162-3
Skeaping, Mary, ballet-mistress, 212
Skoronel, Vera, dancer, 116, 130, 142, 155
Smolova, Esther, dancer, 69
Snell, Gertrud, dancer, 121, 129, 153, 177,
186, 188-91, 199; *39*
and choreology, 142, 150
and notation, 110-12, 122, 131, 133, 141,
151
as a teacher, 118
in Paris, 167, 175
at the Olympics (1936), 194-5, 197
to England (1950), 25
social behaviour in Vienna, 5-6
social dance, 26
social dancing, 6
Soelberg, Louise, dancer, 206, 216
Söhnlein, Kurt, stage designer, 158
solo dance, 46
Spafford, Phyllis, physical educationist, 213
Spies, Daisy, dancer, 161-2; *53*
Spotts, Frederick, historian of Bayreuth, 157
Stalling, Gerhard, publisher, 98

Stammer, Werner, dancer, 117
Stanislavsky, Konstantin, actor, producer
and theatre director, 273
Stansfield, Margaret, teacher, 207
Stattler, Ernst, actor, 91-2
Steiner, Marie, anthroposophist, 20, 29, 59
Steiner, Rudolf, philosopher, 19-20, 29, 38,
59
Stephenson, Geraldine, dancer, producer
and teacher, 215, 238, 246
as a performer, 260-1, 265; *66*
as a teacher, 248-9, 251, 257, 260-1
Sterner, Walter, Dadaist, 56
Stone, Arthur, headmaster and movement
teacher, 249, 262
Strauss, Johann, the younger
Die Fledermaus, operetta, 5
Eine Nacht in Venedig, operetta, 163, 184
'Tritsch-Tratsch', polka, 172
Der Zigeunerbaron, operetta, 164, 168
Strauss, Richard, 186
Josephslegende, ballet, 87
Stravinsky, Igor, 155
Rite of Spring, ballet, 250
Stuttgart, Akademie der Bildenen Künste, 61
Stuttgart, Württemburg Stadtstheater, 60
Suhr, Werner, critic, 164
summer schools, 121
Ascona, Monte Verità: (1913), **28-33**, 150,
206; (1914), **34-7**; (1917), 46-8
Gleschendorf (1922), 74-6; *23*
Blaubeuren (1923), 75
Würzburg (1926), 118
Bad Mergentheim (1927), 131
Berlin and Scheveningen (1928), 141
Burg Lauenstein (1929), 150
Hamburg (1929), 150
Bayreuth (1930), 152-3
Napoule (1932), 171
Essen (1934), 184
Rangsdorf (1936), 192
Dartington (1936), 192
Loughborough (1939), 211
Interlaken (1947), 245
Suschitzky, Olga, dancer, 147
Swaine, Alexander von, dancer, 187
Swallow, Elizabeth, dance teacher, 220
Sykes, Harrison and Co., founders, 235

Tagore, Rabindranath, poet, 205
Talhoff, *Totenmal* (1930), 155-6
Tanz, Der (newspaper), 134, 151, 163-4,
166-7, 176
Tanz Gemeinschaft, Die (journal), 136
Tanzbühne, defined, **279**
Tänzerbund, 140, 143
Tänzerische Zeitfragen, Die (occasional
publication), 88
Tänzerkongresse, *see* Dance Congresses
Tanzschrift (dance notation), 65, 104, 118,

205
Tanzschrift-Schrifttanz, touring exhibition (1931), 167
Tat, Die (cultural journal), 61–2, 72–3, 87, 109, 130, 134
Täuber, Sophie, painter and dancer, 35, 44–6
Taut, Bruno, architect, 27
Taylor, Frederick W., engineer, and 'time and motion' study, 218
Tchaikovsky, Piotr Ilyich
  The Nutcracker, ballet suite, 155
  Serenade for Strings, 86
Tels, Ellen, dancer, 23
Terpis, Max, dancer and ballet-master, 116, 130, 136, 139, 144–5, 163, 201
  Der Letzte Pierrot, 137
Thälmann, Ernst, communist, 82, 140, 170
theatre dance, 153
Theatre Union (amateur drama group), 229–30
Theatre Workshop (Littlewood's), 244–5, 251, 256
theosophy, 19
therapy, *see* art therapy, dance therapy, movement therapy, Withymeade Centre
Therval, Clare, dancer, 89
Thum, Richard, dancer, 189–90, 194, 199
Tietjen, Heinz, conductor and theatre intendant, **158–9,** 162, 174, 178, 202
time and motion study 218, 223–4
Tordis, Ellinor, dancer, 147
Török, Emita, dancer, 95, 103
Toscanini, Arturo, conductor, 157–8, 164, 186
Trevelyan, John, academic, 231, 2⁴8, 254
Trieste, Teatro Nationale, 94
Troplowitz, Hildegard, dancer, 70, 74, 85, 89, 94, 108
Trumpy, Berthe Bartolomé, dance teacher, 103
Tudor, Antony, choreographer, 247
Tudor-Williams, Meg, dancer, 256, 275
Tugal, Pierre, writer on ballet, 201
Tyndale-Biscoe, Veronica, 218, 242–3, 255, 259; *71*
Tyresoles Ltd, 219, 221
Tzara, Tristan, poet and Dadaist, 43–5, 56, 89; *17*

Uhlen, Alice, dancer, 187
Uhlfelder (Munich), Laban's former employer, 39
Ullmann, Lisa, dancer, movement teacher and writer, 219, 221, 229, 232, 245, 268–9, 274
  background and move to England, **206**
  nationality problems, 211, 244
  and the Elmhirsts, 211, 213
  at Dartington, 209–10, 249, 251, 258–60
  at Newtown, 212–21
    at Manchester, 222, 238–9, 244–6, 248, 250
    at Addlestone, 261–4, **272**
  as a teacher: Dartington, 192, 206; London, 212; Manchester, 225–7, 229, 231, 235, 240, 245, 259; elsewhere, 214–16, 220; at courses and classes, 271, 265–7
  Dance Drama Saturdays (1950–51), 257
  on Laban, 72, 120
  protects him, 209, 217–18, 239–40, 244–5
  professional relations, **214–15**
  intimate relations, 244, 248, 262–3
  at his 70th birthday, 251, 253
  edits and publishes his books, 67, 253–4, 272
  dance work, *The Forest* (with Bodmer, 1947), 241–2
unemployment in Germany (1927–32), 140
Universal Edition, publishers, 132–4, 143, 146–7, 151
universality, 229
Urjan, Ida, dancer, 74, 94, 98, 117

Valéry, Paul, poet and writer, 201
Valois, Ninette de, ballet director, 246
van de Velde, Henry, architect, 27, 34
Vaneselow, Maria, dancer, 45
Vaterland, Hans, stage designer, 169
Veith, dancer, 166
Ver Sacrum (from 1898, journal of the Secession), 5
Vera Mystica Lodge (OTO), Monte Verità, 46–7
Verdi, Giuseppe
  Sizilianische Vesper, 170
  Traviata La, 169
Vermey, Ruud, dance teacher, 275
Vienna, the Secession, **6**
Vogel, Dr Carl, sculptor, 219, 228
Vogel, Herbert, and dance notation, 132
Vogelsang, Marianne, dance teacher, 188
Vogt, Karl, rehearsal assistant, 154
Volcard, Mario, dancer, 83, 87

Wachmann, Siegfried, exhibition curator, 7
Wagner, Cosima, Richard's widow, 157
Wagner, Otto, architect, 9
Wagner, Richard, 98, 106–7
  Götterdämmerung, 157
  Die Meistersinger, 180
  Parsifal, 157
  Rienzi, 175, 191
  Tannhäuser, 68–70, 157–8, 164, 180
Wagner, Siegfried, Richard's son, 107, 157–8
Wagner, Winifred, Siegfried's widow, 157–8, 164, 177
Wagner Festival, Bayreuth (1930–1), 107, 152, 157–9, 164
Wagner-Regeny, Rudolf, pianist, 115, 128–9, 186

Walcher, Edith, dancer, 74–5
Walden, Herwath, editor, 153
Wallmann, Margarethe [Margarita], dancer,
    choreographer and teacher
    Orpheus Dionysos (Gluck), 155
Walter, Bruno, conductor, 167, 186
Walther, Clara, dancer, 41–2, 45–7
Warsitz, Eleanor, dancer, 133; *39*
Weber, Carl Maria von, *Oberon*, 167, 180
Wedekind, Frank, dramatist, 87
Wedekind, Lotte, dancer, 87, 206
Weidman, Charles, dancer, choreographer
    and teacher, 226, 271
Weidt, Jean, dancer and choreographer, *La
    Cellule* (1947), 241
Weill, Kurt, composer, 146, 161, 186
Weiss, Peg, writer, 7
Wellesz, Egon, composer, 130, 147
Werefkin, Marianne, painter, 45
Werkbund, *see* Deutsche Werkbund, Munich
    Werkbund
Wernicke, Lotte, dancer and choreographer,
    194–5, 201
    Geburt der Arbeit, 196–7
West Riding Movement Study Group, 233–4,
    262–3, 265–6
Westermeyer, Karl, critic, 177
Westmorland County Education Committee,
    conference (1945), **231**
Weysel, Karl, artist and dancer, 29, 32, 34–5,
    99; *9, 14*
Wiener Neustadt Military Academy, 6
Wigman, Mary [Marie Wiegmann], dancer,
    choreographer and teacher, 90, 99, 169,
    179, 206, 215, 226, 245: *9, 12*
  in America, 171
  in Berlin, 163–4, 172
  in London (1928), 206
  at Monte Verità, **29–30, 35–6**, 37, 249
  in Munich, 27, 32–4, 36, 56, 59: *9*
  in Nuremberg, 49
  in Rome, 108
  in Zurich, 39–42, 44, 46–7, 51–2, 54–5
  avoids Dance Congress (1927), 125, 129–
    30
  touring, 64, 116–17
  at Dance Congresses: (1928), 136–7;
    (1930), 154–6
  at Dance Festival, Berlin (1934), 187
  and the Olympic Games, Berlin (1936),
    193, 197–8
  and her Deutsche Tanz Gemeinschaft, 136
  her archive, xi
  her diaries, 30, 198, 239
  her aims and processes, 56, 60, 95, 109,
    116–17, 136–9, 145
  a freemason, 48
  and the 'High School', 105, 143, 156, 231,
    274

  her influences on dance, 155–6, **270–1**
  her school at Dresden, 132, 166
  her students, 207–8, 220, 270–1
  and Laban, **30**, 52, 66–7, 71, 96, 136, 143,
    145, 187–8, 194
  on Laban, **49, 66–7, 151–2**, 229, 239
  Laban on Wigman, 113, 229
Wigman's dance works
  dance poems (1916), 42
  dance to *Also Sprach Zarathustra* (1915),
    39
  Dances of the Night, 55
  Ecstatic Dances, 55
  Die Feier (1928), 137
  Hexentanz (1914), 33
  Lento (1914), 33
  Totenmal (Talhoff, 1930), 154–5
  Totentanz, 116
  solo performances, 47
Wilckens, Friedrich, répétiteur, 67, 70, 78
Willett, John, historian, 81, 154, 169
Williams, Bronwen Lloyd, school head, 226
Wilson, Lorna, dance teacher, 207–8, 216,
    219, 234; *60*
Winther, Fritz Hanna, writer, 65
  Körperbildung als Kunst und Pflicht
    (1919), 42–3, 62, 99; *9, 12*
Withymeade Centre for Psychotherapy and
    Art Therapy, 222–3, 228, 254–5, 259,
    262, 265
Witt, Traute, dancer, 147
Wolfenberger, Georgio, biographer, 209
  Suzanne Perrottet: Ein Bewegtes Leben
    (1989), 210
Wolf-Ferrari, Ermanno, *Die Schalkhafte
    Witwe*, 167–8
Wolfskehl, Karl, intellectual, 19
Women's League of Health and Beauty, 267
Woog, Heide, dancer, 155, 194–5, 196
work study methods, 218
Workers' Educational Association, 206
Wragge von Pustau, Greta, dancer, 194
Wulff, Käthe, dancer and choreographer, 35,
    48, 59, 87, 96, 155; *14*
  at Zurich, 44–6, 48, 50–2, 56
  at Hamburg, 87
  at Basle, 103
Wundt, Wilhelm, psychologist, 50
Würzburg Stadttheater, 123

Young Dancers' Group (Bodmer's), 249; *68*
Youth Advice Bureau, 268

Zielisch, Fritz, critic, 187
Zimmermann, Lola, at Monte Verità (1913),
    29
Zullig, Hans, dancer, choreographer and
    teacher, 245